College Music Curricula for a New Century

COLLEGE MUSIC CURRICULA FOR A NEW CENTURY

Edited by Robin D. Moore

OXFORD
UNIVERSITY PRESS

OXFORD
UNIVERSITY PRESS

Oxford University Press is a department of the University of Oxford. It furthers
the University's objective of excellence in research, scholarship, and education
by publishing worldwide. Oxford is a registered trade mark of Oxford University
Press in the UK and certain other countries.

Published in the United States of America by Oxford University Press
198 Madison Avenue, New York, NY 10016, United States of America.

Library of Congress Cataloging-in-Publication Data
Names: Moore, Robin D., 1964– compiler.
Title: College music curricula for a new century / Robin D. Moore.
Description: New York, NY : Oxford University Press, 2017. |
    Includes bibliographical references and index.
Identifiers: LCCN 2016037218| ISBN 9780190658403 (pbk.) |
    ISBN 9780190658397 (hardcover) | ISBN 9780190658434 (oxford scholarship online)
Subjects: LCSH: Music in universities and colleges. | Curriculum change. |
    Universities and college—Curricula.
Classification: LCC MT18 .C64 2017 | DDC 780.71/1—dc23
LC record available at https://lccn.loc.gov/2016037218

9 8 7 6 5 4 3 2 1

Paperback printed by Webcom Inc., Canada
Hardback printed by Bridgeport National Bindery, Inc., United States of America

CONTENTS

Disciplinary and Professional Experiments

Best Practices, New Models

CONTRIBUTORS

Juan Agudelo is a former PhD student in ethnomusicology at the University of Texas at Austin. His research has focused on Latin American popular dance music in transnational contexts, and on new forms of digital cumbia produced for contemporary urban dance clubs. Mr. Agudelo has published reviews, translations, and encyclopedia entries in various academic volumes, and he was archivist and research assistant for the PBS documentary series *Latin Music USA*.

Deborah Bradley completed her PhD in the Department of Sociology and Equity Studies, Ontario Institute for Studies in Education (University of Toronto) in 2006. She has published on social justice and music education in many noted journals, including *Philosophy of Music Education Review, Journal of Aesthetic Education, Music Education Research*, and *Action, Criticism, and Theory for Music Education*. Her teaching and research were in the areas of world music education (choral and general music), and antiracism education. Dr. Bradley was appointed editor-in-chief for MayDay Group publications, which include the journals *Action, Criticism, and Theory for Music Education (ACT)* and *TOPICS for Music Education Praxis*.

Katie Chapman received an MM in ethnomusicology and a BM in vocal performance from the University of Texas at Austin. Her master's report demonstrates how the Cuban rumba can be studied to further understand Cuban gender identity by observing the voice. Katie completed two certifications: one in business foundations from the McCombs School of Business and the other in arts and cultural management and entrepreneurship from the LBJ School of Public Affairs. Currently, Katie works as an administrative associate on a $3.5 million grant project studying audience building in performing arts organizations.

Carlos Dávalos is a graduate student in ethnomusicology at the University of Texas at Austin. His research interests are Latin American and Mexican hip-hop and the ways in which migration and technology have contributed to new forms of Mexican identity as manifested through hip-hop cultural practices. Before moving to Austin, Carlos was a journalist and open-media analyst based in Mexico City.

Mark F. DeWitt is professor of music and holds the Dr. Tommy Comeaux Endowed Chair in Traditional Music at the University of Louisiana at Lafayette, where he directs an undergraduate curriculum and degree program in traditional music. His primary research area is Cajun and Creole French music of Louisiana and its diaspora, and he is author of *Cajun and Zydeco Dance Music in Northern California: Modern Pleasures in a Postmodern World* (University Press of Mississippi, 2008). He received a PhD in ethnomusicology from the University of California–Berkeley and an MM in music theory from the New England Conservatory of Music.

Hannah Durham is a PhD student in musicology at the University of Texas at Austin. Her research area includes popular music and American audiences since 1950, disability studies, and genre and performance studies. Her dissertation will investigate the discourses surrounding David Bowie and his music in the post-1970s era—focusing on his work from 1983 *Let's Dance* release through his death and post-death reception. Hannah has played French horn for various UT ensembles and has written, recorded, and performed with several rock bands in and around Austin as guitarist and bassist.

Myranda Harris is percussionist, music educator, and ethnomusicologist based in Austin, Texas. Currently a PhD candidate in ethnomusicology at UT Austin, she holds an MM and BM from the University of North Texas. As a musician, Myranda has built a diverse rhythmic vocabulary by studying percussion in a number of music traditions around the world, and she is an active performer and clinician in the Central Texas area. Her forthcoming dissertation, which focuses on fusion music in South India, examines how music unites people and communities from diverse backgrounds.

Eddie Hsu is a PhD student in ethnomusicology at the University of Texas at Austin. His primary research focus is the musical practices of the Taiwanese aboriginal community and issues of appropriation and revivalism. He received his BA in dizi (Chinese bamboo flute) performance at Tainan National University of the Arts in Taiwan. As a musician with diverse interests, Hsu has collaborated with several groups, including Sangat (collaborative music ensemble with musicians from the National Academy of Performing Arts, Pakistan), Aşk-i Meşk (Arabic and Turkish maqam-based music on the ney), and the UT Javanese Gamelan Ensemble.

Paul Klemperer has a masters degree in ethnomusicology (University of Texas), a BA in sociology (Amherst College), and forty years of professional playing experience. He discovered jazz at an early age, studying with jazz legends Archie Shepp, Max Roach, and Ray Copeland. He has opened for renowned artists such as B. B. King, the Neville Brothers, Ray Charles, Chuck Berry, and James Brown and has appeared on national TV and radio shows in the United States and Europe. He presents workshops, demonstrations, and lectures on a variety of music-related topics. Working as a bandleader, composer, arranger, and freelancer, Paul has produced five CDs of original music and collaborated on over a hundred recording projects.

Emily Kohut graduated in 2016 from Colorado College, where she earned a BA double major in classics and English. A native of London, Ontario, she moved to Colorado Springs with her family in 2001. She focused on classical languages and literature, emphasizing Latin. Her activities at Colorado College included tutoring in classical languages, mentoring first-year students, and serving as Victoria Levine's research assistant from 2014 through 2016. In the summer of 2015, Kohut was an intern for curricular development and programs with Harvard University's Center for Hellenic Studies in Washington, DC. She hopes to attend graduate studies in classics and to pursue an academic career.

Victoria Lindsay Levine is professor of music at Colorado College, where she teaches ethnomusicology and southwestern studies. Her research focuses on Native North American musical cultures and she is the author, coauthor, or editor of numerous publications, including four books. She has received fellowships from the American Council of Learned Societies, the National Endowment for the Humanities, and the Society for Ethnomusicology, among others. At Colorado College, Levine has served as the John D. and Catherine T. MacArthur Professor, the W. M. Keck Foundation Director of the Hulbert Center for Southwestern Studies, and the Christine S. Johnson Professor of Music.

Creighton Moench has a master's degree in ethnomusicology from the University of Texas at Austin and is currently pursuing his PhD at the same institution. During the writing of this volume he served as a research assistant involved with the Butler School of Music's partnership with the National Academy of Performing Arts in Karachi, Pakistan. His research interests include popular music history, African American vernacular traditions, Hindustani classical music, and musical theater. Outside the classroom he often performs in regional and community theater and is an amateur musician in many different world music ensembles.

Robin D. Moore is professor of ethnomusicology at the University of Texas at Austin. His research interests include music and nationalism, music and race, and music of Cuba and the Hispanic Caribbean. His publications include *Nationalizing Blackness* (University of Pittsburgh Press, 1997), *Music and Revolution* (University of California Press, 2006), *Music of the Hispanic Caribbean* (Oxford Press, 2010), *Musics of Latin America* (Norton, 2012), *Danzón: Circum-Caribbean Dialogues in Music and Dance* (Oxford, 2013, cowritten with Alejandro Madrid), and articles on Cuban music in *Cuban Studies, Ethnomusicology, Encuentro de la cultura cubana,* the *Latin American Music Review,* and other journals and book anthologies. Since 2005 he has served as editor of the *Latin American Music Review.*

Justin Patch teaches global and popular music in the music department at Vassar College. His research focuses on the auditory culture of contemporary politics and political campaigns in the United States, on sound studies, and on critical issues in ethnographic research and humanities education. His work has appeared in *American Music, Soundings, European Legacy, International Political Anthropology, Journal of Sonic Studies, Americana, Ethnomusicology Review, Zeteo,* and the edited volume *Critical and New Literacies: Teaching towards Democracy with Popular Culture and Postmodern Texts.*

Ludim Pedroza is associate professor of music at Texas State University. She works primarily in the areas of music history and Latin music studies, teaching undergraduate and graduate courses on a variety of topics. Among these is the survey History of Music in Latin America and specialized seminars on the music and aesthetics of the Caribbean, Mexico, and the nineteenth century. Pedroza's publications include the article "Merengue Meets the Symphony Orchestra" (*American Music,* 2014), various publications on *El Sistema,* and "Music as *Communitas*: Franz Liszt, Clara Schumann, and the Musical Work" (*Journal of Musicological Research,* 2010). Pedroza has recently been named co-coordinator of the Latin Music Studies program.

Brian Pertl is currently the dean of the Lawrence Conservatory of Music. He is a trombonist, ethnomusicologist, former Microsoft manager, didgeridoo player, deep listener, and passionate advocate for music education at all levels. Brian believes that creating music cultures that honor creativity, exploration, and collaboration and play along with teaching exceptional core musicianship and growing intellectual capacity are key to creating musicians who will best overcome the obstacles and capitalize on the opportunities facing today's graduates. Brian is passionate about proactively tackling the challenges that face the world of music education in the twenty-first century and is endlessly optimistic that the properly prepared music graduate will have more opportunities to create a musical life than ever before.

Sonia Tamar Seeman received her PhD from the University of California–Los Angeles in ethnomusicology and has conducted field research in southeastern Europe and Turkey on Romani, Macedonian, Turkish, and transnational musical practices. She taught at UCSB for four years on a postdoctoral faculty fellowship. At UT Austin since 2006, she has served on a variety of arts-wide and campus-wide curriculum committees, has been awarded a teaching excellence award from the school of music and appointed a member of UT's Provost Teaching Fellows. In addition, she has conducted music workshops and founded Bereket, UT Austin's Middle Eastern ensemble. She is the project facilitator for Sangat, a musical fusion project, with members of the Butler School of Music and junior faculty from the National Academy of Performing Arts, Karachi, Pakistan.

Jack Talty is a traditional musician, composer, producer, educator, and ethnomusicologist from county Clare, Ireland. As a performer Jack has traveled extensively throughout Europe, the United States, Australia, and Asia and has contributed to over fifty albums to date as a musician, producer, composer, arranger, and engineer. A frequent contributor to television and radio broadcasts, he performs regularly as a soloist, with his award-winning band Ensemble Ériu, and as a section leader with the Irish Memory Orchestra. In 2009 Jack completed an MA in music at the University of Limerick and is currently completing his doctorate there under the supervision of Dr. Aileen Dillane.

Michael Tenzer is active as a composer, performer, scholar, and teacher. He is editor of *Analytical Studies in World Music* (2006) and *Analytical and Cross-Cultural Studies in World Music* (2011, co-edited with John Roeder), and author of *Gamelan Gong Kebyar: The Art of Twentieth-Century Balinese Music* (2000; winner of the ASCAP–Deems Taylor Award and the Society for Ethnomusicology's Merriam Award), plus other books, chapters and articles. His diverse compositions are available on "Let Others Name You" (2009) in the New World Records Recorded Anthology of American Music series, as well as on numerous other CDs. Involved with Balinese music since 1977 as performer, composer, and researcher, he co-founded Gamelan Sekar Jaya in Berkeley, California, in 1979. His compositions for gamelan since 1982 have been cited in the Balinese press as a "significant contribution to our cultural heritage." Tenzer is professor of music at the University of British Columbia.

ABOUT THE COMPANION WEBSITE

www.oup.com/us/collegemusiccurriculaforanewcentury

The contributors to this volume have created a companion website that can be accessed at www.oup.com/us/collegemusiccurriculaforanewcentury. Most of its materials consist of hyperlinks to the many web pages referenced in the book so that those interested can navigate to them easily. The site also includes sample course syllabi corresponding to material in Chapters 3 and 9, a list of the Carnegie "Basic Classification" discussed in Chapter 4, and curricular outlines corresponding to the BM major in music studies with minor in mariachi music (instrumental and choral concentrations) associated with Chapter 7. Materials available online are indicated in the text with the symbol ⊙ to encourage readers to consult them for further information.

College Music Curricula for a New Century

CHAPTER 1

Introduction

Toward a Model of Reform

ROBIN D. MOORE

This volume offers examples of what a more inclusive, dynamic, and socially engaged curriculum of musical study might look like. Our goal is to create dialogue among educators about what college music instruction should be in the future and how to transition to new paradigms. The book's chapters concentrate primarily on changes to performance degrees rather than other subdisciplines since they constitute the center of activity in most institutions, with some attention to music education, music theory, musicology/ethnomusicology, and other areas. Ethnomusicologists feature prominently among the contributors, but the volume also includes chapters by those with expertise in music education, theory/composition, professional performance, and administration. The project derives from our collective experience over decades in schools and departments of music, and as performers.

Critiques and calls for reform have existed for decades, but few publications have offered concrete suggestions as to how things might be done differently. Our study is motivated by a desire to do just that: to consider what new concepts or guiding principles might be used to reconceive music education at the college level and what the application of such principles might look like in practical terms. It differs from past studies in that it examines existing innovative curricula in programs nationally and internationally and uses them as a point of departure for analysis; its conclusions thus derive from practice.

The chapters have a degree of US-centric bias, as most of its authors are based there. However, whenever possible we incorporate insights from international sources, and six of the contributors are currently based in or were born in other countries (the majority were educated abroad as well). In addition to foregrounding the many domestic curricular initiatives music professionals may not be aware of, we consider it a priority to look beyond musical institutions in the United States.

CHALLENGES TO ARTS EDUCATION

A growing consensus exists that the training of musicians and music educators in universities and conservatories requires fundamental revision. Such concerns are being voiced from national and international music organizations including scholarly societies, from administrators, faculty, private donors, and from students themselves. Many innovative projects have developed in response to such concerns, typically in isolation. But in most institutions, change has been minimal; the dominant model of performance-oriented education is still adhered to, and discussions about what pedagogy should look like in the future are only beginning to attract widespread attention. In the mid-nineteenth century, when schools of music, conservatories, and related programs were first established, far fewer students had access to university education, and elitist, hierarchical notions of good and bad music (the latter frequently associated with "inferior races" or the poor) contributed to the establishment of a canon of elite European works. Wind ensembles, symphonies, and choruses became central to institutional practice as the ensembles used to interpret such repertoire, with most music school activity revolving around them. The model has perpetuated itself and has proven surprisingly resistant to change.

Since the 1940s, university education in the United States and elsewhere has become more accessible to the general public. As a result, the profile of the typical college student has changed radically in terms of race and ethnicity, cultural orientation, income level, and other factors, yet arts curricula as a rule have not responded to such trends. A chasm currently exists between the kinds of music taught in music schools and the music most students hear in their community and/or identify with as individuals (Carson and Westvall 2016, 43).[1] The classical music community's recent emphasis on advocacy and outreach represents a response to this phenomenon; it has become

1. *Slate* magazine notes that classical music accounted for less than 3 percent of national record sales. See Mark Vanhoenacker, "Requiem: Classical Music in America Is Dead," http://www.slate.com/articles/arts/culturebox/2014/01/classical_music_sales_decline_is_classical_on_death_s_door.html (accessed June 4, 2016).

increasingly necessary in order to justify a curriculum whose relevance is frequently apparent to neither audiences nor the agencies that provide financial support to educational institutions (Bowman 2004, 29). Little congruence or alignment exists between the world of academic music instruction, the broader professional world of music performance, and audience interest (Freeman 2014, xviii). While various popular, traditional, and international music forms have achieved limited representation in university courses, one usually finds them discussed in academic rather than performance contexts. Courses on rock music or world music, for instance, tend to appear as academic electives within music schools or as offerings for the general student body rather than part of music performance curricula.[2] With the exception of jazz programs and more recent offerings such as music business or production, the core coursework of most music students remains largely the same as it did a century ago.

Nonprofit policymaking institutions in the United States such as the Rand Corporation and the National Endowment for the Arts have published insightful critiques of the changes in US society in recent years and their implications for the arts sector. They point to trends including increasing cultural pluralism, with 40 percent of recent population growth resulting from immigration, primarily of Hispanics (McCarthy et al. 2001, 34). Note that while African American traditions, such as jazz, have received some recognition in tertiary-level music programs, the music of Hispanics, the country's largest minority, tends to be even more consistently marginalized (Madrid 2011).[3] Other trends noted in recent publications include reduced governmental support for the arts and instead greater private or corporate sponsorship; an increasing tendency for audiences to experience the arts passively rather than actively and in such mediated forms as videos or recordings rather than live concerts; and a marked decline in symphony attendance (McCarthy et al. 2001, iii–iv, 31; Ivey 2008, 171).[4] On the latter point, Ivey (2008, 171) notes that

2. Bradley (2007, 134) discussed this issue some years ago, and it still accurately describes the curriculum at the University of Texas where I teach. Heuser (2014, 108) comes to similar conclusions about present-day curricula. And recent correspondence with faculty and staff at other large institutions devoted to applied music instruction— including the Hartt School of Music, Indiana University's Jacobs School of Music, the Peabody Conservatory, the Boyer School at Temple University, the University of Kansas School of Music, and the University of South Carolina School of Music—suggests that courses on rock or world music are still not a required part of applied music study in most other schools. A few are beginning to include short modules on world music or popular music within their music major history sequence, however.

3. For more on the issue of long-term demographic trends, see also Avlerie B. Morris and David B. Pankratz, eds., *The Arts in a New Millennium. Research and the Arts Sector* (Westport, CT: Praeger, 2003).

4. Regarding passive or mass-mediated consumption of the arts, see the results of the 2015 NEA study suggesting that about 70 percent of audiences' cultural activity in the

audiences at symphonic concerts declined 10 percent between 1993 and 2003 and that 70 percent of orchestras reported deficits during the same period. Opera companies have experienced similar difficulties.[5] Various factors contribute to such trends, but clearly the performing arts need to engage with a broader spectrum of contemporary musical experience in order to remain socially relevant. And it is unethical to continue graduating tens of thousands of students each year with a specialization in European classical performance if the likelihood of employment in that area is minimal.[6] In order to engage modern audiences with compelling live performances, we need to understand what a compelling performance looks like to them.[7] This will undoubtedly involve altering the ways we discuss and present classical repertoire and the extent to which we do so. With past notions of a canon of masterpieces, of artistic genius, and of a "historical teleology with Europe as its point of origin and efflorescence" (Yang 2014, 4) all in question and with European classical music heard more often on smartphone apps or sampled in pop songs than in formal classical concerts, new and more diverse forms of pedagogical practice are called for.

One of the only places where a resurgence of interest in elite European musical repertoire has taken place in recent decades is among middle-class and elite families in East Asian countries such as Japan, China, and South Korea. The presence of Asian performers is significant in the most prestigious conservatories and music schools of the United States, Europe, and beyond, where their tuition dollars have become an important form of revenue. The domestic symphonic performance scene in East Asia continues to be more vibrant than in North America as well. Some of Asian performers' interest in elite European heritage undoubtedly has to do with a profound attraction to the repertoire itself. The respective histories of modernization in East Asian countries (especially Japan and South Korea following World War II and the Korean War, respectively), as well as the music's associations with prestige and with upward social mobility also play an important role in its popularity (Yoshihara 2007, 6, 47).

The United States has proven especially ineffective at promoting its own vibrant and diverse music in institutional settings. It is hard to believe that in the twenty-first century a music student interested in the performance, arranging, or composition of black gospel music, funk, zydeco, bluegrass,

United States is now virtual: https://www.arts.gov/news/2015/surprising-findings-three-new-nea-reports-arts (accessed June 4, 2016).

5. E.g., Michael Cooper, "New York City Opera Files for Bankruptcy," *New York Times*, October 3, 2013, http://www.nytimes.com/2013/10/04/arts/music/new-york-city-opera-files-for-bankruptcy.html?_r=0 (accessed August 5, 2015).

6. Dean Mark McCoy, DePauw University, phone interview, July 22, 2015.

7. Brian Pert, "Twenty-First Century Musicianship at Lawrence," http://www.lawrence.edu/conservatory/21st-century-musicianship (accessed August 5, 2015).

Native American expressive forms, or any number of other US styles has few institutions across the country to enroll where he or she can learn such skills. There exist important exceptions to this tendency, such as the Berklee College of Music and other programs emphasizing discrete regional traditions (DeWitt, Chapter 4 in this volume), but nevertheless, it is striking that the study and performance of historical and contemporary music from the United States has been in large part sidelined rather than celebrated. Most musical institutions appear ideologically colonized in this sense, refusing to valorize such heritage. The contributors to this volume are eager to address this issue going forward.

It is important to consider what applied music majors end up doing with their degrees, what challenges they face as performers after graduation, and what skills might make them more widely marketable. Surprisingly little information on these topics is available; in order to meet the needs of students we need to do a better job of collecting it and considering its implications. The Strategic National Arts Alumni Project (SNAAP), based at Indiana University, has some data that merit consultation.[8] Supported by the Surnda Foundation, SNAAP has conducted surveys of roughly 92,000 graduates in the arts from US institutions. One finds many self-employed individuals among their ranks (roughly 80 percent reported being self-employed for significant periods); many end up working outside the arts sector in order to support themselves, and others remain committed to the arts but aren't paid terribly well. Young musicians often choose alternate forms of employment as they marry and start a family (McCarthy et al. 2001, 37, 42–44). Only a small fraction of aspiring performers succeed in making a comfortable living strictly with their instrument; those involved as part-time performers outnumber full-time performers by a factor of at least twenty to one. Amateurs or nonprofessionals increasing dominate the performing arts, the result of shrinking support for live performance among nonprofit institutions.[9] In the face of these trends, conservatories, music schools, and departments must renew their efforts to critically examine their overall orientation and purpose and modify their offerings.

While the focus of this volume is on applied music instruction, its authors are also concerned with how to reconceive academic musical disciplines such as musicology, ethnomusicology, and music theory so as to make them more relevant to student training.[10] In the same way that applied performance

8. http://snaap.indiana.edu/ (accessed July 22, 2015).

9. See "Performing Artists Compete, Move, Adapt in Tough Economy," *PBS News Hour*, June 27, 2013, http://www.pbs.org/newshour/videos/#53717 (accessed July 22, 2015).

10. Regarding music theory, see Greg Sandow's recent posts on the importance of reform in that discipline: http://www.artsjournal.com/sandow/2015/10/music-the-ory-for-a-new-century.html (accessed December 8, 2015). The *Analytical Studies in World Music* anthologies, edited by Michael Tenzer and John Roeder (Tenzer 2006,

faculty tend to train their students narrowly for ever decreasing numbers of jobs, academic faculty also tend often to train their students in narrow areas of expertise, implicitly grooming them for work as researchers that is difficult to find. The fields of music history and music theory have embraced new topics since the 1980s, yet the focus of most professors in the classroom at major music schools and conservatories (e.g., music schools at the University of Texas where I teach, Indiana University, or the University of Illinois Urbana–Champaign) is on the same European canonical literature. Ethnomusicology, the study of music as a component of social life, is also limited in terms of its relevance to applied pedagogy, though in different ways. In an ongoing effort to engage with the humanities and social sciences, ethnomusicology has foregrounded theory to the extent that its publications frequently have little relevance for performers. Ethnomusicology graduates learn about notions of the black Atlantic, about postmodernity and pastiche, about transnational cultural flows, and so on, but in the process implicitly learn not to discuss music in ways that would be relevant in performance settings or to the broader public. Some programs, especially at exclusive private universities with music departments, do not encourage applied music making of any sort as a required part of training in the discipline (this applies to musicology as well). In general, ethnomusicology undervalues didactic publications and does not dialogue sufficiently with applied music faculty or students. As individuals who study noncanonical music and who represent marginal communities, ethnomusicologists have valuable insights into the confining nature of current musical practice. The following chapters hope to make that apparent.[11]

MOMENTUM FOR CHANGE

To some, interest on the part of ethnomusicologists in applied music pedagogy may seem counterintuitive. In many ways, however, it represents an extension of work that has been conducted for many years. The most obvious early examples of this are the publications by Henry Kingsbury (1988) and Bruno Nettl (1995) on the cultures, discourse, and values of music schools.

Tenzer and Roeder 2011), and the new *Analytical Approaches to World Music* interest group and journal (http://www.ethnomusicology.org/?Groups_SIGsAWM; http://www.aawmjournal.com/; accessed December 8, 2015) have important implications for the field of music theory and ways that it could expand and diversify its repertoires of interest. See also chapters by Michael Tenzer and Sonia Seeman in this volume.

11. Graduate students in ethnomusicology have begun to recognize the lack of their discipline's engagement with mainstream music educators, as evident in the focus of the Fall/Winter 2015 issue of *SEM Student News* (Vol. 11) devoted exclusively to the intersections of ethnomusicology and music education.

Kingsbury's groundbreaking study focused on notions of talent surrounding music, viewing evaluations of it as a means of exercising social power. He examined the ritualistic aspects of classical recitals, their fusion of sacred and secular elements, and their emotional impact on participants, among other topics. Nettl's analysis continued along the same lines in a more lighthearted manner, considering the extent to which art music could be viewed as a religious system and performers and scholars as a priesthood of sorts. He discussed the symphony as the product of industrialization and social hierarchy and notions of canon and exclusion. More broadly, our book project corresponds to the tendency of ethnomusicologists since the 1980s to research "closer to home," to study commercial as well as traditional musics, to consider the politics of world music study within US or other academic institutions (e.g., Wong 2006, Krüger 2009, Guilbault 2014),[12] and to engage in scholarship that engages socially and politically as well as musically (Araújo 2009, Harrison et al. 2010, Krüger 2011, etc.). The discipline of ethnomusicology has always been reflexive; contributors to the book with training in that area expand the focus to include practical reflection over what insights it can provide to musical institutions as a whole.

Despite calls from many organizations to diversify and critically examine music pedagogy beginning in at least the 1960s, efforts at reform had little impact until recently. True, certain programs developed in decidedly innovative ways—the Berklee College in Boston, dating from the 1940s, with its unapologetic embrace of commercial music making, its countless ensembles in a diversity of styles foregrounding US traditions, its emphasis on technology and recording, and significant offerings on non-Western music performance; or the California Institute of the Arts, founded in 1969 with funding from Walt Disney, influenced by Marcuse's theories of radical pedagogy, incorporating social outreach, and offering an impressive array of national and international performance options to music majors, with no orchestral component[13]—but such programs have not been widely emulated. Since the opening years of this century, however, experimentation with curricula and with new types of instruction have become much more commonplace. Many schools have established performance degrees in regional traditional musics in collaboration with local performers, featuring everything from Hawaiian repertoire to bluegrass to salsa. Programs in music technology, recording, and business are developing rapidly. Entrepreneurial initiatives that focus

12. A special edition of the journal *Worlds of Music*, edited by Simone Krüger (Vol. 51 No. 3, 2009), is devoted entirely to the issue of the proper place or function of ethnomusicology within the academy, its future, and problems encountered by researchers.

13. https://calarts.edu/. For further information on the program's origins, see Janet Sarbanes, "A Community of Artists: Radical Pedagogy at Cal Arts, 1969–72" (2014), *East of Borneo*, http://www.eastofborneo.org/articles/a-community-of-artists-radical-pedagogy-at-calarts-1969-72 (accessed August 4, 2015).

on developing new audiences, on finding new ways to productively make music in society, and on stylistic innovation are more common. A familiarity with world music is expected of students in some performance programs as well. Examples of recent innovative experiments (among many) include the University of Miami's Experiential Music Curriculum (2009), which combines the study of interpretive and improvised performance, music history, ear training, music theory, and composition into a single six-hour weekly course;[14] DePauw University's 21st-Century Musician Initiative (2012), with an emphasis on community engagement, promotion, marketing, and exposure to diverse repertoires;[15] the Lawrence Conservatory's 21st Century Musicianship initiative (2013), with its emphasis on combining technical instrumental skill with a rigorous liberal arts education (Lawrence encourages five-year double majors and develops improvisational and compositional skills among all music students, viewing them as key to cross-disciplinary exploration, social engagement, and creative thinking);[16] Illinois Wesleyan University's BM in contemporary musicianship, incorporating music technology, jazz and non-jazz improvisation, and composition (2015);[17] and Cornell University's shift toward greater diversity in repertoire and analytical approaches to musical study (2016).[18]

National music institutions have helped to encourage curricular reform in recent years, in part through policy changes and in part through initiating dialogue with their membership.[19] The National Association of Schools of Music (NASM), founded in 1924, by all accounts acted as a deterrent to curricular innovation for many years in encouraging a focus on canonical repertoire through its accreditation policies. Recent decades have witnessed significant changes in this position, however. Both the NASM website and handbook now

_____

14. http://www.miami.edu/frost/index.php/frost/programs/experiential_music_curriculum/ (accessed August 4, 2015).

15. http://www.depauw.edu/music/21cm/, http://www.depauw.edu/news-media/latest-news/details/31084/ (accessed August 4, 2015).

16. More information on the Lawrence program and philosophy can be found in the online statement penned by Brian Pertl (https://www.lawrence.edu/conservatory/21st-century-musicianship, accessed July 24, 2015) and in his web lecture "Music Education, Improvisational Play and Dancing between Disciplines," https://www.youtube.com/watch?v=UL8iJ4y32Vk (accessed August 5, 2015).

Though not offering a BM degree, Santa Fe University's Contemporary Music program also deserves mention because it engages students in composing and performing a diversity of traditional, commercial, and world music styles in addition to providing instruction in studio production and recording. See http://santafeuniversity.edu/academics/contemporary-music/ (accessed August 6, 2015).

17. https://www.iwu.edu/music/academics/suggested-curriculum-musicianship.html (accessed June 4, 2016).

18. http://as.cornell.edu/news/playing-new-tune-revamped-music-curriculum-reaches-students-diverse-musical-backgrounds (accessed April 11, 2016).

19. These include the American Musicological Society, esp. its Pedagogy Study Group; see https://teachingmusichistory.wordpress.com/.

(Community music?) —

openly encourage music institutions to develop new ideas and experiment in their course offerings. Every national NASM conference since at least 2008 has included prominent presentations on the topic of curriculum reform, including the role of administrators in initiating and facilitating the process, discussion of the importance of community engagement, creative approaches to pedagogy, and so on.[20] At present, such discussion has not yet translated into concrete changes in accreditation guidelines or advocacy for specific curricular policies on the part of NASM, but the sustained focus on the topic suggests this may well occur in the future. Certainly any sort of systemic reform will necessarily involve dialogue with NASM and other accreditation agencies in order to be effective.

The College Music Society has been active in terms of addressing curriculum reform of late. Former president Patricia Shehan Campbell created a task force on the undergraduate music major and charged it with examining systemic deficiencies in pedagogy, as well as means of addressing them. The group produced a thought-provoking document (Campbell et al. 2014), noting among other problems a tendency for performance classes to unnecessarily subordinate the cultivation of new composition and improvisation to the interpretive performance of existing canonical pieces; ethnocentrism; and the unnecessary fragmentation of subjects and skills associated with performance into discrete classes.[21] The authors argue for the creation of new "pillars," or foundational principles, for music pedagogy, much as we do. Specifically, they call for greater attention to creative performance experiences, exposure to a wider gamut of repertoire, and greater integration of fundamental musical skills (ear training, music theory, instrumental performance, etc.) into holistic classroom experiences. The task force calls for jazz and other Afro-diasporic musics to be more central to the pedagogical process and for a curriculum that provides students with "expanded options for navigating their artistic pathways." The former issue is especially important to lead task force author Ed Sarath, who has developed an innovative jazz performance program at the University of Michigan, a BFA in jazz and contemplative studies.[22] Our project draws from many aspects of the task force document, extending some topics

20. Program information about NASM conference proceedings is available on their site (http://nasm.arts-accredit.org/index.jsp?page=Annual%20Meeting%20Papers; accessed August 5, 2015). As examples of the materials presented in the 2012 meeting, see Chattah 2012, Lowe 2012, Rosenboom 2012.

21. The document is available at the website http://www.mtosmt.org/issues/mto.16.22.1/manifesto.pdf, accessed January 3, 2017) as well as at academia.edu and other platforms. A revised version of the chapter is also to appear in a forthcoming (2017) book by Routledge: *Redefining Music Studies in an Age of Change. Creativity, Diversity, and Integration*, by Ed Sarath, David Myers, and Patricia Shehan Campbell.

22. See http://pccs.umich.edu/BFA-in-JCS/index.html and a blog describing the program's development: http://www.pbs.org/thebuddha/blog/2010/apr/8/improvisation-creativity-and-consciousness-ed-sara/ (accessed August 5, 2015).

and documenting in detail the ways in which existing programs have developed innovative initiatives of their own.[23]

The current volume largely avoids critiques of mainstream music pedagogy and its resistance to reform in many cases, largely because these topics have been the focus of others for many years (e.g., Kwami 1998, Sefa Dei and Kempf 2006, Bradley 2007). To the extent that critiques are included, they are discussed in order to more clearly chart a path forward within the particularities of conservatory or music school culture. All suggestions for change are based on certain assumptions, however. We suggest that elite European music, while an important form of heritage, represents but one of many styles of music that present-day performers need exposure to, that they require additional skills and experiences. Similarly, we assume that the large-ensemble paradigm of musical instruction requires modification so as to allow for a greater diversity of performance experiences. In most conservatories and music schools, symphonies, wind bands, and choruses represent the public face of their respective institution. They make wonderful music, yet require such expansive resources that they restrict the development of alternate groups and tend not to allow for much student agency. In order for music schools to re-envision themselves, they must strive to create a more equitable balance between large-ensemble formats and others. It is worth noting that current NASM guidelines do not define "major ensemble" and do not require a minimum number of "major ensemble" or large ensemble credits. For the BM and music education undergraduate degrees, the guidelines simply suggest that "Ensembles should be varied both in size and nature" (*NASM Handbook* 2013–2014, 99). Depending on an institution's current makeup, achieving a more equitable balance between ensemble formats may require policy changes regarding student recruitment, scholarships, admissions, and even faculty hires.

GUIDING PRINCIPLES

As in the case of the College Music Society (CMS) task force, our project proposes a number of new priorities and suggests how they might be used to reorganize curricula. The priorities do not represent an exhaustive list, nor are they entirely independent of one another. Yet all intersect with a number of independent initiatives in recent decades and should serve as a point of departure for fruitful discussion. It is important for music educators to debate

23. The CMS has organized important events on curricular reform more recently as well. These include the June 2016 summit Twenty-First Century Music School Design, in Columbia, South Carolina, and the October 2016 preconference workshop The End of the Conservatory, in Santa Fe, New Mexico.

and eventually agree to curricular priorities such as these; to date, far too few "metadiscussions" of this sort are taking place among faculty as a whole. Reaching a broad consensus represents the only way to enact change across institutions rather than the piecemeal fashion that it has taken place in to date. As a point of departure, we intend to explore how the following might be incorporated into twenty-first-century music curricula:

1. **Commitment to community**. Institutions adopting this priority would engage consistently with styles of music in which the surrounding community or region is strongly invested. Students would learn to perform such repertoire, study its history and prominent performers and innovators, and spend time interacting with local community members themselves as a means of understanding its significance to them. Community would thus become more central to curriculum in helping determine the repertoire and musical projects students engage with. Manifestations of this emphasis might involve ethnographic research and interviews, participation in special ensembles based on local styles, learning to arrange or compose in particular idioms, or inviting guest artists from the community to the university. A stronger local or regional component to instruction has the advantage of helping distinguish repertoires of music learning from one institution to the next, moving away from an overly standardized approach to core repertoire toward a more diverse model.

Examples of institutions choosing to incorporate local heritage into their curricula include the Maui campus of the University of Hawaii,[24] the Irish World Academy of Music and Dance in Limerick,[25] and the Scandinavian folk music program at the Sibelius Academy in Helsinki.[26] Recent academic literature also references the potential benefit of community ties to music pedagogy. Aaron Corn, for instance, discusses courses on traditional Australian music organized in conjunction with cultural festivals in northeast Arnhem Land (Corn 2009). Student participation involves travel to the area, extended stays with native communities and instruction in the arts by local elders alongside Melbourne University faculty. Paulo Costa Lima describes the focus of applied music students in the Federal University of Bahia, Brazil, during his tenure as minister of education there, toward community projects in Afro-Brazilian *terreiros* (religious centers). This took place as part of an initiative he called Curricular Activity in Community. Its intent was to break down barriers of class and race, create a new sense of regional identification among music

24. http://maui.hawaii.edu/ihm/ (accessed August 3, 2015).
25. http://www.irishworldacademy.ie/ (accessed August 3, 2015).
26. http://www.uniarts.fi/en/siba/folk-music (accessed August 3, 2015). See also Juniper Hill's article (2009) on their folk music program.

students, and help musical research emerge in dialogue with the community (Lima 2002). For his part, Samuel Araújo has encouraged students to study marginal forms of music making in their home city of Rio de Janeiro. He and his students examine topics such as the intersections of music and poverty in local communities, mainstream ideologies surrounding working-class music, and notions of symbolic violence (e.g., Araújo and Cambria 2003). Within the United States, the Multicultural Arts Initiative at the University of Wisconsin–Madison supports hip-hop instruction, performance, and activism as a form of community engagement.[27] A recent issue of *MUSICultures*, a publication of the Canadian Society for Traditional Music, is devoted exclusively to "collaborative, community-based and community-engaged research" in institutions of higher education (Ostashewski 2015, 2). Much of the trend among ethnomusicologists in recent decades toward applied, activist, or public sector work similarly intersects with the prioritization of community interaction (e.g., Titon 1992, Alviso 2003); institutions such as the International Council on Traditional Music have partnered with the Society for Ethnomusicology to further community engagement projects as well (Harrison 2015).[28] Of course, the emphasis on outreach, the staging of music in new venues, and dialogue with audiences attests to the importance educators and administrators place on community engagement in many schools of music. What is needed going forward is to situate the music of local communities more prominently within the core curriculum of music majors.

2. **Commitment to the practical concerns of professional musicians**. As mentioned, the performance environment for musicians continues to change, with decreasing opportunities for specialists in western European art music and a growing need for exposure to other styles. Aspiring performers of the future need to be well versed in vernacular music as they search for employment, as many programs now recognize (Patch, Chapter 6 in this volume). They need to be sensitive to changing demographics and audience tastes. Similarly, they will need to have some familiarity with topics frequently associated with entrepreneurship, music business, or music technology/production programs such as basic knowledge of recording, sound and video editing, engraving software, licensing and copyright, and music sales via the internet. Students need to be trained to think creatively about how to engage audiences and find application for their skills. Practical concerns should also include more focus on training from disciplines outside music in order for students to explore new interdisciplinary connections. Many schools offer discrete courses that cover such topics,

27. http://omai.wisc.edu/?p=184 (accessed August 3, 2015).
28. See, e.g., the theme of their joint 2015 forum: http://www.ictmusic.org/joint-sem-ictm-forum-2015 (accessed August 3, 2015).

but they aren't effectively integrated with performance degrees in most cases. The meteoric rise in music business, music technology, music production, popular music performance, and entrepreneurship programs are all related in the sense that they have responded to deficiencies in existing pedagogy and to the inability of performers to support themselves using repertoires and models of concert hall performance dating largely from the nineteenth century. Only more flexible and innovative curricula can effectively respond to such challenges.

The notion of arts entrepreneurship has received a great deal of attention and has led to the creation of at least three new journals in recent years: *Artivate*,[29] the *Journal of Arts Entrepreneurship Education*,[30] and the *Journal of Arts Education Research*,[31] in addition to countless other resources.[32] At present, at least ninety-six tertiary institutions in the United States offer arts entrepreneurship training of some sort (White 2015). Despite this, notions about how to define entrepreneurship and what constitutes appropriate training for it vary widely (Beckman 2015).[33] Theories surrounding entrepreneurship derive ultimately from economic models in which individuals provide specialized services in order to maximize profit. This concept fits poorly when applied to the arts sector, given that most do not pursue the arts primarily for financial return, and in many cases the goods or services they offer have distinct forms of value that may be difficult to evaluate or monetize. Many authors conflate career development, business courses, and arts administration training with entrepreneurship, though others would argue that such topics have nothing in common. Most typically, arts entrepreneurship is defined as the discovery and pursuit of new ideas through artistic expression, or the creative application of resources at hand to new problems or opportunities (Essig 2015, 2, 7). Mark Rabideau similarly views entrepreneurship as perceiving social needs and using "the transformative powers of the arts" to respond to them in innovative ways.[34] An entrepreneurial perspective involves creativity, inquisitiveness, and a willingness to consider new alternatives. It can best be cultivated through the combining of performance with a wide-ranging education (Pertl 2015).

Attempts to incorporate popular music performance into degree programs represent another important way that the practical concerns of performers can be addressed through curricular change. Only in the past decade has

29. http://artivate.org (accessed August 5, 2015).
30. http://jaee.ncsu.edu/ (accessed August 5, 2015).
31. http://jaer.ncsu.edu/ (accessed July 25, 2015).
32. As only a few prominent examples of book publications on the subject, see Beeching 2005, Cutler 2009, and Klickstein 2009.
33. An article in *Artivate* addresses this issue directly. See Chang and Wyszomirski 2015.
34. Mark Rabideau, e-mail communication, July 29, 2015.

Problem not addressed: connection between K-12 mus. Ed. with college perf. curriculum.

notable momentum developed in support of more inclusive BM programs and recognition of the benefits of performing popular music (Green, Lebler, and Till 2015). Such initiatives suggest a model for narrowing the gap between the music of everyday life and that of the academy. At the same time, voices that have denigrated popular music performance for decades seem to be losing ground. The National Association for Music Education published a book (Rodríguez 2004) and has held multiple conferences on the subject of popular music performance; the March 2009 issue of the *Journal of Popular Music Studies* focuses on the same topic, as does the first issue of the 2015 *IASPM* journal (Vol. 5 No. 1). An Association for Popular Music Education (APME) was established in 2010 to advocate for all forms of engagement with such repertoire.[35] And a forthcoming *Ashgate Research Companion to Popular Music Education* (2017) devotes considerable attention to applied performance as well.

Powell, Krikun, and Pignato (2015) provide a useful overview of the history of popular music performance in higher education within the United States. Such experiments date back to the 1930s, with junior colleges among the first to offer courses in jazz arranging and performance, followed by the Berklee College, the University of North Texas, and other institutions. None of them had much effect on degree plans or course offerings in most conservatories and music schools. However, the pace of change is accelerating. In 2009, for instance, Oberlin Conservatory established a Music for Everyone program that centers on songwriting, audio production training, and the foregrounding of student work on a university music label. The initiative is conceived of both as a form of music major training and of community engagement.[36] USC's Thornton School of Music launched a bachelor of music in popular music studies the same year, one of the first offered in a conservatory-style context.[37] It has been overwhelmed by applicants. And the University of Miami's Frost School of Music has developed a Creative American Music program that allows music majors to work together in cooperative groups on project-based assignments.[38] Similar curricula exist at institutions in England, including the University of Chester[39] and the University of Huddersfield, where applied popular music study developed earlier than in the United States and has received greater support. At Huddersfield, for instance, aside from more common technical tracks in popular music production, music technology, film music, and music for TV and games, students also have two distinct popular music

35. http://www.popularmusiceducation.org/ (accessed August 5, 2015).
36. https://new.oberlin.edu/conservatory/music-for-everyone/ (accessed August 5, 2015).
37. http://music.usc.edu/departments/popular-music/ (accessed July 25, 2015). See also Powell, Krikun, and Pignato 2015, 14.
38. http://creativeamericanmusic.net/ (accessed July 25, 2015).
39. http://www.chester.ac.uk/undergraduate/pm (accessed July 23, 2015).

performance emphases to choose from. Both include internships and visits by professionals in the music industry in conjunction with academic coursework.[40] Note that online music pedagogy sites that provide the potential for expert instruction in a variety of vernacular styles to music students and that have the potential to dramatically expand the styles of instruction offered at a given institution have developed of late.[41] Ultimately, institutional music education cannot afford to ignore popular music, the form of expression most students and audiences experience each day and are most comfortable with. The constant shifting of popular repertoires creates challenges for curricula but caters more directly to the cultural and class backgrounds of a diverse student body and allows for the foregrounding of student knowledge (Bowman 2004, 43–35; Wemyss 2004, 145–46).

3. **Commitment to global awareness**. The increasingly global nature of cultural influences and the constant migration and movement of world populations suggests that musicians of the twenty-first century be more aware than their predecessors of international musical forms and practices. A commitment to understanding musical forms outside of one's own culture must be a prominent part of any progressive curriculum and should influence many aspects of pedagogy (performance, composition, ear training, theory,[42] arranging, conducting, etc.). A number of programs have already embraced this emphasis, including those at the Rotterdam Conservatory in the Netherlands and the University of Malmö in Sweden.[43] Many other institutions in Europe, the United States, and elsewhere combine the academic study of global musics with performance training to some degree, though an exclusive or even predominant focus on the performance of such repertoire is less common.[44] A commitment to global musical awareness would of course involve studying world repertoires, analyzing and performing them, as well as learning to compose, arrange, and improvise

40.   http://www.hud.ac.uk/courses/full-time/undergraduate/popular-music-bmus-hons;   http://www.hud.ac.uk/courses/full-time/undergraduate/music-performance-bmus-hons/ (accessed August 3, 2015). The Huddersfield popular music performance program was established in 2004.

41. As one example, consider the variety of music that can be learned on the site artistsworks.com, a service established in 2008. Similar resources could supplement the performance skills of existing faculty, especially in styles that a conservatory background has not prepared them to teach.

42. An example of Victoria Levine's course on world music theory is provided on the companion website to this volume, in the files associated with Chapter 9 ▶.

43. See http://rotterdamconservatory.com/world-music/program/ and http://www.mhm.lu.se/en/education/performance-programmes-in-music-bachelors-level/world-music (accessed August 5, 2015).

44. Representative programs of this nature include UCLA's World Arts and Cultures program, www.wacd.ucla.edu/; and the ethnomusicology program at Wesleyan University, http://www.wesleyan.edu/music/ (accessed July 24, 2015).

in representative styles. Expanded ensemble options support this goal, as well as guest artist programs and study-abroad options. In terms of the latter, extending ties between local and international music institutions would potentially benefit student professional development and support broader campus initiatives involving global awareness. The study of world cultures provides a compelling point of entry into understanding alternative perspectives, values, histories, aesthetics, and ways of life abroad, as well as compelling macro-level social and political trends that affect us all.

The field of music education has the longest history of advocacy for the inclusion of world music repertoire and performance into degree plans, dating back at least to the 1960s. Music education specialists continue to be at the forefront of this discussion, though until recently they have had mixed success in making global music awareness a central priority within their discipline. Therese Volk (1998) provides a useful overview of the movement to include diverse repertoires in music programs in the United States that emerged in the wake of the civil rights movement, the founding of the International Society for Music Education (1953), the Tanglewood Symposium (1967), and subsequent initiatives of the 1980s and 1990s. Volk notes throughout her discussion a consistent gap between the ideals of the MENC leadership and their implementation (e.g., 1998, 84). Contemporary authors dwell on many of the same issues (Jorgensen 2003; Campbell 2005, Drummond 2010). Even so, the extent of applied publications and conference activity surrounding world music pedagogy continues to accelerate, suggesting a more widespread sensitivity to this priority.[45] The final roundtable of the 2016 conference Analytical Approaches to World Music, with many contributions by composers, performers, and theorists, suggests that interest in the incorporation of world music repertoire to other fields is growing as well.[46]

Ethnomusicology as a discipline devoted largely to the study of world musics continues to grow, and the increasingly visibility of such faculty in music programs (as performers as well as academic instructors) has contributed to greater curricular diversity. What is needed going forward is an embrace of diverse repertoire as a component of all applied degree plans. Several chapters in this volume make suggestions as to how it might be practically implemented. In some cases this may involve expanding current

45. E.g., consult recent issues of the *International Journal of Music Education* (http://www.isme.org/publications), recent conference proceedings of the International Society for Music Education (http://www.isme.org/publications/28-world-conferences/50-isme-world-conference-proceedings), and resources compiled by UNESCO's Centre for Arts Research in Education, http://www.unesco-care.nie.edu.sg/events/cultural-diversity-music-education-conference-cdime-11 (all accessed August 5, 2015).

46. See, e.g., p. 10 in the conference program for the 2016 conference: http://aawm-conference.com/schedule.html (accessed July 20, 2016).

offerings in music education (Bradley, Chapter 11, and Pedroza, Chapter 7, in this volume), reemphasizing transcription and ear training (Tenzer, Chapter 9 in this volume), or training students in popular music performance as well as in other traditions (Patch, Chapter 6 in this volume). More broadly, it will require restructuring existing performance degrees so as to accommodate new experiences, repertoires, and skills alongside those of the standard music degree (Chapters 13 and 14).

4. **Commitment to social justice**. This issue was discussed at the first-ever International Conference on Music Education, Equity, and Social Justice that took place in October 2006 at Columbia University. Social justice can be conceived in various ways, such as the foregrounding of historically marginal forms of music; the incorporation of repertoire into the classroom that raises awareness of social concerns; recognition of implicit bias regarding gender, race, class, or other factors in existing musical practice (e.g., Heth 2013, 6); and in general learning to think critically about the social circulation of all music, its public meanings, and the broader issues surrounding it. A commitment to social justice need not involve the creation a specific course to address the issue but ideally should influence a variety of coursework, applied and academic.

Of course, many efforts already undertaken by music institutions support progressive social agendas such as interacting with local communities in respectful ways, providing students more control over the content and direction of their musical education, and engaging in a sustained fashion with the musical practices of other cultures. Each institution must determine for itself how best to provide an education sensitive to such concerns. A social justice agenda could inform choices about guest artist residencies or institutional affiliations in addition to decisions about coursework content and repertoire. It might influence the final independent projects of advanced students, perhaps in conjunction with research on particular musical communities, their concerns, and their histories. Regardless of how the goal of musical equity and social justice is achieved, we agree with Timothy Rice (2016, 2) that "North American music schools need to be rebuilt on a foundation that takes their ethical responsibilities to all the citizens of their region, state, and nation" seriously and prioritizes an aesthetics of inclusion. When institutions fail to take the music of their surrounding communities seriously, underprivileged or otherwise, "they also fail to take the peoples and communities seriously who make it" and are implicitly establishing an unethical relationship with the society in which they will practice their musical life (Rice 2016, 6).

A surprising amount on the topic of social justice has been written of late, also largely by those in music education. Many such articles appear in the journals *Action, Criticism, and Theory for Music Education*, the *International Journal of Music Education*, and the *Philosophy of Music Education Review*.[47] Interest in social justice has led to applied and public sector projects as well.[48] Musicologists and ethnomusicologists have rarely adopted the term social justice per se, but trends in those disciplines and in anthropology toward activist scholarship conceived in collaboration with and of direct benefit to particular communities, as well as with issues of cultural rights, share many commonalities with advocates of social justice (e.g., Weintraub and Young 2009; Harrison, MacKinlay, and Pettan 2010; Angel-Ajani 2006). Bowman (2007) provides a useful introduction to the ways the term "social justice" has been conceived, including ideas drawn from academic writing and from Eastern and Western philosophy. He emphasizes a concern for others and their heritage as central to the concept, as well as space for multiple points of view and productive dialogue. Vaugeois (2007) provides a useful critique of the multiculturalism movement within music education from the same perspective. She notes that while ostensibly committed to inclusion, multiculturalism has often functioned less productively owing to a lack of attention to legal, material, or other forms of oppression that have framed relations between the West and others (173, 183). The author calls for scrutiny of the hierarchical relations that exist between various forms of music making in existing institutions and that are manifest constantly in decisions about curricula. And Bradley (2006, 141), discussing music pedagogy as racial project, examines the ways in which nonwhite peoples and their music can be used to challenge the values, structures, and behaviors that perpetuate inequality. A majority of this literature, while insightful, focuses on critiques of existing practice rather than discussing how social justice might be more fully incorporated into curricula today. Several of our chapters address the latter issue.

5. **Commitment to creative, student-driven projects and practices.** This priority involves greater space for creative musical expression, such as composition and improvisation, but also creative academic musical experiences of all sorts, including flipped classrooms, integrated approaches to pedagogy, and an option-rich curriculum, designed in part by students, that would allow them to conceive their own artistic initiatives, help select their own repertoire, and perhaps arrange, write, record, and market it as well. This emphasis reflects in part the findings of the CMS task force, whose members correctly stress that the interpretive performance of canonical repertoire should not have the same importance in the future

47. See also Benedict, Schmidt, Spruce, and Woodford 2015.
48. See, e.g., the Shifting Perspectives project that explores social equity issues through cross-discipline and cross-cultural collaborations: http://www.tylercessor.com/#!shifting-perspectives/c1b9r (accessed July 24, 2015).

that it currently does. Instead, music pedagogy needs to more consistently valorize the experiences and preferences of students themselves and to foster creative experimentation. Such ideals align with the findings of specialists in music pedagogy, who suggest that learning is an inherently active process that involves guided exploration and engagement (Duke 2005, 12). They also resonate with the position of Giroux and Freire that the curriculum needs to be vitally connected to everyday life, that it should blur distinctions between high and popular culture, and that educators should strive to create "a public sphere of citizens who are able to exercise power over their own lives" and "over the conditions of knowledge productions and acquisition" (1989, viii).

Literature on option-rich music curricula is not extensive, yet many suggest in passing that student interests and expertise deserve greater recognition. Some of the strongest statements along these lines have come from music theorists, who increasingly recognize that the models and materials they present to students do not prepare them adequately for twenty-first-century musical life. Kulma and Naxer (2014) stress that students are frequently accomplished instrumentalists before they enter a given program and that faculty must "acknowledge their extensive musical experience as listeners and performers." Others advocate even more directly for a student-centered and inclusive approach to theory pedagogy, one that involves giving students control over learning processes, content, and assessment and that finds other "ethnically responsible ways to share power" with them (Weimer 2012; see also Poundie Burstein 2013). The ideal teaching environment from this perspective is one that is more collaborative, both between students themselves and between students and faculty.

Recent interest in peer instruction, flipped classrooms, and inquiry-based learning apply to this priority in that they all involve more active, interactive, and creative approaches to teaching than are found in many institutions. The peer instruction paradigm (Mazur 1997) and the flipped classroom and inquiry-based models derived from it encourage students to spend class time wrestling with problems or issues and to seek their resolution independently or in small groups. All such models presuppose that basic background reading on a particular subject be undertaken independently so that the crucial concepts behind them can be explored and internalized in class (DeClerq 2013). They attempt to put student inquiry rather than the presentations of an instructor at the center of class activity. While not necessarily allowing for student input in the orientation of instruction, they suggest approaches that would engage students more actively in learning, often through applied performance. Shaffer and Hughes (2013) use the example of teaching about a particular style of music by asking students to collectively compile observations that define it, then compare notes and only afterward consult the insights of specialist authors on the topic.

Integrated pedagogical models represent an important related emphasis; they have the advantage of allowing for creative experimentation on the part of students and also free up (inevitably overloaded) music curricula so as to provide more option-rich alternatives. Sarath is a strong proponent of integrated learning (2013).[49] His model is centered on improvisation, composition, performance, and analysis as a composite activity, with black Atlantic musics holding a prominent place in assigned repertoire. While students would continue to take private studio instruction, musicianship skills would be acquired through small-group classes meeting for extended sessions each week and stressing the practical application of theory, analysis, and ear training simultaneously. The Experiential Music Program at the University of Miami has implemented many of these same concepts. All incoming freshmen enroll in the program during their first year; they study performance, music history, music theory, and composition simultaneously in six hours of weekly applied chamber music sessions. Jazz, world music, film music, and other styles are included in course assignments. Ensemble exercises in which students perform, conduct, create, improvise, discuss, and analyze music have largely replaced aural skills courses (Chattah 2012, 14). In recognition of the practical concerns of aspiring musicians, freshmen also take a year of music technology coursework and a yearlong music business course.

Educators raised with the Western canon may be apprehensive about the broad strokes of changes proposed in this chapter and in particular may wonder what the potential disadvantages may be to a less exclusive focus on common-practice repertoire. They may believe that something is lost when in-depth of study in a single style of music is lessened so as to accommodate diversity. Undoubtedly, loss and gain are associated with any paradigm shift. To those concerned with the future of the canon, I suggest two points to consider. First, putting canonical repertoire more directly in dialogue with diverse traditions through curriculum reform is a net positive, as the possibilities for cross-cultural or cross-repertoire experiments can potentially enrich all forms of music making. Interactions between art music and other forms of expression date back centuries in any case (e.g., Bellman 1998) and have only accelerated of late. Second, though the proposed reorientation of music curricula may further change the nature of classical music performance, the reality is that the classical performance scene is already changing. The interventions suggested here and in the following chapters are intended to revitalize formal music instruction and ensure its relevance into the future. If the Western art music tradition is to remain an important part of social life, it will occur only

49. See esp. ch. 10.

by grounding future composition and performance in all facets of contemporary experience. Art music must become a modality through which we naturally choose to express ourselves, in respectful dialogue with others (Moore 1992, 82).

While this introduction has touched on many topics in its overview of curriculum reform literature, the following chapters consist of case studies devoted to ongoing experiments at specific institutions. By examining existing programs and their respective strengths, the contributors hope to provide tangible examples of how reform can take place rather than remaining at the level of abstraction. Educators in the United States may not be aware of all programs discussed in the following pages, especially those based abroad (e.g., Hsu, Chapter 8, and Talty, Chapter 5); hopefully the information provided will lead to greater dialogue between schools internationally on the topic of curriculum and suggest modifications to individual programs.

Many questions remain about music curricula going forward, in part because serious attempts at reform are only now beginning. The chapters that follow do not consider what the role of the performance studio should be in the future, for instance, beyond the suggestion that a greater variety of instruments and compositional techniques be offered to students. It appears that the intensive student-teacher mentoring relationship currently employed may be less central to institutional education in the future and/or may be modified to include new modalities of instruction, but to date few if any programs have attempted reform along those lines. Chapters 13 and 14 do, however, provide curricular models that may help studio instructors incorporate new repertoire, expose their students to new instruments or vocal styles, embrace new technologies, accommodate more diverse forms of professional training, and emphasize independent projects of the students' own design into their studies.

Our volume considers primarily the reform of applied music major curricula but does not devote nearly as much attention to the broader question: whom should music institutions be teaching? It is worth considering how much of a program's energies—especially in smaller institutions (Levine and Kohut, Chapter 3), but even that of a music school or conservatory—should be devoted to amateur performance or non-major instruction, for instance. Given the need to cultivate future audiences for the arts and in light of the ongoing difficulties facing aspiring full-time performers, one could argue that a much greater percentage of institutional energy should be devoted to the teaching of nonspecialists. But again, few music programs have attempted reform of this sort, perhaps because the instruction of amateurs is perceived as less prestigious and may result in less polished performances. Similarly, it remains unclear what the relationship of an applied music degree should have to academic pursuits beyond music. Most curricular reform continues to focus on technical training on an instrument and related musical skills. But music majors of the future will likely need to be more versatile (in their entrepreneurial savvy as self-employed professionals, drawing on business and technical as well as musical skills), more cosmopolitan (conversant in the music of other cultures, able to function in a variety of social settings), and more socially engaged (involved in the community not only economically but as an artistic participant in civil society) in order to succeed in their chosen career. And indeed a music degree should help them succeed even if they ultimately choose not to pursue music professionally. The priorities described above and the chapters that follow suggest how music curricula of the twenty-first century can address these needs.

A final topic for future discussion concerns the relationship between music making in and outside academia. So much of what is truly innovative and exciting in the world of music performance is taking place outside institutional contexts, a humbling reality for music educators. Music departments and schools have much to learn from artists who have opted for nontraditional forms of education. We must critically examine our broader institutional purpose and consider what we can productively offer students that less academic music experiences cannot. Greater respect for and dialogue with existing musical scenes beyond academia will do much to overcome our current limitations.

CONTRIBUTIONS TO THE VOLUME

The contents of this book have been organized into four distinct sections. Part 1, "Institutional Structures," concerns itself with a broad overview of musical institutions of varying types and the ways they might be modified so as to incorporate some of the discussed progressive changes. Brian Pertl's chapter, "Reshaping Undergraduate Music Education in Turbulent Times Through Cultural Rather Than Curricular Change," is written from the perspective of a senior administrator. Noting the many challenges to existing programs and the radical shifts in musical employment opportunities in recent years, Pertl advocates change derived from the cultivation of new institutional attitudes. His suggestions do not involve formal modifications of degree plans primarily and thus have the potential to be implemented quickly. By creating an environment that celebrates creative, collaborative change, he suggests much can be accomplished to reform existing practice within existing curricular models.

While Pertl reflects on changes within conservatories and schools of music, Victoria Levine and Emily Kohut, in "Finding a Balance," focus instead on music programs within liberal arts institutions. They compare degree programs in many peer institutions and note that all struggle to maintain a balance between courses that simultaneously offer preprofessional music training and that engage with socially aware, global, and inclusive curricular priorities.

While noting the difficulties of instigating rapid changes in liberal arts institutions given their small size and reduced faculty, the authors advocate the creation of a "lean" curricular model that is more flexible and responsive to diverse student interests. Mark F. DeWitt's chapter, "Training in Local Oral Traditions," provides an overview of music programs within the United States that have foregrounded various styles of regional community music. His analysis underscores the surprising extent to which such engagement already exists and emphasizes successes and challenges facing the institutionalization of music originally associated with nonnotated learning. Its content provides an introduction to themes explored later by Eddie Hsu and Jack Talty.

Part 2, "Case Studies," considers specific examples of curricular change nationally and internationally. Jack Talty's chapter, "Noncanonical Pedagogies for Noncanonical Musics," examines European programs foregrounding various styles of traditional music, with special emphasis on the Irish World Academy at the University of Limerick. He examines the tendency of musical institutions to canonize certain kinds of traditional repertoire, noting the ways that their coursework diverges from more traditional pedagogy and how neighboring music communities have reacted to them. Justin Patch's chapter, "The Case for Pop Ensembles in the Curriculum," discusses the advantages associated with a more central focus on commercial music, including an ability to attract larger numbers of students to music programs, new and important forms of professional training provided to future music educators, and greater support for the cultivation of creative, student-led projects among majors and non-majors alike. He examines representative institutions as a means of exploring how such engagement can be accomplished in practical terms.

Ludim Pedroza takes a different approach in Chapter 7, using her intimate familiarity with the Latin music program at Texas State University–San Marcos as a means of considering the specific coursework and curricular modifications to standard music education degrees that best suit students specializing in mariachi and salsa music. Pedroza examines the politics of curricular expansion within mainstream music institutions from the perspective of a faculty member at an officially recognized Hispanic-serving institution. She also examines issues of canonization, standardization, and virtuosity within European canonical repertoire and mariachi repertoire, noting that many of her students support the creation of a recognized body of "classics" in genres other than that of Western art music. Her analysis forces us to consider the most appropriate balance between interpretive performance and creative experimentation in institutional contexts. Concluding Section 2, Eddie Hsu's chapter, "Traditional Music for the People," examines the presence of Asian court and traditional/folkloric music in Chinese and Taiwanese conservatories. He notes that many such programs developed in conjunction with governmental efforts to inspire regional or national pride and to formally recognize each country's ethnic diversity. Hsu examines the efficacy of artist-in-residence programs as a means of bridging the divide between academic institutions and the community and of providing conservatory students exposure to nonnotated forms of musical training and performance.

Part 3, "Disciplinary and Professional Experiments," considers the ways that particular subfields of music might be modified so as to more consistently engage with some of the priorities discussed above. Chapter 9, "In Honor of What We Can't Groove To Yet," by Michael Tenzer, focuses on integrating close listening and music transcription into courses across the curriculum, to soften the disciplinary divide between the oral and written, and the Western and non-Western. He argues that transcription and analysis in numerous forms cultivates musicianship and embodiment without sacrificing the university's core focus on literacy. He notes they could help create a more equitable balance between the study of European canonical and other repertoire and serve as a means of fostering broader appreciation for all styles of music. Chapter 10, Sonia Seeman's "Embodied Pedagogy," encourages those in academic musical disciplines to theorize their own pedagogical practices more actively and consider their ultimate goals as they contribute to the education of music majors and non-majors alike. She advocates a form of pedagogy that helps bridge and de-exoticize differences between Western and other cultures even as it accentuates commonalities in usage or meaning and thus sheds new light on familiar musical forms.

Deborah Bradley begins Chapter 11, "Standing in the Shadows of Mozart," by discussing various structural reasons why the field of music education has been slow to become more inclusive and socially engaged and why it is still dominated in general by discourses of whiteness. She goes on to survey progressive experiments in the field of music education at the University of Washington and elsewhere and to outline her vision for programs in which inclusivity and social justice would serve as central guiding principles. Paul Klemperer's "Making a Living, Making a Life" (Chapter 12) offers the insights of a professional performer on the issue of what applied music pedagogy should consist of and what skills performers need in order to succeed. He describes how the music industry has changed radically in recent years and how performers have been forced to shift from aspiring to sign with a major label or land a job in an established musical institution to greater reliance on marketing and entrepreneurial skills. Klemperer thus notes a need to balance artistic goals with an at-times unrelated practical skill set. He underscores the importance for younger performers of working with professional mentors and suggests that universities could do much to establish such relationships in surrounding communities to the benefit of their graduates.

The book concludes with a synthesis of best practices and innovative experiments in various national and international institutions, considering primarily the curricula of large conservatories and schools of music. Chapter 13 begins by discussing potential changes to performance and music education degrees and continues by examining various ways the priorities discussed earlier could be (or have been) implemented. Specifically, it examines progressive forms of local community engagement and various ways that the practical concerns of professional musicians are being accommodated through attention to entrepreneurship, technological training, and greater engagement with commercial repertoire. The book's final chapter provides four potential models that could be used to restructure existing music performance degrees for the twenty-first century based on existing degree plans. These include (1) an enhanced core model that endeavors to expand and diversify the content of courses while maintaining existing structures; (2) a pluralist model in which students are obliged to enroll in a diversity of distinct performance and academic courses during their first two years in the degree prior to choosing a concentration; (3) an integrated curriculum that endeavors to combine instruction in ear training, music theory, keyboard skills, and potentially other areas in a single classroom experience; and (4) a capstone model that emphasizes work toward self-directed, individualized student projects involving composition, improvisation, the use of technology, public speaking, and other elements.

REFERENCES

Alviso, J. Ricardo. 2003. "Applied Ethnomusicology and the Impulse to Make a Difference." *Folklore Forum*, Vol. 34 Nos. 1–2, 89–96.

Angel-Ajani, Asale. 2006. *Engaged Observer. Anthropology, Advocacy, and Activism*. Rutgers, NJ: Rutgers University Press.

Araújo, Samuel. 2009. "Ethnomusicologists Researching Towns They Live In: Theoretical and Methodological Queries for a Renewed Discipline." *Muzikologija/Musicology*, Vol. 9, 33–49.

Araújo, Samuel, and Vincenzo Cambria. 2003. "Sound Praxis, Poverty and Social Participation; Perspectives from Collaborative Study in Rio de Janeiro." In *Yearbook for Traditional Music*, Vol. 45, 28–42.

Araújo, Samuel, and José Alberto Salgado e Silva. 2009. "Musical Knowledge, Transmission, and Worldviews: Ethnomusicological Perspectives from Rio de Janeiro, Brazil." *World of Music*, Vol. 51 No. 3, 93–110.

Beckman, Gary. 2015. "What Arts Entrepreneurship Isn't." *Journal of Arts Entrepreneurship Research*, Vol. 1 No. 1. http://jaer.ncsu.edu/volume-1-number-1-2015/what-arts-entrepreneurship-isnt/ (accessed 29 December 29, 2016).

Beeching, Angela Myles. 2005. *Beyond Talent: Creating a successful career in music*. Oxford: Oxford University Press.

Bellman, Jonathan, ed. 1998. *The Exotic in Western Music*. Boston: Northeastern University Press.

Benedict, Cathy, and Patrick Schmidt, Gary Spruce, and Paul Woodford. 2015. *The Oxford Handbook of Social Justice in Music Education*. New York: Oxford University Press.

Bowman, Wayne D. 2004. "'Pop' Goes . . .: Taking Popular Music Seriously." In Carlos Xavier Rodríguez, ed., *Bridging the Gap. Popular Music and Music Education*. Reston, VA: National Association for Music Education, 29–50.

———. 2007. "Who's asking (Who's answering): Theorizing social justice in music education." *Action, Criticism & Theory for Music Education* vol. 6 no. 4, 1-20.

Bradley, Deborah. 2007. "The Sounds of Silence: Talking Race in Music Education." *Action, Criticism, and Theory for Music Education*, Vol. 6 No. 4, 132–162.

———. 2009. "'Oh that Magic Feeling!' Multicultural Human Subjectivity, Community, and Fascism's Footprints." *Philosophy of Music Education Review*, Vol. 17 No. 1 (Spring), 56–74.

Campbell, Patricia S., et al., eds. 2005. *Cultural Diversity in Music Education. Directions and Challenges for the Twenty-First Century*. Brisbane: Australian Academic Press.

Campbell, Patricia S., et al. 2014. "Transforming Music Study from Its Foundations: A Manifesto for Progressive Change in the Undergraduate Preparation of Music Majors." Missoula, MT: College Music Society. http://symposium. music.org/index.php?option=com_k2&view=item&id=11118:transforming-music-study-from-its-foundations-a-manifesto-for-progressive-change-in-the-undergraduate-preparation-of-music-majors&Itemid=126. Accessed December 28 2016.

Carson, Charles, and Maria Westvall. 2016. "Intercultural Approaches and 'Diversified Normality' in Music Teacher Education: Reflections from Two Angles." *Action, Criticism, and Theory for Music Education*, Vol. 15 No. 3, 37–52.

Chang, WoongJo, and Margaret Wyszomirski. 2015. "What Is Arts Entrepreneurship? Tracking the Development of Its Definition in Scholarly Journals." *Artivate*, Vol. 4 No. 2 (Spring), 11–31.

Chattah, Juan. 2012. "Case Studies on Developing Synthesis Capabilities in Undergraduate Students I." *Proceedings of the 88th Annual Meeting of NASM*. Reston, VA: National Association for Music Education, 13–21.

Corn, Aaron. 2009. "Sound Exchanges: An Ethnomusicologist's Approach to Interdisciplinary Teaching and Learning in Collaboration with a Remote Indigenous Australian Community." *World of Music*, Vol. 51 No. 3, 21–50.

Cutler, David. 2009. *The Savvy Musician. Building a Career, Earning a Living, and Making a Difference*. Pittsburgh: Helius Press.

DeClercq, Trevor. 2013. "Towards a Flipped Aural Skills Classroom: Harnessing Recording Technology for Performance-Based Homework." In *Engaging Students*, Bryn Hughes, ed. *Essays in Music Pedagogy*, Vol. 1. http://flipcamp.org/engagingstudents/toc.html. Accessed July 1, 2015.

Drummond, John. 2010. "Re-thinking Western Art Music: A Perspective Shift for Music Educators." *International Journal of Music Education*, Vol. 28 No. 2, 117–126.

Duke, Robert A. 2005. *Intelligent Music Teaching. Essays on the Core Principles of Effective Instruction*. Austin: Center for Music Learning.

Essig, Linda. 2015. "Means and Ends: A Theory Framework for Understanding Entrepreneurship in the US Arts and Culture Sector." Paper read at the biannual AIMIC conference. Available at http://aimac2015-aix-marseille.univ-amu. fr/themes/aimac/papers/PS1_track7/369.pdf. Accessed December 28 2016.

Freeman, Robert. 2014. *The Crisis of Classical Music in America. Lessons from a Life in the Education of Musicians*. Lanham, MD: Rowman and Littlefield.

Giroux, Henry, and Paolo Freire. 1989. "Pedagogy, Popular Culture, and Public Life: An Introduction." In H. Giroux and R. Simon, eds., *Popular Culture, Schooling, and Everyday Life*, vii–xii. Granby, MA: Bergin and Garvey.

Green, Lucy, Don Lebler, and Rupert Till, eds. 2015. "Editorial Introduction." *Journal of the International Association for the Study of Popular Music*, Vol. 5 No. 1, 1–3.

Guilbault, Jocelyne. 2014. "Politics of Ethnomusicological Knowledge Production and Circulation." *Ethnomusicology*, Vol. 58 No. 2, 321–326.

Harrison, Klisala. 2015. "The Second Wave of Applied Ethnomusicology." *MUSICultures*, Vol. 41 No. 2, 15–33.

Harrison, Klisala, Elizabeth MacKinlay, and Svanibor Pettan, eds. 2010. *Applied Ethnomusicology. Historical and Contemporary Approaches*. Newcastle upon Tyne: Cambridge Scholars.

Heth, Charlotte. 2013. "Charlotte Heth Interviewed by Victoria Levine." *SEM Newsletter* Vol. 47 No. 3 (June), 1, 6.

Heuser, Frank. 2014. "Juxtapositional Pedagogy as an Organizing Principle in University Music Education Programs." In *Promising Practices in Twenty-First-Century Music Teacher Education*, Michele Kaschub and Janice Smith, eds. Oxford University Press Online.

Hill, Juniper. 2009. "The Influence of Conservatory Folk Music Programmes: The Sibelius Academy in Comparative Context." *Ethnomusicology Forum*, Vol. 18 No. 2 (November), 207–241.

Ivey, Bill. 2008. *Arts, Inc. How Greed and Neglect Have Damaged America's Cultural Heritage*. Berkeley: University of California Press.

Jorgensen, Estelle. 2003. *Transforming Music Education*. Bloomington: Indiana University Press.

Kingsbury, Henry. 1988. *Music, Talent, and Performance*. Philadelphia: Temple University Press.

Klickstein, Gerald. 2009. *The Musician's Way. A Guide to Practice, Performance, and Wellness*. New York: Oxford University Press.

Krüger, Simone, ed. 2009. "Ethnomusicology in the Academy: An Introduction." *World of Music*, Vol. 51 No. 3, 5–16.

———. 2011. "Democratic Pedagogies: Perspectives from Ethnomusicology and World Music Educational Contexts in the United Kingdom". *Ethnomusicology*, Vol. 55 No. 2, 280–305.

Kulma, David, and Meghan Naxer. 2014. "Beyond Part Writing: Modernizing the Curriculum." In *Engaging Students. Essays in Music Pedagogy*, Vol. 2. http://flip-camp.org/engagingstudents2/essays/kulmaNaxer.html. Accessed December 28 2016.

Kwami, Robert. 1998. "Non-Western Musics in Education: Problems and Possibilities." *British Journal of Music Education*, Vol. 15 No. 2 (July 1998), 161–170.

Lima, Paulo Costa. 2002. "Formação cidadã, reforma curricular e Extensão Universitária." In *Reforma do Pensamento, Extensão Universitária e Cidadania* (Francisca Nazaré Liberalino, Org.), XXVI Fórum de Pró-Reitores de Extensáo das Universidades Públicas Brasileiras—Regional Nordeste. *Natal-RN, EDUFRN*, 37–54.

Lowe, Melanie. 2012. "Case Studies on Developing Synthesis Capabilities in Undergraduate Students II." *Proceedings of the 88th Annual Meeting of NASM*, 21–24. Reston, VA: National Association for Music Education.

Madrid, Alejandro. 2011. "American Music in Times of Postnationality." *Journal of the American Musicological Society*, Vol. 64 No. 3, 699-703

Mazur, Eric. 1997. *Peer Instruction. A User's Manual*. Upper Saddle River, NJ: Prentice Hall.

McCarthy, Kevin, et al. 2001. *The Performing Arts in a New Era*. Santa Monica, CA: Rand Corporation.

Moore, Robin. 1992. "The Decline of Improvisation in Western Art Music since 1840: An Interpretation of Change." *International Review of the Aesthetics and Sociology of Music*, Vol. 23 No. 1 (June), 61–84.

Morris, Avlerie B., and David B. Pankratz, eds. 2003. *The Arts in a New Millennium. Research and the Arts Sector*. Westport, CT: Praeger.

National Association of Schools of Music. 2013–2014. *Handbook 2013–14*. http://nasm.arts-accredit.org/site/docs/Handbook/NASM_HANDBOOK_2013-14.pdf. Accessed June 4, 2016.

Nettl, Bruno. 1995. *Heartland Excursions*. Urbana: University of Illinois Press.

Ostashewski, Marcia. "Engaging Communities and Cultures in Ethnomusicology: An Introduction." *MUSICultures*, Vol. 41 No. 2, 1–14.

Pertl, Brian. 2015 "Twenty-First Century Musicianship: Articulating a New Vision for Undergraduate Music Training at the Lawrence Conservatory of Music." https://www.lawrence.edu/conservatory/21st-century-musicianship. Accessed December 28 2016.

Poundie Burstein, L. 2013. "Music Theory Pedagogy in the iPhone Generation." In *Engaging Students. Essays in Music Pedagogy*, Vol. 1, Bryn Hughes, ed. http://flip-camp.org/engagingstudents/toc.html. Accessed July 2, 2015.

Powell, Brian, Andrew Krikun, and Joseph Michael Pignato. 2015. "'Something's Happening Here!': Popular Music Education in the United States." *Journal of the International Association for the Study of Popular Music*, Vol. 5 No. 1, 4–22.

Rice, Timothy. 2016. "Diverse Musical Exposure." Unpublished paper, College Music Society 21st-Century Music School Design conference, Columbus, SC, June 3-5.

Rodríguez, Carlos Xavier, ed. 2004. *Bridging the Gap. Popular Music and Music Education*. Reston, VA: National Association for Music Education.

Rosenboom, David. 2012. "Fostering and Supporting Student Creativity and Innovation." Case Studies on Developing Synthesis Capabilities in Undergraduate Students I. *Proceedings of the 88th Annual Meeting of NASM*, 43–54. Reston, VA: National Association for Music Education.

Sarath, Edward. 2013. *Improvisation, Creativity, and Consciousness. Jazz as Integral Template for Music, Education, and Society*. New York: SUNY Press.

Sefa Dei, George J., and Arlo Kempf, eds. 2006. *Anti-Colonialism and Education. The Politics of Resistance*. Toronto: Ontario Institute for Studies in Education, University of Toronto.

Shaffer, Kris, and Bryn Hughes. 2013. "Flipping the Classroom: Three Methods." In *Engaging Students. Essays in Music Pedagogy*, Vol. 1, Bryn Hughes, ed. http://flip-camp.org/engagingstudents/toc.html. Accessed July 1, 2015.

Tenzer, Michael, ed. 2006. *Analytical Studies in World Music*. New York: Oxford University Press.

Tenzer, Michael, and John Roeder, eds. 2011. *Analytical and Cross-Cultural Studies in World Music*. New York: Oxford University Press.

Titon, Jeff Todd, ed. 1992. *Ethnomusicology*, Vol. 36 No. 3, Special Issue, "Ethno-musicology in the Public Interest."

Vaugeois, Lise. 2007. "Social Justice and Music Education: Claiming the Space of Music Education as a Site of Postcolonial Contestation." *Action, Criticism, and Theory for Music Education* vol. 6 no. 4, 163-200.

Volk, Therese. 1998. *Music, Education, and Multiculturalism. Foundations and Principles*. New York: Oxford University Press.

Weimer, Maryellen. 2012. "Five Characteristics of Learner-Centered Teaching." *Faculty Focus*. http://www.facultyfocus.com/articles/effective-teaching-strategies/five-characteristics-of-learner-centered-teaching/. Accessed July 2, 2015.

Weintraub, Andrew, and Bell Yung, eds. 2009. *Music and Cultural Rights*. Urbana: University of Illinois Press.

Wemyss, Kathryn L. 2004. "Reciprocity and Exchange: Popular Music in Australian Secondary Schools." In *Bridging the Gap. Popular Music and Music Education*, Carlos Xavier Rodríguez, ed., 141–155. Reston, VA: National Association for Music Education.

White, Jason. 2015. "Toward a Theory of Arts Entrepreneurship." *Journal of Arts Entrepreneurship Education*, Vol. 1 No. 1. http://jaee.ncsu.edu/volume-1-number-1-2015/toward-a-theory-of-arts-entrepreneurship/. Accessed December 28 2016.

Wong, Deborah. 2006. "Ethnomusicology and Difference." *Ethnomusicology*, Vol. 50 No. 2 (Spring/Summer), 259–279.

Yang, Mina. 2014. *Planet Beethoven. Classical Music at the Turn of the Millennium*. Wesleyan, CT: Wesleyan University Press.

Yoshihara, Mari. 2007. *Musicians from a Different Shore. Asians and Asian Americans in Classical Music*. Philadelphia: Temple University Press.

Institutional Structures

CHAPTER 2

Reshaping Undergraduate Music Education in Turbulent Times Through Cultural Rather Than Curricular Change

BRIAN PERTL

Change is in the air, and all of higher education is in the process of redefining itself. At colleges and universities across the nation and the world, external and internal forces are compelling reflection, prompting self-assessment, and exerting pressure to reform. Yet it can be difficult to instigate reform even so, as the obstacles are many, daunting, and very real. In this chapter I share strategies for implementing meaningful institutional change by focusing on culture rather than curriculum. I do not mandate what that change should look like or how it should be approached. Instead I use my seven years of leadership experience at the Lawrence University Conservatory of Music as a case study to suggest what may work at other institutions. I hope the lessons I have learned will serve as a practical guide to implementing meaningful institutional change in turbulent times.

THE LANDSCAPE

Since the late 1990s we have experienced phenomenal change in nearly every aspect of the music world. From digital downloads to orchestras and opera companies in distress; from changing royalty models to increased pressure on public school music programs; from online learning to new models of philanthropic funding, the world that awaits our music graduates is very different from what came before. This new landscape demands new kinds of preparation. Our world today requires a daunting array of skills that go well beyond exceptional technique and musicality. We need musicians who can act, dance, play multiple instruments, and sing. We need collaborators, improvisers, entrepreneurs, marketers, and impresarios. We need graduates who are comfortable performing in multiple styles and in nontraditional situations (how about an opera in a parking terrace or a virtual improv session in the online world of Second Life?[1]). It is little wonder that the future for musicians seems at the worst overwhelming and at the best unclear. If, however, we push beyond the fear and uncertainty and consider what's unfolding around us, then like the awesome beauty of a tornado or the terrifying splendor of an avalanche, there is great wonder to behold in the collapse and reshaping of our music world.

The uncertainty that the music industry is currently experiencing can be considered part of a Kuhnian paradigm shift. Thomas Kuhn, in his book *The Structure of Scientific Revolutions* (Kuhn 1962), details the traumatic process involved in shifting from one scientific model to the next. An inertia surrounds all accepted paradigms and an unwillingness to discard them. Evidence that contradicts the current theory tends to be ignored or rationalized away for some time. Eventually, the anomalies can no longer be ignored. A state of crisis then develops as new approaches and theories are proposed to resolve the discrepancies. The eventual shift to a new paradigm is often contentious and rarely quick, as supporters of the old battle supporters of the new. Kuhn's work on paradigms focused solely on examples from the hard sciences, yet there are clear similarities to what the music industry is experiencing. We aren't seeing the end of music or of people loving music or of society needing music or even of consumers purchasing music. We are seeing only a transition between the old way of mediating music and the new. It is critically important to realize that we are still in a state of transition.

We occupy a liminal space between what was and what will be. The liminal, the in-between, can be unsettling and scary. When fear, panic, and worry take over, transitions can feel like a collapse, an end. Such fear prompts articles about the imminent demise of classical music, the end of live music, or speculations that e-courses will completely supplant live classroom instruction. It prompts parents and potential students to question the relevance and value of a college education in music. From this perspective, a career in music might look bleak indeed, but occupying the liminal space between the old and the new can also be exhilarating and wildly productive. Untethered by the conventions of old models and not yet constrained by the structure of new models, creativity, innovation, and playful improvisation can flourish. This in turn can

1. See http://secondlife.com/ (accessed 28 December 28, 2016).

help shape the future for college music programs in radical ways. I see the current situation as a rare opportunity to act as the catalyst for completely reimagining how we train the music graduates of the future.

RECOGNIZE THE INHERENT INSTABILITY OF PARADIGM SHIFTS

As new paradigms begin to emerge, there is a tendency to feel that if your institution doesn't act immediately, it will be left behind. There have been numerous examples of this over the past few years; for instance, in the area of e-courses, MOOCs,[2] and online learning. There is no doubt that online learning will play an increasingly important role in higher education, but the initial dash on the part of universities to stake a claim in the e-course gold rush was as chaotic and unfocused as a thousand puppies released in a field of butterflies. In the headlong rush to be a part of a new magical world, institutions, instead of carefully analyzing how online learning could best serve their particular institution and enhance educational offerings, let the fear of being left behind drive decision making.

This tendency is clearly illustrated by a conversation I had with a faculty colleague in 2011. I asked if our institution could design an e-course that would enhance the student experience and yet remain true to our institutional identity. His response was, "That train has already left the station!" He went on to explain that so many other institutions were already creating such courses that our time to act had passed. Again, we spoke in 2011, before the real e-course and MOOCs craze even started. Our conversation perfectly illustrates how panic changes perception in unproductive ways. My colleague read about all the things other institutions were doing and drew the conclusion that we were so far behind it wasn't even worth exploring e-learning options. In reality, even four years later, the proverbial train is just starting to leave the station. It's still missing a few wheels, it doesn't know where it's headed, and the tracks haven't been laid yet.

The scenario described above applies beyond the world of online learning. It is easy to look around at other music schools and feel as if you are being left behind in other areas. "Quick, we need a course on entrepreneurship!" "Where is our e-course offering in online marketing for musicians?" "Oh no! Beluga State University is requiring that all incoming performance majors take Advanced Composition in Garage Band, what is our response?" These reactions are normal but to be avoided. It not that urgency is bad, but that one must cultivate a thoughtful instead of a panicked urgency.

2. Massive open online courses.

First relax and take a deep breath. Achieving real, meaningful, and rapid change requires a period of institutional self-reflection. The process isn't necessarily easy, especially when it seems like time is of the essence. Imagine trying to meditate in that field of puppies chasing butterflies. That is what I am asking you to do. Ignore the puppies! I see this initial phase of change-planning as a four-step process.

1. Strive to deeply know your institutional identity, its strengths, weaknesses, and culture. Take a cold, honest look at who you really are. This is often harder than it sounds. What we perceive our institutional identity to be is often quite different from what it actually is. Include all of your institution's constituencies in the process: faculty, staff, and students. If you have the time and resources, bring outside experts into the conversation. Having an external voice you trust take a look under the hood can be invaluable. If you don't know your institutional identity with crystal clarity, meaningful change will be difficult to achieve.
2. Once you have a clear sense of who you are as an institution, consider the musical world of today that your students will be entering. What are the challenges today's young musicians will face? The list may be exhaustive. Group the list into related areas.
3. Then ponder what the ideally prepared graduate needs to thrive in this world of challenges you previously identified. What are the skills, knowledge, and mindset needed to be successful in the musical landscape of today?
4. Now start defining how to best prepare this ideal graduate. For now avoid thinking about specific classes and instead identify key areas of focus that you feel all students will need to best prepare them for a musical career today.

At Lawrence we came up with seven main areas of focus that reflect our vision for what a twenty-first-century music education should include (see Figure 2.1). The diagram outlines our particular areas of focus, all aligned with our institutional identity and values. For example, we are a conservatory within a liberal arts college. We believe that to be best prepared for the challenges of twenty-first-century musical life, a music student must also expand her intellectual capacity through an immersion in a liberal arts curriculum. This is represented through the diagram in that all other areas of focus are embedded in the larger circle of the liberal arts model. Since liberal arts training is already a key institutional strength, the likelihood of success in this area is great; we are building on who we already are. The other areas represented include Core Musicianship, Creative Impulse (the cultivation

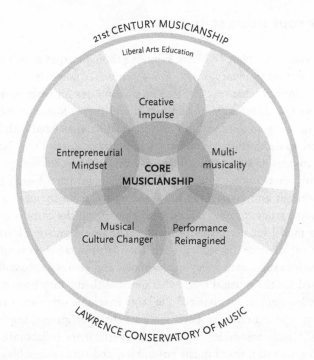

Figure 2.1. Twenty-first century musicianship.

of creative musical abilities), Multi-musicality, Entrepreneurial Mindset, Performance Reimagined, and Musical Culture Changer. Core Musicianship lies at the center of the model and represents much of the training that traditionally formed the foundation of a conservatory education: building technical facility, tone quality, musicality, ensemble work, along with extensive training in theory and musicology. Notice how in our diagram the newer initiatives intersect and extend from the core. Our goal is for all of our focus areas to integrate seamlessly into all aspects of our core music training and, by doing so, radically extend the very definition of Core Musicianship. Many of our focus areas align closely with the three pillars of the College Music Society (CMS) document (see Campbell et al. 2014)—creativity, diversity, and integration—but some don't. Each institution needs to create its own vision for change. Although there are sure to be areas of overlap with other institutions, the vision for your music school should uniquely reflect your identity, strengths, and beliefs. If your team finds itself wondering how your institution could be more like Conservatory Y or Music School X, then it is probably time to refocus on how your institution can be more like itself. Identifying your institution's key areas of focus will give you a valuable roadmap for change. As your school begins to implement changes, they should always align with the key areas of focus.

Now that you have a plan, I'd like to suggest a thought experiment inspired by Ed Sarath and his visionary works on institutional change. It will help shake the foundations of what was and free up possibilities for what could be. The rules are simple: blow up your institution and curriculum. Pretend you are starting from a clean slate without any constraints associated with buildings or physical space, faculty, administration, staff, or curriculum! Now imagine what courses of study and hands-on experiences would best prepare the ideal twenty-first-century graduate. This encourages participants to bypass current realities and gives them full freedom to create something radically new. A recent student group tasked with blowing up the conservatory came up with a model for performance majors that would greatly diversify their ensemble experience. The students felt that future graduates would need a much broader exposure to as many ensembles and genres as possible so as to be prepared for the musical world that awaited them. They proposed a program that kept but de-emphasized the large ensemble experience and added many more opportunities to participate in chamber groups, improvisation ensembles, small ensembles in which the performers collaborate to write their own repertoire, world music ensembles, and small ensembles that collaborate with other artists like dancers, actors, and cinematographers. It was a surprisingly forward-thinking and comprehensive result from a session that lasted all of seventy minutes. At Lawrence, we have done this thought experiment with student and faculty groups, and the results are always fascinating. Interestingly, the new models, no matter how different from what currently exists, seem to further define our unique institutional identity. The great thing about the exercise is that you can look either at the whole institution or at a small part of it. Soon, Lawrence's choral ensemble directors will be meeting to blow up the choral ensemble program! They will envision the ideal ensemble experience with none of the constraints that have defined the program for the last seventy-five years and formulate an experience that best serves the needs of our twenty-first-century students. I anticipate a lively, productive conversation.

THE BARRIERS TO CHANGE—REAL AND IMAGINED

Why go to the trouble blowing up institutional models and dreaming up new curricular scenarios when our institutional realities seem as rigid and fixed as the Rock of Gibraltar? I love the experiment discussed above because it gives us a glimpse of what could be. Having a clear vision of what could be can help us push through change. Yet everything about the structure of colleges and universities is built to resist rapid change. The thick walls of our ivory towers are meant to insulate educational goals from the whims and fads of the outside world. The monumental steadfastness of required curricula and the glacial pace of shared governance are perfect examples of our structural resistance to change. Shared governance models force conversation and reflection. This is a good thing. It sets universities apart from corporations, where the CEO can mandate change unilaterally. Our university structures are a beautiful thing, even though they might not seem quite so beautiful at the end of a two-hour faculty meeting in which the only actual accomplishment was the approval of the minutes!

Other institutional structures unwittingly discourage change as well. Every ten years a NASM[3]-accredited institution undergoes a self-study in preparation for an external site visit and accreditation review. NASM has gone out of its way of late to create guidelines that allow for great flexibility in meeting accreditation goals. NASM has made great strides in encouraging institutions to innovate. For example, an integrated model that combines theory and history into one sequence, as suggested in the CMS manifesto, does not fall outside of NASM guidelines. In fact, it is a perfectly acceptable approach as long as the institution can demonstrate that it is giving students an appropriate grounding in both theory and history. Therein lies the rub. At its best the NASM self-study is an opportunity for institutional self-reflection, a time to assess the need for change, a time to make decisions that will move an institution forward. The reality is that the self-study is a year-and-a-half-long process that is typically looked upon with dread by music departments. For many music departments, it is seen, not as a tool for self-reflection and change, but as a difficult hoop to jump through. So while an institution can create all sorts of cool, cutting-edge, integrated curricular models and although the NASM guidelines are set up to accommodate those models, the amount of work involved to document that a student is getting the required grounding in each of the integrated subject areas can be daunting and creates another barrier to change. If it is easier to get through the review by having a class in theory and a class in history, an institution may decide to stick with the tried-and-true instead of being wildly creative. In this instance, it isn't the NASM self-study itself that suppresses change but institutional perceptions regarding how best to get through what seems like an overwhelming process.

It's all about human psychology. Often when a person is confronted with a changing paradigm, his first thoughts are not about embracing the excitement of the new but are profound worries about change making his position more difficult if not entirely obsolete. For example, the collapse of the CD industry wasn't caused just by the overwhelming superiority of digital file sharing. Equally complicit were the tens of thousands of small decisions made by

3. National Association of Schools of Music.

mid-level recording company managers desperately worried that if digital file sharing supplanted the CD industry, it would put their jobs at risk. Time after time, these managers decided to ignore or actively fight against the new technology in order to protect their ever-shrinking CD revenues instead of finding ways to thrive as part of the new paradigm. Ironically their steadfast refusal to find ways to partner with the upstart file-sharing companies hastened rather than slowed the demise of the CD industry. Humans crave stability, the known and the understandable. We avoid the unknown and unstable.

Change in the form of new priorities can also imply to some that what came before is of little or no value. Let's assume a professor is nearing the end of her career. She has single-handedly built the music education curriculum over the past twenty years. Now there is a move to make radical changes to the program. Our professor may wholeheartedly embrace those changes, or she may feel completely devalued and see the proposed changes as condemning her lifetime of work to meaninglessness. Depending on her point of view, she may be a change leader or a change blocker. What looks like forward-thinking, innovative change to one set of professors may look like an all-out attack on the foundations of a quality education to another group. This is what makes change so desperately hard.

In 2009, I experienced at first hand how all of these factors could converge into a debilitating logjam. Our Brass Department was proposing to add a three-unit requirement (half of a full course) in brass pedagogy for its majors because the previous NASM review had concerns that students weren't receiving enough instruction in this area. Previously, brass pedagogy had been integrated into private studio lessons. During the NASM review, it had proven difficult to clearly show in our integrated model that students in each studio were getting the required grounding in pedagogy, so a stand-alone course was proposed. It was felt that having a course in the catalog that specifically addressed an NASM-required area would make things easier to explain for the next review.

Not wanting to add to additional credits to the degree requirements, the Brass Department proposed removing one of three upper-level elective course requirements in musicology or theory. Thus ensued a multiple-month debate, not about the addition of the pedagogy course but solely about the proposed elimination of the third elective. The discussions, intense and emotional, seemed to suggest that the very essence of our music program would be compromised by dropping one upper-level elective. Having one department (in this case, Brass) suggest modifications to requirements in another department rarely goes well but is a common occurrence when a music program is trying to make radical changes. Psychology in action! In the end, after three months, the course was added and nothing was taken away. It was at that point that I realized how many forces conspire to prevent change, particularly on the curricular level. I also realized that if it took three months to get one three-unit course approved that was in no way radically new or boundary-pushing, meaningful, timely change would not happen through formal curricular change—at least at first.

A FOCUS ON INSTITUTIONAL CULTURE

When you sidestep the minefield of trying to implement sweeping curricular change and the potentially divisive arguments, debates, and hard feelings that go along with it, opportunities to achieve successful change increase exponentially. By focusing on changing your music institution's culture, you avoid directly challenging any specific curricular requirements. There may be some professors who aren't wildly enthusiastic about all of the new focus areas your institution chooses, but as long as the proposed changes aren't perceived as negatively impacting how their department teaches its material, few professors will become active adversaries of change. I can't stress how important that is. Remember the three months it took to add one three-unit class to our required curriculum? It doesn't take many people who are violently opposed to some aspect of change to stop it dead in its tracks. A focus on culture can diffuse potential deadlock. This may seem antithetical to the "blow up your curriculum" approach, but in some ways it isn't. By changing your institutional culture, all of the monumental curricular pillars you envisioned still exist, but now the students are dancing around them, leaping between them, and discovering secret passages to them that no one knew existed. The truth is that amazing institutional change can happen without ever touching the curriculum.

Here is an example. One of our areas of focus in Lawrence's 21st Century Musicianship initiative is multi-musicality. We believe that learning other musical languages and dialects is critical preparation for the global, interconnected world of today. We also believe that exposing violin students to the immersive, highly collaborative, aural pedagogy of a Balinese gamelan will help them bring new rhythmic depth, melodic understanding, and cohesive ensemble playing to a performance of a Mendelssohn string quartet. Here is what we did without adding one new requirement. Our Percussion Department and our amazing percussion professor, Dane Richeson, have offered Brazilian samba drumming and Ghanaian Ewe drumming and dancing for over two decades. Historically these ensembles were populated primarily by percussion students. When I arrived, our new ethnomusicology professor, Sonja Downing, and I added Balinese gamelan and didgeridoo instruction to the mix. Then an Afro-Cuban ensemble was created. We showed clear institutional support for these ensembles. We found more prominent showcases for world music performances, including university-wide convocations. Both the dean of the conservatory and his wife went to every performance.

Lawrence was demonstrating that it embraced and celebrated world music traditions. As a result, more and more nonpercussionists began joining the groups. Now, out of a conservatory population of 350, in any given term there are around 100 students participating in one or more of the five world music ensembles. We created a culture that encouraged musical exploration and gave students the permission to explore. The fun really began when students began getting into the action by creating their own groups: HMELU (Heavy Metal Ensemble of Lawrence University), electronic music club, fiddle club, klezmer collective, polka band, a deep listening club, a half-dozen jazz combos, and numerous student rock and pop groups. Our students are also more deeply exploring the Western tradition through the creation of a madrigal group and the baroque ensemble. Again, institutional support was shown from the top for these musical explorations. I was the faculty adviser for the heavy metal ensemble, fiddle club, deep listening club, and baroque ensemble. Having the conservatory dean as faculty adviser for the heavy metal ensemble sends a clear message that an institution's culture is changing drastically. By creating an environment that honors musical diversity rather than sticking its nose up at it, we have reached a point of focusing on the musicianship of any endeavor rather than on the appropriateness of a particular musical genre. We have created an option-rich environment that gives our students the autonomy to explore. Without adding a single requirement, the vast majority of our music majors now participate in ensembles that fall outside of the Western classical tradition. This raises a vitally important related issue: how does it change the educational experience when students broaden their musical experiences because they choose to do so rather than being required to do so?

SUPPORT YOUR CHANGE MAKERS

Even if you have broad institutional buy-in from all your key constituencies—administration, faculty, staff, and students—change will not just happen. There will always be a small number of change leaders. To lead successful change, a person needs to be passionate about achieving the end goals. When you find your passionate change makers, supporting them in their efforts is critical. As soon as a music school has four or five change leaders from two or more constituencies (including students), then active change begins to emanate from the school itself instead of being imposed from the top down. In this scenario, change becomes part of the institutional culture and encourages more forward-thinking ideas to emerge. Imagine the excitement this type of institutional creativity can foster in students, staff, faculty, and administration! At Lawrence we are lucky to have passionate change makers in the faculty, staff, and student body leading experimentation in each of our six main areas of focus. I will focus on just one area below to illustrate the impact that motivated leaders can have.

Two of our faculty, Dr. Erin Lesser, assistant professor of flute, and Dr. Michael Mizrahi, associate professor of piano, were part of Carnegie Hall's Academy Program and Teaching Artists Collaborative. These programs bring high-level performing artists into New York public schools for ongoing residencies and on a broader scale promote live performance and audience engagement as a powerful vehicle for social change. Alumni of these programs, wanting to continue the work they had begun, created a new ensemble, Decoda. Decoda has been a leader in redefining the performance of classical music, especially in terms of where it should be played. It frequently plays gigs in food pantries, warming shelters, and halfway houses and accepts extended residencies in prisons. Erin and Michael, as members of Decoda, wanted to bring the spirit of Decoda to Lawrence and the greater Appleton community. So they did just that by creating the Music for All project. It started small, as Michael and Erin began working with four student chamber music groups. Instead of just focusing on the technical and musical aspects of the repertoire, they tasked students with creating an outreach program that incorporated meaningful ways to engage audiences and draw them into the performance. The process and performances were a revelation for our students, who began working towards a goal much larger and more meaningful than simply performing an end-of-term chamber music recital at the conservatory, frequently to a small, disengaged audience. Since the project started two years ago, the number of participating student groups has grown; so too has the number of participating faculty groups. Additional members of Decoda have been to campus on four separate occasions for residencies, performances, and workshops, teaching faculty and students how to incorporate new models for audience engagement into their applied study. The Music for All model also breaks down institutional hierarchical power structures. During the last Decoda visit students partnered with faculty and our visiting artists in an ensemble to prepare and perform Jennifer Higdon's *Zaka* and Missy Mazzoli's *The Sound of the Light*, both challenging pieces for mixed instrumentation. The ensemble performed the pieces at schools and a community center, with audience interaction a key element of the event. For our students, partnering with their professors and working professionals to prepare and perform these challenging works in nontraditional venues was a transformative experience. Here are a few student comments: "The interactive element of the performance was new to me and much more effective than I anticipated." "It was enlightening to hear how more experienced performers approach a difficult piece with minimal rehearsal time." "This approach made the music newly relevant not only for the audience but also the performers." The ideas embodied in the Music for All project are becoming a part of our institutional DNA.

Our goal has been to incorporate the audience-engagement approach into all chamber music experiences and become part of how every studio teacher works with students as a means of ensuring meaningful, engaging recitals. Furthermore, as our large ensembles begin adopting this paradigm, the way in which we had traditionally approached performance, audience engagement, appropriateness of venue, and appropriateness of audience is being turned on its head. The really amazing thing about this sweeping institutional change is that it didn't depend on radical curricular reform. The course catalog today is identical to what it was ten years ago; the contents of the courses is where real innovation has taken place. When changing the boxes is difficult or impossible, think about changing what is contained in the boxes. Once the content of the boxes has changed, the shape and nature of the boxes will begin to change as well.

CULTURE CHANGE TO CURRICULAR CHANGE

Given my nearly gleeful take on how the Music for All project is profoundly transforming Lawrence's conservatory culture without radically changing curricular requirements, it may seem like I oppose sweeping curricular change. I am actually wildly in favor of curricular change. I just get excited about approaches that create tangible results quickly. The reality is that thoughtful culture change can lead to rapid curricular change. One of our focus areas at Lawrence is nurturing the creative impulse, particularly through composition and improvisation. As an example of how this can happen, let me discuss improvisation. Improvisation is a foundation of our jazz program, but we wanted to make it a pervasive part of our entire conservatory culture. We began by finding like-minded colleagues who were passionate about the power of improvisation in all of its forms—music, dance, theater arts, spoken word, even business initiatives—and we started to weave it into our classes. For instance, improvisation plays a central role in my Entrepreneurial Musicianship class. How can one "think outside of the box" and be boldly innovative and creative if one never has a chance to practice being boldly innovative and creative in other contexts? Thus, students in my class spend as much time experimenting in the dance studio, participating in sonic meditations, and improvising in racquetball courts as they do preparing marketing strategies, high-level strategic plans, and three-year budget projections. Releasing the creative impulse through improvisation directly impacts how students approach and execute their business proposals. Improvisation is also finding its way into our large ensemble rehearsals, music education classes, opera training classes, and even some musicology classes. It also has a home in IGLU, the Improvisation Group of Lawrence University, an ensemble with about twenty participants led by Matthew Turner, improvising cellist and one of the leading pedagogues in the field of improvisation. Through the summer of 2014, Matt worked only part time at Lawrence leading IGLU.

In the fall of 2014, we found an opportunity to bring him on full time and the impact has been striking. He is now offering Intro to Non-Jazz Improvisation classes that are quickly changing the musical lives of our students.

Matt has offered such classes only twice so far, with a grand total of about twenty-three students participating. But what the numbers don't show is that the students who took the course were the school's musical leaders. Word has spread, and the interest in improvisation has exploded. This past spring term IGLU enrollment ballooned from twenty to nearly forty! Four students took advantage of our self-designed major program to create majors in Contemporary Improvisation. The curricular implications of this cultural shift are enormous. If one student creates a self-designed major in a particular area, it isn't a big deal; the faculty don't necessarily take notice. Even if two students do, it doesn't suggest much curricular impact. But when four or more self-designed major proposals are submitted in the same area and they are all approved, how can an institution possibly turn down the fifth, sixth, or seventh proposal? Student interest has created such momentum in the area of improvisation that we are compelled to seriously consider what a major in Contemporary Improvisation should look like. If our institution decides not to define and create a Contemporary Improvisation major, the next half-dozen proposals for student-designed majors will do it for us. Cultural change can indeed drive rapid curricular change. Now that the celebration of improvisation and creative collaboration are embedded into our culture, I can't wait to see where the next five years will take us!

THE ROAD FORWARD

I've shared some thoughts and observations on leading institutional change based on my experiences at Lawrence University. It is important to remember that we are still in the middle of this muddle, trying to figure things out, trying to find the most effective pathways to meaningful change, doing our best to enjoy the creative, electric excitement that the process has created and use that energy to drive even more change. Our path at Lawrence won't be your path, our goals might not be your goals, our areas of rapid change might not be the same as yours, but I do think that following a few key steps can greatly facilitate the process.

1. Know your institution: Don't wait for a NASM review to reflect deeply and engage in your own self-study. If you are preparing for a NASM self-study, use it to your best advantage. Use the opportunity to discover your institutional identity and what it should strive to become.
2. Know the musical landscape: Look around at the world today and consider what the musical worlds of tomorrow might be.

3. Define the ideal graduate: What will your graduates need to be successful today and into the future?

4. What experiences will help create this graduate? Remembering your institution's unique identity, create a roadmap for success that best utilizes your institutional strengths and honors your institutional culture.

5. Create a culture that honors and embraces change: From the top down, brainstorming, innovative ideas, and lively discussion all need to become part of the institutional culture. This also means that pre-tenure faculty can't be terrified to suggest anything even slightly innovative for fear of not receiving tenure. A culture that celebrates creative, collaborative change is vital, whether that change is driven by students, staff, faculty, or administration.

6. Support your change leaders: Let these folks lead the charge. Do whatever you can to support them. Knowing that their ideas and direction are honored is often more important to them than financial support. Once a network of change leaders is distributed throughout different areas of your institution, the excitement for what they are doing and the excitement for new types of creative change will begin to grow. Even the most change-averse faculty can get swept up in the excitement, as long as they are part of the conversation and aren't being told that they must change.

Once you have created a culture that supports, nurtures, and celebrates forward-thinking change, then don't forget to enjoy the ride. There is nothing better than coming in to work each day, whether you are an administrator, faculty, staff, or student, and feeling that palpable electricity generated by an institution in the midst of creative, collaborative, meaningful experimentation. There is a potential for amazing things to happen and everyone can feel it. It can influence how students approach leaning, how faculty approach teaching, and how administrators approach leading. When everyone is excited about what their institution can be and wondering how they can be a part of getting it there, then real and meaningful change is inevitable.

REFERENCES

Campbell, Patricia, et al. 2014. "Transforming Music Study from Its Foundations: A Manifesto for Progressive Change in the Undergraduate Preparation for Music Majors." Missoula, MT: College Music Society. http://symposium.music.org/index.php?option=com_k2&view=item&id=11118:transforming-music-study-from-its-foundations-a-manifesto-for-progressive-change-in-the-undergraduate-preparation-of-music-majors&Itemid=126. Accessed 28 December 2016.

Kuhn, T. 1962. *The Structure of Scientific Revolutions*. Chicago: University of Chicago Press.

CHAPTER 3

Finding a Balance

Music at Liberal Arts Colleges

VICTORIA LINDSAY LEVINE AND EMILY KOHUT

Liberal arts colleges focus on undergraduate education, emphasizing the development of critical thought, of the whole person, and of values consistent with ethical participation in a civil society. Traditionally, their mission was to prepare students for public service or a profession rather than technical or vocational training, but the mission has shifted since 1970 toward more comprehensive and preprofessional curricula (Pfnister 1984, Delucchi 1997, Kushner 1999, Lang 1999). By the late twentieth century, the curricula of liberal arts music departments reflected that shift. Liberal arts music departments were once programs designed to cultivate aesthetic appreciation and skilled community musicians as part of a broader education. Most students enrolled in music courses for personal enrichment, although some majored in music. Curricula emphasized interpretive performance of the Western canon, supported by courses in music theory and history. During the 1970s, liberal arts music curricula gradually became more professionalized, reflecting the programs offered at conservatories and schools of music but on a smaller scale. By the 1970s some departments had introduced courses in ethnomusicology and experimental music. The multicultural movement of the 1980s and rapid technological innovations of the 1990s resulted in further additions to the liberal arts music curriculum. In less than fifty years, the emphasis within liberal arts music departments shifted from Western music connoisseurship to professionalized training to coverage of multiple disciplines within the field of music.

The horizontal expansion of the liberal arts music curriculum has begun to threaten its coherence. Melinda Russell (Carleton College) explained that by the start of the twenty-first century, liberal arts music faculty had adopted "the inoculation model," meaning that students get a small shot of everything that might broaden their educational experience.[1] Moreover, the culture of liberal arts colleges has also evolved in other ways. Institutions that were once the province of the elite began to diversify in terms of their student body by the 1990s. By 2010, the soaring cost of college coupled with an economic downturn steered undergraduates toward majors with solid earning potential (cf. NPR Staff 2011). Whereas enrollments in music courses and co-curricular programs remain strong at liberal arts colleges, the number of students who major in music is low because the degree is perceived as impractical. Liberal arts music faculty therefore find themselves at a crossroads. They recognize the need to remap the music major and transform the way music is taught and learned at small colleges in order to remain relevant in the current cultural and economic climate, but the process is challenging given the competing demands of contemporary musical life. It is no longer enough for aspiring professional musicians to master the European concert repertory. Twenty-first century musicians must also become adept at performing and creating music cross-culturally in diverse genres, repertories, venues, and contexts (cf. Solís 2004, Tenzer 2006). They must acquire facility with music technology to produce and distribute their own work and need entrepreneurial skills to build and maintain an audience. Covering such broad content is difficult enough at schools of music, but it poses an even greater challenge at liberal arts colleges, where the pace of curricular change is slow due to the small size of the faculty, limited resources, and finite facilities. This chapter explores how faculty members at thirteen colleges are striving to meet the challenge.[2] Our twin goals are to provide a snapshot of current trends in liberal arts music education and to stimulate productive discussion around curricular change.

Developed as a faculty-student collaborative research project, our methodology in this chapter combines an analysis of music department websites, interviews with faculty, and a qualitative exploratory survey. We collected data over the course of the 2014/15 academic year. We analyzed department websites during the summer of 2014, administered an electronic survey questionnaire in September, and interviewed department chairs or their representatives the following spring. We sent the survey questionnaire to

1. Telephone interview, May 14, 2015.
2. Initially, we collected data from the websites of fifteen comparable colleges and also sent the survey questionnaire to their full-time music faculty. However, we were unable to interview department chairs at two of those colleges, and therefore we are presenting information only from the thirteen colleges whose faculty we were able to interview.

more than one hundred full-time music faculty at the colleges included in our study: Amherst, Bowdoin, Carleton, Colorado, Davidson, Grinnell, Hampshire, Macalester, Pomona, Reed, Skidmore, Smith, and Williams. Survey responses were organized thematically by Dr. Amanda Udis-Kessler, the Colorado College director of Assessment and Program Review, in order to preserve the anonymity of the respondents (Udis-Kessler 2014). We reference the survey where appropriate throughout the chapter. The information we collected indicates that in the early twenty-first century, liberal arts music departments are revising their curricula toward a flexible major with a "lean" required core that accommodates changing student culture and prepares students for lifelong involvement in music. Each of the departments in our study is finding its own balance between the Western-oriented, conservatory-style curriculum and a commitment to liberal education as well as to global musical styles, practical musicianship, music technology, and popular music. We begin with a discussion of the liberal arts tradition in the United States and consider the role of music departments in private undergraduate institutions.

MUSIC AT LIBERAL ARTS COLLEGES

Liberal arts colleges occupy a specialized niche in higher education. Students who attend these colleges prioritize general education, residential campus life, individualized attention from faculty and administrators, and discussion-based instruction (Pfnister 1984, Carnegie Foundation 1985). Liberal arts colleges differ from public or private research universities and community colleges in several ways. They are private and nonprofit, operate independently of larger institutions, enroll fewer than about three thousand students, have a history rooted in the eighteenth or nineteenth century, and emphasize baccalaureate education but may confer a small number of graduate degrees (Kushner 1999). They have a low student-to-faculty ratio and classes usually seat fewer than thirty students. Liberal arts colleges trace their philosophical roots to "a tradition that began in New England over three hundred years ago with the establishment of the first enclaves for educating privileged white males ... in a tightly disciplined Anglo-Saxon educational tradition that was presumed to instill qualifications for leadership in a theocratic community" (Lang 1999, 134). Yet the liberal arts tradition has undergone continual change. For example, women began to be admitted to liberal arts colleges in the nineteenth century at around the same time that women's colleges, such as Smith, were founded. Liberal arts colleges made significant efforts to recruit and retain domestic students of color, first-generation college students, and students from middle- and working-class economic backgrounds beginning in the late twentieth century, and these efforts continue.

Following the adoption of more comprehensive and preprofessional curricula in the 1970s, liberal arts colleges more recently began "to redefine their missions in contemporary terms," in part by invoking "a philosophy of enlightened self-interest that clearly makes 'social ideas and action' and 'external engagement' the subjects of aggressive attention" (Lang 1999, 140). Liberal arts colleges have generally lagged behind public universities in educating for social justice and social action but began to address this gap through curricular change by the 1980s. Initiatives include general education requirements designed to increase awareness of social inequality and global cultures, courses and internships that involve community partnerships and community-based research, and co-curricular programming, including public lectures, panel discussions, film screenings, and art exhibitions, that explores pressing social issues such as racial, ethnic, and economic inequality. In other words, liberal arts faculty are transforming their curricula and teaching methods in order to educate for social change, including upward mobility for previously underrepresented and marginalized groups.

Music faculty at liberal arts colleges have responded to broader institutional imperatives by expanding the scope of their departments to encompass four main roles according to our survey respondents. First, they promote musical performance among both music majors and general students. Second, they serve general students, leading them "to a critical understanding of the role of the arts in human societies," in the words of one respondent. Third, they prepare music majors for graduate study within the field of music through courses in Western music history and theory, composition, music technology, performance, and ethnomusicology. Finally, they contribute significantly to the cultural vitality of the campus and surrounding community each year by sponsoring community-inclusive ensembles as well as numerous public concerts that feature faculty, students, and visiting artists. We would add that they also serve other academic departments, interdisciplinary programs, and study-abroad initiatives through courses cross-listed in the humanities, social sciences, and natural sciences. Jenny Kallick (Amherst) remarked that for liberal arts music faculty, "Our true mission is to bring music to as many people as we can."[3] Interestingly, only one survey respondent suggested that the role of liberal arts music departments is to train professional performers.

Many liberal arts music departments had begun to diversify their curricula by the 1990s through the introduction of electives in ethnomusicology and popular music. According to Virginia Hancock (Reed), "Diversity is part of the college's mission statement, so adding courses in African American music allowed our department to support that mission."[4] Similarly, Victoria

3. Telephone interview, May 20, 2015.
4. Telephone interview, May 2, 2015.

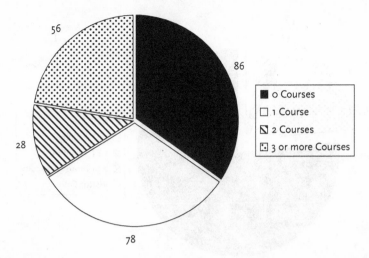

Figure 3.1. Courses in ethnomusicology or popular music taught at liberal arts colleges in 2014/15.

Malawey (Macalester) noted that "We really try to tie into the college's mission statement regarding multiculturalism and internationalism. The faculty is proactively invested in musical diversity, and this benefits the students."[5] All of the survey respondents indicated that they are working to diversify their music curricula and that they support this effort. In 2014, roughly two-thirds of the 248 colleges identified as liberal arts institutions by *US News and World Report* offered at least one course in ethnomusicology or popular music (Figure 3.1); roughly one-fourth of those colleges had hired an ethnomusicologist (Figure 3.2).[6] The designation "1FT Faculty +" in Figure 3.2 indicates the presence of one full-time faculty member plus one or more part-time faculty members in ethnomusicology, including world music ensemble directors.

Despite initiatives to diversify the music curriculum, incorporating inclusive content into core courses for the major remains a challenge. Music departments at liberal arts colleges operate with a small full-time faculty that is stretched thin; they have little time and few resources to retool in areas outside their professional training. Most academic classes, especially core courses, are taught by full-time faculty members. Other than studio teachers

5. Telephone interview, May 19, 2015.
6. We based this number on information provided by *US News and World Reports*, including its lists of both ranked and unranked colleges (see http://colleges.usnews. rankingsandreviews.com/best-colleges/rankings/national-liberal-arts-colleges/ spp%2B50, accessed January 2015). As of 2010, the Carnegie Classification of Institutions of Higher Education identified 233 liberal arts colleges in the United States (see http://carnegieclassifications.iu.edu, accessed August 31, 2015).

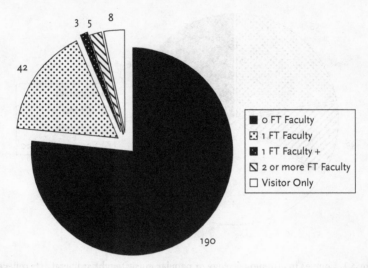

Figure 3.2. Full-time faculty members in ethnomusicology at liberal arts colleges in 2014/15.

and ensemble directors, we hire few part-time or contingent faculty. New full-time faculty lines are rarely created because of financial and facility restrictions, and faculty turnover is slow. Curricula are therefore shaped largely by faculty specialties, abilities, and interests. Changes in student culture further complicate matters. As Mauro Botelho (Davidson) remarked, "[Our] music program depended on students entering with years of prior instruction that no longer exists. The talent has not changed, but the students no longer arrive having taken eight years of private piano lessons. [We are] adapting to students who are more diverse in terms of the musical background they bring with them. The liberal arts music department should be welcoming to students who come in with considerable talent as vocalists and instrumentalists, but who do not read music notation."[7] Alfred Cramer (Pomona) added that "The challenge is to welcome [all] students into the department and to make a place for them."[8] Welcoming all students into the liberal arts music department involves offering academic, performance, and creative opportunities in curricular areas that may be beyond the expertise of the existing faculty. As some respondents to the survey questionnaire explained, diversifying the curriculum necessitates strategic hiring, patience, and a gradual shift in department priorities.

Finding a balance within the liberal arts music major between professionalized music training, general education, and a more socially aware, global, and inclusive program requires remapping the curriculum. To illustrate various

7. Telephone interview, May 6, 2015.
8. Telephone interview, May 20, 2015.

approaches to this project, we compared the structure of the undergraduate music major at thirteen liberal arts colleges and collected data on enrollments, staffing patterns, music courses offered, and similar information. Initially, we collected information from department websites, which we confirmed through telephone interviews with the chair or another faculty member from each department. The colleges in our sample employ different academic calendars (quarters, semesters, or blocks) and represent various geographic regions throughout the United States, from the Southeast to the Pacific Northwest. They include both rural and urban institutions. Some belong to either the Five Colleges Consortium in western Massachusetts or the Claremont Colleges Consortium in southern California. Whereas these colleges have much in common, we found that each music department has adapted to its unique institutional challenges in unique ways.

REMAPPING THE MUSIC MAJOR AT LIBERAL ARTS COLLEGES

The music departments we compared share many similarities (Tables 3.1a and 3.1b). During the 2014/15 academic year, each department employed between four and eleven full-time faculty members in music and graduated between four and sixteen music majors and minors. Only the number of graduating seniors appears in Table 3.1a because the number of music majors and minors can fluctuate from year to year at liberal arts colleges. Full-time faculty includes those who are tenured or tenure-track along with full-time lecturers, performance faculty, and artists-in-residence with continuing contracts. The size of the music faculty does not correlate with the number of graduating music majors and minors. For example, Hampshire has one of the smallest music faculties in this sample but graduated among the most music majors in 2015. Similarly, the number of full-time faculty in a department does not necessarily correlate with the number of academic courses offered in a given year. For example, Smith has more than eleven full-time faculty members but offered fewer academic classes than the other colleges in our sample because more than half of Smith's full-time music faculty teach private lessons or direct ensembles as part or all of their load. Otherwise, music departments with more faculty members tend to offer more ensembles and academic classes, and students at colleges in local consortia have additional options through campus exchange programs. The ensembles available include choirs, orchestras, concert bands, jazz bands, chamber music groups, and a variety of world music ensembles such as gamelan, bluegrass, taiko, Scottish pipes, and ensembles in African, Arabic, Chinese, Irish, and South Asian musics. At urban liberal arts colleges, part-time studio faculty and ensemble directors teach most of the performance classes, whereas full-time faculty teach most

Table 3.1a. LIBERAL ARTS MUSIC DEPARTMENTS IN COMPARISON

College	Campus Enrollment[a]	FT Faculty	Ensembles	Academic Courses[b]	Majors	Minors
Amherst	1,790	9.5	7[c]	27	10	0[d]
Bowdoin	1,800	7	8	24	8	15
Carleton	2,000	8	9	21	5	0
Colorado	2,060	7	9	29	7	14
Davidson	1,900	6	8	19	4	5
Grinnell	1,720	7	13	27	6	0[d]
Hampshire	1,490	4	5[c]	17	13	0[d]
Macalester	2,040	9	11	20	10	10
Pomona	1,610	9.5	7[c]	29	5	4
Reed	1,380	4	5	17	5	0[d]
Skidmore	2,800	16	8	32	16	6
Smith	3,030	11.5	7[c]	19	7	10
Williams	2,150	11	15	37	7	0[d]

[a] We obtained these numbers from college websites and rounded them to the nearest ten.
[b] In counting the number of academic courses offered by a given music department in 2014/15, we did not include short winter term classes, independent studies, ensembles, or private lessons; we did include aural skills and theory labs. The number of academic classes offered in a given year varies according to how many faculty members are on sabbatical or research leaves and whether there is a postdoctoral teaching fellow.
[c] Students have access to additional ensembles at other colleges through the campus exchange program.
[d] These colleges do not offer minors.

of these at rural colleges such as Grinnell, where it is difficult to hire part-time faculty locally.

At nine of the colleges in our sample, more than 50 percent of all music majors are double-majoring, and fewer than 40 percent pursue careers or advanced degrees in music after graduation.[9] Hampshire is the exception, where roughly half of all music majors continue in music-related careers or graduate study. This trend reflects Hampshire's interdisciplinary, individualized curricular style and its emphasis on internships and project-based learning. Despite the relatively small number of music majors that graduated in 2015 from the colleges in our sample, roughly one-third of the entire student body participated in their music departments. Precise data on the number of students enrolled in academic classes, lessons, and ensembles in a given year are hard to pinpoint, especially because students may not register for

9. Liberal arts colleges do not have systematic methods of tracking alumni careers after graduation, and therefore data on the number of music majors who pursue careers or advanced study in music after graduation are anecdotal.

Table 3.1b. LIBERAL ARTS MUSIC DEPARTMENTS IN COMPARISON

College	Double Majors	Campus-wide Student Involvement in Music Department	Alumni Who Pursue Careers in Music
Amherst	80%	590 (33%)	25%
Bowdoin	60%	650 (36%)	25%
Carleton	60%	660 (33%)	No data
Colorado	30%	700 (34%)	30%
Davidson	25%	450 (23%)	15%
Grinnell	50%	919 (53%)	20%
Hampshire	80%	385 (26%)	50%
Macalester	70%	1,130 (55%)	26%
Pomona	40%	615 (38%)	40%
Reed	0	330 (24%)	25%
Skidmore	50%	1,600 (57%)	No data
Smith	50%	1,000 (36%)	No data
Williams	60%	460 (21%)	25%

ensembles in which they participate in order to avoid exceeding credit limits. Nevertheless, our numbers suggest an impressively high percentage of student involvement. These numbers do not even account for the many students who attend department concerts or who perform independently of the department in bands and a cappella groups. The correlation between the relatively small number of music majors and relatively high involvement of general students underscores the prominent service role of music departments at liberal arts colleges, which typically attract students with strong interests in music and other fine or performing arts.

Five of the colleges in our sample offer a traditional music major, which channels the curriculum offered at schools of music (Table 3.2). By our definition, the traditional music major requires eleven or more prescribed classes supporting performance of the Western canon and sixteen or more requirements in all. We counted actual courses rather than credit hours to facilitate the cross-college comparison. For example, one semester of private lessons counted as one required course, just as one academic class in music theory counted as one required course. The prescribed classes in the traditional major center on Western music history and theory and include one course in ethnomusicology or popular music as well as one or more years of participation in both ensembles and private lessons, a capstone, and other requirements that vary by department. The integrative exercise required of music majors at Carleton is a significant senior project comparable to what is called a senior

Table 3.2. THE TRADITIONAL MUSIC MAJOR

Requirements	Carleton	Macalester	Pomona	Skidmore	Williams
Theory	2	4	4	3[a]	4
Musicianship[b]	2	0	0	0	0
Music history	1	2	2	1	3
World/popular	1	1	1	1	1
Composition	1	0	0	0	0
"New" music	0	0	1	0	0
Advanced seminar	1	0	0	1	0
Junior/senior seminar	0	0	1	1	0
Electives	2	3	0	1	1
Music technology	0	0	0	0	0
Integrative exercise	2	0	0	0	0
Capstone	0	1	1	0	1
Ensemble	2	4	4	3	4
Private lessons	2	2	4	3	2
Total courses	16	17	18	15	16
Piano proficiency	No	Yes	No	Yes	No

[a]Many colleges integrate musicianship and music theory; therefore, the total number of course hours dedicated to musicianship may appear low.
[b]Three semesters of music theory at Skidmore involve the same number of credit hours as the previous four-semester version of the requirement.

capstone or thesis at other liberal arts colleges. Although the precise format differs somewhat among the institutions in our study, senior capstones in music generally involve one of three options: an extended paper (fifty pages or more) based on original research and analysis in theory, history, or ethnomusicology; a one-hour public recital of advanced repertory accompanied by oral and/or printed program notes, and a research paper that contextualizes the works performed; or an original composition accompanied by a reflective paper. The senior integrative exercise or capstone project usually grows out of courses students have taken and reflects their individual interests and focus within the music major. In most cases, two faculty members direct the project as first and second readers, and completion of the project usually involves a presentation for the department.

The traditional major provides room for few electives. Beyond the academic and applied music requirements, two of the five colleges with traditional majors require piano proficiency, which can add as many as four semesters of piano lessons to a music major's load. The traditional music major can be hard to complete in four years, since liberal arts students usually devote two years to general education while also meeting the course requirements for one or more majors. The many requirements in a traditional curriculum are a deterrent to potential majors, especially because most of them have no intention of pursuing careers in music. The strength of the traditional major is that it provides a solid foundation in Western classical music and prepares students (the relatively small number who are interested) for advanced training at the graduate level.

Eight of the colleges in our sample offer a compact music major (Table 3.3). By our definition, the compact major includes ten or fewer prescribed courses and eighteen or fewer requirements in all. Prescribed courses include Western music theory and history along with other requirements that vary by department. Some require a course in ethnomusicology or popular music, some require participation in ensembles and/or private lessons, and some require seminars or capstone projects. However, none of these departments requires piano proficiency, and the compact major provides room for as many as eight electives. A weakness of the compact major is that it mandates particularly close advising for those students who plan to pursue careers in music to ensure they can qualify for admission to graduate or professional training programs. Its strength lies in its flexibility. It accommodates individual student interests, facilitates the completion of double majors, and encourages cross-disciplinary training, which, as our survey respondents agreed, is a hallmark of liberal education. Music departments that feature a compact major may also be more agile in remapping the curriculum according to ongoing changes in the field of music.

We asked the faculty members we interviewed to comment on the rationale behind their adoption of a compact music major. Jenny Kallick (Amherst) explained, "We used to have a heavily proscriptive major that colored [it] in a way that did not reflect our philosophy. The leanness of the [current] requirements allows students to create their own areas of interest as a focus."[10] Along the same lines, Mauro Botelho (Davidson) stated that "The old major was very prescriptive and biased toward classroom instruction. The new major envisions pathways such as performance, composition, history, world music, possibly digital music in the future."[11] These comments reflect the flexible, individualized nature of the compact major and its potential to incorporate emerging disciplines within the field of music. Distilling the core of the music major allows students to create their own emphases, since they have the opportunity to take many more electives than in the traditional major. Individualized emphases in turn increase the likelihood that alumni will pursue music-related careers. At Hampshire College,

---

10. Telephone interview, May 20, 2015.
11. Telephone interview, May 6, 2015.

Table 3.3 THE COMPACT MUSIC MAJOR

Requirements	Amherst	Bowdoin	Colorado	Davidson	Grinnell	Hampshire	Reed	Smith
Theory	2	3	1	1	2	4	2	1
Musicianship[a]	0	0	0	0	2	0	0	0
Music history	1	3	3	1	2	3	2	1
World/popular	1	0	2	1	0	0	1	0
Creative course	0	0	1	0	0	0	0	0
Electives	2	3	3	6	8	7	3	6
Advanced seminars	2	0	2	0	0	0	0	0
Hybrid course	0	0	1	0	0	0	0	0
Junior/senior seminar	0	0	0	1	1	0	1	1
Capstone	0	1	1	0	0	1	0	0
Ensembles	0	2	2	2	0	0	2	0
Private lessons	0	2	2	0	4	2	2	0
Total courses	8	14	17	12	18	17	14	10
Piano proficiency	No	No	No	No	No	No	No	No

[a]Many colleges integrate musicianship and music theory; therefore, the total number of course hours dedicated to musicianship may appear low.

for example, students have created interdisciplinary emphases in music and film, dance, political science, economics, cultural studies, and social action. Music alumni from Hampshire have entered careers in music journalism, arts administration, music therapy, music education, composition, and studio teaching, among others.

Several of the music departments in this study offer discrete concentrations within the music major. Students at Amherst, Hampshire, and Pomona may concentrate in musicology or ethnomusicology, and both Pomona and Smith offer concentrations in performance. Carleton offers a concentration in American music that permits courses outside the music major to count toward the degree. The American music concentration is largely an academic degree and is open to students without formal musical training. It includes a gateway survey of American music history and styles, a course in critical perspectives on American culture, three courses on specific American musical traditions, a course on particular social institutions that shape musical life, and a capstone seminar. The option to concentrate in a specific discipline within the field of music provides more focused preparation for students planning to attend graduate school. Concentrations also permit students who are majoring in a field other than music to demonstrate competence in a certain aspect of music. In addition, as this chapter was in preparation (2016), the faculties at Carleton and Colorado were in the process of developing a minor or certificate program in music performance. The certificate or minor in performance will recognize the achievements of students who complete a course of private lessons at the intermediate or advanced level and who participate in specified numbers and kinds of departmental ensembles and public concerts. It also requires at least one academic music course. Concentrations, certificates, and focused minors represent progressive adaptations to changing student culture at liberal arts colleges; they offer distinct pathways through the music department and permit students to define both the major and performance in their own ways. Russell commented that "The direction we are moving will take us closer to the amazing students we have who are interested in music. In the past, if students played bluegrass or started a rock magazine, we didn't have a way to recognize them or form scholarly communities around their interests. We are heading toward a [curriculum] that is more welcoming to the students who already see themselves in our courses."[12]

Regardless of whether music departments offer a traditional or compact major, interdisciplinary concentrations, or minors and certificates in performance, liberal arts music faculty are transforming the way they teach through

12. Telephone interview, May 14, 2015.

innovative courses designed to prepare students for lifelong engagement with music. The next section discusses some of the approaches taken and courses taught at the colleges in our study.

TRANSFORMING MUSIC PEDAGOGY AT LIBERAL ARTS COLLEGES

The introduction to this volume outlines five priorities for undergraduate music education in the twenty-first century: commitment to community, commitment to the practical concerns of professional musicians, commitment to global awareness, commitment to social justice, and commitment to creative, student-driven projects and practices. These five priorities resonate clearly with the educational mission of liberal arts music departments. Our curricula reflect a commitment to active engagement with the local and regional community through course offerings that address local musical cultures. We invite local and regional artists to give workshops and concerts on campus, and we encourage student projects that involve local music makers and musical institutions. Few of our alumni become professional musicians, but increased inclusion of courses and ensembles focused on world or popular music and music technology reflects our commitment to comprehensive practical musicianship. Many liberal arts colleges now include a commitment to global awareness in their mission statements, which music supports through curricular and co-curricular programming as well as inclusive course design. Many liberal arts colleges have also begun to address social justice through courses, co-curricular activities, and offices of community-based research. However, music departments have been slower to embrace the last initiatives, with the notable exceptions of Amherst, Carleton, and Hampshire. Finally, liberal arts music faculty excel at facilitating creative, student-driven projects. We often employ what might be called integrative pedagogy, which involves the synthesis of two or more modes of music learning within a single course, particularly in hybrid courses and courses that involve project-based or field-based learning. Respondents to the survey questionnaire indicated that they are actively seeking ways to strengthen inclusive course design and integrative pedagogy.

Inclusive course design incorporates the musical styles of domestic peoples of color as well as world musics into courses required for the major such as music theory, aural skills labs, and music history. The goal of inclusive course design is to move beyond the single course in ethnomusicology or popular music that many departments added onto the major and to work instead toward diversifying everything we teach. The need for inclusive course design also applies to ethnomusicology classes, which sometimes privilege international musical styles while neglecting those of domestic peoples of color. Courses in music theory are prime candidates for inclusive course design.

At Bowdoin, for example, faculty members incorporate as many styles as possible into first- and second-level theory classes, and they avoid drawing sharp distinctions between classical and vernacular musics. Vineet Shende stated that "Secondary dominants exist as much today as they did two hundred years ago," explaining that he teaches music theory using student iPod song collections as well as pieces from the Western canon.[13] Similarly, theory courses at Carleton feature examples from the Beatles, gamelan, and South Asian traditions. Russell remarked that "Our theory faculty have remade theory so that it is relevant to and inclusive of a broader set of musical interests."[14] Michael Tenzer's chapter in this volume describes specific strategies for inclusive design in music theory as well as in music courses for general students.

We define integrative pedagogy as the synthesis of two or more modes of music learning within a single course. Integrative pedagogies occur in hybrid courses as well as courses that involve project-based or field-based learning. Hybrid courses engage students in research, writing, critical reading, and discussion, along with music analysis, performance, composition, and arrangement. Hybrid courses culminate in a concert of the music learned, composed, and arranged during the class. For example, Russell teaches a course at Carleton titled the US Folk Music Revival in collaboration with Mark Kreitzer, Carleton's instructor in American folk instruments. Students in the class engage in the kind of reading, writing, and discussion that would normally occur in an academic class. In addition, during one session each week, students divide into two groups. Those without prior musical background receive beginning guitar lessons from Russell, while students with at least one year of experience playing the guitar, banjo, mandolin, fiddle, or other stringed instrument work with Kreitzer. At the end of the class, the students recreate a folk music coffeehouse and perform for one another. Russell has written that

> Whereas losing a third of the lecture and discussion time has necessitated some sacrifice of course content, there is no question that student benefit from the applied sections is enormous. Playing the music of the folk revival, and playing it with others, rewards them with a deeper knowledge of repertory, technique, and performance practice. Students notice similarities and departures in song form and harmony. They are able to think in some detail about individual performance styles. They hear and feel connections between songs in a way that was not prompted by listening exams, but rather by their own intellectual paths. Engaging the music as players helps them as scholars; their study of the period, in turn, informs their playing. (Russell 2015, 343)

13. Telephone interview, May 11, 2015.
14. Telephone interview, May 14, 2015.

Figure 3.3. Colorado College students conclude the 2015 American Folk Music course by performing at a national bluegrass festival in Durango, Colorado. Photo courtesy of Kendall Rock; used by permission.

Other examples of hybrid courses include American Folk Music, taught by Ryan Bañagale and Keith Reed at Colorado (Figure 3.3), Irish Traditional Music, taught by Levine and Mick Bolger at Colorado (see the companion website for the syllabus ▶),[15] and Jazz Seminar, taught by Marty Ehrlich at Hampshire. These courses differ from the integrated pedagogies developed at schools of music, such as the University of Miami, in that they are not theory or musicianship courses. Rather, they are designed for both music majors and general students, although they may carry prerequisites, such as the ability to play a relevant instrument or sing at an intermediate level. Hybrid courses include focused work on performance, arrangement, and composition within the appropriate style but are offered as electives within the music major rather than as core requirements. These pedagogical methods mirror those used in noncanonical ensembles, as Justin Patch describes elsewhere in this volume, and constitute another way to encourage greater participation in music making within the undergraduate music curriculum.

Project-based courses involve collaborative, experiential learning that results in a multifaceted production demonstrating the application of several different skills. An example of a project-based course is Pioneer Valley Soundscapes, taught at Amherst by Jeffers Engelhardt and Jason Robinson (see the companion website for the syllabus ▶). In this class, students document the musical life and acoustic terrain of the Pioneer Valley region of

15. Another hybrid course taught at Colorado College is Indonesian Music (team-taught by Levine and I Made Lasmawan), which engages students in the composition, arrangement, and public performance of original music for Javanese gamelan ageng. Levine has also taught World Music as a hybrid course.

western Massachusetts by making ethnographic films. The course begins with critical reading of, writing about, and discussion of scholarly articles on sonic environments, community music making, local histories, ethnographic methods, and approaches to cultural representation. During the second part of the course, students conduct ethnomusicological fieldwork with musicians and musical communities in the Pioneer Valley. Working in pairs or small groups, students contribute fifteen-minute films to a web-based documentary archive.[16] Staff members from Amherst's Center for Community Engagement and Information Technology unit provide assistance in arranging transportation to field sites and in the use of audio and video equipment and editing. Engelhardt's syllabus explains that

> The rewards of this course are substantial and perhaps unlike anything you have encountered at Amherst—getting to know people whom you would have never otherwise met, forming new musical relationships and friendships, coming to know and appreciate more about your sonic and social surround, investing yourself in creating something of use and lasting value for others in the community ... deepening your understanding of musics that already mean a lot to you, or learning new technologies. A basic premise of this course is that you will learn by doing, experimenting, being open to the unexpected, and seeking out people and sounds that promise to tell interesting, important stories. (Engelhardt 2015)

Additional project-based learning courses include Making Opera, taught by Jenny Kallick (Amherst), Music Journalism for Radio, taught by Rebecca Miller (Hampshire), and Beatlemore Skidmania, taught by Gordon Thompson (Skidmore). In Kallick's course, students learn about opera history, musical style, and theatrical production while preparing an opera for public performance on campus. Kallick's students collaborate with young singers, costume and set designers, and directors who live in the Northeast corridor, many of whom participate in the summer Glimmerglass Festival near Cooperstown, New York. Miller's class capitalizes on Hampshire's strong film, photography, and journalism programs, and subsequently some alumni have embarked on careers in music journalism. Skidmore offers a minor in arts administration and has a long connection to the music industry. Thompson's course contributes to these initiatives by engaging a small group of students in the planning, organization, and production of a concert of music composed or inspired by the Beatles. Thompson establishes a theme for each concert that requires students to research a particular album or year in Beatles history. Students learn to recruit, audition, and

16. The documentary films produced by students in this class may be accessed at http://www.pioneervalleysoundscapes.org/.

select performers, design the concert program and related merchandise such as posters and T-shirts, advertise the concert, and stage-manage the event. This is the largest annual event on campus other than commencement.[17] Project-based learning also occurs in music courses at Colorado, Smith, and Williams, among others.

Field-based learning immerses students in a domestic or international musical culture by moving the classroom off-campus for an extended period; these kinds of courses support the development of intermusical competence and promote intercultural communication. Field-based learning occurs in a course titled Music, Culture, and Performance: Bali, team-taught by Elizabeth Macy (Skidmore) and I Made Lasmawan (Colorado). Students travel to Bangah, a farming village in central Bali, where they live at the Lasmawan family compound. They study the history and culture of Balinese music while learning to perform gamelan angklung, gamelan gong kebyar, gamelan gender wayang, gamelan balaganjur, and gamelan joged bumbung. They also attend a wide range of concerts and temple ceremonies, participate in lecture demonstrations led by guest artists (Figure 3.4), and ultimately perform for the community. A main focus of the class is the critical analysis of the impact of colonization, globalization, and tourism on the arts and environment in Bali (see the companion website for the syllabus) ⓟ.[18]

The pedagogical methods described here illustrate approaches to transforming the way music is taught and learned at liberal arts colleges along the lines proposed by Moore and the other contributors to this volume. Inclusive course design interweaves diverse content into the fabric of the liberal arts music major, whereas hybrid, project-based, and field-based courses inspire student creativity and synthesize academic content and skills with embodied musical practice. However, these kinds of curricular transformations are expensive in terms of both resources and time. They often require team teaching and can incur additional cost, which demands a commitment from the music department as a whole when allocating operating budgets and endowment funds. Individual faculty members must often seek funds outside the music department to support curricular innovations. Perhaps most importantly, the specialties, capabilities, and interests of the existing faculty must be foregrounded in the curriculum, and not everyone feels comfortable teaching inclusive content and hybrid, project-based, or field-based courses.

17. Additional information and concert programs for "Beatlemore Skidmania" may be found at http://www.skidmore.edu/music/events/skidmania.

18. Examples of field-based courses taught at Colorado College include the Arts and Culture of Bali, team-taught in Bali by Levine or Macy with Lasmawan, Irish Traditional Music, team-taught in Ireland by Levine with Mick Bolger, and In the Footsteps of Bach, team-taught in Germany by Ofer Ben-Amots and Michael Grace.

Figure 3.4. Skidmore students enrolled in Music, Culture, and Performance: Bali participate in a Balinese dance workshop led by Ibu Suasti Bandem in the village of Bangah (2015). Photo courtesy of Elizabeth Macy; used by permission.

FINDING A BALANCE

Finding a balance between the conservatory-style curriculum and new curricular models in liberal arts music departments presents a significant challenge. Some survey respondents mentioned the difficulty their departments have in covering the array of theory and musicianship courses needed to prepare majors for graduate school. Others discussed the wish to expand course offerings in ethnomusicology, popular music, and music technology but felt constrained by personnel, budgets, and physical space. Some raised concerns about connecting studio and ensemble work to academic studies. "We need much better coordination between classroom and performance teachers," wrote one respondent; "we neglect the powerful potential collaboration between classroom and studio teachers to support students' theory and musicianship studies." Additional concerns revolved around the difficulty of attracting liberal arts students to the music major despite curricular flexibility. "From my interactions with students," a respondent stated, "it is clear that the majority of our Western approach to music does not necessarily allow for the creative approach that students desire." Another wrote that "It's very hard to get students whose main interest is popular music / cultural studies in music to actually major."

Conflicting values and worldviews among individual faculty members can pose a challenge to curricular change in liberal arts music departments. Faculty who themselves were trained in conservatories or schools of music tend to value professionalized training focused on interpretive performance, theory, composition, and history within the Western canon. By contrast, those who themselves completed double majors, attended liberal arts colleges, or took graduate training in music that was interdisciplinary and noncanonical tend to favor an individualized major. Russell commented that "You're up against everyone's bottom line when it comes to making room for change. It bumps up against everyone's core values, and there are generational differences. It can feel very personal at times."[19] Thompson echoed this sentiment, stating that "Curricula represent faculty turf. The curriculum is the battleground for ideology and personal status. Including what one does in the [requirements for the major] means that one is more important. It is a reality."[20] Tony Perman (Grinnell) provided a slightly different perspective: "Achieving curricular balance is so difficult because what has held the major together is the Western music canon; now that the canon is breaking down, it's hard to maintain cohesion."[21] Yet curricular change can be managed by "caring about teaching, committing oneself to it, willingness on the part of a collegial faculty to change and adapt, and talking to students," according to a survey respondent. In Chapter 2 in this volume, Brian Pertl discusses specific strategies for managing curricular change.

Despite the challenges, most survey respondents and the faculty members we interviewed expressed enthusiasm for new directions in music curricula at liberal arts colleges. Finding curricular balance does not imply replacing or superseding the Western concert tradition. Rather, it involves responding proactively to broader changes in the musical lives of our students, our society, and the world at large. It also requires recognition of the role of music in a liberal education oriented toward the development of critical thought, the whole person, and ethical values. As one respondent wrote, "Every value judgement we instill, question, or reinforce has ethical consequences. The most ethical choice music departments can make would be to validate and support all musical experiences, regardless of their place in a received musical canon. This is why it is so important that our curriculum reflect the inclusivity

19. Telephone interview, May 14, 2015.
20. Telephone interview, May 19, 2015.
21. Telephone interview, May 13, 2015.

we desire in the student body and the world around us." Perhaps Jenny Kallick (Amherst) said it best: "Being open to all possibilities is a good way to be a musician."[22]

ACKNOWLEDGMENTS

We presented preliminary versions of this work in Levine 2014, at the 2014 meetings of the Society for Ethnomusicology, and in webinars sponsored by CMS in 2014 and 2015. We are grateful to Colorado College for generous financial support from a Mellon Faculty-Student Collaborative Research Grant, a Venture Grant, and the Christine S. Johnson Professorship. We thank student research assistants Tabetha Katz, who initiated the web-based analysis of liberal arts music departments, and Breana Taylor, who supported manuscript preparation. We also thank Dr. Meghan Rubenstein, Colorado College Visual Resources Curator, who helped to format the figures, and Dr. Amanda Udis-Kessler, the Colorado College director of Assessment and Program Review, who assisted with design, administration, and analysis of the survey questionnaire in compliance with the college's institutional review board. We appreciate all who completed the survey questionnaire and those who participated in telephone interviews: Jenny Kallick (Amherst), Vineet Shende (Bowdoin), Melinda Russell (Carleton), Ofer Ben-Amots (Colorado), Mauro Botelho (Davidson), Tony Perman (Grinnell), Rebecca Miller (Hampshire), Victoria Malawey (Macalester), Alfred Cramer (Pomona), Virginia Hancock (Reed), Gordon Thompson (Skidmore), Margaret Sarkissian (Smith), and Anthony Sheppard (Williams). Finally, we thank those who served with Levine on the CMS Task Force on the Undergraduate Music Major: Patricia Shehan Campbell, Juan Chattah, Lee Higgins, David Myers, Timothy Rice, David Rudge, and Ed Sarath (cf. Campbell et al. 2014). Special thanks are due to Tamara Bentley, Colorado College professor of art, for her inspiration as Levine's writing partner.

We dedicate this work to our friend and colleague, Dr. Katherine Hagedorn (1961–2013). Katherine was a founding member of a peer-mentoring group formed in 1997 with Levine, Melinda Russell, Margaret Sarkissian, Gordon Thompson, and Roger Vetter, the scant handful of ethnomusicologists who were then teaching at liberal arts colleges. As a professor of music and associate dean at Pomona College, Katherine was known as an innovative, inspirational teacher and a brilliant scholar. We remember her energy, humor, and ebullience, and we miss her sorely.

22. Telephone interview, May 20, 2015.

REFERENCES

Campbell, Patricia S., et al. 2014. "Transforming Music Study from Its Foundations: A Manifesto for Progressive Change in the Undergraduate Preparation of Music Majors." Missoula, MT: College Music Society. http://symposium.music.org/index.php?option=com_k2&view=item&id=11118:transforming-music-study-from-its-foundations-a-manifesto-for-progressive-change-in-the-undergraduate-preparation-of-music-majors&Itemid=126. Accessed December 28, 2016.

Carnegie Foundation for the Advancement of Teaching. 1985. "Change Trendlines: The Liberal Arts Perspective." *Change*, Vol. 17 No. 4, 31–33.

Delucchi, Michael. 1997. "Liberal Arts Colleges and the Myth of Uniqueness." *Journal of Higher Education*, Vol. 68 No. 4, 414–426.

Kushner, Roland J. 1999. "Curriculum as Strategy: The Scope and Organization of Business Education in Liberal Arts Colleges." *Journal of Higher Education*, Vol. 70 No. 4, 413–40.

Lang, Eugene M. 1999. "Distinctively American: The Liberal Arts College." *Daedalus*, Vol. 128 No. 1, 133–150.

Levine, Victoria Lindsay. 2014. "Making the Music Major Relevant at Liberal Arts Colleges." *College Music Symposium*, Vol. 54. http://symposium.music.org/index.php?option=com_k2&view=item. Accessed August 31, 2015.

NPR Staff. 2011. "College Student Debt Grows: Is It Worth It?" *All Things Considered*, May 16. http://www.wbur.org/npr/136214779/college-student-debt-grows-is-it-worth-it. Accessed May 6, 2015.

Pfnister, Allan O. 1984. "The Role of the Liberal Arts College: A Historical Overview of the Debates." *Journal of Higher Education*, Vol. 55 No. 2, 145–170.

Russell, Melinda. 2015. "Finding and Recovering Musicality in a College Folk Music Class." In *This Thing Called Music. Essays in Honor of Bruno Nettl*, Victoria Lindsay Levine and Philip V. Bohlman, eds., 342–353. Lanham, MD: Rowman and Littlefield.

Sarath, Ed. 2014. "Transforming Music Study from Its Foundations: A Manifesto for Progressive Change in the Undergraduate Preparation of Music Majors." Report of the College Music Society Task Force on the Undergraduate Music Major.

Solís, Ted, ed. 2004. *Performing Ethnomusicology. Teaching and Representation in World Music Ensembles*. Berkeley: University of California Press.

Tenzer, Michael, ed. 2006. *Analytical Studies in World Music*. Oxford: Oxford University Press.

Udis-Kessler, Amanda. 2014. "Liberal Arts College Music Department Survey Thematic Organization." Unpublished report.

CHAPTER 4

Training in Local Oral Traditions

Analysis of Postsecondary Music Programs

in North America

MARK F. DEWITT

Increasingly in recent years, instruction in the making of folk and traditional music has appeared in higher education in the United States, where Euro-American art music (along, more recently, with jazz) has held exclusive sway. At some colleges and universities, this development has taken the form of engagement with local communities of musicians whose music is identified with the region where the institution is located—for example, indigenous music in Hawaii, Cajun music in Louisiana, and old-time and bluegrass music in Appalachia—a context different in goals and impact from the typical world music ensemble. This chapter documents and advocates this small and growing trend.

In the mid-twentieth century, jazz became the first vernacular music to make inroads in the curricula of community colleges and four-year colleges and universities in the United States. Since then, jazz in the academy has gone from a largely oral tradition with high commercial success and low social status to an increasingly literate tradition with low commercial prospects and much higher social status, accepted as an art alongside classical music in several of the nation's top conservatories and schools of music (Wilf 2014, 53–81). After tastes in commercial popular music moved on in the 1950s to other genres such as rhythm and blues, rock, and country music, further opportunities to study vernacular music began to appear in conjunction with the development of music industry programs in higher education (Powell, Krikun, and Pignato 2015; Patch, Chapter 6 in this volume). Meanwhile, departments and schools of music began hiring ethnomusicologists on their faculties and starting graduate programs that featured one or more performing ensembles of music from another part of the world, often an oral tradition or one in which a music student's prior training was of little use (Solís 2004; Schippers 2010).

Performance training programs in folk and traditional music began to emerge in North America in the 1980s, on a parallel time frame with some in Scandinavia and the British Isles (Hill 2009; Keegan-Phipps 2007; Talty, Chapter 5 in this volume). Here I examine degree programs at accredited two- and four-year postsecondary institutions in the United States, Canada, and Mexico, especially but not exclusively those that focus on traditions that developed in the region where the institution is located. In addition to conducting a broad overview of such programs, I draw from my own experience working at the University of Louisiana at Lafayette with its traditional music program.

This study relates to the College Music Society's task force report (Campbell et al. 2014) in that the programs covered here support at least two of the authors' "core pillars of reform": diversity and integration. Specifically, such programs address the following symptoms that the report attributes to the problem of ethnocentrism in music curricula: "The fact that music majors commonly spend many years on campus without even a nod to surrounding multicultural communities, and that practitioners from these communities are rarely invited to engage with university students of music, underscores the extent to which this problem manifests itself locally and practically as well as more philosophically" (Campbell et al. 2014, 19). Many of the vernacular music programs that are the subject of this chapter strive to achieve integration with the rest of the music curriculum, such that the diversity achieved surpasses token representation. The CMS task force's third pillar of reform, creativity, is not a focus here, due to time and space limitations. It is not a given that such programs foster musical creativity, although some of them clearly do.

In this chapter I am also following the lead of editor Robin Moore, whose introduction touches on a number of values embodied by degree programs centered on oral traditions. I have already mentioned the commitment to community. Commitment to the practical concerns of professional musicians varies according to the presence or absence of professional music degrees at a specific institution. At institutions where professional degrees in music (and also, often, in music business) are offered (see Tables 4.4 and 4.5), the study of oral traditions will inevitably have a greater impact on future professional musicians, whether they concentrate on folk and traditional music or simply gain fluency in traditional music through participation in an ensemble or applied lessons. The commitment to social justice is embedded in the act of adding historically marginal forms of music to the curriculum as music to be played, not simply heard from a playback system for a music appreciation class. A curriculum centered on oral tradition(s) also removes an entry barrier for the considerable number of students who play music but who never learned how to read Western staff notation, a skill which itself is correlated with social class (Southgate and Roscigno 2009).

The chief intended audience of this chapter consists of faculty and administrators of schools and departments of music, especially those who are contemplating the addition of local oral tradition music to their curriculum or at least open to the idea of doing so. The opportunities to create new ties with the community are numerous and energizing, not to mention the interdisciplinary connections that can be made with other departments in your institution. Talented students who happen not to read music will walk through the door and enrich the soundscape of the music building. The students you already have will gain new skills for the marketplace and new ideas for their art.

This chapter is a benchmarking study in the sense that it provides points of reference, through descriptions of over two dozen programs, for a variety of institutional contexts. My experience with working for large organizations in the for-profit, nonprofit, and education sectors is that for every person who has an idea for a new way of doing things, there is a cautious manager looking over her shoulder and asking, "Well, how are other people doing it?" and "How does that apply to us?" In these pages most readers should be able to begin to answer these questions for themselves and their superiors, since many different kinds of institutions are represented as well as several musical traditions. The multiplicity of cases testifies to the fact that there is no one way to build a curriculum. Some programs have grown from small, grassroots beginnings gradually over decades, while others have been created as the result of a top-down administrative decision or large institutional gift. Some spring from vocational or professional degree programs, while others thrive in a liberal arts environment at a small college or large research university. Some coexist peacefully in a school of music alongside classical music and jazz, while others have had to take refuge in a vocational division or area studies department. Whatever the reader's situation, there is probably a solution that one or more of the institutions listed in Table 4.1 has found. It is beyond the scope of this study to pronounce which solutions have worked best, and in most cases (including mine) these programs are too new to be able to evaluate them definitively. My hope is that anyone who wants to start a curriculum can begin with this study, identify a set of comparable benchmark programs, and do one's own additional research to assess what will work best at his or her institution.

Table 4.1 NORTH AMERICAN INSTITUTIONS WITH A PROGRAM IN TRADITIONAL MUSIC OR NOTABLE ASPECTS THEREOF.

Institution Name	Location	Level	Control	Students[a]	NASM Accred	Basic[b]	Undergrad Profile[c]	Size & Setting[d]
Appalachian State University	Boone, North Carolina, USA	4-year[e]	Public	16,968	✓	Master's/L	FT4/MS/HTI	L4/R
Belmont University	Nashville, Tennessee, USA	4-year	Private NFP[f]	5,424	✓	Master's/L	FT4/MS/HTI	M4/R
Berea College	Berea, Kentucky, USA	4-year	Private NFP	1,548		Bac/A&S	FT4/S/LTI	S4/HR
Berklee College of Music	Boston, Massachusetts, USA	4-year	Private NFP	4,145		Spec/Arts[g]	Spec/Arts	Spec/Arts
Cape Breton University	Sydney, Nova Scotia, Canada	4-year	Public	2,943	N/A	N/A[h]	N/A	N/A
Cégep régional de Lanaudière à Joliette	Joliette, Québec, Canada	2-year	Public	2,650	N/A	N/A	N/A	N/A
College of William and Mary	Williamsburg, Virginia, USA	4-year	Public	7,874		RU/H	FT4/MS/LTI	M4/HR
Columbia College Chicago	Chicago, Illinois, USA	4-year	Private NFP	12,127		Master's/M	FT4/I	L4/NR
Denison University	Granville, Ohio, USA	4-year	Private NFP	2,267		Bac/A&S	FT4/MS/LTI	S4/HR
East Tennessee State University	Johnson City, Tennessee, USA	4-year	Public	14,421	✓	DRU	FT4/S/HTI	L4/NR
Glenville State College	Glenville, West Virginia, USA	4-year	Public	1,721		Bac/Diverse	FT4/I	S4/R
Hazard Community Technical College	Hyden, Kentucky, USA	2-year	Public	4,713		Assoc/Pub-R-M	PT2	M2
Morehead State University	Morehead, Kentucky, USA	4-year	Public	8,822	✓	Master's/L	FT4/S/LTI	M4/R
Northwest Indian College	Bellingham, Washington, USA	4-year	Public	609		Tribal	MFT4/I	VS4/NR
Palo Alto College	San Antonio, Texas, USA	2-year	Public	8,335		Assoc/Pub-U-MC	PT2	M2
South Plains College	Levelland, Texas, USA	2-year	Public	10,011		Assoc/Pub-R-L	Mix2	L2

Institution	Location	Level	Control	Student population	NASM	Basic	Undergraduate Profile	Size & Setting
Texas State University	San Marcos, Texas, USA	4-year	Public	30,803	✓	Master's/L	FT4/S/HTI	L4/NR
Texas Tech University	Lubbock, Texas, USA	4-year	Public	30,049	✓	RU/H	FT4/S/HTI	L4/R
Universidad Nacional Autónoma de México (UNAM)	Mexico City, Mexico	4-year	Public	197,594	N/A	N/A	N/A	N/A
University of California, Los Angeles	Los Angeles, California, USA	4-year	Public	38,550		RU/VH	FT4/MS/HTI	L4/R
University of Hawaii at Manoa	Honolulu, Hawaii, USA	4-year	Public	20,435	✓	RU/VH	FT4/S/HTI	L4/NR
University of Hawaii Maui College	Kahului, Hawaii, USA	4-year	Public	4,114		Assoc/Pub4	PT4	S4/NR
University of Louisiana at Lafayette	Lafayette, Louisiana, USA	4-year	Public	16,361	✓	RU/H	FT4/S/LTI	L4/NR
University of Virginia-Main Campus	Charlottesville, Virginia, USA	4-year	Public	24,355		RU/VH	FT4/MS/LTI	L4/R
Volunteer State Community College	Gallatin, Tennessee, USA	2-year	Public	8,430		Assoc/Pub-S-SC	Mix2	L2
Warren Wilson College	Asheville, North Carolina, USA	4-year	Private NFP	1,028		Bac/A&S	FT4/MS/LTI	S4/HR

[a] Level, Control, and Student population data, as well as the three rightmost columns of classifications, were gathered for US institutions from the Carnegie Classifications of Institutions of Higher Education website using its Institution Lookup facility; ttp://carnegieclassifications.iu.edu/lookup_listings/institution.php (accessed August 4, 2015).

[b] For an explanation of the Carnegie "Basic" Classification and its categories, see chapter appendix.

[c] For an explanation of the Carnegie "Undergraduate Profile" Classification and its categories, see chapter appendix.

[d] For an explanation of the Carnegie "Size & Setting" Classification and its categories, see chapter appendix.

[e] Meaning "4-year or above."

[f] Private not-for-profit.

[g] As a "Special Focus Institution," Berklee did not receive normal ratings for these classifications.

[h] NASM membership and Carnegie Classifications do not apply to institutions outside of the United States.

RESEARCH BASIS

The foundation of this chapter is my personal experience of stewarding the introduction of local oral traditions into the School of Music and Performing Arts at the University of Louisiana at Lafayette, a second-tier public research university with a high percentage of commuting students that is taking steps to develop a more residential campus and attain the highest research rating in the Carnegie classification system.[1] In 2008, an endowed chair in traditional music was established at the university after eleven years of community fundraising and matching grants from the state, and I was hired as the first holder of the chair in 2010. The Dr. Tommy Comeaux Endowed Chair in Traditional Music affords an annual budget that pays for adjunct instructors, artist residencies, guest lecturers, and other associated expenses. The school began offering a bachelor of arts in music with a concentration in traditional music in the fall of 2012 after obtaining approvals from the Louisiana Board of Regents and the National Association of Schools of Music (NASM).

Additional research for this chapter includes site visits to East Tennessee State University (ETSU) in 2012 and Texas State University in 2015, a visit with Le Centre de Formation des Musiciens Intervenants (CFMI) at Université Rennes 2 in France in 2012, reciprocal visits from ETSU Director Daniel Boner and CFMI-Rennes 2 students and faculty to our campus, Internet research on institution websites, e-mail correspondence with program directors and colleagues on the Society for Ethnomusicology's e-mail discussion list (SEM-L), and panel discussions at meetings of the International Council for Traditional Music (2011) and the Society for American Music (2015).[2]

SYNOPSIS OF NORTH AMERICAN PROGRAMS

As stated in the introduction, the focus of this volume is on applied instruction; that is, training in musical performance. In looking for programs parallel to ours at UL Lafayette, I developed criteria for inclusion in this study. Some

1. http://carnegieclassifications.iu.edu/ (accessed August 30, 2015). See Tables 4.6–4.8 online, ▶
2. I would like to further acknowledge first Dr. Len Springer, our university's bluegrass ensemble founder, who represented our program at the International Bluegrass Music Association's 2014 annual meeting and who pointed me to the list of university programs that the IBMA maintains on its website. Thanks also to Chris Smith at Texas Tech, who helped me organize the 2011 ICTM panel, and to Greg Reish at the Center for Popular Music at Middle Tennessee State University, who invited me into the Society for American Music panel. Additional thanks go to some SEM-L correspondents who opened my eyes to some additional programs, including Alex Rodriguez, Elizabeth Clendenning, Susan Oehler, Joel Rubin, Gayle Murchison, Anne Rasmussen, and Rolf Groesbeck.

of these refer to curricular policy and practice specific to the United States and its accrediting organization for music, NASM. Most music curricula in the United States include the core elements of general education (outside of music), applied instruction, ensemble performance, musicianship / music theory / composition, and music history and repertory. Additional elements take on prominence at some but not all colleges and universities, most commonly music education (teacher training), music business, and music technology. The following questions suggest the extent to which oral traditions are integrated into curricula.

1. Are there ensemble classes for credit dedicated to traditional music of some kind? I used a somewhat loose notion of traditional music to cast a broad net and looked especially for programs that drew on community resources for instructors, students, or audiences.
2. Do the traditional music ensembles count toward the mandatory ensemble requirement for music majors of any concentration? Candidates for a bachelor of music degree typically must enroll in at least one ensemble each semester for eight semesters. If a BM student majoring in bass performance took only one ensemble in a given semester, could the school's bluegrass ensemble (for example) be that ensemble?
3. Is applied or studio instruction offered for the instruments used in the traditional music ensembles? This most commonly takes the form of private lessons with a teacher but at the beginning or intermediate stages may involve group instruction. If standard music school instruments, such as the violin, are used in the ensemble, is applied instruction offered in the style of music that the ensemble plays, such as Cajun or bluegrass fiddle?
4. Can applied instruction in an oral tradition, vocal or instrumental, count as the primary instrument for music majors of any concentration?
5. Are there courses or tracks in music theory and music history geared for students who want to concentrate their studies on the oral tradition(s) related to their ensemble work and/or applied instruction?
6. Does the institution offer a degree, minor, diploma, or certificate centered on the performance of traditional music?

Programs did not need to meet all of these criteria to appear in the tables below, but they did need to meet more than one of them. The importance of these issues, in addition to others, such as audition and scholarship policies, has slowly come into focus at UL Lafayette. In some cases, it is a question of having access to the same types of resources as other programs within the School of Music; in other cases, essential differences in pedagogy between written and oral traditions must be recognized.

I find the term "traditional music" problematic, both for purposes of this study and generally. The International Folk Music Council changed its name to the International Council for Traditional Music (ICTM) circa 1981, presumably because the term "folk music" had been captured over twenty years earlier by the commercial music industry to mean something else and because scholars who studied elite non-Western traditions felt that "folk music" was not an accurate representation of their interests. Without necessarily knowing the history of ICTM, founders of programs at UL Lafayette, Morehead State University, and other schools chose "traditional music" to describe what they do. Yet when discussions were underway at UL Lafayette to form a traditional music program, a historical musicologist on the faculty objected, maintaining that traditional music was what *he* taught.[3] Indeed, college music instruction has *traditionally* consisted of Western art music, and my colleagues and I trip over this dual meaning of the word frequently. At the College of William and Mary, the Appalachian Music Ensemble is considered a "nontraditional ensemble" (along with world music and performance art groups) as opposed to the more customary wind ensemble, choir, orchestra, and jazz groups.[4] Warren Wilson College works around the issue by offering two music minors: a conventional music minor for those who want to study classical music or jazz, and a traditional music minor for old-time Appalachian and bluegrass music.[5] The word "vernacular" is sometimes used (but mostly by academics) to encompass both folk and popular music; Texas Tech's Vernacular Music Center is the only organization that uses it of those identified here.[6] The bluegrass genre straddles the blurry semantic boundary separating traditional music from popular music (also known here as commercial music), as do others, including Cajun, zydeco, blues and gospel music. Bluegrass was born as commercial music and later acquired a more egalitarian participant base (Kisliuk 1988, 142), while other styles began as community-based oral traditions that were later commoditized. Most school mariachis learn from published sheet music, for example. In light of these complexities, concentrating on community-based oral traditions without regard to the level of commercialization seemed a practical way forward.

When I polled the SEM-L e-mail list asking for information about programs I did not already know about, the majority of responses concerned the existence of an ensemble at one school or another, reflecting the preoccupation that ethnomusicologists have with world music ensembles as part of their teaching responsibilities (Solís 2004, Titon 2009, Dor 2014). Ted Solís makes the distinction between "realization ensembles," in which student musicians realize/apply their existing skills in the performance of canonic repertoire

3. Susanna Garcia, private communication, August 2015.
4. http://www.wm.edu/as/music/ensembles/index.php (accessed August 22, 2015).
5. http://www.warren-wilson.edu/academics/warren-wilson-college-catalog/music#minor (accessed August 22, 2015).
6. http://www.vernacularmusiccenter.org/ (accessed October 24, 2015).

(choirs, bands, orchestras, chamber music, jazz combos), and "experience ensembles," in which students first experience an unfamiliar music culture. In the latter, performance standards tend to be low and turnover high, which is typical of the world music ensemble (Solís 2004, 6–14). While there is certainly a place for the "experience ensemble," there are other situations in which we as educators should expect more from our administrations and students.

I propose we reconsider our notion of the "realization" ensemble to include those based on prevailing local cultural practices. These might include the Texas State University mariachi ensemble, populated with Texas natives who played in their high school mariachi bands (Pedroza, Chapter 7 in this volume), or a Cajun band of university students who learned to play their instruments among friends and family before attending college, or performance courses taught by instructors immersed in traditions of blues and gospel music in Chicago (Jones 2009). However, the path to curricular reform requires more than having an ensemble. Integration of oral traditions and the mindset they require into the music major curriculum, which has historically been predicated on the ability to read, perform, and analyze music in Western staff notation, must entail a more holistic and far-reaching plan. Moreover and (I think) very importantly, that path need *not* require that oral traditions be written down.

The place of music literacy in a university curriculum dedicated to oral traditions is a burning question related to a larger issue that community members raise when such curricula are established. The fact is that until a quarter century ago or so, oral traditions everywhere that were surviving were doing so with the benign neglect of the academy, training generations of practitioners through decentralized networks of autodidacts, private teachers, and community schools, with mediation playing an increasing role through the availability of audio and video recordings and the Internet. The fear is that the university, with its power and prestige, will centralize the transmission of tradition and turn out cohort after cohort of graduates who all sound the same, echoing past criticisms of jazz as taught in the academy (Alper 2007, 157) as well as folk and traditional music programs in Europe and Asia (Hill 2009, 215–216; Talty, Chapter 5, and Hsu, Chapter 8, in this volume). In other words, there is a fear of codification of oral tradition; a folklorist colleague of mine with a flair for metaphor likens this tendency to displaying a once-living being in amber. Music literacy plays into this debate with its implied authority of correctness: this is the way to play this song. A related fear is that certain teachers will require all of their students to play like them: if I employ just one fiddle teacher to teach all of our private fiddle students, will an identifiably academic style of fiddling result? Traditional music programs have a responsibility of conscious stewardship, lest they kill the very traditions they are trying to sustain. Mentors must allow students to find their own styles, nurture their creative voices within the traditions under study, and teach them to use any source material (whether it is a piece of sheet music or a recording) as just a starting point for learning a tune or song.[7]

The place of music literacy in the pedagogy of folk and traditional music is, it seems, still being worked out. Applied instructors at ETSU revealed a variety of attitudes towards it when interviewed (Frank 2014, 65–69). At UL Lafayette, I have actively discouraged the use of sheet music and tablature in most cases (except for Cajun French texts for singers), although some of the instructors I employ have felt free to disregard those wishes. In the context of applied group instruction with diverse learning styles among the students, some instructors view notation or tablature as an expedient for those who cannot keep up when learning by ear. Music literacy is also built into the structure of applied instruction in the School of Music: in order to advance through a professional degree program, a student must pass a sequence of juried exams ("juries") that are graded by standardized levels using benchmarks of music literature, repertoire graded by level of difficulty. Without notation, the association of difficulty with certain songs in the Cajun and Creole French repertoire is problematic, since almost any repertory item can be played simply or with virtuosic elaboration. How to grade memorization also comes into question with oral traditions, as does the playing of scales. Therefore we are in the process of reinventing the jury system for our traditional music majors to take these things into account. Looking in this level of detail at what other programs do regarding juries, while crucial to effective curricular reform, is beyond the scope of this study; the same goes for auditions, placement tests, scholarships, and credentials required for instructors.

Table 4.1 lists public and private North American institutions with a program in traditional music or notable aspects thereof, meaning that the program can answer yes to at least two of the questions posed above.[8] The list is undoubtedly not exhaustive. In terms of the Carnegie Basic Classification, the institutions represent a wide range of orientations from community colleges to baccalaureate institutions with no graduate programs to tier 1 research universities ("RU/VH"), and several gradations in between. This institutional overview provides valuable context. As anyone who has received doctoral training at a research university and then gone to teach at another type of school knows, the kind of instruction that is desirable and appropriate at a given institution varies widely according to such parameters as admissions requirements, the percentages of students that live off-campus or attend

7. These concerns have come up in conversations not only with community members in Louisiana but also when speaking with colleagues at East Tennessee State University (see also Frank 2014, 65–79).

8. A key to the abbreviations used by the Carnegie Classifications of Institutions of Higher Education can be found at http://carnegieclassifications.iu.edu/descriptions/ (accessed November 20, 2015). See also the "Carnegie 'Basic' Classification" table uploaded to the companion website ▶.

part-time, the presence or absence of graduate students, and the educational focus of the institution as a whole. Table 4.1 dispels any assumptions that institutions offering performance instruction in oral traditions are limited to a certain type, size, or level of academic rigor.

Of the twenty-one four-year institutions shown in Table 4.1, eight are accredited by NASM in the United States. To readers unfamiliar with the structures of American higher education, a few words of explanation are in order. Public institutions are all administered by state governments except for tribal colleges[9] and military academies, which are administered by the national government. All colleges and universities, public and private, are examined periodically by regional accreditation agencies that span several states. These institutions may pursue additional accreditations in various disciplines from a discipline-specific agency such as NASM, but an institution is not required to do this in order to maintain its overall accreditation. The presence of NASM accreditation may indicate a certain level of quality in a school's music program, but its absence does not necessarily imply a lack of quality. Several prominent music institutions have decided not to maintain NASM accreditation, including Oberlin Conservatory of Music in Ohio, Juilliard, Yale School of Music, New England Conservatory, and University of Southern California.[10]

Colleges and universities usually model their music curricula after NASM's *Handbook*, even if they have not sought its accreditation. The handbook describes two basic kinds of undergraduate music degrees: liberal arts degrees and professional degrees. While it is not completely strict about numerical percentages, NASM characterizes liberal arts degrees as requiring between 30 and 45 percent music content. In other words, for a university in which a four-year degree requires 120 credit-hours to graduate, a liberal arts music major will require between 36 and 54 credit-hours of music classes. For professional degrees, NASM looks for music education and music therapy concentrations to have at least 50 percent music content and for concentrations not requiring work in other disciplines, such as education or psychology, at least 65 percent music content (NASM 2014, 85–90).

9. Across its several campuses, Northwest Indian College, a small tribal college near Bellingham, Washington, offers courses in Northwest Coast Indian song and dance traditions, along with courses on the making of Native American dance regalia, drums, and flutes. These are purely elective and not organized as a curriculum (www.nwic.edu, accessed July 13, 2015; Ted Williams, private communication, July 2015). The scope of this study did not permit a thorough look at all thirty-seven tribal colleges listed by the American Indian Higher Education Consortium (http://www.aihec.org/who-we-serve/TCUmap.cfm, accessed August 11, 2015).

10. http://news.oberlin.edu/articles/oberlin-conservatory-withdraws-national-association-schools-music/ (accessed August 7, 2015).

For two-year degrees, while the liberal arts / professional distinction still applies in the abstract, the more relevant differentiation is between music major transfer programs (for students planning to transfer to a four-year institution and complete a bachelor's degree) and vocational programs whose degrees are designed as ends in themselves (NASM 2015, 90–93). Table 4.2 gives information about a handful of institutions awarding two-year (in the French Canadian case, three-year) degrees in which oral traditions play a significant or integral role. The column labeled Trad Music Centric reflects my interpretation of how integral oral traditions are to the degree or certificate offered. In cases where the word "traditional" or the name of a traditional genre appears in the full degree name, the Trad Music Centric designation is clear. Where traditional music is one of multiple options used to fulfill the performance portion of a curriculum but is not required, I have classified those programs as *not* Trad Music Centric.

When looking at curricula, it is important to view each in its larger institutional context: what other kinds of music are taught and what other kinds of music-related degrees are offered at that institution? Program structures and departmental affiliations can provide indirect evidence of histories of administrative resistance to the development of oral-tradition music programs and subsequent growing pains (Hebert 2011). Moreover, peer networks will influence a student who is working toward a degree concentration in oral traditions, so the existence of these other degree programs (and their students) make a difference in the informal learning environment as well as the local patterns of social stratification. I hypothesize that students quickly learn which programs have the upper hand in terms of wealth, power, or prestige, based simply on their interactions with other students. This can have an effect on their approach to and attitude towards their studies.

At Volunteer State Community College, oral traditions are integrated in the music major transfer degree programs (associate of arts or associate of science). The college has several music-related degrees weighted toward commercial music.[11] With the other schools in Table 4.2, the study of oral traditions is part of a vocational degree or certificate program. In the case of Hazard Community Technical College, the Kentucky system offers transfer degrees in preparation for university study but nothing specifically for music majors, so the bluegrass program at Hazard stands out all the more.[12] According to instructor J. P. Mathes, "It was part of a movement throughout the whole region of eastern Kentucky to look towards different jobs and different industries because of the decline of coal" (Frank 2014, 54). This decision parallels that of community leaders in south Louisiana in the 1980s, when a recession

11. http://www.volstate.edu/Music/index.php (accessed November 20, 2015); Frank 2014: 52–53.
12. http://ksbtm.hazard.kctcs.edu/ (accessed June 27, 2015).

Table 4.2 PROGRAMS AT INSTITUTIONS OFFERING TWO-YEAR DEGREES

Institution	Program Name	Department	Offers Related Degrees	Prep for 4-yr	Offers Certificate	Trad Music Centric	Program Comments	Degree Name
Cégep à Joliette	Techniques professionnelles de musique et chanson	Département de Musique	✓			✓	Offers trad music option as a three-year vocational degree (which also has a jazz option)	Diplôme d'études collégiales, Techniques professionnelles de musique et chanson, profil musique traditionnelle
Hazard CTC	Kentucky School of Bluegrass & Traditional Music	Division of Heritage, Humanities & Fine Arts	✓		✓	✓	In addition to AAS degree are offered a Studio Artist Diploma (35–45 hours) and a Certificate (14–15 hours)	Associate in Applied Science, Professional Studio Artist, Bluegrass and Traditional Music Track
Palo Alto College	Music	Fine and Performing Arts / Speech Communication			✓		Ensembles include three levels of mariachi plus one conjunto ensemble	Local Certificates in Conjunto and Mariachi Performance

(*Continued*)

Table 4.2 (Continued)

Institution	Program Name	Department	Offers Related Degrees	Prep for 4-yr	Offers Certificate	Trad Music Centric	Program Comments	Degree Name
South Plains College	Commercial Music	Creative Arts Department	✓		✓		Commercial Music ensembles include bluegrass, country, jazz, and rock; applied lessons include all bluegrass instruments.	Associate of Applied Arts in Commercial Music
University of Hawaii - Maui College	Institute for Hawaiian Music	Humanities			✓	✓	38 credit-hour certificate. Guitar, 'ukulele, voice, keyboard, composition, music theory, dance, music business and technology, Hawaiian language and singing.	Academic Subject Certificate in Hawaiian Music
Volunteer State CC	Bluegrass Music Program	Department of Visual and Performing Arts	✓	✓		✓	"for students planning to continue their education to earn a bachelor's degree in the field of Bluegrass."	Associate of Arts in Bluegrass Associate of Science in Bluegrass

in the oil-based economy led them to develop cultural tourism as an alternative revenue stream (DeWitt 2008, 198–203), which in turn created an economic justification for establishing the traditional music program at UL Lafayette over two decades later.

At South Plains College in Texas, the Creative Arts Department has a commercial music program that offers a two-year vocational degree emphasizing bluegrass and country music. The Technical Education Division administers this department and all of the college's vocational programs, while the Arts and Sciences Division oversees all of the university transfer curricula (AA and AS), including the Fine Arts Department's music major transfer degree. The two curricula have essentially no overlap. Commercial music majors take music theory fundamentals and class piano in the Fine Arts Department (basic courses that a music major transfer student could skip), then the rest of their courses through Technical Education, including a year of music theory, sight-singing and ear training; history of popular music and bluegrass, songwriting, and music technology.

The consideration thus far of two-year colleges already brings to light a number of oppositions that recur with oral tradition programs in higher education: vocational versus academic orientation, bureaucratic integration versus separation of vernacular and cultivated (classical and jazz) music studies, and establishing a programmatic identity with a specific degree or concentration versus the offering of electives in the context of general education or a general music degree. These same oppositional tendencies appear in the four-year programs (and a very few graduate programs) summarized in Tables 4.3, 4.4 and 4.5. Due to space limitations, a few remarks on general trends and notable features of these programs must suffice.

Table 4.3 summarizes four-year institutions that include oral traditions in their curricula and offer liberal arts degrees in music but no professional degrees, especially no professional performance degrees (some offer music education). These include not only liberal arts colleges but also some research universities with graduate programs in ethnomusicology or music scholarship of some kind. Of the seven institutions, five are located in or near the Appalachian Mountains and offer music associated with that region, either old-time music or bluegrass or both. While NASM offers standards for liberal arts programs, its main function is to sanction professional music degrees, so it is not surprising that none of the schools in Table 4.3 is accredited by NASM.

The requirements for applied instruction and ensemble work in a general liberal arts degree with no concentration are often conflated into a single performance requirement of two to four credit hours, requiring one course a semester for a year or two (College of William and Mary, University of Virginia). Berea College requires more (eight semesters of private lessons, six semesters of ensemble). Readers in the United Kingdom and Ireland, where the BA is often the degree awarded for undergraduate professional degrees in

Table 4.3 LIBERAL ARTS PROGRAMS AT FOUR-YEAR INSTITUTIONS NOT OFFERING PROFESSIONAL MUSIC DEGREES

Institution	Program Name	Department	Offers Related Degrees	Offers Minor	Trad Music Centric	Program Comments	Degree/Minor Name
Berea College	Music Program	Music Department	✓		✓	BA general music degree applied instruction includes banjo, mandolin, fiddle, and folk guitar (not for music education concentration). Major ensembles include bluegrass and folk ensembles.	Bachelor of Arts (BA) in Music
Cape Breton University	Folklore and Ethnomusicology	Department of History and Culture			✓	Study of traditions local to Cape Breton, especially Gaelic and Acadian, including performance of step dancing, Gaelic song, percussion with master musicians. Optional business minor.	Bachelor of Arts Community Studies (BACS) in Music
College of William & Mary	Undergraduate Program	Department of Music		✓	✓	Ensembles include Appalachian, Middle Eastern, North Indian. Applied instruction includes banjo, mandolin, flat-pick guitar.	BA in Music
Denison University	Bluegrass	Music	✓		✓	Holds an annual bluegrass festival in February. Major is structured with Western art music as the core, with bluegrass concentration added. Private lessons offered in bluegrass guitar, mandolin, banjo, fiddle.	BA in Music with a Concentration in Bluegrass

Institution				Description	Degree
UCLA	World Music Concentration	Ethnomusicology	✓	Theory & composition classes are mostly jazz, which is the other BA concentration offered by this department. Wide range of world music ensembles. Credit for applied instruction is offered for study with community musicians not on the faculty.	BA in Ethnomusicology, World Music Concentration, Performance and/or Composition Emphasis
University of Virginia	Undergraduate Program	McIntire Department of Music	✓	Private instruction offered in banjo and mandolin by a staff instructor, plus a Bluegrass Workshop ensemble class offered each spring. Other ensembles include African Music & Dance and Klezmer Ensemble.	BA in Music with a Concentration in Music Performance
Warren Wilson College	Appalachian Music Program	Music Department	✓	Ensembles include old-time string band and bluegrass band. Applied instruction in fiddle, banjo, mandolin, guitar, vocals. Home of the Swannanoa Gathering, an annual summer music camp.	Minor in Music with a Concentration in Traditional Music

traditional music with very little coursework outside of music, will note that this same degree in the United States generally connotes far less intensive musical study.

When schools add a concentration or emphasis to a liberal arts degree, they can prescribe a more performance-intensive program. UL Lafayette's concentration in traditional music requires eight hours of lessons and four hours of ensemble. The University of Virginia's performance concentration requires twenty-one credit hours of performance-related study, including applied lessons and ensembles, in addition to the two hours required by the general BA in music. Students who study banjo or mandolin and play in the university's bluegrass ensemble are just as eligible for this concentration as any other music major.[13]

Cape Breton University's School of Arts and Social Sciences offers a bachelor of arts community studies (BACS) degree that has less of a liberal arts orientation than the bachelor of arts degrees the school offers in folklore and ethnomusicology. Rather, the BACS emphasizes experiential learning through its core courses and two community internships in concentrations such as sports management, business, police work, and music. The BACS in music emphasizes study of musical traditions of Cape Breton (Gaelic, Acadian, Mi'kmaq) that includes academic courses, optional performance training, and work internships in the music industry.[14]

Several of the liberal arts programs at institutions that also offer professional music degrees (Table 4.4) are more like Cape Breton University's BACS music program in that they offer concentrations, beyond the general BA in music, that provide necessary vocational skills or specialized training of some kind. Some of these curricula do not neatly fit the focus of this chapter but have notable community-based features. The Vernacular Music Center at Texas Tech has guided the creation of undergraduate certificates in world music and in community arts entrepreneurship, the latter of which provides a track for students wishing to develop entrepreneurship skills which can be employed in developing their own careers, in promoting community arts initiatives, or as the foundation for graduate work in arts administration. The vast majority of those earning the community arts entrepreneurship certificate (which consists mostly of courses outside of music) have been music majors.[15]

A BA program at a school where a professional music curriculum exists can take advantage of some of the resources available to professional music students, including music business and technology courses, though in some

13. Joel Rubin private communication, July 15, 2015.

14. http://www.cbu.ca/academic-programs/program/school-of-arts-social-sciences/bachelor-of-arts-community-studies/2256-2/ (accessed November 1, 2015); Heather Sparling, private communication, November 2015.

15. http://www.vernacularmusiccenter.org/ (accessed August 8, 2015). Christopher J. Smith, private communication, August 16, 2015.

Table 4.4 LIBERAL ARTS PROGRAMS AT INSTITUTIONS THAT ALSO OFFER PROFESSIONAL MUSIC DEGREES

Institution	Program Name	Department	Offers Related Degrees	Offers Minor	Trad Music Centric	Program Comments	Degree/Minor Name
Appalachian State U.	Appalachian Studies	Center for Appalachian Studies		✓	✓	Undergraduate minor includes some group instruction, no lessons or ensembles. A Master of Arts degree with this concentration has no performance component.	Appalachian Music: Roots & Influences Minor
Columbia College Chicago	Contemporary, Urban, and Popular Music	Music	✓			Ensembles: blues, rhythm & blues, gospel band, gospel repertory and choir, folk, country music, Latin pop, hip hop, and several other pop and classical groups.	Bachelor of Arts (BA) in Music with Contemporary, Urban and Popular Music concentration
East Tennessee State U.	Bluegrass, Old-Time and Country Music Studies	Department of Appalachian Studies	✓	✓	✓	Old-time, bluegrass, country music, Celtic ensembles. Applied instruction in guitar, fiddle, banjo, bass, mandolin, vocals, dobro. Bluegrass theory and history.	BA in Bluegrass, Old Time, and Country Music Studies
Glenville State College	Bluegrass Music	Department of Fine Arts	✓		✓	Bluegrass major curriculum allows for two semesters of Bluegrass music history in place of Western music history and bluegrass ensemble as alternative to large ensemble. Music theory optional; required are digital media, internship, recording & engineering.	BA in Music with a Concentration in Bluegrass Music

(Continued)

Table 4.4 (Continued)

Institution	Program Name	Department	Offers Related Degrees	Offers Minor	Trad Music Centric	Program Comments	Degree/Minor Name
Morehead State University	Kentucky Center for Traditional Music	School of Music, Theatre and Dance	✓	✓	✓	Old-time, bluegrass, Celtic, blues, trad vocal ensembles. Applied instruction in guitar, fiddle, banjo, bass, mandolin, vocals, dobro, dulcimer, others. Music theory and history tailored to major.	BA in Traditional Music Studies
Texas Tech	Vernacular Music Center	School of Music		✓		World music and dance ensembles with some applied instruction. Certificate in Community Arts Entrepreneurship with courses in business, communications, psychology.	Undergraduate Certificate in Community Arts Entrepreneurship
University of Hawaii at Manoa	Hawaiian Music	Music Department	✓		✓	Hawaiian music ensembles include Hawaiian Chorus, Hawaiian Ensemble, Hula and Chant, and Slack Key Guitar. Other Asian/Pacific ensembles offered with the graduate program in ethnomusicology.	BA in Music with a Hawaiian Music Emphasis
	Hawaiian Studies	School of Hawaiian Knowledge	✓			Program focus on Hawaiian language, history, literature, and culture. Performance courses in hula and chant; lecture class on Music and Native Identity.	BA in Hawaiian Studies
UL Lafayette	Traditional Music	School of Music & Performing Arts	✓	✓	✓	Practical instruction offered in Cajun, zydeco, blues, and bluegrass styles. An 18-hour minor is required in a field related to the major.	BA in Music with a Concentration in Traditional Music

cases the bureaucratic separation of the school of music and the study of local oral traditions is almost total. This can be seen in two programs housed in Appalachian studies units: Appalachian State University's relatively modest Appalachian music minor[16] and East Tennessee State University's well-developed four-year degree program in bluegrass, old-time, and country music studies. ETSU's program began small in the Department of Music in the 1980s: a few elective ensembles, instrument lessons, and one country music course. In 1999 it changed its departmental home to Appalachian Studies, where it grew to offer a minor in 2005 and then in 2010 a major in bluegrass, old-time, and country music.[17]

ETSU's major curriculum is notably free of requirements to study music theory or music history related to classical or jazz music; all of its courses are focused on the major's highlighted genres. Music theory instruction, for example, does not include sight-reading from staff notation, but it does teach the Nashville Number System, a method developed in professional recording studios to represent song arrangements compactly using chord numbers, section designations, repeat signs, and the like (Williams 2012). The bluegrass program also has its own recording studio where students create a senior capstone project, as well as its own practice rooms and classrooms.[18]

At most other institutions, oral and literate traditions reside in the same school or department of music but with a wide variety of approaches for achieving coexistence. Consider a hypothetical liberal arts degree, a general BA in music designed decades ago with Western art music in mind and the basic elements of lessons, ensembles, theory and history. All of the bachelor of arts degrees listed in Table 4.4 indicate a concentration or emphasis in traditional music. The comments in the table only begin to indicate which programs simply added oral traditions to an existing BA degree and which programs created new BA degrees in which some or most of the basic courses in literate traditions have been replaced with comparable content concerning oral traditions. The most common substitutions are in the ensemble and applied instruction requirements; music history and especially music theory requirements have been resistant to change. For example, at the University of Hawaii at Manoa all BA music students are required to take the same two-year sequence of music theory and aural training and one-year sequence of Western music history. This includes students who pursue the Hawaiian music emphasis through applied instruction, ensembles including multiple levels of hula/chant ensemble, and more advanced courses in music history and

16. http://appstudies.appstate.edu/ (accessed June 23, 2015).
17. Daniel Boner, private communication, December 11, 2015.
18. http://www.etsu.edu/cas/das/bluegrass/default.php (accessed November 8, 2015). Additional insights about the ETSU program have come from several conversations I have had with ETSU students and faculty.

ethnomusicology.[19] The same university formed the Hawai'inuiakea School of Hawaiian Knowledge in 2007, which separately offers performance courses on hula and chant and a lecture course on music and native identity.[20]

At UL Lafayette, the music school did not offer any kind of liberal arts degree in music at the time that we submitted a proposal for a BA in music with a concentration in traditional music, together with a proposal for a concentration in music business. We devised a simplified music theory and musicianship sequence for BA students that was appropriate for the music business students, the only music majors not required to audition for admission. UL Lafayette's traditional music concentration moves toward a professional music curriculum in that it requires an audition, an additional music theory class focused on oral traditions, and restricted general education electives.[21]

The professional music degree programs described in Table 4.5 represent a variety of institutional approaches rather than common trends. Columbia College's offerings span performance and composition in classical, jazz, and popular music, with a partially integrated curriculum and the opportunity to study blues and gospel music. Texas State University (see Pedroza, Chapter 7 in this volume) builds its mariachi studies program on top of the conventional music education degree that requires full musical literacy and knowledge of Western music history and theory; it also offers a masters in salsa performance suitable especially to students with educational backgrounds in jazz.[22] Like UCLA, Universidad Nacional Autónoma de México, the sole Mexican representative in this North American study, offers an undergraduate degree in ethnomusicology with a significant applied instruction component, but UNAM's curriculum is more intensively focused on music research (requiring some thirty courses combined in music history, ethnomusicology, transcription, analysis, organology, folklore, and anthropology), without the general education component of a liberal arts degree.[23]

The Berklee College of Music has effectively reinvented a conservatory model (Wilf 2014) where popular music and jazz studies predominate and in which students major in performance or composition without, for the most part, a necessary concentration in a specific genre such as bluegrass or rock. Berklee does not make special use of *local* oral traditions—most of the genres

19. http://manoa.hawaii.edu/music/about-us/degrees-programs/ba/ (accessed August 16, 2015).

20. http://www.catalog.hawaii.edu/schoolscolleges/hawaiian/kamakakuokalani.htm (accessed August 16, 2015).

21. http://music.louisiana.edu/curr_traditional15-16.html (accessed November 8, 2015).

22. http://latin.music.txstate.edu/ (accessed November 8, 2015); Ludim Pedroza, private communication, July and August 2015.

23. http://www.fam.unam.mx/campus/licenciaturas.php#demoTab6 (accessed November 8, 2015); Gonzalo Camacho, private communication, August 2015.

Table 4.5 PROFESSIONAL MUSIC DEGREE PROGRAMS

Institution	Program Name	Department	Offers Related Degrees	Offers Minor	Trad Music Centric	Program Comments	Degree/Minor Name
Belmont University	Commercial Music	School of Music	✓			Ensembles include bluegrass, rock, several jazz. Applied instruction in banjo; mandolin; commercial voice guitar, violin, and bass; some classical study also required.	Bachelor of Music (BM) and Master of Music (MM) in Commercial Music with Performance Emphasis
Berklee College of Music	American Roots Music Program	Strings		✓	✓	"Focused Area of Study" sponsors artist residencies, produces concerts, sponsors performance opportunities for students. Minor consists of two lecture courses, 3 ensembles, plus ensemble and instrumental lab electives.	Minor in American Roots Music
Columbia College Chicago	Contemporary, Urban, and Popular Music	Music	✓			More applied study, aural skills, keyboard and ensemble work than parallel BA degree, plus classes in music business, technology, improvisation, and songwriting. Internship; senior recital.	BM in Contemporary, Urban, and Popular Music

(*Continued*)

Table 4.5 (Continued)

Institution	Program Name	Department	Offers Related Degrees	Offers Minor	Trad Music Centric	Program Comments	Degree/Minor Name
Texas State University	Latin Music Studies	School of Music	✓	✓		Mariachi minor open only to music education majors who start as freshmen. Mariachi ensemble, arranging, and pedagogy; applied instruction in mariachi voice, violin, trumpet, vihuela, guitarrón, harp	BM in Music Studies (Choral or Instrumental Concentration with teacher certification in Music, Grades EC–12) with a Mariachi Minor
			✓	✓	✓	Salsa history, ensemble, arranging, pedagogy, Afro-Cuban hand drumming and other applied instruction. Music literacy requirements analogous to a professional music degree in jazz.	MM in Salsa Performance
			✓	✓	✓	Three-summer program designed for working teachers. Mariachi history, ensemble, arranging, and pedagogy; applied instruction in mariachi voice, violin, trumpet, vihuela, guitarrón, harp	MM in Music Education - Concentration in Mariachi
UNAM	Etnomusicología	Escuela Nacional de Música	✓		✓	Two years of applied instruction in traditional instruments of Mexico, including harp, guitarron, vihuela, jarana, and more. Courses on ethnomusicological analysis and musical transcription, Mexican music history, world music, anthropology of music	Licenciatura en Etnomusicología [undergraduate degree]

covered in its American Roots Music Program are rural southern ones, far from its Boston location—but it cannot be ignored due to its size and influence. Whenever I speak with a music scholar or professional performer about the traditional music program at UL Lafayette, if that person knows of any comparable programs, the Berklee name is the one most often mentioned. Berklee has over four thousand music students, while by comparison Indiana University's Jacobs School of Music has sixteen hundred and the New England Conservatory and the Juilliard School well under a thousand each.[24]

To understand how the American Roots Music program functions, one needs to know something about Berklee's unusual institutional structure. There are twelve undergraduate majors, of which only Jazz Composition implies a genre by name. Departmentally, the college is organized in three divisions: Professional Education, Professional Performance, and Professional Writing and Music Technology. The Performance division is largely organized into departments by instrument type (guitar, bass, strings, brass, woodwinds, percussion, piano, and voice) and also has separate departments for ensembles and ear training. Banjo and mandolin are available for study as a student's principle instrument.[25] On the fall 2015 class schedule, the ensemble department offers 423 sections of 145 different ensemble courses; another hundred ensembles for credit involving instruments of a single type are offered by other performance departments: saxophone quartet in woodwinds, steel pan ensemble in percussion, banjo improvisation in strings, and so on. Berklee also has an unconventional type of musicianship class called an instrumental lab, offered in 164 different courses and a total of 317 sections in fall 2015. Instrumental labs focus on particular instrumental techniques and musical styles, such as slide guitar or Native American drumming. The range of musical styles offered in the ensembles and instrumental labs is vast, and performance majors are required to take several of each.[26]

Somewhat independent of its academic departments and degree programs are Berklee's nine "focused areas of study," some geographically focused (American roots, Africana studies, Berklee Indian exchange) and some with global and interdisciplinary missions. The American Roots Music Program "explores America's musical and cultural heritage, focusing on styles such as country, folk, bluegrass, Cajun, Tex-Mex, and others. The program's curriculum focuses on ensemble playing and nontraditional improvisation, and will present visiting artists, concerts, and symposiums."[27] The main focus is

24. http://music.indiana.edu/about/welcome.shtml and http://carnegieclassifications.iu.edu/lookup_listings/institution.php (accessed August 18, 2015).

25. https://www.berklee.edu/principal-instruments (accessed August 22, 2015).

26. https://www.berklee.edu/registrar/current-schedule-courses (accessed July 30, 2015). The counts of the numbers of classes and sections of various kinds constitute my own analysis of the schedule data.

27. https://www.berklee.edu/focused (accessed August 22, 2015).

on identifying and bringing visiting artists to perform and to interact with students on an informal basis, including occasional individual lessons (not for credit). The program director told me that he selects the artists purpose-fully to diversify the experiences of his students, who would otherwise want "all bluegrass all the time."[28] An American Roots minor consists of one lecture course supported by the program, combined with a list of related courses offered by other units.

CONCLUDING OBSERVATIONS

To analyze further the curricula of the several programs discussed here, let us return to the question of motivation. Why introduce folk and traditional music into the music performance curriculum? Is it to add a new set of skills for music majors to learn to make them more employable? Or is it an opposite motivation, to preserve art forms that are no longer in demand in the market-place? Are we trying to add diversity to our student body by bringing in first-generation college students, talented musicians with high school educations who don't read music and might not otherwise attend university at all? Or are we starting with an intellectual agenda, based in the discipline of ethnomusi-cology or folklore, and using performance training as a way to engage students more fully in the intellectual and social issues that we care about? The programs mentioned in this chapter do not all have the same goals, and of course even within a single program individual actors will differ in their motivations.

The opposing goals of providing employable skills versus preserving waning art forms is reflected in the existence of commercial and vocational music degree programs in traditional music as compared to liberal arts programs that have a broader educational mandate. Given that tradition bearers in many oral traditions have historically not had extensive formal education, especially in music, the vocational degrees offered by two-year colleges as ends in themselves would seem a logical first step toward creating an academic program in traditional music. Hazard Technical and Community College's artist diploma contains as many credit hours of music study as a general BA in music at a four-year school, as does UH-Maui College's Hawaiian music certificate. Yet compared to the two-year programs, the four-year programs are far more numerous, many of them at schools with commercial music and music business programs that can balance a liberal arts degree with practical training.

This study has only scratched the surface in portraying the depth (and possibly also the breadth) of instruction in oral traditions that is already taking place in North American colleges and universities. Time did not permit the

28. Matt Glaser, private communication, July 2014.

collection of additional quantitative information such as the age of each program, the number of students currently enrolled, the number per year who graduate, and the total number of graduates. In most cases, however, the programs are less than twenty years old; a study of what graduates do with a degree or certificate in traditional music would be worthwhile but would not have much longitudinal depth.

We have no graduates yet with a bachelor of arts in music with a concentration in traditional music at UL Lafayette. We anticipate that they may go on to be professional musicians, to work in the music industry or nonprofit arts administration as experts on traditional music genres, or to continue their studies in graduate professional school (business, law) or in doctoral programs in ethnomusicology or related social-science fields. With the liberal arts education and communication skills they receive, they will also be positioned to contribute to the preservation and promotion of traditional music, which contributes significantly to Louisiana's cultural economy. I have read similar justifications for degree programs at other schools, such as ETSU, that can point to successful alumni in the performing and recording fields.

Qualitatively, I know from personal experience that the types of sources from which I gathered most of my information—websites, brief e-mail correspondence, a few telephone calls—convey no more than an approximate suggestion of institutional politics, community relations, and how teachers and students engage with local oral traditions and each other on a daily basis. A few telling details from the first five years of developing our program at UL Lafayette may give some idea of the complexities that attend any such program.

Cajun and Creole music in Lafayette and neighboring rural south Louisiana towns and parishes is in no danger of dying out, given the number of younger Cajun and zydeco bands currently active. At the same time, on the university campus this music is not highly popular, even if it is familiar to the predominantly local student body through exposure on local television, radio, and live entertainment at public events. In 2012 we created a bachelor of arts in music degree with two concentration options: traditional music and music business. Over the last three years, music business has grown to have 88 majors, whereas traditional music has one. The first traditional music class we offered was a Cajun ensemble; its enrollment has waxed and waned from a dozen full-time degree-seeking students (most of them not music majors) down to two. Over its first ten semesters, the Cajun band for credit has several times more closely resembled an "experience ensemble" (going back to Solís's terminology) than I would have expected or preferred. When we added a bluegrass ensemble, suddenly more bachelor of music students were interested. Bluegrass has a more exotic appeal in Lafayette, something rarely seen locally, and perhaps also there is a perception (misguided, in my opinion) that it possesses a complexity more worthy of study than Cajun music. Meanwhile, most of our applied courses in accordion, fiddle, and French vocals are under-enrolled. Community members who enroll in group instruction tend to have very different learning styles and needs from full-time degree-seeking students; the challenge this presents to teachers is sometimes downplayed by advocates of community music (Carruthers 2005). UL Lafayette students who are already playing Cajun music professionally have no interest in obtaining a traditional music degree, and only a few have played in our Cajun ensemble; their mission in college is to study engineering or business to maximize their future income potential. The cultural precedent of Cajun and Creole musicians who make their livelihood outside music remains strong, despite several notable exceptions. Tried-and-true high school recruitment strategies used by my School of Music colleagues have no meaning for me because the high schools in our state do not offer classes in the types of music that we teach, so I am casting about for new approaches. On a positive note, I have been able to recruit students from our growing music business program to play in some of our ensembles, and I am in a position to help my music business colleagues start some commercial music ensembles that their program currently lacks. Indeed, based on the results of this study, I suspect the future vitality of the traditional music program will depend on more collaboration with our music business curriculum and our professional degree in music media.

The most significant conclusion I draw from data collected for this project is that there is a surprising amount of vernacular music education already taking place at North American colleges and universities. Such programs appear especially but not exclusively at institutions that also offer instruction in music business or commercial music. Clearly, some schools did not need a College Music Society task force to tell them that they needed to diversify the curriculum, and some have done it with little fanfare. The trajectory of oral-tradition musics in North American higher education is one of gradual acceptance through many disconnected local efforts, resulting in a variety of solutions to problems inherent in reforming a curriculum that does not meet their needs. My hope is that music educators at more colleges and universities will draw upon these examples and expand this movement for the sake of their students and the vitality of local music making in their communities.

REFERENCES

Alper, Garth. 2007. "Towards the Acceptance of a Bachelor of Music Degree in Popular Music Studies." *College Music Symposium*, Vol. 47, 156–166.

Campbell, Patricia Shehan, Task Force Convenor; David Myers, Task Force Chair; Ed Sarath, Lead Author; Juan Chattah, Lee Higgins, Victoria Lindsay Levine, David Rudge, and Timothy Rice. 2014. "Transforming Music Study from Its Foundations: A Manifesto for Progressive Change in the Undergraduate Preparation of Music Majors." Report of the Task Force on the Undergraduate

Music Major. College Music Society. http://www.mtosmt.org/issues/
mto.16.22.1/manifesto.pdf (accessed January 2, 2017).

Carruthers, Glen. 2005. "Community Music and the "Musical Community": Beyond Conventional Synergies." *International Journal of Community Music*, Vol. C.

DeWitt, Mark F. 2008. *Cajun and Zydeco Dance Music in Northern California. Modern Pleasures in a Postmodern World*. Jackson: University Press of Mississippi.

Dor, George Worlasi Kwasi. 2014. *West African Drumming and Dance in North American Universities. An Ethnomusicological Perspective*. Jackson: University Press of Mississippi.

Frank, Alexandra. 2014. "'That's the Way I've Always Learned': The Transmission of Traditional Music in Higher Education." Master of Arts in Liberal Studies thesis, School of Continuing Studies and Academic Outreach, East Tennessee State University.

Hebert, David G. 2011. "Originality and Institutionalization: Factors Engendering Resistance to Popular Music Pedagogy in the U.S.A." *Music Education Research International*, Vol. 5, 12–21.

Hill, Juniper. 2009. "The Influence of Conservatory Folk Music Programmes: The Sibelius Academy in Comparative Context." *Ethnomusicology Forum*, Vol. 18 No. 2, 207–241.

Jones, Fernando. 2009. "Teaching the Blues Effectively." *Journal of Popular Music Studies*, Vol. 21 No. 1, 108–112.

Keegan-Phipps, Simon. 2007. "Déjà Vu? Folk Music, Education, and Institutionalization in Contemporary England." *Yearbook for Traditional Music*, Vol. 39, 84–107.

Kisliuk, Michelle. 1988. "'A Special Kind of Courtesy': Action at a Bluegrass Festival Jam Session." *TDR: The Drama Review*, Vol. 32, No. 3, 141–155.

NASM. 2015. *National Association of Schools of Music Handbook 2014–15*. Reston, VA: National Association of Schools of Music.

Powell, Bryan, Andrew Krikun, and Joseph Michael Pignato. 2015. "'Something's Happening Here!': Popular Music Education in the United States." *IASPM@ Journal*, Vol. 5 No. 1, 4–22.

Schippers, Huib. 2010. *Facing the Music. Shaping Music Education from a Global Perspective*. Oxford: Oxford University Press.

Solís, Ted, ed. 2004. *Performing Ethnomusicology. Teaching and Representation in World Music Ensembles*. Berkeley: University of California Press.

Southgate, Darby E., and Vincent J. Roscigno. 2009. "The Impact of Music on Childhood and Adolescent Achievement." *Social Science Quarterly*, Vol. 90 No. 1, 4–21.

Titon, Jeff Todd. 2009. "Teaching Blues and Country Music, and Leading an Old-Time String Band—at an Ivy League University." *Journal of Popular Music Studies*, Vol. 21 No. 1, 113–124.

Wilf, Eitan Y. 2014. *School for Cool. The Academic Jazz Program and the Paradox of Institutionalized Creativity*. Chicago: University of Chicago Press.

Williams, Chas. 2012. *The Nashville Number System*, 7th ed. Nashville, TN: http://nashvillenumbersystem.com/.

Case Studies

CHAPTER 5

Noncanonical Pedagogies for Noncanonical Musics

Observations on Selected Programs in Folk, Traditional, World, and Popular Musics

JACK TALTY

INTRODUCTION

Conventional mainstream music education often attaches a certain prestige to the Western canon not enjoyed to the same extent by other genres. As a result, musical styles outside the Western conservatory are often made to "march to the drummer of the central classical tradition" (Nettl 1995, 144). Courses on other repertoires may be offered, but frequently with the implicit understanding that they do not equal the Western classical tradition in terms of sophistication and artistic merit. The very term "music" is often conflated with Western classical music in educational environments and modifiers such as "serious music" and "good music" function to differentiate it from other genres (Kingsbury 1988, 17). Such perceptions are a source of contention among those who write about folk and traditional music pedagogy, and many are skeptical of the suitability of applying dominant Western classical music educational models to folk and traditional musics that largely emanate from oral, extra-institutional, community-based contexts (Smith 1999, McCarthy 1999, Doherty 2002, Hill 2005).

In this chapter I explore how folk and traditional music pedagogy in Western Europe negotiates two prominent themes. First, I discuss how educators problematize "canonicity," the construction and maintenance of musical canons. Unchallenged, canonicity can potentially confine our experiences of the musical world within narrow norms and conventions. It contributes to textbook narratives of musical orthodoxy. The inherent disposition of educational structures to codify and organize knowledge suggests that music education plays a potentially significant role in the promotion and/or confrontation of canons. Can music pedagogy interrogate perceptions of what a music canon is, or is it invariably complicit in narrowing and systematizing our experiences of music? Second, I examine the ways in which traditional music pedagogy in western Europe negotiates the needs and expectations of musical communities. Traditional musics are communal, extra-institutional forms of expression associated with unique processes of transmission, enculturation, and social interaction. How are these cultural processes represented in higher education? What aspects of community music making do traditional music curricula hope to impart to their students? What is the purpose of such programs? Although the institutions referenced throughout this chapter locate music studies within discrete pedagogical frameworks, similarities can be observed in how each one promotes pedagogical flexibility, curricular diversification, the fostering of critical engagement with music repertoires, professional industry training, and community engagement. The concepts explored here are informed by discussions with pedagogues involved with the following programs: the BA in Irish music and dance at the Irish World Academy at the University of Limerick, Ireland; the BM at the Folk Music Department of the Royal College of Music in Stockholm, Sweden; the BA in Scottish music at the Royal Conservatoire in Glasgow, Scotland; the BM in folk music at the Sibelius Academy in Helsinki, Finland; the BM in world music at Codarts Rotterdam; the BM in world music at the Malmö Academy at Lund University, Sweden; the BA in popular music performance at the University of Chester; and the BA in popular music at the Institute of Popular Music at the University of Liverpool. In addition, I draw heavily on my doctoral fieldwork and on my experiences as an educator and a professional practitioner of Irish traditional music.

PROBLEMATIZING CANONICITY IN MUSIC EDUCATION

Many authors are critical of how Western classical music pedagogy constructs canons by privileging certain composers and masterworks over others. Canonicity is for Caswell "a flawed paradigm for pedagogy" that is "destructive of our critical faculties," as it tells consecutive generations what we *should* study and what we *should* perform (Caswell 1991, 12). Entire music histories and narratives can be created and sustained through canonicity. Discussing the institutionalization of jazz, Marquis asserts that its introduction in American higher education has led to the development of an "official history and an official canon, perhaps even an official music" (Marquis 1998, 121). Nettl's observations on the convenient "six-period-plan" associated with European classical repertoire (medieval, Renaissance, baroque, classical, romantic, and twentieth century) highlights the propensity of music education to categorize and codify musical knowledge, quite possibly at the expense of presenting diverse and nuanced educational experiences.[1] Perhaps the codification and systematization of musical knowledge is an inevitable consequence of music pedagogy. However, educators must be vigilant so that the systematization of knowledge does not facilitate the construction of an accepted or official music that conflicts with how such music is experienced by practitioners outside formalized education systems.

Critics of nonclassical music education are also dubious of alternate forms of canonicity in music education; see, for instance, Pedroza's discussion of the canonization of mariachi repertoire (Chapter 7 in this volume). For many, canonicity manifests itself through homogeneity and standardization of repertoire; it threatens stylistic individualism, a hallmark of most traditional musics (Doherty 2002, Hill 2005, Keegan-Phipps 2007). In his study of the institutionalization of English folk music, Keegan-Phipps discusses the homogenization of its musical style in performance. This "clone" phenomenon appears to result from students "engaging in the emulation of an unhealthily small number of musicians" (Keegan-Phipps 2007, 102). Similarly, some suspect that a pedagogical "feedback loop" is created when graduates of the Sibelius Academy are engaged to teach Finnish folk music at the same institution where they studied and advance only the pedagogical practices they received as students (Hill 2005). Formalized and structured music curricula inevitably prioritize certain components of a musical culture over others. The extent to which they accommodate diverse perspectives on a given music determines the extent to which music education eschews the construction of inflexible canons.

Music pedagogues must also be mindful of the power relations inherent in all educational settings. The seminal studies of Kingsbury (1988) and Nettl (1995) suggest how ideologies and biases are disseminated, as exemplified by the hierarchical relationship between students and teachers. At one particular Irish institution I overheard a lecturer using colorful language to comment disapprovingly upon the selection of Irish music recordings a student had just acquired from the university library. In this case, the subjective values expressed by the lecturer revealed his personal biases regarding what the student should be listening to. Conversely, pedagogues at the Sibelius Academy's

---

1. In *Heartland Excursions: Ethnomusicological Reflections on Schools of Music*, Bruno Nettl suggests that the oversimplified delineation of what he terms the "six-period plan" in music historiography is evidence of canonicity in action. In his opinion, transition periods occurring between the "six-period plan" are neglected due to music historians' emphasis on stability rather than change (Nettl 1995; 99).

folk music department attempt to limit the influence of their own biases by encouraging students to continually question what they are taught and avoid being "too obedient" (Ilmonen, cited in Hill 2009, 89).[2] Regardless of whatever policies are adopted by music institutions to safeguard against the promotion of canonicity and ideological biases, faculty may unconsciously disseminate their own musical canons through interactions with students. Since canonicity is frequently constructed (and occasionally challenged) through pedagogy, faculty should be conscious of their influence.

Musical canons and "official" music narratives, histories, and practices are also created and maintained outside educational and institutional contexts. Topics such as authenticity, tradition, and other constructs of inherited value are prevalent in discourses surrounding many traditional musics. Given the ubiquity of such attitudes, can music pedagogy hope to confront canonicity rather than construct it? At the Irish World Academy at the University of Limerick, ethnomusicologist and musician Aileen Dillane endeavors to instill critical engagement, academic rigor, and curiosity in her BA students; she encourages them to honor the tradition they study while being "unafraid to interrogate it" or even creatively alter it.[3] Similarly, Niall Keegan, associate director of the Irish World Academy, believes that it is important to encourage students to broaden their musical horizons and that higher education is an appropriate sanctuary within which to experiment.[4] Pedagogues at the Royal College of Music in Sweden view their work as an opportunity to challenge what they perceive as the "mystification" of Swedish folk music through a variety of cultural narratives.[5] Music pedagogy can and should question

2. Kristiina Ilmonen describes the democratic dynamic fostered at the Sibelius Academy through teacher-student relations. Students are encouraged to think critically and creatively at all times: "We don't give any kind of orders about what is the right way to play, what is the right way to make music, what is the right music. . . . If we say "this is the right thing to do, this and this and this," it would maybe make people more obedient and we don't like them to be too obedient. We like them to be a little crazy and creative and have a mind of their own" (Kristiina Ilmonen, interview with Juniper Hill, July 2004).

3. Dillane firmly believes that pedagogues have a responsibility to encourage students to critically engage perceptions of what traditions are; "We don't do our job as university lecturers if we don't do that" (Aileen Dillane, in discussion with the author, April 2015). See Dillane (2013) for further discussion on the critical distance ethnomusicology can offer the study of Irish traditional music.

4. Keegan describes his ethos towards artistic experimentation and encouraging his students to push musical boundaries in the following way: "I do like putting students into situations where they do things that are a little bit off the wall or a little bit different just for the heck of it, and see what they think, and what people think. That's the beauty of an Ivory Tower" (Niall Keegan, in discussion with the author, October 2014).

5. Renowned pedagogue and fiddler Sven Ahlbäck learned folk music aurally in rural Sweden. He uses this background to deconstruct and challenge what he believes are unrepresentative and exclusionary ideologies about who can and cannot learn folk music. Likewise, Ahlbäck's colleague at the Royal College of Music, Ellika Frisell, suggests that we must also be cognizant of changing contexts for the transmission of folk

ideological biases existing outside educational structures while avoiding the creation of internal biases.

The rejection of inherited musical canons can lead to the construction of alternative pedagogical approaches that are more sympathetic to artistic innovation than "straight ahead" interpretations of a music genre. The critical and somewhat rebellious ethos endorsed by Dillane and Ilmonen safeguard against cultural and institutional stasis. However, folk and traditional music communities sometimes perceive such dispositions towards experimentation as misrepresentative of extra-institutional practices. In Finland, despite the general approval of the Sibelius Academy's Folk Music Department, some decry the institution's appetite for innovation, yearning instead for more "honest, straightforward Finnishness" rather than "noise and cacophony" (Hill 2005, 334). Likewise, in Ireland, Irish higher education is regarded in some quarters as more inclined toward innovation than cultural representation (given the nature of academic enquiry); consequently, practitioners lament the proliferation of what is perceived as a homogenous "university style" (discussed below). The interrogation and critique of musical canons invariably challenge inherited conventions and how we perceive music traditions. It is important for such a process to remain as impartial as possible if we are to eschew replacing one manifestation of canonicity with another.

Notwithstanding the complexities of the situation, I believe there are a number of ways music pedagogy can confront canonicity and safeguard against authoritative and confined "textbook" definitions of a given genre. Promoting a critical and creative environment, as Dillane, Keegan, and Ilmonen suggest, is an important first step. In practice, I see much to be gained from the rigorous and detailed study of diverse aspects of music cultures, a commonplace approach in programs of ethnomusicology. In Ireland, for instance, young practitioner-researchers are engaging in "ethnomusicology at home" at an unprecedented rate. Their research projects explore cultural and musical aspects of Irish traditional repertoire in great detail and in the process diversify students' understanding of it within and beyond academic institutions. Another useful approach involves community collaboration, inviting nonacademic performers and folklorists to interact with students. This takes place at the Irish World Academy to an extent, usually in the guise of extra-curricular seminar fora. Developing a sustained collaborative relationship with nonacademic stakeholders enriches the pedagogical resources available to a music

and traditional musics in contemporary society when she states: "sometimes people have a very romantic view about folk music, [believing] it is something that you have to learn [while] milking a cow with your fiddling teacher. The problem is that the fiddling teachers are not milking cows any more, they are living in the cities" (Ellika Frisell, in discussion with the author, May 2015).

program and, again, militates against overly authoritative and narrow "text-book" definitions of music.

NEGOTIATING THE NEEDS AND EXPECTATIONS OF MUSICAL COMMUNITIES

As we have seen, the incorporation of folk and traditional musics into higher education has frequently been a source of contention among performers, educators, and community practitioners (Keegan 2011, Doherty 2002).[6] My ongoing work in this area has uncovered a wide array of opinions about the institutionalization of Irish traditional music. Perhaps of most relevance here is how selected programs negotiate the relationship between undergraduate music education and extra-institutional community practice. Scholarship on the pedagogy of folk and traditional musics includes commentary about authority and power relations, academic prestige and social hegemony, and perceptions of ideological bias towards musical innovation and cross-genre musical experimentation, all of which are described by some in Ireland as "university style." Although the institutionalization of community-based musics is a potentially problematic process in aesthetic and social terms, cultivating a respectful, collaborative relationship with surrounding musical communities can ensure that diverse perspectives on music are represented in curriculum design. As noted, extra-institutional practitioners can share perspectives on their respective areas of expertise and can offer institutions insights into new areas of enquiry. Collaboration between communities or regional music "scenes" and higher education institutions keeps music pedagogy relevant to the needs and expectations of everyone.

One particular source of community concern involves the extent to which music institutions draw upon, adapt, or depart from conventional Western educational models in their teaching of traditional music. How does a system that has relied heavily on music notation and codified theory tackle aural musical transmission, for example?[7] Implementing appropriate pedagogical

6. In the *Companion to Irish Traditional Music*, Niall Keegan refers to suspicions in the Irish music community that higher education institutions have a "stylistic and aesthetic agenda which favours third-level classical music values and is dismissive of traditional-music values" (Keegan 2011). Liz Doherty believes one of the main concerns of the traditional community is that "homogeneity and uniformity will replace individualism as the main characteristics of the music" (Doherty 2002, 18).

7. See also Mark DeWitt's comments on the subject (Chapter 4 in this volume). Here I use the term "aurality" to refer to methods of transmitting musical knowledge by listening and repetition. Thérèse Smith observes challenges inherent in recontextualizing oral music traditions in academic environments that primarily emphasize the value of the written text. She suggests that resolutions of the perceived orality-literacy binary are further complicated by the fact that oral traditions (including Irish traditional music) frequently lack a comprehensive catalog of "masterpieces" or an

methodologies specific to folk and traditional musics is a universal challenge, as noted in Eddie Hsu's discussion of coursework in the People's Republic of China and Taiwan (Chapter 8 in this volume). The programs I have reviewed deal respond to the unique qualities of aurally transmitted repertoire in a number of ways. Many do not require prospective students to demonstrate knowledge of Western music notation or theory prior to enrollment. For example, the Irish World Academy does not have a music theory or literacy component to its entrance exams. In addition, music tutors there (in instrumental and vocal music, dance, etc.) are not required to use Western notation; instead, many transfer musical knowledge in ways similar to those found outside higher education structures.[8] Although the Irish World Academy provides for music notation and theory training in the curriculum of the BA, traditional methods of musical transmission are also facilitated.

Adopting Western classical music notation in the instruction of aural musical cultures is a divisive practice. Western notation can be viewed as a common musical lingua franca with which to engage with other musics globally, but it is also commonly regarded as an inappropriate tool with which to transmit traditional and world music idioms.[9] For example, Leo Vervelde at the University of the Arts in Rotterdam accepts that each form of world music has "its own set of codes and conventions" but believes that students should be familiar with Western music theory and notation in order to provide them with a common analytical language.[10] The world music program at Lund University in Malmö

abundance of biographical information on individual composers (Smith 1999, 209). According to Smith, this can result in a lack of understanding or appreciation for the artistic depth of an oral music form.

8. BA students of Irish music and dance do encounter Western music notation and theory on a regular basis, however, in mandatory notation and theory classes, where sight-reading is included in all end-of-semester assessments. Teaching contexts for Irish traditional music performance (both within and outside higher education) vary considerably and depend on the idiosyncratic approaches of individual teachers. This trend is mirrored in the Irish World Academy by allowing experienced tutors to teach using whatever methodologies they deem appropriate.

9. This is particularly true in Ireland. Marie McCarthy's historical survey of when and how school music and traditional music transmission have interfaced makes many references to ideologues who impose the perceived "high art" ethos of classical music upon Irish music (McCarthy 2013, 220). Decrying the formalization of the "Irish Traditional music canon," Seán Corcoran feels that "'Classical' music techniques, intonation, timbral preferences, and aesthetics have been foregrounded over vernacular practices" (Corcoran 2013, 282). Similarly, Matt Cranitch exemplifies fundamental differences between Western classical music and Irish traditional music by recounting many of the challenges faced by classical violinists learning Irish traditional music. Such challenges include a reliance on staff notation, a lack of familiarity with the musical style, detached bowing, and an emphasis on vibrato (Cranitch 2013). Paul McGettrick warns against imposing classical assessment templates on Irish traditional music, calling for a more creative and idiomatic approach to evaluating such performance (McGettrick 2013, 197).

10. Leo Vervelde, in discussion with the author, July 2015.

uses Western music theory to an extent. Pär Moberg encourages his students to engage with Western classical theory on their own terms; his faculty teaches Swedish folk music using traditional methodologies, such as learning by ear, but also by means of Western classical notation and theory when they are perceived to be of benefit.[11] Both of the examples above highlight the potential of balancing Western notation systems with more idiomatic approaches drawn from conventional, genre-specific methodologies. Flexibility is key, and providing students with a plurality of methods and approaches to analyzing and communicating musical ideas ensures they are equipped to view music through a variety of lenses.

Sven Ahlbäck, at the Royal College of Music in Stockholm, has been a central figure in designing and implementing a nuanced music theory system that adequately represents what he feels are the idiomatic characteristics of Swedish folk music. Ahlbäck set about designing his system in order to analyze the music of Sweden's master fiddle players whose music features microtonality and unique rhythmical elements. Ahlbäck's system, which remains in use at the Royal College of Music, has successfully equipped students with a means of analyzing Swedish folk music that was not possible by means of Western classical music theory and notation. Microtonality and unusual rhythmic techniques are now discussed, notated, and performed as part of a unique musical language. Ahlbäck's achievement exemplifies the importance of interrogating the suitability of Western classical theory and notation in the analysis of musics from outside the Western classical tradition.

Pedagogues have noted that students respond most effectively to music theory classes when they are presented in conjunction with performance. Joshua Dickson of the Royal Conservatoire of Scotland believes that the best guarantor that students of the BA in Scottish music will engage effectively with Western music theory and appreciate its relevance is to align it more closely to how they experience performance on their principal instrument and/or voice. The BA in Scottish music curriculum at the RCS (currently undergoing revision) hopes to further incorporate this approach to theory through folk ensemble class sessions: students will engage in describing and understanding

11. Pär Moberg expands on the extent to which the department draws on conventional Western music theory and notation: "We use sheet music. We want our students to know something about Western music theory, of course, but we try to do it our own way, with lots of emphasis on playing by ear. We have our own Swedish folk music theory classes, and they're of course based [largely] on modal music since much of our music is modal originally. But then [our approach to analysis can be] very different also depending on what needs people have and what kind of music they play. We want to have the opportunity to study theory on our own terms. But on the other hand, since we are at an institution in which [other genres are played], we also benefit from that. We can use those resources when it suits us. I think it's a really good combination. We have the opportunity to have our own theory but we can also use theory teachers from other genres when it is suitable to us" (Moberg, interview with the author, July 2015).

the theoretical manifestations of the many musical phenomena that they explore as a group. The approach is similar to that taken by proponents of an integrated curriculum, such as Ed Sarath and Juan Chattah (Moore, Chapter 1 in this volume). It also aligns with my attempts to use motifs of familiar traditional melodies as a means of helping students identify and memorize melodic intervals at the Irish World Academy. Consequently, students understand theoretical concepts in a more practical and digestible manner. Such an approach resonates with that of Susanne Rosenberg of the Royal College of Music in Stockholm. For her as well, it is essential to develop performance pedagogies drawn from specific genres or musical traditions. Rosenberg feels that techniques such as vocal inflection and string bowing or articulation drawn from the Western classical tradition can fail to sufficiently express the characteristics of Swedish folk music style. For example, fiddle students are encouraged to avoid bowing with a whole bow (as promoted in classical violin technique) and instead use idiomatic quick bowing techniques and directional changes appropriate to playing rhythmical dance music. Approaches such as these, explored by the RCS and the Royal College of Music, exemplify the many benefits of tailoring curriculum design to reflect the idiomatic ways that musicians learn and teach traditional musics.

INTEGRATING INSTITUTIONAL AND COMMUNITY PRACTICE

Some believe that the presence of traditional musics in higher education contributes to a hegemonic division between program graduates (practitioner-academics) on the one hand and nonacademic amateur and professional practitioners on the other.[12] In Ireland, this division is somewhat diffused by the appointment of expert musicians from surrounding music communities in university departments to provide performance instruction. Institutes such as the Irish World Academy at the University of Limerick and the Department of Music at University College Cork employ instrumental, vocal, and dance tutors based on their expertise as practitioners rather than their academic qualifications. This trend originated in University College Cork in the late 1970s, when Professor Mícheál Ó Súilleabháin (now Professor Emeritus of the Irish World Academy) began hiring traditional musicians. Finding a precedent in the employment of native speakers of French and Italian by the French and

12. Keegan-Phipps argues that the processes inherent in institutionalizing folk and traditional musics in higher education systems invariably construct hierarchical barriers, such as those created between teacher and student and between professional musician and audience or the community, for example. "Wedges" between student and teacher, according to Keegan-Phipps, are facilitated by the "top-down" knowledge transfer processes inherent in educational structures (Keegan-Phipps 2007, 89).

Italian language departments, Ó Súilleabháin insisted that music practitioners from the community be employed on an equivalent basis. Despite early resistance, the model has now been widely adopted. Moreover, many musical institutions now highlight the fact in their marketing and promotional materials. Apart from functioning to redress power imbalances between higher education and musical communities, this approach also ensures that institutions remain in close contact with how musics are performed outside of academia.

For faculty, satisfying the many divergent views as to how the study of traditional music should be incorporated into curricula is an unenviable task. Nevertheless, soliciting input from students and community practitioners helps to ensure that formal pedagogy remains relevant. Joshua Dickson of the Royal Conservatoire of Scotland has collected extensive feedback on pedagogical practices there from a range of individuals and groups using a combination of online questionnaires, student feedback forms, and focus group discussions with musicians, teachers, students, prospective applicants, and professional organizations. Dickson engages in this process to "get a range of opinion so as to conclude definitively what we do well, what we don't do so well, and, crucially, what works well in other aspects of the conservatoire's teaching and learning." Developments are currently underway at the RCS to integrate much of the feedback received through this consultation process into the undergraduate curriculum.[13] Topics raised include suggestions as to how pedagogy could better reflect the historical development of Scottish traditional music; belief that in a conservatory environment a bachelor of music should be offered in traditional music rather than a bachelor of arts; and calls for greater emphasis on creativity in all facets of coursework.[14] By consulting a variety of resources, diverse insights into what educational approaches practitioners value are accumulated, guaranteeing a locally grounded perspective[15].

13. As a visitor to the RCS, I was invited to attend a curriculum design meeting with members of the conservatoire's faculty. There I observed firsthand the ways in which staff discussed feedback they had received from various sources with a view to implementing curricular changes. Examples of feedback received through the consultation process include opinions on balancing the teaching of performance skills with theoretical knowledge, providing students appropriate sight-reading skills, and the importance of optimizing graduates' career prospects following graduation.

14. The Royal Conservatoire of Scotland's undergraduate program in Scottish music is currently in a state of significant transition from a BA program to a BM. Other feedback received from the consultancy process will be incorporated into the curriculum in the near future.

15. While Dickson and his team strive to embrace practitioners' voices and local musical perspectives, the process of collaborative consultancy employed at the RCS circumvents any form of pedagogical provincialism. Various authors have written on the scholarly pitfalls that can arise from an overreliance on practitioner perspectives

Literature on folk and traditional music pedagogy has frequently called for more contact between higher education and the professional music industry (see Doherty 2002). The programs and institutions consulted for this chapter share an emphasis on equipping students with the skills required to seek employment as performers but also as professionals in the music industry. Where possible, they simulate real-life scenarios students might encounter following graduation and integrate them into coursework and assessments. Many programs promote the development of entrepreneurial and business-related skills, for instance. At the Sibelius Academy's Folk Music Department, recitals take the form of public concerts that students produce and promote by themselves. Kristiina Ilmonen believes that this enhances their career prospects, which is especially important given that full-time folk music performance, education, or research positions rarely become available in universities. At the Royal Conservatoire of Scotland, Hamish Napier and Jenn Butterworth conduct ensembles as they would rehearsals for one of their own professional bands. They provide students with insights into work in professional contexts and develop associated skills, such as stagecraft. These skills are enhanced when the RCS Scottish traditional music students perform tours as part of their undergraduate studies. For its part, the popular music department at the University of Chester demonstrates a focus on the music business by referring to students as "professionals in training."[16] Similar efforts are described by Patch (Chapter 6 in this volume) in conjunction with popular music pedagogy in the United States.

As mentioned, one of the thorniest questions faced by pedagogues is how best to locate aural musics within educational structures that have traditionally emphasized music notation and theory systems. It seems natural that the teaching of nonliterate musics should de-emphasize music notation. However, in order to optimize how students engage with the analysis and communication of their chosen music, I suggest adopting an approach similar to that of Sven Ahlbäck and his colleagues and creating genre-specific systems of music notation and theory. Perhaps an introduction to foundational Western theory during year one can be augmented by further core studies in customized or genre-specific music theory and notation in subsequent years. This would certainly alleviate some of the frustration I witnessed among students at the Irish World Academy, who did not find aspects of Western theory pertinent to their studies. Perhaps the approach advocated by Pär Moberg is the best way

exclusively. See, e.g., White (1984), on the importance of developing a critical academic methodology for understanding the sociology of Irish folk music, and O'Connell (2010), on the tendency of locally focused practitioner perspectives to sometimes advance the subjective cultural and political baggage so often embedded in folk and traditional musics.

16. Ruth Dockwray, in discussion with the author, July 2015.

of thinking about Western notation and analytical techniques; they can be advantageous under certain circumstances, but they should not be the only tools adopted in the instruction of traditional musics.

The consultancy process instigated at the Royal Conservatoire of Scotland, although not fully implemented as yet, appears to be an effective way for pedagogues to evaluate what students and other practitioners perceive as central to traditional music pedagogy. Similar policies adopted in other institutions could only benefit curricular planning. Finally, the touring component within the RCS undergraduate curriculum undoubtedly enriches students' training, and this model should be considered for adoption by all pedagogues who train aspiring music professionals.

CONCLUSIONS

Approaches to the pedagogy of traditional, world, and popular musics must be flexible in order to adequately represent and interpret such repertoire and cultural context. I have suggested that the ways in which European programs problematize canonicity in music education and negotiate the needs and expectations of musical communities offer important insights into how we can best provide diverse, representative, and relevant musical education to students. In particular, fostering critical engagement and creativity in the curriculum helps prevent the perpetuation of unchallenged narratives about tradition and authenticity. Consultation with practitioners operating outside higher education and the incorporation of their feedback into curricula helps make music education more relevant to surrounding communities and mitigates against cultural, social, and musical disconnects between music programs and others.

ACKNOWLEDGMENTS

I would like to thank Mícheál Ó Súilleabháin, Aileen Dillane, Niall Keegan, Sven Ahlbäck, Suzanne Rosenburg, Ellika Frisell, Joshua Dickson, Hamish Napier, Kristiina Ilmonen, Pär Moberg, Leo Vervelde, Ruth Dockwray, Marion Leonard, and Freya Jarman for contributing their time and expertise to this discussion. I would also like to thank Robin Moore for his guidance and patience throughout the writing process.

REFERENCES

Caswell, Austin B. 1991. "Canonicity in Academia: A Music Historian's View." *Journal of Aesthetic Education*, Vol. 25 No. 23, 129–145.

Corcoran, Sean. 2013. "Canons, Curricula and Power in Irish music." In *Crosbhealach an Cheoil, the Crossroads Conference 2003. Education and Traditional Music*, Fintan Vallely, Liz Doherty, Thérèse Smith, Paul McGettrick, Eithne Vallely, Desi Wilkinson, and Colette Moloney, eds., 277–284. Dublin: Whinstone Music.

Cranitch, Matt. 2013. "Learning and Teaching 'Outside the Tradition.'" In *Crosbhealach an Cheoil, the Crossroads Conference 2003. Education and Traditional Music*, Fintan Vallely, Liz Doherty, Thérèse Smith, Paul McGettrick, Eithne Vallely, Desi Wilkinson, and Colette Moloney, eds., 76–83. Dublin: Whinstone Music.

Cranitch, Matt. 2013. "Learning and Teaching 'Outside the Tradition.'" In *Crosbhealach an Cheoil, the Crossroads Conference 2003. Education and Traditional Music*, Fintan Vallely, Liz Doherty, Thérèse Smith, Paul McGettrick, Eithne Vallely, Desi Wilkinson, and Colette Moloney, eds., 76–83. Dublin: Whinstone Music.

Dillane, Aileen. 2013. "Ethnomusicological Theory and Practice: Towards an Irish Ethnomusicology." In *Crosbhealach an Cheoil, the Crossroads Conference 2003. Education and Traditional Music*, Fintan Vallely, Liz Doherty, Thérèse Smith, Paul McGettrick, Eithne Vallely, Desi Wilkinson, and Colette Moloney, eds., 184–191. Dublin: Whinstone Music.

Doherty, Liz. 2002. "A Needs Analysis of the Training and Transmission of Traditional Music in University and Professional Level Education throughout Europe." Commissioned by the European Network of Traditional Music and Dance Education Working Group. Unpublished MS.

Hill, Juniper. 2005. "From Ancient to Avant-Garde to Global: Creative Processes and Institutionalization in Finnish Contemporary Folk Music." PhD diss., University of California, Los Angeles.

Hill, Juniper. 2009. "Rebellious Pedagogy, Ideological Transformation, and Creative Freedom in Finnish Contemporary Folk Music." *Ethnomusicology*, Vol. 53, 86-114.

Keegan, Niall. 2011. "Postgraduate studies". In *Companion to Irish Traditional Music*, Fintan Vallely, ed., 234. Cork: Cork University Press.

Keegan-Phipps, Simon. 2007 "Déjà Vu? Folk Music, Education, and Institutionalization in Contemporary England." *Yearbook for Traditional Music*, Vol. 39, 84–107.

Kingsbury, Henry. 1988. *Music, Talent, and Performance. A Conservatory Cultural System*. Philadelphia: Temple University Press.

Marquis, Alice Goldfarb. 1998. "Jazz Goes to College: Has Academic Status Served the Art?" *Popular Music and Society*, Vol. 22 No. 2, 117–124.

McCarthy, Marie. 1999. *Passing It On. The Transmission of Music in Irish Culture*. Cork: Cork University Press.

McGettrick, Paul. 2013. "Third-Level Education in Irish Traditional Music: Challenges, Opportunities and the Impact of Technology." In *Crosbhealach an Cheoil, the Crossroads Conference 2003. Education and Traditional Music*, Fintan Vallely, Liz Doherty, Thérèse Smith, Paul McGettrick, Eithne Vallely, Desi Wilkinson, and Colette Moloney, eds., 195–202. Dublin: Whinstone Music.

Nettl, Bruno. 1995. *Heartland Excursions. Ethnomusicological Reflections on Schools of Music*. Urbana: University of Illinois Press.

O'Connell, John Morgan, and Salwa El-Shawan Castelo-Branco, eds. 2010. *Music and conflict*. Urbana: University of Illinois Press.

Smith, Thérèse. 1999. "The Challenge of Bringing Oral Traditions of Music into an Academic Teaching Environment." In *Crosbhealach an Cheoil, the Crossroads Conference. Tradition and Change in Irish Traditional Music*, Fintan

Vallely, Hammy Hamilton, Eithne Vallely, and Liz Doherty, eds., 206–210. Dublin: Whinstone Music.

White, Harry. 1984. "The Need for a Sociology of Irish Folk Music. A Review of Writings on 'Traditional' Music in Ireland, with Some Responses and Proposals." *International Review of the Aesthetics and Sociology of Music*, Vol. 15 No. 1, 3–13.

CHAPTER 6

The Case for Pop Ensembles in the Curriculum

Amateurism, Leadership, Civics, and Lifelong Learners

JUSTIN PATCH

Music is about communication.
I'm sorry, Mr. Cage, it just is.

—Arnold Friedman

It was not a typical Wednesday night rehearsal for the students at the Austin Live Music Academy. The end-of-semester showcase at the Dirty Dog Bar was a week and a half away, and all that remained was to run the set top to bottom a few times, decide on a final set list, and discuss set-up and take-down protocol to get the ensemble on and off the stage smoothly. Unlike previous semesters, the entire hour-long set consisted entirely of original tunes written and arranged that semester by ensemble members. The songs ran the gamut from instrumental prog-rock to roots country, punk, and Americana. As we wrapped up the first hour, the students were feeling confident—the run-through was smooth, the mix was balanced, and the singers' background harmonies added delicious depth to the group's overall sound. As the ensemble concluded the final song, I looked at my watch, "We're at about fifty-two minutes, so we're still under an hour. Do you guys feel like working up a cover or something fun to close with?" I asked.

"Mike's got a new tune that we can do," Nate said, gesturing towards our resident lead guitar shredder, who had never sung a tune with the group.

"No, no. It's not ready," Mike demurred. "And who's going to sing it? You?"

"I heard you sing it in class, you sound great. We can totally do it."

Mike looked hesitant, but the group had already taken Nate's side. Mike pulled out his chart, made copies, and put the changes up on the chalk board. He walked the group through his arrangement, repeats, solo sections, and bridges and discussed the tempo, shape and tone that he wanted. The ensemble listened intently, made pencil marks on their charts, and then tuned up. Mike took a deep breath and counted off.

After the song ended and congratulatory words from his bandmates, the coaching started. The group discussed tempo and contour, and one chorus and bridge were eliminated. Meggan, the only woman in the group, suggested three-part harmony on the chorus that she and Nate took a few minutes to work out. Andrew, another guitarist, suggested that he play the main rhythm guitar riff, leaving Mike to concentrate on vocals and the lead guitar parts. Daniel proposed hi-hat, kick, and ride cymbal variations during the chorus, solo, and bridge sections, offering Mike samples to choose from. Adjustments were made to the chart on the board and Mike counted off the tune again.

During the second run-through Patrick, the ensemble's co-coach, snuck in to the rehearsal room, fresh from a happy hour gig. When the tune ended, he asked, "Whose song is that?" The surprise registered on his face when Nate gleefully pointed out that it was Mike's freshly penned original. "Let me hear it top to bottom," Patrick asked, and with a smile Mike counted it off again.

INTRODUCTION

This vignette about the construction of one song in a single rehearsal does not provide basis for a wide-ranging theory of popular music pedagogy in higher education. But its contours and characters speak volumes about the ways pop ensembles augment the musical, intellectual, and social experience of student musicians. Pop/songwriting ensembles (referred to here simply as pop ensembles) keep music education relevant by better preparing students for professions in music and music industry and add practical depth by providing students the opportunity to assume leadership roles and apply competencies learned in theory, aural skills, and arranging courses. Pop pedagogy also nurtures interdisciplinary connections to creative writing, law, business, media studies, and technology, expands the music curriculum in ways that speak to contemporary concerns for diversity and social justice, and helps institutions meet goals of developing future leaders and teaching critical communication skills. The anecdote above reveals ways that pop and songwriters' ensembles can and do contribute both to music curricula and to the development of students as musicians, music professionals, leaders, communicators, and critical thinkers.

Mike was an unusual student in the ensemble, part of the now-defunct Austin Live Music Academy (ALMA), a post-secondary program designed to provide training for students interested in popular music careers in Austin, Texas. Mike was a decade older than his peers, a married college graduate with a career in health care, a mortgage, and future plans that included having children. He did not plan on having a career in popular music and doubted whether he would ever play in a rock band again. But he was passionate about making music, and as he transitioned away from heavy metal and got more interested in songwriting and home recording, he wanted to develop new tools to help him stay musically involved. For these reasons, he took a year of voice lessons and spent time working on his songwriting instead of studying the guitar, his primary instrument. Mike is like a multitude of amateur musicians—full of enthusiasm and the desire to continually improve their craft outside of the professional sphere. Music making is an integral part of his identity and an important aspect of his life. He is also the kind of student who routinely slips through the cracks in collegiate curricula.

Mike and others like him are the type of students that many music departments are not attuned to: those who are not interested in a professional career as a canonical musician, music educator or therapist, or an industry professional. Mike's musical passions—80s metal, classic rock, flamboyant electric guitar playing, and blues-based hard rock—are rarely taught or discussed outside of History of Rock courses. His chosen vocal style had little in common with the art song, opera, or choral repertoire that features prominently in most curricula. He would probably not have flourished in the competitive, concert-based atmosphere common to many music departments, nor would he be afforded a creative outlet within standard ensemble offerings.

While establishing a career in music is a competitive endeavor and students need to experience such pressures and learn to play music they are less familiar with, excessive competition creates an environment that is unwelcoming to amateur musicians and musicians of noncanonical forms. It also artificially limits the range of musical and creative expression available to young musicians. I believe that a competitive canonical orientation is detrimental to music departments and their graduates. By limiting participation in performance programs or by funneling students exclusively to ensembles like wind bands, orchestras, jazz bands, and choirs, music departments are doing a disservice to students and to the many musical communities in their midst (see Moore, Chapter 1, Pedroza, Chapter 7, and Bradley, Chapter 11, in this volume).

Apart from making Mike a synecdoche for musicians not served by standard music curricula, the vignette above provides insights into the ways pop ensembles benefit not just a music department but the university as a whole. The ALMA students encouraged and supported each other, learned to give and receive criticism, experimented with musical ideas, learned to communicate and articulate their ideas, and applied lessons from their songwriting and theory classes. Pop ensembles cultivate skills that are relevant to more than careers in music: leadership, confidence, self-actualization, teamwork, and critical engagement with others. They also prepare students for a life that is attuned to musical practices in twenty-first century communities.

The ALMA ensemble had two coaches, but often students chose repertoire and worked out arrangements themselves, particularly during their second semester together, when they were more comfortable with each other. The students composed original songs, took turns directing and submitting to peer criticism, learned to offer constructive suggestions and evaluate their results, and worked together towards a common end product: a concert in front of friends, family, and bar patrons. While these skills benefit career-minded musicians, they are applicable to other career paths and are essential to the practice of democratic life. It is no overstatement that playing in pop ensembles can make for better civic leaders; as philosopher John Dewey insisted, there is a correlation between democracy and creativity. For Dewey, the practice of art teaches experimental relationships between individuals and their world and between individuals themselves as they collectively alter sound, space, and images through art (Dewey 2005, Goldblatt 2006). Making art teaches students to experiment with the structures of the world and the materials that are available to them. Pop ensembles provide an opportunity for creative, intersubjective experiences through which students learn to cooperatively produce by taking commonly known musics and remaking them or by composing in familiar idioms. In these endeavors, students learn civics, self-actualization, and critical pedagogy while enriching the musical life of the community.

This chapter examines the ways in which pop ensembles intellectually nurture their members by providing skills necessary for future professional endeavors. Pop pedagogy, which I define as a serious engagement with applied popular music performance, opens a music program to a host of students who might never have taken a music class, enables participants to build a foundation for lifelong musical engagement, enhances self-knowledge, and teaches leadership and communication skills. Pop pedagogy augments the music curriculum in ways that maintain relevance and enhance real-world preparation. Evidence suggests that a popular music and music industry emphasis greatly enhances student employment prospects (Smilde 2008) and augments existing curricular structures. For music majors, the experience of playing in a pop ensemble teaches professionalism through learning efficient rehearsal technique, verbal communication, and critical listening skills. For music educators and therapists, pop ensembles provide an opportunity to teach and perform popular music, songwriting, and arranging, essential skills for professionals who work with youth and young adults. For students whose professional aims involve the music industry, conducting, or composition, pop pedagogy offers practical experience in music directing, arranging, studio, and post-production work. In all of these facets, pop pedagogy brings the opportunity for the flipped classroom, in which students have the opportunity to experiment, apply, and theorize learning from other music courses, enhancing their creative and problem-solving abilities. Pop pedagogy develops music majors as complete musicians, ensuring that they possess knowledge of contemporary styles and practices and encouraging them to develop relevant skills that are rarely cultivated through standard curricula. Pop pedagogy also develops leadership skills and offers practical lessons in civics and communication that are necessary for success in nearly any field and are therefore relevant to any student regardless of major. This chapter concludes with thoughts on best practices derived from interviews with pedagogues who are currently engaged in pop pedagogy.

THE SCHOOL OF SOMEONE ELSE'S MUSIC

Current music curricula emphasize repertoire that is removed from the everyday experience of most listeners (Green 2005, Rodriguez 2004, Ruthmann 2007). While critiques of esoteric bias could also be leveled at programs in Arabic literature, modern dance, or fluid dynamics, there are key differences. First, nearly all students consume music. It is constitutive of their identity and part of their daily routine. Literature from the sociology and anthropology of music (see Stokes 1994, Frith 1996, North et al. 2000, Turino 2008) and music education (North and Hargreaves 1999, Phelan 2008, Dabback 2008, Bell 2008, Mixon 2009) attests to the importance of music in social life and identity formation. Musical engagement during the college years can be especially important, as students experience intense personal growth and change. If avenues for expression are absent at this time, young performers may become discouraged or choose to develop other facets of their personality. Expanding the curriculum to include pop ensembles encourages students who do not have professional aspirations to continue making music and to solidify their creative identity, keeping them involved in music and encouraging continued participation.

One can argue that collegiate classes should provide students with musical experiences other than the ones they already know, in the same way that learning a new language or studying new novels does. Walker (2005) provides compelling evidence that, when presented effectively, Western art music can be meaningful to all students and contribute to a comprehensive education. The counterargument is that in a society cognizant of the myriad musical forms present, allocating value only to canonical repertoire represents a failure of vision and obligation, not to mention ethnocentric bias (see Moore, Chapter 1, and Bradley, Chapter 11, in this volume). Additionally, learning pop music, local popular musical traditions, and musics from around the globe can be meaningful for those preparing to perform in the Western art music idiom and other canonical forms, as modern composers often use idioms derived from popular and global music. Just as creative writing programs provide fundamental grammatical skills but ultimately push students to realize their own voice, music departments have an obligation to do the same. As Scott Shuler and Lucy Green emphasize, any experiences that allow for creativity, improvisation, self-realization, and self-assessment facilitate profound musical learning. As I discuss below, pop pedagogy is particularly suited to facilitate these goals—and for a wider range of students.

LIFELONG MUSICIANS

A great deal of literature on K–12 music education discusses how to develop lifelong music makers, creators, and active listeners (e.g., Ernst, 2001; Shuler 2011, 2012; Lamont, 2011). Unfortunately, on the post-secondary level, music learning continues to be conceived of in binary fashion, as either vocational or avocational, with heavy curricular emphasis on the former. Avocational music learning tends towards music studies, music appreciation, nonperformance electives, and opportunities to perform canonical repertoire with jazz and wind bands, orchestras, chamber music, and choirs. The purpose of a professional track is obvious: to prepare students for work as music professionals. The purpose of supporting amateur musicians is also clear but is rarely addressed. It allows amateurs to express themselves creatively, just as intramural sports enable less dedicated or skilled athletes to participate in athletic competition. However, canonical ensembles are no longer representative of the modern amateur musical experience, and participation in these ensembles does not best prepare musicians for engagement with twenty-first century musical communities. This reality means that many music departments fail to facilitate lifelong musical engagement for amateur musicians.

Community orchestras, choirs, and wind bands are playing a smaller role in shaping the musical worlds and creative imaginations of young performers. The most common collegiate ensembles appeal to musicians with specific skills and training and often require high proficiency, at minimum the ability to read standard notation. They also represent a small fraction of the musical world outside the academy. In contrast, pop ensembles—like a cappella choirs that sing popular hits, singer-songwriter courses, rock bands, or hip-hop and turntable/laptop/iPad ensembles—promote familiar genres and have broad appeal and stylistic flexibility. These ensembles can accommodate a wide range of musical abilities, and with proper oversight and coaching, they can adopt repertoire appropriate to the skills of their participants. While community wind bands, orchestras, and choirs are not as common as they once were, other structures have sprung up to take their place. Jam sessions, pub sessions, open mic nights, bar bands, and virtual/online musical communities represent the new face of community music making. In a recent article on the recruitment of music teachers (specifically those choosing to major in music education) only 8 percent cited participation in institutionalized community ensembles as a source of inspiration (Bergee and Demorest 2003). Young music education majors appear not to be thinking of canonical community ensembles as creative outlets or as relevant spaces for music making and identity formation. This suggests a disconnect between the skills passed along in collegiate music education programs and those needed to participate in and sustain contemporary musical communities. Colleges and universities must consider how to respond to changes in community music making and in students' musical interests with the goal of teaching independent participation outside established institutionalized structures.

In "Five Guiding Principles for Music Education," Scott Shuler writes about approaches that encourage "a lifetime of involvement" that are ideological rather than prescriptive (see also Shuler 2011). Shuler's key is teaching independence—the ability for musicians of any level to create, respond, and perform music without direct guidance. He believes that young musicians must be taught with the goal of attaining musical independence and that the path involves teaching skills that are authentic and transferable. For Shuler, authenticity means teaching music that corresponds to students' own musical reality, and transferability refers to teaching musical concepts in such a way that they can be broadly applied outside the specific context in which they are learned. Few courses currently foreground such principles, and thus if collegiate music curricula hope to cultivate lifelong musicians, they must expand their course and ensemble offerings. An exclusionary performance curriculum is unresponsive to contemporary communities and can result only in young musicians looking elsewhere for musical training, intellectual satisfaction, and professional employment.

Regarding community engagement, Cindy Bell (2008) points out that many music teachers who are trained in the Western canon are unprepared to engage with musicians who lack knowledge of Western art music and its cultural practices. In one case study, the author recounts the story of a once successful chorus that was floundering, despite a talented conductor and enthusiastic but not necessarily talented singers. After attending several rehearsals, Bell "realized that our conservatory-type music [education] program had failed to prepare [the conductor] to work with the average adult learner" (2008, 236). In a study of community choirs, she also notes troubling demographic trends (Bell 2004). She describes the typical chorus as consisting of "twice as many women as men," primarily white, over forty years of age, with a college education, and previous choral experiences (46). The author worries that choruses, many of which are directed by individuals grounded in canonical practice, are becoming mini-cultures removed from most forms of community music. For Bell, promoting only elite music represents the abandonment of a democratic calling. Following John Dewey, she sees the nurturing of a creative public as the heart and soul of education. She pointedly asks of music educators: "Are they prepared to respect the amateur musical experience, to crave and successfully direct such an experience?" (238). These questions underscore the problematic hierarchies of social value that inform current music curricula.

Mantie and Tucker (2008) point out that music education is not typically geared towards encouraging lifelong engagement but rather towards the imparting of discrete skills that may not transfer outside of institutional settings. This leaves amateur musicians who do not practice canonical forms with no collegiate outlet to develop their musicianship. However, there are attempts being made to remedy this situation. Deb Bradley (Chapter 11 in this volume) outlines curricular changes in music education programs that are aimed at remedying such problems. The University of Washington and UCLA have both made community involvement a priority of music teacher education through programs of homestays and fieldwork, courses and workshops with local musicians, and requirements that foreground noncanonical musical forms that are representative of global, regional, and youth musics. Perhaps the most radical program that Bradley outlines is Arizona State University's, which makes access and diversity priorities. At ASU students pursue an individual track in music studies, allowing them to specialize in an instrument of their choice, including instruments like turntables, laptops, and accordion, under the guidance of a chosen faculty member. Likewise, the music program at the University of Louisiana–Lafayette has added performance of Cajun music to its curricular offerings (see DeWitt, Chapter 4 in this volume), and the University of Texas at San Marcos has added Mariachi as a possible emphasis for music education majors (Pedroza, Chapter 7 in this volume). Pop music programs, from the highly professional training at colleges like Berklee College of Music, the University of Southern California, and Belmont University to the amateur-centered like those of UNC Greensboro and East Tennessee State, are at the cutting edge of experimenting with pop ensembles as both professional training and as tools to encourage lifelong musical participation.

TAKING A LESSON FROM PRIMARY AND SECONDARY MUSIC EDUCATION

Concern for inclusion, access, and dynamism in higher education is often shared by colleagues in primary and secondary schools. In searching for ideas and models that integrate pop into a musical curriculum, some of these experiments in process can serve as crucial departure points. One such case is that of Alex Ruthmann and his experience with his Composer's Workshop in a Michigan middle school. His class represented a creative solution to teaching students whose musical skills were deemed insufficient for chorus or band (2007). Ruthmann successfully engaged them by having them compose with computer loops, simple recording technology, and basic software. His model imitated writing instructors who coach students to create stories by inventively combining familiar words and phrases: he had them compose using familiar bits of recorded music in a familiar electronic pop style. By being sensitive to his students' musical habits and emulating the popular music that surrounded them, Ruthmann created an environment in which students collectively made music. His innovative technique allowed them to find creative outlets through nontraditional instruments and musical forms. More importantly, his students' experience was what Schuler would deem authentic: it resonated with students' lived musical experience outside the classroom.

Pop pedagogy on the tertiary level, like Ruthmann's middle school experiment, can help ameliorate some of the problems identified by Bell in community music making that is narrowly modeled on collegiate musical practices. Through pop pedagogy, music educators learn about the preferences of local music communities and gain familiarity with the noncanonical musics that are regionally significant. This knowledge enables pedagogues to creatively engage with musicians whose interests are not geared towards concert music. Applied pop pedagogy broadens music educators' horizons, presents new pedagogical tools, provides an opportunity to work with enthusiastic musicians who lack formal knowledge of Western art music, and teaches pedagogues to manage ensemble members with diverse skill sets.

MAKING MUSIC IN CHANGING COMMUNITIES

One of the difficulties in evaluating literature on community music making is that conceptions of community continue to change. Talk of virtual communities, which began in the 1990s (see Wellman et al. 1996), expanded as social networking and mobile connectedness became part of everyday life for many. Wellman and Gulia (1999) note that community has become more about network than geography. Today, one's village can stretch around the world.

Increasingly, young musicians find their musical outlets via electronic networks like YouTube, Facebook, and SoundCloud. These outlets are well utilized by pop musicians, but noted performers of Western art music like Renée Fleming, Deborah Voigt, the Philadelphia Orchestra, and Eric Whitacre have effectively harnessed the possibilities of online communities as well, as has the American Composers Forum. The platforms mentioned above offer musicians ample ways to connect to friends, fans, and collaborators. As Cayari (2011) notes, YouTube now provides what physical communities once did: a creative space, opportunities for professional networking, and connection to fans. New media and dramatic reductions in the cost of recording technology also encourage virtual strategies of self-marketing and collaboration. While Cayari's study of YouTube is based on a single individual, his conclusions are not unique to his subject. The various virtual social networks that accommodate music and video allow millions to upload their music and share it with friends and strangers.

If we accept Chorus USA's estimate that 23.5 million individuals currently sing in choirs in the United States and compare that figure to participation in online music services, it is obvious that communities are trending towards the virtual (Bell 2004). In 2013 Ryan Mac reported that online music interface SoundCloud passed 38 million users in 2013 and was likely to have over 55 million users soon (Mac 2013). Globalwebindex.net claims that one in ten web-connected adults between sixteen and sixty-four use SoundCloud each month, a staggering number. While much of that activity involves listening to and not uploading music, it does suggest involvement in a musical community, much of which is dedicated to pop music. Musical institutions concerned with service to their community must consider their relationship to virtual musicians and listeners. One could also make a strong argument for the inclusion of electronic recording and computer-based music in future curricula along with songwriting and arranging.

THE INVERTED CLASSROOM

In the past decade and a half, many educators have expressed interest in the inverted classroom and in a more interactive, experimental, and application-based learning environment. The premise of their argument stems from the idea that the hierarchical transfer of information—as in an uninterrupted lecture—does not facilitate the most effective forms of learning. Lecturing does not afford students the opportunity to discuss, question, apply, or experiment with concepts. It requires only that they listen and memorize. Since not all students learn in the same fashion, the use of multiple methods of engagement with an emphasis on in-class responsiveness is preferable and statistically more successful than lectures (see Moore, Chapter 1 in this volume). According to Bramsford and colleagues, "To develop competence in an area of inquiry, students must: a) have a deep foundation of factual knowledge, b) understand facts and ideas in the context of a conceptual framework, and c) organize knowledge in ways that facilitate retrieval and application" (quoted in Brame 2013). The authors suggest that "a 'metacognitive' approach to instruction can help students learn to take control of their own learning by defining learning goals and monitoring their progress in achieving them." While Brame admits that metacognition is not always inherent in the flipped classroom, metacognition is necessary for developing Shuler's ideal independent musician. By taking control of their own learning, experimenting with, and applying new information to their practices, students acquire the cognitive tools to continue learning and creating music apart from formal educational structures and institutions.

Most common collegiate ensembles function hierarchically, similar to academic lectures. Each group has a director or conductor who chooses the repertoire and communicates the interpretation to the ensemble. Often this top-down guidance is appropriate and necessary, as students enter higher education without the requisite skills to direct, artistically manage, or compose for large canonical ensembles. However, smaller pop music ensembles provide an ideal space for students to gain the kind of individual competencies Bramsford and his colleagues advocate, along with metacognitive self-knowledge. Unlike more formal ensembles and world music ensembles, the pop classroom inverts easily and lends itself to peer-to-peer instruction and interactive and/or experimental learning. Ideally, musicians work in small groups, learn their parts before attending rehearsal, and come together ready to experiment. The small-group format allows for democratic participation and input into the artistic process. The short duration and repetitive form of pop songs provide opportunities for experimentation and the application of skills like songwriting and arranging beyond that of canonical ensembles. Students may choose their own repertoire, write for the ensemble, arrange or rearrange songs in class, and lead rehearsals. Most music students enter college with the necessary skills to make quality pop music, so more time can be devoted to the advanced skills of application and experimentation. While some students engage in such activities outside the classroom, I believe professional oversight greatly improves their experience. Not only can instructors push them into new artistic territory, even when performing cover tunes, but an instructor can help them more effectively manage rehearsal time, provide additional input on creative work, or develop a greater appreciation of musical elements such as dynamics and form, ensemble balance, and use of vocal harmony.

For music majors, taking a leadership role in an ensemble under the guidance of an experienced pedagogue provides opportunities to develop directing and interpersonal communication skills early on in their collegiate career. Students can choose appropriate repertoire and assess the ensemble and individual participants for strengths and weaknesses. While performing in string quartets or piano trios provides similar opportunities, pop ensembles can offer them earlier in their collegiate education.

The less hierarchical nature of a pop ensemble also lends itself to experimentation and creative dialogue. Cover tunes can be reworked and combined in unusual ways, and a single song can be used as an in-depth teaching tool. In addition, involvement in pop ensembles teaches critical problem-solving skills and the direct application of musical knowledge like part writing, arranging, and scoring. For instance, if a songwriter desires horn parts or string arrangements, it creates an opportunity for a budding arranger not only to practice her craft but to learn about transposition, low third limits, cross-voicings, and other musical intricacies.

For students pursuing music education or planning a career with an applied music education component, working with a pop ensemble provides an invaluable pre-professional experience. Advanced majors playing pop music together are able to experiment and push their own levels of musicianship in ways that go beyond what a canonical education provides. An example from 2015 is *Queen Boudicca: A Metal Opera*, performed at Berklee College of Music. The opera, written entirely by students under the direction of Robert Schlink, combines early Celtic repertoire, chamber and choral music, heavy metal, and death metal.[1] This kind of virtuosic, creative play, sometimes on new instruments (e.g., iPads, turntables, laptops, and samplers), adds an entirely new dimension to applied music education.

As Robin Moore suggests, canonical ensembles have tended to emphasize standard interpretations rather than improvisation and intuitive engagement with musical material (1992). As European art music became available to the masses, more performers learned from media—sheet music, radio, and recordings. This has led to inflexible performance practices that do not allow for improvisation or creative engagement. Making pop ensembles available to canonically trained performers affords them an intuitive engagement with music making that is often not present in the early and intermediate stages of their education.

CRITICAL COMMUNICATION

In an era of partisanship and vehement political disagreement, it is incumbent on educators in all fields to teach and inspire civility. Allegheny College has gone so far as to give public figures awards for civility in public life.[2] The model of deliberative democracy (Young 2000) is imperiled when young people are not provided a space in which to learn critical listening and communication skills. In a deliberative democracy, citizens join in public discourse about matters of public policy and work toward consensus. Similar skills are essential in musical production and other professional pursuits. The art of communication requires sensitive, clear, and informed articulation, but also critical listening and independent contemplation. While some might say that such skills need to be learned through political and civic practice, I believe that critical listening and communication skills are transferable. Learning to present and defend ideas in public and to accept criticism of even one's most treasured

1. Private communication, March 17, 2015
2. http://sites.allegheny.edu/civilityaward/.

ideas requires practice. All of this can be undertaken through ensemble partic-ipation. Learning to experiment and to articulate aesthetic preferences is part of learning about civic and professional life. Pop pedagogy teaches these skills and the leadership, civics, and respect that institutions pride themselves on.

ENSEMBLES IN PRACTICE

The umbrella genre of pop music is immense, ranging from rock and metal to roots, folk, and Americana, country, electronica, hip-hop, reggaeton and R&B, and myriad forms of global pop. Therefore, approaches to pop pedagogy vary widely and are affected by local taste, instructor preferences, and institutional structure and mission. A comprehensive overview of pop ensembles in higher education is beyond the scope of this chapter, but it is necessary to take time to outline some representative programs and discuss the steps being taken to integrate pop pedagogy into the music curriculum. Although the sample I dis-cuss is small, it illustrates the diversity of existing approaches, methods, and goals of existing programs and also suggests commonalities between them. The pop ensembles discussed come from a variety of institutional settings: specialized institutions like Berklee College of Music; music industry programs housed within schools of music, as is the case in the University of Miami and Belmont University; large schools of music with many different majors and courses of study, like UNC Greensboro, the University of Memphis, and the University of Louisiana at Lafayette; and music studies programs like blue-grass, old-time, and country music studies at East Tennessee State University. While these programs have adopted different approaches to pop pedagogy and ensemble practices, there are key similarities. All instructors emphasize the real-world nature of the ensemble and model their practice on the work that professional ensembles or songwriters do. They also emphasize the com-prehensive, humanistic aspects of pop pedagogy, placing the development of the person on a par with, if not ahead of, the acquisition of musicianship and professional acumen.

The most expansive suite of existing pop ensembles is found at Berklee College of Music in Boston, which offers some 350 options.[3] Many of these focus on a specific artist or genre; for example, Pop Icons: The Music of Michael Jackson, Prince, and Whitney Houston; Techno-Rave Ensemble; and Turntable Ensemble. The tremendously varied selection is supported by a large and diverse faculty that prides itself on being at the vanguard of contem-porary musical practices of musicianship, the music business, and industry. Berklee is a unique institution, one that was founded in the mid-twentieth

---

3. https://www.berklee.edu/ensemble (accessed January 3, 2017).

century to teach jazz and popular music of the African diaspora. The institution's nearly exclusive devotion to popular and commercial music allows this complex network of ensembles to work to the benefit of its students. Many graduates have gone on to become top names in pop music internationally.

Other institutions orient themselves toward regional musics or prioritize specific genres. For example, Belmont University in Nashville hosts a number of pop ensembles including Phoenix, a pop/rock ensemble; Rock Ensemble, which covers rock of the 1960s to the present; and Southbound, dedicated to the Nashville top 100.[4] Henry Smiley, the director of Southbound and a seventeen-year faculty member at Belmont, emphasizes two elements of the ensemble work: professionalism on par with Nashville industry standards, and Southbound's pedagogical context within a liberal arts degree. Southbound is a competitive audition ensemble that features eight singers supported by a seven-piece band performing contemporary country styles. Ensemble members are mostly students in the music department. Many of them are music industry majors who aspire to careers in Nashville, Los Angeles, New York, and other major musical centers, but the group also attracts students from outside the music department who have a passion for country.[5]

In early August, Southbound members meet to discuss the semester's repertoire and solicit unrecorded songs from local Nashville publishers. Group members arrange, rehearse, and perform upwards of four hours' worth of material over the course of the semester and attend image and branding workshops with local professionals. Every element of performance is rehearsed and critiqued, even patter with the audience between songs. However, Smiley is careful to note many of the transferable skills learned through this process. He insists that the confidence, creativity, and communication skills students learn through participating in Southbound constitute the most important part of their education. Through this experience, particularly learning from bad performances or rehearsals, he believes that students learn to successfully face life's challenges. He says, "We're making great music . . . we're also making better people," highlighting the humanistic elements of pop pedagogy.[6]

Similar rigor and professionalism is found in the University of Memphis's SoundFuzion ensemble, a pop band that travels to local schools and does recruiting on behalf of the university. Longtime director Lawrence Edwards emphasizes the city of Memphis as an American melting pot for musical styles, a meeting place of blues, rhythm and blues, soul, and funk alongside country,

4. http://www.belmont.edu/Catalog/undergrad2015jun/cvpa/som/ensembles.html (accessed January 3, 2017).

5. Belmont University requires ensemble participation for all music majors but allows them to participate in only one ensemble per semester. The university hosts some thirty-one different ensembles, including a rock ensemble, but the pop ensembles are greatly outnumbered by canonical groups like orchestra, choruses, and jazz ensembles.

6. Private communication, May 20, 2015.

rock, hip-hop, and pop. In putting together a set list that will appeal to a wide swath of high school students, he suggests the key is to be on the cutting edge, to know the latest pop radio hits, and to include a few throwback tracks that have remained popular with local high schoolers. Edwards tasks his fourteen-piece ensemble, which consists of eight voices, two keyboards, two guitars, bass, and drums, with knowing the contemporary music scene. Collectively, the ensemble works to formulate a set list that reflects such knowledge at the beginning of each semester. Members are responsible for assembling a complete hour-long show in three weeks and are constantly adding new repertoire. As in the case with Southbound, many of SoundFuzion's musicians are studying music business or industry and aspire to careers in popular music.

For both SoundFuzion and Southbound, student participation is required for repertoire selection, arranging, rehearsing, and performing. Edwards states that "students become producers"[7] through working with the ensemble, including four weeks spent rehearsing through a dedicated PA system to perfect the band's mix and blend, and set-up and take-down assignments to expedite travel. Edwards emphasizes the positive effect that this level of professionalism has on his students. He insists that when students know what it takes to prepare and have the confidence to perform at professional level, they continue making music for the rest of their lives. Those who do not pursue careers in America's urban musical centers often play in church bands or teach young people in music academies and schools, where their pop training is highly valued.

More financially modest but no less vibrant expressions of pop ensembles are exemplified by ensembles at East Tennessee State University and the University of North Carolina at Greensboro. In both of these institutions, ensembles focus on regional styles of old-time music while simultaneously accommodating diversity of expression and pedagogical flexibility. According to Professor Lee Bidgood, ETSU supports some forty bands, including duos, a mandolin orchestra, typical old-time string bands, a Celtic ensemble, and modern country bands. Bidgood and other coaches depend on student input when choosing repertoire for these ensembles, which are composed of majors, non-majors, community enthusiasts, and local professionals. Bidgood encourages students to arrange for their groups and to experiment, expand their horizons, and learn the complex histories of the music they play. His goal is to get young musicians to think about what they're doing and to say something through the music they perform. He believes that ensemble coaching teaches intentionality and purpose and a conscientiousness about performance and interaction with community, culture, and history.[8] The bluegrass, old-time, and country program at ETSU is housed within Appalachian studies and is offered as both a major and a minor. Within this structure, students

7. Private communication, May 27, 2015.
8. Private communication, May 20, 2015.

participate in seven semesters of ensemble playing bluegrass, old-time, country or Celtic music.

Revell Carr at UNC Greensboro combines performance and songwriting in one ensemble, an approach that has met with some success. His techniques are aimed at teaching songwriting as an integrated part of performance, as a collective rather than a top-down process. He also takes pains to introduce music majors to teaching and learning through the oral tradition. Students in the old-time ensemble are given the option of writing new songs in the idiom (ranging from bluegrass and string band to blues and folk-pop). Carr found that this alleviated much of the struggle with form that challenges young songwriters because old-time musical forms are well known to most students and provide a rough frame to work within. In this respect, Carr's approach is similar to Alex Ruthmann's Composer's Workshop. Rather than ask students to pen new songs without guidance, Carr offers them the option of writing songs in an already familiar musical idiom. As 2015 marked the fiftieth anniversary of the formation of the Grateful Dead, Carr based much of his ensemble's repertoire on the Dead, a band that had roots in Americana and translated it into an electric pop idiom. In keeping with oral tradition, Carr required each student to learn a song and teach the class by ear and example. Following that, those who wanted to play original music brought in their own songs and taught them in much the same way. Approximately half of the students participated. By making the point that most of the world's music makers don't have institutional teachers, prospective educators are encouraged to rethink their roles within communities and develop a tool kit of pedagogical strategies. But Carr is quick to say that even though he has serious goals for his students, his ensemble is, at the end of the day, about the joy of making music.

Miami University's pop pedagogy is highly structured and features a songwriting and performance curriculum aimed at producing music professionals. It adapts classical concepts of form, structure, and idiom analysis, as well as aural skills, to pop idioms. Students study and perform pop music written by Elvis, Johnny Cash, the Beatles, Hart, John Legend, Lourde, and others. In the process, students learn to recognize and perform basic chord structures, modes, and modulations, eventually transforming them into increasingly complex compositions. They also learn terminology used in professional songwriting and studio environments. Miami's music department hosts a number of popular ensembles, including pop, musical theater, and a cappella. Anna Flavia Zuim's pop and songwriting ensemble, like the others, requires an audition.[9] It consists of six to eight singers and a full rhythm section, along with a DJ. Performers are required to participate for a full year and compose their own music, while also cultivating their professional image and stage

9. Anna Zuim is now on music faculty at New York University.

presentation skills. In the context of Zuim's ensemble, members wears many hats: composer, arranger, director, promoter, and performer. They learn to be well rounded, to communicate, think, and listen critically, and to collaborate and support each other. Coached to be bold and unafraid to take artistic chances, they risk making productive mistakes, which provide opportunities to grow musically and personally.

For Zuim, the ensemble serves as a liaison between student life and the professional world; the members are challenged to elevate their musical and professional skills but have the aid of a professional, supportive, and knowledgeable coach. Zuim emphasizes the ensemble's role in helping students find their musical and intellectual voice, to locate their strengths and weaknesses on stage and in the lab. Students also learn metacognitive skills, such as recognizing how they learn and produce music best and how to work with others who have different musical strengths and weaknesses. In this way they maximize their potential for personal growth and artistic independence.[10]

A completely different approach to songwriting has been practiced by Ed Snodderly at ETSU for close to two decades. Snodderly's classes are open to anyone who is interested, and his students run the gamut from prolific and experienced performers and composers to novices. He emphasizes the creation of community in the classroom, making students comfortable enough to share their work in a rigorous but safe environment. Using a realistic, manageable approach, working in small steps, often going through songs phrase by phrase, he emphasizes the importance of progressive experimentation through trial and error. He has students workshop compositions line by line in front of their peers, often accompanied only by guitar or piano. Participants learn to perform with confidence and take pride in their work while also giving and accepting honest criticism. Through songwriting, students grasp and articulate what makes a good song and come to better understand their own processes of making music.[11]

CONCLUSION

As this small sampling of programs demonstrates, there is no single approach to pop pedagogy and songwriting ensembles in higher education. Each of the ensembles and programs discussed has developed unique guidelines and goals established by their instructors. Each director emphasizes professionalism and intellectual growth and works to create a musical experience that corresponds to students' daily lives and communities. The programs strive to develop high levels of creativity, professionalism, and musicianship but also

10. Private communication, July 9, 2015.
11. Private communication, July 3, 2015.

place responsibility for the quality of performance, repertoire selection, and artistic direction on the students' shoulders. Students learn leadership skills and walk away with the ability to continue creating, performing, and reacting to music independently. What was most compelling about all of these pedagogues was that despite their success stories—and all of them had students who had gone on to play and write professionally—they all emphasized the importance of the emotional and intellectual advancement of their students through pop pedagogy. They believed that the pop ensemble experience made students more self-actuated, sensitive, and conscientious, and developed their emotional and intellectual strength in unique ways. Each echoed Henry Smiley's compelling dictum: participating in a pop ensemble made students better people, and that is the point of all education.

ACKNOWLEDGMENTS

I extend my sincerest gratitude to Henry Smiley, Lawrence Edwards, Lee Bidgood, Mark Dewitt, Ed Snodderly, Ana Flavia Zuim, Arnold Friedman, and Revell Carr for taking time out of their busy schedules to share their pedagogical processes with me. I also extend my thanks to Robin Moore for supporting this project and tirelessly working through drafts and ideas.

REFERENCES

Bell, Cindy L. 2004. "Update on Community Choirs and Singing in the United States." *International Journal of Research in Choral Singing*, Vol. 2 No. 1, 39–52.

———. 2008. "Toward a Definition of a Community Choir." *International Journal of Community Music*, Vol. 1 No. 2, 229–241.

Bergee, Martin J., and Steven M. Demorest. 2003. "Developing Tomorrow's Music Teachers Today." *Music Educators Journal*, Vol. 89 No. 4, 17–20.

Brame, C. 2013. "Flipping the Classroom." Vanderbilt University Center for Teaching. http://cft.vanderbilt.edu/guides-sub-pages/flipping-the-classroom/. Accessed August 15 2015.

Cayari, Christopher. 2011. "The YouTube Effect: How YouTube Has Provided New Ways to Consume, Create, and Share Music." *International Journal of Education & the Arts*, Vol. 12 No. 6, 1–30.

Dabback, William M. 2008. "Identity Formation through Participation in the Rochester New Horizons Band Programme." *International Journal of Community Music*, Vol. 1 No. 2, 267–286.

Dewey, John. 2005. *Art as Experience*. New York: Penguin Books.

Ernst, Roy. 2001. "Music for Life." *Music Educators Journal*, vol.Vol. 88 no.No. 1, 47–51

Frith, Simon. 1996. "Music and Identity." In *Questions of Cultural Identity*, Paul Du Gay and Stewart Hall, eds., 108–127. London: Sage.

Goldblatt, Patricia F. 2006. "How John Dewey's theories underpin art and art education." Education and Culture Vol. 22 No. 1 17-34.

Green, Lucy. 2005. "The Music Curriculum as Lived Experience: Children's 'Natural' Music-Learning Processes." *Music Educators' Journal*, Vol. 91 No. 4, 37–42.

Lamont, Alexandra. 2011. "The Beat Goes On: Music Education, Identity and Lifelong Leaning". *Music Education Research*, Vol. 13, No. 4, 369–388.

Mac, Ryan. 2013. "Upload and Share Music—or Any Noise: The Beauty of SoundCloud." *Forbes*, May 6, 2013.

Mantie, Roger, and Lynn Tucker. 2008. "Closing the Gap: Does Music-Making Have to Stop upon Graduation?" *International Journal of Community Music*, Vol. 1 No. 2, 217–227.

Mixon, Kevin. 2009. "Engaging and Educating Students with Culturally Responsive Performing Ensembles." *Music Educators Journal*, Vol. 95 No. 4, 66–71.

Moore, Robin D. 1992. "The Decline of Improvisation in Western Art Music: An Interpretation of Change." *International Review of Aesthetics and Sociology of Music*, Vol. 23 No. 1 (June), 61–84.

North, Adrian C., and David J. Hargreaves. 1999. "Music and Adolescent Identity" *Music Education Research*, Vol. 1 No. 1, 75–92.

North, Adrian C., David J. Hargreaves, and Susan A. O'Neill. 2000. "The Importance of Music to Adolescents." *British Journal of Educational Psychology*, Vol. 70, 255.

Phelan, Helen. 2008. "Practice, Ritual and Community Music: Doing as Identity." *International Journal of Community Music*, Vol. 1 No. 2, 143–158.

Rodriguez, Carlos Xavier. 2004. *Bridging the Gap. Popular Music and Music Education*. Lanham, MD: Rowman and Littlefield.

Ruthmann, Alex. 2007. "The Composers' Workshop: An Approach to Composing in the Classroom." *Music Educators Journal*, Vol. 93 No. 4, 38–43.

Shuler, Scott C. 2011. "The Three Artistic Processes: Paths to Lifelong 21st-Century Skills through Music." *Music Educators Journal*, Vol. 97 No. 4, 9–13.

———. 2011. "Music Education for Life: Building Inclusive, Effective Twenty-First-Century Music Programs." *Music Educators Journal*, Vol. 98 No. 1, 8–13.

Smilde, Rineke. 2008. "Lifelong Learners in Music: Research into Musicians' Biographical Learning." *International Journal of Community Music*, Vol. 1 No. 2, 243–252.

Stokes, Martin, ed. 1994. *Ethnicity, Identity and Music. The Musical Construction of Place*. Oxford: Berg.

Turino, Thomas. 2008. *Music as Social Life. The Politics of Participation*. Chicago: University of Chicago Press.

Walker, Robert. 2005. "Classical versus Pop in Music Education." *Bulletin of the Council for Research in Music Education*, 53–60.

Wellman, Barry, et al. 1996. "Computer Networks as Social Networks: Collaborative Work, Telework, and Virtual Community." *Annual Review of Sociology*, 213–238.

Wellman, Barry, and Milena Gulia. 1999. "Net Surfers Don't Ride Alone: Virtual Communities as Communities." In *Networks in the Global Village*, Barry Wellman, ed., 331–366. Boulder, CO: Westview Press.

Young, Iris Marion. 2000. *Inclusion and Democracy*. New York: Oxford University Press.

CHAPTER 7

Latin Music Studies at Texas State University

The Undergraduate Minor in Mariachi and Its Implications for Expansive Curricula in Mainstream Institutions of the United States

LUDIM PEDROZA

The Latin Music Studies (LMS) area at the Texas State University School of Music represents one of a handful of *degree-granting* programs currently specializing in the study of Latin American popular music repertoires in the mainstream US academy.[1] The LMS undergraduate curriculum was not conceived in an institution dedicated to the study of popular music (such as Berklee College of Music), nor did it emerge with the help of endowed funds (such as the Traditional Music program at UL Lafayette directed by Mark

---

1. Our Lady of the Lake University in San Antonio offers a bachelor of music in sacred music with a Concentration in mariachi. California State University Los Angeles offers a master of music with an option in Afro-Latin music. The Conservatorio de Música de Puerto Rico (San Juan) offers a BM in performance of jazz and Caribbean music with concentrations in bass, drums, Puerto Rican cuatro, guitar, piano, Latin percussion, saxophone, trombone, and trumpet. I am not aware of other degree-granting programs with specific options in Latin American music in the United States or its territories. A variety of tertiary-level programs are developing in Mexico, Central America, and South America under essentially different historical and cultural circumstances than those in the United States; they deserve a study of their own.

F. DeWitt).[2] LMS operates strictly within the overall administrative and financial framework of a mainstream School of Music and thus partakes of the same pool of resources (ensemble budgets, scholarship aid, funds for faculty lines, etc.) allotted to all music programs. This condition lends itself to gradual curricular expansion or diversification rather than radical overhaul of the core structure.[3] It is my hope that the history, analysis, and recommendations I share in this chapter will be useful to those embarking on gradual yet progressive curricular expansion within mainstream institutions.

After defining the terms *mainstream, interpretive performance*, and *canonization*, I briefly describe the history and components of the LMS area and then proceed to analyze LMS's degree-granting undergraduate curriculum, which currently consists of a minor in mariachi. LMS founder John Lopez designed the minor to accompany the BM in music studies (music education) as a way of providing mariachi players already bound to the public school system with fundamental skills in ensemble management and mariachi pedagogy, as well as enhancement of their performance skills through applied lessons. My analysis probes the curricular and administrative conditions that have allowed certain components of the minor—particularly the mariachi ensemble and applied lessons—to substitute in some cases for the standard requirements of band, choir, orchestra, and applied lessons. Because the minor's goal is contingent upon the public school job market, options for credit-hour substitutions are limited, as music educators are expected to gain competency in conducting one or more mainstream ensembles (choir, band, or orchestra). Thus, credit hours of specialization in mariachi repertoire must be added to the already voluminous music studies degree plan. Ideally this results in more marketability and versatility for graduates since they are able to teach both mariachi and other ensembles.

In the section entitled "Expansive Curriculum," I describe how John Lopez, in collaboration with the music studies and voice areas, has successfully implemented an option for mariachi vocalists in the BM degree to fulfill all their applied lesson credits within the mariachi vocal studio. I also discuss how the development of the mariachi vocal studio at Texas State has important implications for the expansion of performance practices in academia and provides context for understanding the conditions that make such expansion possible

2. For more information on the Dr. Tommy Comeaux Memorial Endowed Fund for Traditional Music at UL, visit https://music.louisiana.edu/music/undergraduate/traditional-music/tommy-comeaux-endowed-chair (accessed January 31, 2017).

3. Administrative and curricular autonomy is possible when a singular mission converges with sizable donations and endowments. Indeed, if the funds are donated by an individual or entity invested in the academic development of a particular genre of music, the donation may require the exclusive earmarking of funds to provide faculty lines for specialists, scholarship funds for prospective students, and resources for the rapid development of radically innovative curricula. Mainstream music units in higher education rarely encounter such convergences.

in mainstream music departments. My closing remarks probe the future development of ensembles and curricula within an expansive vision of interpretive performance and offer several practical recommendations based on LMS's experiences with the mariachi ensemble and applied-lesson curriculum.

TERMINOLOGY

I use the adjective *mainstream* to denote the prevailing model of tertiary-level music institutions in which curriculum is centered on the large-ensemble trio (choir, band, orchestra) and applied lessons. *Interpretive performance* is a concept advanced by the CMS task force, whose "Manifesto" is cited throughout this volume (Campbell et al. 2014). The CMS task force does not explicitly define the concept of interpretive performance, yet its critique does, albeit obliquely. In proposing "three pillars" that will "ensure the relevance, quality, and rigor of the undergraduate music curriculum," the CMS task force "takes the position that improvisation and composition provide a stronger basis for educating musicians today than the prevailing model of training performers in the interpretation of older works." In turn, when identifying "core deficiencies in the conventional model of music study," the task force contrasts interpretive performance with jazz and "older" European practices of improvisation, idealizing the latter. Interpretive performance appears to be, in the task force's view, not conducive to "the creation of new work;" it is also associated with ethnocentrism (it appears culturally inseparable from canonized European repertoires and its derivatives). Building on these premises, Moore's introduction to the present volume proposes that "the interpretive performance of canonical repertoire should not have same importance in the future that it currently does." In the context of the goals of the present volume and those of the CMS task force, I understand the phrase *canonical repertoire* to refer precisely to a limited body of eighteenth- and nineteenth-century European works, which are often taught through very strict forms of interpretive performance. Nevertheless, in part because I will be concentrating my discussion on mariachi repertoire and ensembles, I find it necessary to define interpretive performance and canonization in relation to a broader set of genres and tendencies.

My analysis incorporates the concepts of interpretive performance, the canonization of European repertoires, and other forms of canonization as distinct tendencies (i.e., each can occur independently of the others). My definitions rest on the premises 1) that interpretive performance and canonization are found in an array of music genres and cultures including jazz, mariachi, and many world and popular music genres; and 2) that interpretive performance involves a broad spectrum of practices, including improvisation in some cases. My definitions are informed by my past research on the historical formation of the concept of the musical work among pivotal figures such as Franz Liszt and Clara Schumann, by my ongoing research on genre theory in relation to salsa music, by my extensive experience as a solo pianist and as an accompanist for various applied music studios, and ongoing analysis of the LMS programs at Texas State University.[4]

In the CMS task force document, interpretive performance appears collapsed with pseudo-romantic philosophies that hyperidealize some (not all) European repertoires,[5] the composer's intentions, and the "authentic performance" (or "historical performance") doctrine. I propose that, although tacitly accepted in many academic circles, such philosophies are not tantamount to interpretive performance. Rather, they represent the extreme end of a spectrum that also includes philosophers suggesting composer and performer bring music to life in partnership and that old repertoires can be actualized and/or fused with other genres for contemporary audiences and contexts. I suggest we embrace a broader conception of interpretive performance that presumes all creative negotiations between composers and sound realizers (regardless of whether they are the same person) include a degree of interpretation and of creative variation. From this perspective, jazz and many other Western and world genres embrace interpretive performance, albeit placing higher value on *intended indeterminacy* and improvisation. In short, I use the phrase *interpretive performance* to denote a continuum between composition and performed realization. I refer to *closed forms of interpretive performance* when alluding to the extreme pseudo-Romantic philosophical attitudes described above that CMS task force critiques are leveled against.

I use the term *canonization* to denote *standardization*, a practice that closely relates to genre codification and the idealization of works, personalities, and musical elements. The canonization of particular works (often deemed

---

4. See Pedroza (2010) for an in-depth study of the legacies of Franz Liszt and Clara Schumann in present forms of interpretive performance favored particularly by academic piano studios. A quote from this article is relevant to the discussion provoked by the CMS task force: "Clara Schumann thus exemplifies an extraordinary juncture in pianistic mythology and pedagogy: She was taught *to make music*—composition, theory, improvisation, and counterpoint were all part of her training, and she was an adept improviser to the end of her life—yet, she taught her students *to play musical works*, as indicated by their own remarks." (320). This article built on various philosophical and historical sources, and particularly on Lydia Goehr's *The Imaginary Museum of Musical Works* (1992).

5. As explicitly identified in current standard histories of music, such as that of Burkholder, Grout, and Palisca (2014), the notion of canonization in classical music is historically tied to romantic aesthetics, particularly to what we could call the "aesthetic sanctioning" led by Austro-German philosophers, critics, and composers throughout the nineteenth and early twentieth centuries. Beethoven, Bach, Mozart, Schumann, and Brahms, in particular, stand at the top of the list of canonized composers, a list that admits additional composers and nationalities insofar as they cultivate the aspects of thematic development, pitch manipulation (melodic, harmonic, and post-tonal), and formal coherence idealized by related romantic-modernist values.

"masterpieces," "standards," or "classics"), composers, and historical record-ings is evident in jazz, rock, Indian classical music, mariachi, and many other genres. I refer to the entrenchment of eighteenth- to early-twentieth-century European repertoires within certain academic spaces in precisely such descrip-tive, if unwieldy, terms.

During the years I worked as a piano accompanist for vocal and instrumental studios in north and central Texas institutions, I observed that individual studios and instructors (at least in this region) have distinct philosophies of interpre-tive performance. For instance, brass, percussion, and woodwind studios tend to be relatively versatile; while cultivating some standard repertoire, these stu-dios greatly favor experimental compositions and arrangements, a philosophy of performance founded in partnership and collaboration with living composers, and a relatively low penchant for canonization. Many instructors on such instru-ments encourage their students to acquire skills in multiple genres and thus to expand their spectrum of interpretive performance. This is particularly evident in trumpet, trombone, and saxophone studios, whose students often enroll in jazz ensembles and take applied jazz lessons.

By contrast, piano studios tend to perpetuate the composer-as-authority style of interpretative performance and the canonization of eighteenth- to early-twentieth-century European repertoire. Piano studios present these tendencies with surprising consistency; prominent performers who digress from the model stand out as eccentrics (e.g., Glenn Gould) or as specialists (e.g., David Tudor).[6] Piano studios across the country also continue to gradu-ate pianists who are capable of performing an impressive portfolio of standard, very difficult works but who would struggle if asked to play "Happy Birthday" in any major key as part of an impromptu social gathering. These are per-formers who can *play musical works* but who cannot creatively manipulate the elements of any one particular music genre.[7] The situation is often perpetu-ated through the curriculum: while non-piano majors take several semesters of piano proficiency, many programs exempt pianists from this requirement.[8]

<hr>

6. Pianists such as André Previn (classical-jazz crossover) and Keith Jarrett (jazz-classical crossover) are considered exceptional artists in both genres, although ver-satile profiles such as theirs are far more common outside the academy than critics, historians, and artists in the same genres would like to admit.

7. Among the notable piano pedagogues who have polemicized academic clas-sical training is Marienne Uszler, whose article "Fin de Cycle?" (*Piano & Keyboard* 2000) bluntly asked the question: "What are all these pianists being trained to do? We already have an over-supply of degreed, tolerable players and teachers seeking posi-tions that are disappearing or being diluted. Is it more important to sustain the status quo so that we can feel good now, or had we better face the music?" (7).

8. The subject of keyboard skills for piano majors is greatly underresearched. One of the few studies is Steven Ray McDonald, "A Survey of the Curricular Content of Functional Keyboard Skills Classes Designed for Undergraduate Piano Majors" (PhD diss., University of Oklahoma, 1989). McDonald found that "approximately one fourth of the four-year degree-granting institutional members of NASM *offer* functional

Conversely, while instrumentalists and vocalists (other than pianists) have to fulfill a piano proficiency requirement, they do not have to demonstrate "creative proficiency," so to speak, on their own principal instrument. As I discussed earlier, such experiences with creativity and multigenre experimentation are pursued to varying degrees by instructors who choose to do so within the historical, regional, and individualistic domain of their own experiences. In short, in arguing against interpretive performance, the CMS task force is effectively arguing against closed forms of interpretative performance that teach students to perform a handful of canonized works without the opportunity to create and/or manipulate the musical elements that constitute those works. Such experiences with creation, manipulation, and indeed, improvisation, should be crucial in the musicianship of the twenty-first century, as argued by the manifesto.

All in all, further study of the various shades of interpretive performance evident in the academy would be beneficial; doing so would help identify areas of the curriculum that are ripe for expansion and avoid undue generalizations about academic musicians. Mariachi musicians also cultivate a broad spectrum of interpretive performance practices. Their aesthetic inclinations, discussed below, provide unique insights into issues of canonization, indeterminacy, and interpretive performance.

LATIN MUSIC STUDIES AT TEXAS STATE UNIVERSITY SCHOOL OF MUSIC: A BRIEF HISTORY

Texas State University is an Emerging Research University with a student population of approximately 38,000. In 2011 Texas State University was officially designated HSI, a "Hispanic-Serving institution"; as of 2015, 32 percent of its students were Hispanic.[9] The School of Music serves a population of approximately six hundred and offers degrees up to the master's level. Latin music studies comprise both degree-granting programs and community outreach initiatives. Graduate degrees include the master of music in music education with a concentration in mariachi music education and the master of music with a concentration in Latin music performance. At the undergraduate level, the minor in mariachi was recently approved, a program that students

keyboard skills classes designed for the undergraduate piano major" (108; emphasis added).

9. The offices of University Marketing and University News Service publish all data pertaining to the university; see http://www.umarketing.txstate.edu/resources/facts.html, http://www.txstate.edu/news/news_releases/news_archive/2011/March-2011/HSIRelease032411.html, and http://www.txstate.edu/news/news_releases/news_archive/2012/January-2012/EmergingResearch011212.html (accessed June 20, 2015).

can pursue only in conjunction with the BM in music studies (i.e. music education) ⓘ. Three main ensembles associated with the program are open to all students in the university, through audition: Salsa del Río, Orquesta del Río, and Mariachi Nueva Generación.

Community outreach programs also affiliated with LMS at our institution include the Mariachi Infantil and the Mariachi Feria. The first is an after-school weekly workshop that provides mariachi instruction and ensemble experiences for children in the Central Texas area for a fee. The Mariachi Feria is an annual event that welcomes middle school and high school mariachi ensembles, predominantly from Texas, to the School of Music for workshops and competitions. Feria, which has been in place since 1999, also features professional mariachi artists who perform in a public concert.

Texas State University Associate Professor of Percussion John Lopez founded all programs within the LMS area. Lopez was born in San Antonio; his late father was director of the San Antonio–based Mariachi Chapultepec and his mother, Beatriz Llamas, "La Paloma del Norte," is a Conjunto Hall of Fame–inducted singer. Lopez created the ensembles Salsa del Río (1995) and Mariachi Nueva Generación (1997) as elective but for-credit courses. Shortly after, he created a second ensemble in each genre, intending the top ensembles to be competitive and the other ensembles to be primarily preparatory. This two-prong model is consistent with the culture of the School of Music, which, as with so many music institutions in Texas, places a premium on ensemble competitiveness. Lopez's own identity as ensemble director informs the high performance standards he requires of his ensembles. The salsa bands perform in local dance clubs three to four times a semester, and the mariachi ensembles perform in official university events, national competitions, and civic celebrations, such as Cinco de Mayo.

In 2003, Lopez created a seventeen-credit undergraduate mariachi teaching certificate (MTC). The recently approved minor in mariachi has now replaced the MTC and is available to undergraduates in music studies. In 2007, Lopez created graduate concentrations in Latin music. Up to 2011, all LMS programs were described as a "multicultural studies area," at which point the faculty generated the current designation, "Latin music studies."

Among undergraduates, the minor in mariachi (formerly MTC) attracts mostly Hispanic students from Texas high schools that have strong band, choir, and mariachi programs; some of them are members of community, or "gigging," mariachis and wish to be music educators. Among graduate students, the program has attracted practicing salsa and Latin jazz musicians from various states, as well as academically trained percussionists seeking to expand their repertoire and techniques. A relatively high number of undergraduates audition yearly for the MTC (often requiring selective admission), and the new minor is expected to attract large numbers of students in the same way. In short, interest in mariachi education correlates with the widespread presence of mariachis in Texas high schools. In terms of shared interests, mariachi musicians seem strongly attracted to mainstream ensemble formats, while *salseros* value crossover experiences with jazz. All students accepted into the graduate program have an undergraduate degree in music, as it is required for the MM.

FROM THE MTC TO THE MARIACHI MINOR: THE LMS UNDERGRADUATE CURRICULUM

University music departments with long-established music education programs tend to develop powerful ties to the public school system and to university sports. Primary and secondary schools, the main job market for music educators, strongly emphasize wind bands, choirs, and orchestras and thus ensure the prominence of these ensembles at the university as well. These large ensembles function as training arenas for music educators, competitive performance venues for the student population, and as the public face of the music program in a variety of contexts. Degree requirements and, in particular, scholarships and performance grants keep such ensembles not only populated but also performing at peak level.[10] As Robin Moore states in the introduction to this volume, "they make wonderful music, yet require such expansive resources that they restrict the development of alternate groups and tend not to allow for much student agency." Moore also reminds us that NASM does not define "major ensemble" and in fact requires variety in the size and nature of ensembles for the professional degrees in music. Yet, the band-choir-orchestra trio dominates the music curriculum thanks largely to persistent networks of internal and external institutional interdependences. It is in relation to these complex realities that we must situate the emergence of the MTC and its development into the minor in mariachi.

The earlier MTC required six credits in mariachi ensemble, three in mariachi arranging, two in mariachi history and methods,[11] one in *guitarrón* and *vihuela*

10. For example, in many music departments degree plans require a mix of "major" ensembles and chamber or smaller ensembles (e.g., four semesters of band, choir, or symphony orchestra and four semesters of chamber or alternative ensemble). Nevertheless, a highly competent, say, violin player will frequently participate in the symphony orchestra for all eight semesters (in addition to the chamber/alternate ensemble) because her music scholarship or grant requires it.

11. The methods component of the course required students to evaluate current mariachi method books and learn teaching techniques for solo, trio, and ensemble formations; for *huapango, son*, bolero, *ranchera valseada*, and other subgenres; vocal phrasing in various subgenres; and several other aspects of performance practice on melodic and *armonía* (rhythm section) instruments. Due to credit-number restrictions, the LMS faculty approved the removal of the history component during the design of the mariachi minor. As of now, only the graduate degree plan includes history of music in Mexico.

group class instruction, and three in group guitar class. To these, instrumental majors would add two credits in mariachi voice, while vocalists would split their ensemble credits with solo voice requirements and take only two credits of instrumental methods (one in strings and one in brass). After 2012 the MTC became available only to students pursuing the BM in music studies, a condition established by Lopez himself. He believed the MTC to be most effective in the hands of certified music teachers who could obtain full-time jobs in the school system and handle both mainstream and mariachi ensembles. His comments indicate additional concerns:

> For too long, school administrators have disrespected the mariachi tradition by hiring non-certified mariachi musicians so that they can pay them a fraction of what certified music educators receive. Don't misunderstand me; I am not saying that these mariachi musicians are necessarily unqualified to teach mariachi; I am saying that some administrators take advantage of the fact they are not certified teachers in order to save themselves some money. I created the mariachi certificate program precisely to change this situation. Ideally, we want all our mariachi certificate graduates to also have the BM in Music Studies so that they can be paid accordingly and help legitimize mariachi music.[12]

In linking the MTC to music studies, Lopez hoped to correct the persistent situation that places mariachi ensembles in the schools as an inexpensive add-on to the conventional ensemble trio of band, choir, and orchestra. Nevertheless, the MTC (seventeen credits) itself was an add-on to the music studies degree that even without the mariachi specialization requires 129 to 131 credits. As discussed above, MTC candidates could not substitute their band, choir, or orchestra credits for mariachi ensemble credits and thus found themselves in two or more demanding ensembles simultaneously. In addition, mariachi instruments are not currently designated as "principal instruments," making it impossible for the study of guitarrón or vihuela, for instance, to apply toward studio requirements. The large number of credits required of those in the MTC program caused emotional stress and a heavy financial burden for some students. In addition, restrictions regarding the number of credits an undergraduate on financial aid could accumulate prior to graduation created additional pressures.[13]

The audition and acceptance process further impacted MTC students negatively. As in many music departments, applied studio faculty members accept or reject prospective music majors into the school. This is primarily because

12. Mariachi Teaching Certificate Open Forum, minutes. Texas State University, March 5, 2012. Lopez's statement came in response to one of the student's questions regarding the goals of the MTC.

13. See http://www.finaid.txstate.edu/graduate/maintain.html (accessed January 31, 2017).

all professional music degrees (BM) and, in some cases, the BA as well require a significant number of applied studio credit hours. Though students interested in the MTC auditioned for the LMS faculty, applied studio faculty made the ultimate decision regarding their acceptance into the School of Music. As opposed to violinists, trumpet players, guitarists, or vocalists, guitarrón and vihuela players have no chance of entering the music program unless they audition on an instrument associated with the mainstream applied studios. In turn, only these studios can grant music scholarships; not being an independent degree, the MTC was not entitled to dedicated scholarship funds.

Informally named after LMS's mariachi vocal instructor, Michelle Quintero, the 2013 Quintero Proposal manifests some of the ways in which Lopez has negotiated these academic realities. The proposal establishes that mariachi vocalists—and only vocalists—can now audition exclusively for the LMS faculty for acceptance into the BM in music studies if they adhere to certain parameters: 1) only vocalists with strong mariachi technique but little "classical" training qualify for Michelle Quintero's studio; 2) vocalists under this option complete all of the required applied studio credits with Quintero and thus are allowed to count the MTC applied lessons toward their BM in music studies; 3) students admitted into Quintero's studio fulfill their recital requirement with a program that includes both pieces from the canonized European art song repertoire and a variety of other Latin American music (including mariachi repertoire).

In addition to creating the Quintero Proposal—effectively, an option for mariachi vocalists to integrate their training with the requirements of the BM—Lopez recently converted the MTC into a minor in mariachi. The new minor expands on the pedagogy of mariachi methods and ensemble teaching associated with music education credentials and moves the heaviest specialized requirements to summer workshops, thus significantly relieving students' course load during the academic year. Specialized summer offerings include Mariachi *Armonía* Techniques, a course that covers performance, pedagogy, and stylistic issues related to the rhythm section of the mariachi (guitarrón, vihuela, guitar, and harp). Mariachi *Melodía* Techniques offers the same sort of instruction but focuses on the melodic components of the ensemble. Mariachi Arranging considers traditional and innovative approaches to that topic, and Mariachi Ensemble Teaching Lab complements other coursework by focusing on the broader skills of ensemble management, performance, and curriculum creation. All courses mentioned will be offered over three consecutive summers, with each session focusing on a segment of mariachi repertoire (huapango, ranchera, bolero, etc.). During the academic year, students will enroll in mariachi ensemble and take applied voice, brass, and strings with a focus on mariachi.[14]

14. Complete degree plans and course descriptions of the BM in music studies with the minor in mariachi are available for download at the companion website

The minor in mariachi is attached to the BM in music studies, and therefore instrumental majors pursuing it continue to enroll in multiple ensembles simultaneously during the academic year and in two sets of applied studios. Nevertheless, most vocal majors in the future will be able to complete all their applied studio credits with a mariachi specialist and perform recitals of notable versatility. In addition, mariachi vocalists will audition for LMS directly and potentially partake of general music scholarship funds. In the case of both vocalists and instrumentalists, student transcripts will henceforth recognize the minor in mariachi as a separate degree.

EXPANSIVE CURRICULUM: THE IMPLICATIONS OF THE QUINTERO PROPOSAL

Several aspects of the Quintero Proposal merit further discussion, among them its implications for the continued expansion of interpretive performance in academia and the conditions that allow for the inclusion of instructors capable of enacting such expansion. The proposal creates the conditions for the execution of recital programs that showcase a broad array of practices associated with interpretive performance. Quintero assigns students mariachi pieces, works from European, Mexican, and Latin American art song repertoire, and songs that resist classification.[15] The art song repertoire requires interpretive performance, with a particular emphasis on vocal projection valued by mainstream applied vocal studios. The mariachi component also involves the interpretive performance of works by composers and arrangers canonized in that repertoire (José Alfredo Jiménez and Rubén Fuentes, among many others). Standard mariachi pieces allow students to cultivate specific virtuosic techniques such as the falsetto, the long vibrato, and the fierce *estilo*

for this text ▶ and at http://latin.music.txstate.edu/degrees-programs/mariachi-minor.html. For a description of Quintero's studio option, see http://latin.music.txstate.edu/degrees-programs/mariachi-vocal-ed.html (accessed January 31, 2017). To see the graduate MM in music education / mariachi education concentration, go to http://www.music.txstate.edu/prospectivestudents/graduatedegreeplans/latin-musiceducation (accessed January 31, 2017).

15. The description of Quintero's use of repertoire is based on my observations of her lessons and seminars for MTC undergraduates and an examination of recital programs from graduate students. I have also observed Quintero teaching mariachi voice students who are not necessarily enrolled in degree-granting mariachi programs but who wish to develop their mariachi voices and compete in various mariachi national events. These observations allow me to infer how the undergraduate recitals associated with the minor in mariachi will take form. I reiterate that the minor is a new program; the first student recital associated with it was scheduled for the spring of 2016. (To an extent, my description is also based on my awareness of the preparations and draft program for this recital, which are taking place concurrently with the writing of this chapter.)

bravío. On the other hand, mariachi works are often published only in lead-sheet format; they require instructor and student to listen to and study both canonized and contemporary recordings and to decide upon a given arrangement or create their own. Such decisions involve choosing an instrumental ensemble to accompany the song (which could be either a full or a "chamber" mariachi ensemble). I have particularly enjoyed seeing how Quintero and the students take advantage of each other's singular talents. Harp and accordion players, for example, although engaged officially as music majors on other instruments, pair with the vocalists to accompany them as stylistically appropriate. Figure 7.1 showcases two of Quintero's voice students teaming up as vocalist and accordionist; although this performance took place in a competition rather than a recital, it clearly exemplifies Quintero's general approach.

Latin American art song repertoire presents students with unique challenges as well. For example, standard arrangements for "Estrellita" by Mexican composer Manuel M. Ponce feature a fully written out piano accompaniment and vocal line, not unlike a song by Schubert. Because of the piece's distinctive appeal and difficult range, singers strive to execute it faithfully. Yet "Estrellita" can be performed to a variety of instrumental accompaniments, including solo piano, guitar, or various chamber ensemble combinations. Compositions by Agustín Lara, Alberto Aguilera Valadez (Juan Gabriel), or composers from the Trova Yucateca tradition have also been published in lead-sheet form and are covered by a multitude of singers from both academic

Figure 7.1. Texas State University students Karen Zavala and Robert Casillas, with Mariachi Nueva Generación at the Mariachi Vargas Extravaganza (San Antonio, Texas, 2012). Photograph and © by David F. Martinez.

and popular backgrounds. They further challenge the art/popular dichotomy, requiring instructors and students to exercise creativity in terms of determining arrangements, ensemble format, vocal ornamentation, and other aspects of performance. From the moment Quintero begins work with students, they collectively select and study repertoire required for the BM recital. At the end of their degree, Quintero's students add a printed recital program and a final recording showcasing a rich variety of works to their performance portfolio. In support of their recitals, undergraduate vocalists write program notes describing the creative processes involved in its realization (including arranging and ensemble design for each work performed) as well as some history of the composers and genres included.

All in all, future recitals associated with the minor in mariachi will showcase the elements discussed above in conjunction with Quintero-led lessons, seminars, and mariachi concerts: 1) a variety of vocal techniques including some derived from outside the European tradition; 2) an assortment of ensemble accompaniment, ranging from a single piano, guitar, or harp to a full mariachi ensemble; 3) repertoires that straddle several countries and continents and that derive from both popular and academic contexts; 4) program notes that illuminate the student's own artistic decisions or contributions; and 5) in some cases, the student's own arrangements. If this model is successful, it may in turn convince voice faculty in mainstream studios that singers can be educated to perform a variety of techniques and genres.[16] Finally, a program that features Latin American art song and additional versatile repertoires may serve as a model for vocal studios to experiment with recitals that feature the rich US repository of song, the spirituals of Harry Burleigh, and many other song repertoires. I also believe this model can be further developed into the type of student-driven project Moore explores in chapters 13 and 14 and that can be easily extrapolated to instrumental studios, as a growing number of instructors are highly qualified to experiment with these ideas.[17]

Michelle Quintero's advanced vocal training greatly facilitated her integration into existing institutional contexts. In most college-level institutions, instructors are required to have academic credentials that popular music artists often lack. Without advanced degrees, directors and graduate studies coordinators must justify their hire through special procedures. Applied lessons offered by those without advanced degrees frequently require special oversight; in addition to supervising the artist's teaching, a faculty adviser

16. This is a delicate topic for many singers; indeed, I have met only few who are open to educating voices in multiple genres.

17. My colleague and viola studio instructor Ames Asbell, for instance, regularly performs across genres in baroque and popular music and is a founding member of the self-defined "crossover" Tosca String Quartet (http://www.toscastrings.com/about. html (accessed January 31, 2017)). The Tosca is a successful example of the many such experimental chamber music ensembles developing in the United States and the world.

must often oversee their grading, syllabi creation, and other actions. The adviser (who often carries a full teaching load in addition to other responsibilities) thus expends considerable effort serving as a mentor. In short, the hiring of specialized artists quickly becomes complicated and demanding. In the mariachi world, this situation is mitigated because many musicians now hold graduate degrees and have the potential to become "dual-genre" pedagogues. Thus, the Quintero Proposal was successful largely thanks to the fact that 1) Quintero holds degrees in classical vocal performance (BA in music) and music education (BM and MM) in addition to her lifelong and distinguished experience as mariachi performer and pedagogue; and 2) she is well versed in the day-to-day business of academia.[18] Quite simply, the credentials of dual-genre musicians allow for easy integration into academic life.

It is important to consider how Quintero, who grew up deeply embedded in the mariachi world, came to acquire credentials from the mainstream music academy. She earned her BA with concentration in vocal performance and the BM with all-level certification in music education from the University of the Incarnate Word in San Antonio (Incarnate Word College, at the time of Quintero's graduation). She recounts that she auditioned for the faculty there in the genre she knew best: mariachi. She performed on guitarrón, vihuela, violin, guitar, and voice and earned a scholarship substantial enough to allow her to pursue music studies.[19] According to Quintero, voice professor Deborah Bussineau-King was instrumental in her crossover success because she trained Quintero in academic vocal techniques (i.e., those related to opera and art song repertoires) and at the same time encouraged her to continue cultivating her mariachi voice. For her part, Quintero asserts she welcomed academic training wholeheartedly because, above all, she wanted to be treated and recognized as "a musician, period." Quintero explained to me that she transferred aspects of academic training to her mariachi technique: these include "diaphragm support, centering the vibrato, good flow of air, control of change

18. Among Quintero's prominent students is Sebastien de la Cruz, the young mariachi vocalist whose performance of the national anthem on June 11, 2013, at the NBA finals, was received with both positive and hostile comments by the public and media. Sebastien was also a semifinalist in NBC's *America's Got Talent* 2012.

19. It is important to emphasize that this open audition process and awarding of music scholarships at the University of the Incarnate Word (UIW) was likely possible thanks to the fact that the degree was a bachelor of arts in music and that the institution had not at the time renewed its NASM accreditation (it has recently regained such accreditation). I am familiar with the infrastructure of the Department of Music at UIW, as I was employed there from 2003 to 2011 (after Quintero's graduation, I should add). In general, the curricular structure of the BA presents interesting opportunities for expansive curricula, and, at the same time invites us to further investigate the ways in which NASM guidelines have been and continue to be interpreted and enforced in relation to both the BA in music and the BM—the *professional* degree in music.

from chest to head voice, and finding the best color of her voice."[20] In short: an operatically trained professor accepted her into a mainstream applied studio with scholarship funding even though Quintero auditioned with "nonclassical" repertoire; the professor introduced Quintero to classical vocal techniques while neither prohibiting her from continuing to pursue mariachi nor systematically trying to morph Quintero's mariachi voice into an operatic or art song voice; Quintero herself adopted a selection of techniques best suited to mariachi singing, style, and repertoire. She continues to develop this approach in her studio at Texas State University, which is populated mostly with singers trained in mariachi performance. Her students eagerly absorb the technical tools from both the academic and the mariachi worlds, just as she did.

CLOSING REMARKS AND PRACTICAL RECOMMENDATIONS

A curricular model that allows mariachi musicians to integrate their training with the BM requirements may be applied to instrumentalists in the near future if LMS can hire more dual-genre instructors. Under these conditions, the eventual recognition of vihuela, guitarrón, Mexican harp, and mariachi guitar as principal instruments is also possible. Nevertheless, a freestanding BM in mariachi music studies is neither viable nor desirable at Texas State University. As already stated, students graduating with exclusive expertise in mariachi would not fare well in a local job market in which the band-choir-orchestra trio dominates. Yet mariachi ensembles are proliferating at all academic levels. According to the Texas Music Office, 131 mariachi ensembles have registered on their site since 1995, the vast majority in high schools. Although the data may require updating, it documents a substantive mariachi ensemble presence in Texas schools.[21] Other indicators of the extent to which mariachis are accommodating themselves within academic culture can be glimpsed from data provided by the Texas Association of Mariachi Educators

20. Although I have collected data about Quintero's approach and education over the last three years, I obtained most of the information related here during formal conversations on the topic on November 9, 2015. In turn, Bussineau-King had the following to say about her experience with Quintero: "My goal with Michelle was to put in place a technique that would give her the tools to avoid the vocal damage that frequently occurs in that genre of vocal singing, i.e. straining for high notes, vocal dysfunction and vocal nodules. I didn't want to change her. I wanted to add to her. I wanted to make her performance skills multifaceted. I wanted her to continue to love the music she sang when she first came into my studio but open her eyes to other styles so she could adapt what she wanted into her style of Mariachi" (Email communication, November 22, 2015).

21. See http://governor.state.tx.us/music/education/mariachi/ (accessed June 12, 2015). Approximately ninety high school mariachis are listed, along with twenty-four middle school ones, fifteen university and community college ones, and two at the elementary school level.

(TAME). The TAME Mariachi Director's Handbook provides evidence of pedagogical and aesthetic codification and the creation of standards for eligibility in UIL and TMEA All-State competitions in relation to instrumentation, repertoire, and arranging. Participation is allowed only in the "small ensemble" category, however; time will tell whether the mariachi becomes a stand-alone category in the near future.[22] Interestingly, in certain regions of Texas mariachi ensembles have budgets that significantly surpass that of standard public school and college-level ensembles.[23]

It may be that mariachi ensembles will eventually coexist with the standard ensemble trio as an equal. In this hypothetical future, a BM in music studies could offer a dual specialization in band-mariachi, choir-mariachi, or orchestra-mariachi. Yet would the addition of mariachi to the current ensemble trio alter the emphasis on large ensembles and closed forms of interpretive performance in fundamental ways? A BM in music studies with a specialization in band and mariachi might well expand the cultural community of academia, shift the allocation of financial aid toward small or medium-sized ensembles, and, at Texas State University and other mainstream institutions, relieve add-on credit hours for students, all potentially beneficial. The effects of institutional mariachi groups on practices of interpretive performance and other general tendencies are less clear. Mariachis cultivate a range of orientations of interpretive performance techniques, as musicians in all genres do. Some mariachis focus on canonized mariachi repertoires and composers[24] and eschew improvisation in favor of competitive consistency. For example, Mariachi Vargas is often perceived as canon-oriented, while other contemporary mariachis describe themselves as avant-garde or experimental.[25] Thus,

22. http://texasmariachi.us/ (accessed June 12, 2015). UIL (University Interscholastic League) and TMEA (Texas Music Educators Association) are the powerful organizations that drive competitive standards for public school ensembles in the state of Texas.

23. During its year of establishment (2009–2010), the mariachi program at Roma High School (Roma, Texas) boasted an annual budget of $100,000. After the purchase of instruments, uniforms, and other essentials (2010-2013), the budget was reduced to $40,000, a number still far higher than any college-level mariachi I know of. Dr. Noe Sanchez provided this data; he was the mariachi director at the institution from 2009 to 2013. Dr. Sanchez speculates the budget to have significantly increased once more. (e-mail communication, October 7, 2015).

24. See Jáuregui (2010) and Hutchinson (2003) for mutually complementary perspectives on the canonization and standardization of "Son de la negra." This song is required repertoire in mariachi curriculum at all levels; it is often an audition piece for both academic programs and competitions.

25. E.g., the all-female small ensemble trio Ellas fuses mariachi with bluegrass, flamenco, and popular trends and clearly cultivates various form of improvisation (http://www.trioellas.com). José Hernandez's Mariachi Sol de Mexico, on the other hand, because of famous experiments with contemporary genres and symphonic music, is often informally branded an avant-garde group, although improvisation receives little attention in this rather large and arrangement-oriented mariachi.

mariachi directors have some prerogative to choose the orientation of their ensembles, one that could easily favor closed forms of interpretative performance and a focus on canonized mariachi works.

In turn, historians of music education could argue that the repertoire of many mainstream wind bands and choirs is more fluid than that of canon-oriented mariachis in that they cultivate arrangements of music from many genres, including the popular. William R. Lee and Michael D. Worthy conclude the following in their contribution to the 2012 *Oxford Handbook of Music Education*, vol. 1:

> School ensembles in North America are school-community blends, with function, size, and musical emphases peculiar to their community and region. In general, they have strong connections to the community, and intense group values predominate. School ensembles have become part of popular culture, with only [a tangential relationship to] classical art music.[26]

Indeed, at least in some institutions, music history professors probing their undergraduate students will note that it is through participation in symphonic bands and choirs that many undergraduates receive first aural and performative exposure to everything from Charles Ives and Silvestre Revueltas to arrangements of popular and traditional musics from the United States and the world. Questions we ask about ensembles might then shift away from the size or mainstream versus nonmainstream status of the ensemble and toward its versatility of genre coverage and interpretive performance practices.

Ultimately, all ensembles, regardless of size, could explore greater genre diversity, a wider range of interpretive performance practices, and appropriate improvisational practices. We may find that ensembles embracing such practices acquire open identities; rather than monolithically representing one genre and one way of making music, these ensembles can connect with audiences through a variety of genres and repertoires.

I close by sharing some concrete ideas the LMS faculty has collected over the past few years in conjunction with their undergraduate and graduate

26. William R. Lee and Michael D. Worthy, "North American School Ensembles," in *The Oxford Handbook of Music Education*, vol. 1 (Oxford: Oxford University Press, 2012), 808. Lee and Worthy historicize the post-1930s rise of band programs in US schools in relation to wind instrument manufacturers and public relations negotiations, among other factors. Lee and Worthy describe band culture in general, including programs at the college level. It is important to note that some symphonic band conductors in large, prestigious college-level music departments would problematize Lee and Worthy's assessments, as their programs are largely autonomous from the music education curriculum; these bands are aestheticized more as symphonic "art music" ensembles and less in the more populist orientation observed by Lee and Worthy.

programs.[27] Although I discuss them in relation to mariachi ensembles, many are applicable to other ensembles and to the general music curriculum:

- Although it is important for students to know and cultivate standard repertoire and established forms of interpretative performance, mariachi ensembles can avoid extreme tendencies toward canonization by reserving part of their budgets for annual commissions from living composers. Mariachi Nueva Generación uses such commissions to acquire fresh arrangements of familiar works as well as new compositions, all of which are often featured in competitions such as the Mariachi Vargas Extravaganza.
- Music majors who are also mariachi musicians often have hidden skills on instruments such as the harp and the accordion. Although no applied studios exist (yet) for these instruments, ensemble directors have a unique opportunity to produce fresh arrangements and feature these alternative instruments in their ensembles. Mariachi Nueva Generación has indeed enjoyed an array of talented instrumentalists that provide opportunities to explore new repertoires, fresh arrangements, and improvisational practices in this way.
- Improvisational practices for any given ensemble are often codified; in mariachi, improvisation is cultivated through trumpet *floreos* (melodic embellishment), poetic and witty improvised dialogue with the audience, virtuoso displays on certain instruments (violins, vihuelas, voice), individualistic cultivation of timbre and rhythmic inflections (both vocal and instrumental), and in the interplay between the ensemble and the idiosyncrasies of the singer's timing or rubato. As LMS deploys the minor in mariachi and the MM in music education / mariachi music concentration, it will be critical that mariachi instructors maintain such practices in performance, examine them in critical historical perspective, and create flexible platforms for their development in pedagogical and lab courses.
- In arranging courses, students acquire the ability to adapt musical works from a distant genre to a mariachi or salsa ensemble. This exercise forces them to manipulate the essential elements of a genre (form, rhythmic treatment, contrapuntal textures, timbre treatment, choreographic and vocal shading, the range of determinacy and indeterminacy invested in all of these, etc.) independently of canonized mariachi and salsa recordings (which ultimately present a single manifestation of musical elements). As I stated earlier, this experience is crucial in developing students' creative skills.

27. Visit http://latin.music.txstate.edu/ to see samples of programs from student recitals, media, detailed descriptions of degree plans and courses, and other resources that may provide perspective on the continuing development of the LMS program and ideas for those experimenting with music curricula. We also welcome questions and suggestions.

- Large ensembles lend themselves to experimentation with composition and arrangement, but small ensembles are crucial in allowing students to explore more daring forms of expansion in everything from genre delimiters to interpretive performance practices. LMS has recently created an Afro-Caribbean Lab for the advanced exploration of arranging, composition, improvisation, and fusion in the broad spectrum of local and transnational circum-Caribbean genres (in which Afro-Caribbean percussion is prominent). We look forward to achieving similar goals in the future with the foundation of a Latin American chamber music ensemble that can experiment with codified genres such as *son jarocho*, conjunto, *joropo*, and others in which string instruments predominate. Student-led creativity and management will be central elements in the learning outcomes of these ensembles. Such elements already are among the central goals of our graduate LMS programs. Just as Patch argues in this volume (Chapter 6) in relation to pop ensembles, mariachi and salsa ensembles require student leadership, and the acquisition of such skills must be integrated into the overall curriculum of professional music degrees (the BM).

Although LMS has not created a BM in Latin music performance, the insights we have acquired from our experience with the mariachi minor may eventually inform such a degree. For this to occur, we would need applied studios and dual-genre instructors specializing in instruments not currently part of mainstream music departments. We would also need explicit delineation of the aspects of interpretive performance and improvisation within the curriculum. Nevertheless, the following general insights based on our current experiments may prove useful to others.

- An instructor who does not see himself/herself as adept in improvisation can still expand students' exposure to repertoires outside the classical, romantic, and post-romantic canon and support creative experimentation. Simply exploring the rich array of works in post-1920s Inter-American repertoires (experimental, crossover, neoclassicist, minimalist, electronic, etc.), collaborating with living composers, and delving into repertoires that challenge the classical-popular dichotomy will greatly enhance the student's ability to make critical, creative decisions as musicians.
- Pedagogies in applied studios should systematically and integrally involve the exercise of critically listening to multiple instances of the same canonized work. Such an exercise helps prevent students from adopting closed forms of interpretive performance that overidealize the composer's intentions (an ultimately elusive goal), the notion of a single ideal "correct" iteration of the work, and extreme doctrines of historical performance. Once performers expand their conception of interpretative performance,

they will more easily venture into genres that welcome and/or require improvisation.

• For those experimenting with the inclusion of popular and traditional musics in mainstream institutions where curricular expansion (rather than radical overhaul) is the norm, the cultivation of a diversity of repertoires is greatly encouraged, as opposed to iconoclastic reactions against "classical" music. Most students are omnivores, tacitly or explicitly; they want to dominate the virtuosic, formal, and harmonic aspects associated with so-called classical repertoires as well as others. Conversely, some choose to segue into classical repertoires after years of practice in popular music genres. These students are, potentially, the dual-genre academics of the future. Their multiple forms of expertise may help us transition to pedagogical models in which the very notion of a dual-genre musician will be unnecessary.

REFERENCES

Burkholder, Peter J., Donald Jay Grout and Claude V. Palisca. 2014. *A History of Western Music*. 9th edition. New York: W.W. Norton & Company.

Campbell, Patricia, et al. 2014. "Transforming Music Study from Its Foundations: A Manifesto for Progressive Change in the Undergraduate Preparation for Music Majors." College Music Society.

Goehr, Lydia. 1992. *The Imaginary Museum of Musical Works. An Essay in the Philosophy of Music*. Oxford: Oxford University Press.

Hutchinson, Sydney. 2003. "Standardization and Canonization in Mexican Mariachi Music: A Historical Analysis of the Son de la Negra." Unpublished paper.

Jáuregui, Jesús. 2010. "El son mariachero de *La negra*: de gusto regional independentista a aire nacional contemporáneo. *Revista de literaturas populares*, Vol. 10 Nos. 1–2 (January–December), 807–825.

Lee, William R., and Michael D. Worthy. 2012. "North American School Ensembles." In *The Oxford Handbook of Music Education*, Vol. 1, 807–825. Oxford: Oxford University Press.

McDonald, Steven Ray. 1989. "A Survey of the Curricular Content of Functional Keyboard Skills Classes Designed for Undergraduate Piano Majors." PhD diss., University of Oklahoma.

Pedroza, Ludim R. 2010. "Music as *Communitas*: Franz Liszt, Clara Schumann, and the Musical Work," *Journal of Musicological Research*, Vol. 29 No. 4, 295–321.

Uszler, Marienne. 2000. "Fin de Cycle?" *Piano & Keyboard*, No. 203 (March–April), 7.

CHAPTER 8

Traditional Music for the People

Chinese Music Departments in the PRC and Taiwan

EDDIE HSU

INTRODUCTION

Western-style music conservatories have provided the predominant model for musical instruction in East Asia since the early twentieth century and thus shape the way traditional music is taught and perceived there (Nettl 1985, Stock 2004). In many cases, the goal of traditional music pedagogy in East Asia is not primarily to teach musical heritage from the past in its original form but rather to adapt the practices of traditional music to present circumstances, including the mandates of particular institutional ideologies or governmental initiatives. This process involves negotiating authenticity, creating wider conversations between musical institutions and the public, and connecting the goals of music pedagogy to those of the music industry, as in the case of the Irish institutions discussed by Jack Talty (Chapter 5 in this volume). Using Chinese music programs in the PRC and Taiwan as case studies, this chapter explores how the institutionalization of traditional music in the region has led to the formalization of unique curricula, teaching methods, and materials. It suggests that Chinese music programs increasingly develop pedagogical practices that engage local music traditions and surrounding communities as a central element. First, I explain how governmental interventions have fundamentally shaped the course design and methods associated with Chinese music instruction. Second, given the increasing tendency to promote local music traditions in East Asia, I explore how music programs have developed models that attempt to reach diverse audiences and create a broad range of experiences for students through interdisciplinary performances. Finally, I argue that institutions must encourage robust collaboration between institutions and music communities in order to ensure the appropriate representation of all musical forms and diversify students' experiences outside academic settings.

MUSIC INSTITUTIONS IN THE PRC AND TAIWAN

In East Asia, the adoption of Western-style music education can be traced to the early twentieth century, when modernist reformists trained in Europe first adopted formalized curricula. Since then, Western-style training has strongly influenced all music programs in East Asia. Nearly all institutions of higher education there offer degrees in Western classical music; only a few have programs in Chinese or traditional music.[1] Music institutions for many years thus unintentionally deepened the urban disdain for peasant cultures and traditional repertoire by contributing to their graduates' lack of experience with traditional folk arts. Although since the 1980s some knowledge of local music has become essential for conservatory-trained artists to compose and perform in a national style (*minzufenge*), most incorporate Western harmonies and styles of orchestration into such works (Mittler 1997, 290–291). Dominant Western ideologies foregrounding the importance of canonical European repertoire also help explain why numerous institutions offer individual courses but not specialized degrees in traditional music. To the extent that such classes exist, most are electives and not terribly popular among music majors. Only a few programs focus on popular music of any sort, and thus students interested in the pop music industry tend to work outside the formal educational system. This strong institutional focus on Western classical music has marginalized traditional and popular music in the PRC and Taiwan, just as in the United States and elsewhere.

---

1. There are nine music conservatories and numerous regional music institutions in China; Taiwan is home to three major national universities of the arts and twenty-six comprehensive universities offering degrees in music (BA, BM). However, most programs in Chinese traditional music are offered by conservatories or national universities of the arts. All conservatories in the PRC offer degrees in traditional Chinese music: the China Conservatory of Music, Central Conservatory of Music, Shanghai Conservatory of Music, Tianjin Conservatory of Music, Shenyang Conservatory of Music, Sichuan Conservatory of Music, Xinghai Conservatory of Music, Xi'an Conservatory of Music, and Wuhan Conservatory of Music. In Taiwan, in addition to the Taipei National University of the Arts Department of Traditional Music, other institutions offering Chinese music include Taiwan National University of the Arts, Tainan National University of the Arts, Chinese Culture University. The Hong Kong Academy for Performing Arts is the only institution providing instruction in Chinese music in that city.

To the extent that traditional music instruction is offered in East Asia, the adoption of Western-style instruction has resulted in the systemization of its pedagogy. Since the 1950s when they were first established, programs of Chinese music have prepared students to become professional performers or teachers on their instruments by means of specialized theory and repertoire courses.[2] The introduction of Western notation and music theory to Chinese music instruction and the embrace of staged performance contributed to the canonization of such repertoire, its style and technique. By contrast, traditional music learning outside institutions has historically been passed on either through oral/aural transmission or with the aid of traditional notation systems.[3] Although the government has funded initiatives and events promoting traditional music, especially those that present a "refined" image of the national heritage,[4] faculty in Chinese music programs have struggled to develop a music pedagogy that strikes a balance between Western theory and traditional approaches to music learning.

Ethnographies on music programs in Scandinavia (Hill 2005), England (Keegan-Phipps 2007), and Indonesia (Stock 2004) have focused on the institutionalization of folk music and its relationship to governmental and nationalist initiatives. Similarly, state intervention and official ideologies are the dominant forces in shaping musical institutions in the PRC (Rees 2000, Wong 2006) and Taiwan (Wang 2012) that incorporate regional genres in order to promote local identities. However, despite government funding, traditional music programs still struggle to attract students.

The PRC's Ministry of Culture has been central in developing traditional programs in numerous provincial and local institutions, as well as mechanisms for the dissemination of state ideology (Lau 1991, 88).[5] After 1978 as the Chinese Cultural Revolution ended, the government began to reform arts education.[6] It revitalized musical exchanges between the PRC and the West and re-established Western-style curricula, techniques, and teaching content. Nonetheless, the Ministry of Education still shapes the politics and ideology

2. The study of traditional music was initially instituted at the Central Conservatory of Music in Beijing in 1950. In 1956, the Chinese Music Department at the Shanghai Conservatory was founded.

3. *Gongchepu*, a Chinese character notation system, for instance, has been widely used in traditional Han Chinese music.

4. The ROC state's support of *nanguan* (a Taiwanese traditional music genre), which led to the professionalization of its performance (Wang 2012, 161), is one example of such an initiative.

5. The PRC has been officially defined as a "unitary multiethnic state" (*tongyi de duominzu guojia*) by the Communist Party since 1949.

6. During the Cultural Revolution (1966–1976), Mao Zedong and his allies sought to eliminate Chinese court music instruction (viewed as elitist) and Western musical influences of all sorts within the PRC, as they clashed with his interpretation of socialist ideology.

of school programs and promotes arts in the interest of national defense (Ho and Law 2004, 150). Beijing's official stance on multiculturalism underscores ethnic harmony within the PRC and is deeply rooted in socialist ideology; it emphasizes similarities among all national ethnic groups by situating them under the tutelage of the Communist Party (Chou 2014, 28). Thus, by incorporating the music of various ethnic groups into curricula and using musical diversity to represent a unified nation, they hope to encourage patriotism (Ho 2010, 76). Recent decades have witnessed overt governmental initiatives to promote Chinese folk and traditional music for this reason,[7] and music institutions have been enlisted in support of such goals.[8] In 2006 the PRC listed fourteen regional genres as part of a national "cultural protection" effort (Lau 2008, 61); music in some of these regions has been recognized as UNESCO Intangible Heritage (Rees 2012, 26). Curricula in Chinese music institutions such as Peking Opera and *kunqu* tend to foreground repertoires recognized by UNESCO.[9]

In Taiwan, the Kuomintang (KMT) nationalist government controlled most cultural initiatives following Japanese colonization (1895–1945) and sought initially to situate Taiwanese heritage as part of Chinese culture in order to contest mainland discourse and reclaim the legitimacy of the Chinese past for themselves (Guy 1999).[10] Thus, the KMT advocated a curriculum featuring Chinese history, culture, geography, literature, and other traditions. It also promoted Western classical music by implementing a conservatory-style system and supporting a national symphony orchestra (Wang 2012, 164). However, a series of movements advocated a "return to native" (*huigui xiangtu*) practices in Taiwan in the 1980s and marked a transition. In response to a growing Taiwan-centered identity, the government began to support Taiwanese cultural study as well. The Ministry of Culture increased its support of local

7. According to ethnomusicologist Qiao Jianzhong, the phrase "folk music" (*minjian yinyue*) in China refers to all traditional music performed by the people in the present day. On the other hand, "traditional music" refers to those that existed in China before the onset of Western influence (Rees 2012, 24).

8. E.g., the China Conservatory of Music's philosophy includes strong support for the study of traditional/folk music. The Shanghai government also allocated the equivalent of $1,454,604 for ten training programs in Beijing Opera, *Kunqu* opera, and folk songs and dances (Ho 2010, 75).

9. Recognized in 2008 as Intangible Cultural Heritage of Humanity, *Kunqu* opera is a theatrical genre that developed under the Ming dynasty (fourteenth to seventeenth centuries) in the city of Kunshan, located in the region of Suzhou in southeastern China http://www.unesco.org/culture/ich/?RL=00004 (accessed August 25, 2015).

10. Almost all publications, performances, and art work supported by the KMT were expected to oppose the mainland PRC regime by emphasizing Taiwanese patriotism and even the eventual recovery of the mainland from the Communists. The KMT government therefore supported Mandarin as the island's national language, suppressing the Taiwanese dialect, and presented Peking opera as a national genre.

musical forms such as *beiguan* and *nanguan*,[11] and the Ministry of Education implemented policies that required elementary, junior high, and high schools to include local Taiwanese arts in their curricula.

Musical instruction at institutions of higher education has become an essential part of the government's new celebration of local heritage. During the 1990s, performing arts institutions were founded that claimed to be "traditional" or "Taiwanese." The National Taiwan College of Performing Arts, founded in 1994, includes a Department of Taiwanese Opera (*gezaixi xuexi*) featuring works and music in Taiwanese dialect.[12] The Ministry of Education founded a Traditional Music Department (*chuantong yingyuexi*) at Taipei National University of the Arts in 1995, the only department of its kind in Taiwan.[13] In addition, Chinese music departments have encouraged the promotion of local music.[14]

Since the nineteenth century, music schools and conservatories have been hegemonic sites that shape musical meaning, in the West and elsewhere. As Bruno Nettl (1985) notes, institutions in some parts of Asia demonstrate how Western-style curricula can be applied to programs that focus on folk/traditional repertoire. Western influence in Asia has led to new expectations of professionalism among the graduates of such programs (Stock 2004). Chinese music departments (*minyuexi* or *guoyuexi*) in the PRC and Taiwan offer degrees in Chinese instrumental (e.g., *erhu, dizi, pipa, suona, yanqin, yuan, sheng, qin, zheng*) and vocal performance; a few also have majors in composition and conducting for the modern Chinese orchestra.[15] Most undergraduates complete their degrees in four years, with coursework centered on private lessons. Major course requirements usually include solo exams and/or recitals and participation in the modern Chinese orchestra and in small *sizhu* (silk and bamboo) ensembles. In addition, the coursework

11. Both *beiguan* and *nanguan* originated in Fukien province in southeastern China but were brought to Taiwan by Chinese immigrants in the eighteenth century. *Beiguan*, a genre of vocal and ensemble music, was popular throughout Taiwan on occasions such as temple festivals. *Nanguan* is a kind of classical ensemble music that has been transmitted by means of amateur music clubs and a form of self-cultivation (Wang 2012, 161).

12. The official website of the Department of Taiwanese Opera, National Taiwan College of Performing Arts, is: http://www.tcpa.edu.tw/files/11-1000-1118.php (accessed February 2, 2017).

13. The official website of Department of Traditional Music, Taipei National University of the Arts is: http://trd-music.tnua.edu.tw/en/news/a.html (accessed February 2, 2017).

14. In Taiwan, traditional music departments (*chuantong yingyuexi*) offer majors in local traditional genres such as *beiguan* and *nanguan*, as well as on instruments originally associated with mainland court traditions such as *qin* and *pipa*. Chinese music departments (*minyuexi* or *guoyuexi*) in both the PRC and Taiwan offer majors in Chinese vocal and instrumental performance, focusing on *guoyue* (the modernized/Westernized version of Chinese music).

15. The modern Chinese orchestra is a twentieth-century invention that uses Chinese instrumentations but is modeled on the structure of a Western symphony orchestra (Lau 2008, 36).

includes standard Western musical training in theory, music history, sight-singing, and dictation. Because Chinese music departments train students to become professional musicians, the adoption of Western training and a Western-style canon is essential to create a body of modernized traditional/folk music for staged performance. Many traditional Chinese genres emphasize the importance of *jixing jiahua* (improvised ornamentation), yet the embrace of Western models of fixed/notated composition has led to the decline of improvisation.

The institutionalization of traditional music has deepened the dichotomy between formally trained professional musicians (*zhuanye*) and amateurs (*yeyu* or *minjian*) who perform for fun or as a hobby. In general, the growth of professionalism fostered by institutions has led to the standardization of solo repertoire, the emergence of new performance techniques, new forms of tone production, and musical style (Lau 1991, Stock 2004).[16] For instance, almost all the instrumental repertoires of traditional music in music schools have shifted toward a focus on equal-tempered tuning, homogenous timbres, and standard approaches to articulation in order to support the efforts of the modern Chinese orchestra and large-ensemble performance. Such changes support an ideology of traditional/folk music as an elite art form. While many intellectuals and musicians in the past viewed community-based traditional music as outdated and backward, the professionalization of regional folk traditions has created a new body of Chinese repertoire that is perceived as highly sophisticated.

Since regional music traditions are an important source of inspiration for modern instrumental performance of all kinds, music departments encourage their preservation by offering a variety of core courses on the subject. These are typically organized into courses on folk songs (*minge*), Chinese instrumental music (*chiyue*), theatrical genres (*xiqu*), and narrative music (*shuochang*), as well as courses on traditional music history and on the music of ethnic minority groups. More advanced courses specialize in regional genres or styles, such as Traditional Chinese Music in Fujian Province, depending on the repertoires found in surrounding communities. The Department of Chinese Music at the Hong Kong Academy for Performing Arts, for example, has incorporated the singing of *yueyue* (Cantonese music) into course requirements. Music faculty frequently help construct the categories of the music they teach about and compile related course materials, thus allowing institutions to claim authority in shaping traditional/folk music pedagogy.

16. Frederick Lau (1991) has written an informative study about how new techniques on *dizi* (Chinese bamboo flute) adopted those of the Western flute. E.g., because traditional *dizi* is a keyless instrument (six-hole), a new fingering exercise was invented to accommodate Western scales and half-steps. As another example, violin-style vibrato techniques have been adopted on the *erhu* (Stock 2004, 21).

The China Conservatory of Music (CCM), a government-sponsored conservatory whose mandate is to promote traditional music as a form of patriotism, offers introductory courses in traditional Chinese music designed for all first- and second-year undergraduate students.[17] Additionally, it provides more theoretically advanced courses for third- and fourth-year music majors (Yao 2012, 183). All students at the conservatory, including those not specializing in Chinese music, are required to take introductory courses in that area.[18] Composition students at the CCM and other conservatories must conduct fieldwork and collect elements of regional music that they later incorporate into their compositions (Lau 2008, 29). In addition, the CCM has established relationships with numerous folk artists as part of its traditional music program, similar to the initiatives discussed by Talty (Chapter 5 in this volume).[19] Students interested in continuing their study of traditional music as an area of future research are thus well positioned to do so and to contribute to the preservation and promotion of traditional music in the region. Such partnerships are essential in fostering not only institutional collaborations with local communities outside the concert hall but also in expanding students' musical experiences. In short, the foregrounding of traditional/folk music highlights the conservatory's use of traditional repertoire to enrich new compositions and support the perpetuation of traditional music in contemporary settings.

NEGOTIATION BETWEEN INSTITUTIONS AND THE COMMUNITY

Although institutions and governmental policies are decisive in shaping traditional music pedagogy, musicians working outside institutional contexts have their own approaches to teaching such repertoire. In Taiwan, for instance, most activities involving traditional/folk music have been limited to temple festivals (miaohue) or the clubhouses (guange) of veteran folk musicians, but this is changing as they interact more directly with music schools. Formally trained performers can read Western notation and interpret compositions based on Western techniques but do not necessarily specialize in traditional genres, as mentioned.[20] They now have additional opportunities to interact

17. For an English introduction to the China Conservatory of Music, see http://old-web.ccmusic.edu.cn/ccmusic/yingwenwang/About_Conservatory/n8730409585.html (accessed February 2, 2017).

18. Peng Liu, personal interview, February 12, 2015. The introductory courses usually include the main four categories of Chinese music (folk song, theatrical, narrative, and instrumental music).

19. Interview with Yao Yi-Jun (August 2015), a professor at the CCM.

20. Lu Chue-Kuan (2005). Beiguan Yishi: Yeh Mei-Ching, Wang Song-Lai, and Lin Sui-Chih shenmingshi [The Biographies of Three Beiguan Masters: Yeh Mei-Ching, Wang Song-Lai, and Lin Sui-Chin]. Taipei: National Center for Traditional Arts. Here the Western technique refers to harmony, orchestration, etc.

with traditional music specialists. An increasing number of departments encourage students' involvement in traditional music ensembles; and since regional genres have historically been taught through aural transmission, music schools often hire local artists as instructors or coinstructors in order to bridge the gap between traditional and institutional music learning. The artist-in-residence model creates a more versatile learning context that balances Western-style training with other techniques. The Department of Chinese Music at Tainan National University of the Arts (TNNUA), for instance, has established a core curriculum that requires students to take multiple courses in traditional/folk music.[21] Local guest instructors offer courses including *Beiguan* (gong-drum) Performance and Classics of *Nanguan* Ensemble Repertoire. Other courses on *Beiguan chuida* (traditional Taiwanese percussion and wind ensemble music) are highly recommended for those majoring in wind and percussion instruments.

Luogujing, a mnemonic technique for percussion in which rhythmic patterns are chanted, has been used for centuries to memorize rhythms associated with regional genres such as *jingju* (Peking opera), *yueju* (Cantonese opera), and *beiguan*. The approach relies on the lead drummer's hand signals and on imitation of the actual sounds of each instrument; it is learned through face-to-face demonstration, repetition, subtle interaction among musicians, and critique on the part of master teachers. Students internalize the rhythmic and melodic patterns of *beiguan* by listening to and imitating instructors with the aid of a Chinese notation system called *gongchepu*. Playing *beiguan* thus enriches students' musicianship and aural training, providing a complement to their experience with notated music in large ensembles.[22] Other programs invite guest instructors into the classroom as well, deepening the collaboration between them and surrounding communities. For example, Yunnan Art Institute invited several folk musicians to offer guest lectures and teach traditional music and dance to undergraduates in 2004 (Rees 2012, 34).[23] Similarly, the Department of Chinese Music in TNNUA has invited *nanguan* artists from Tainan Nanshengshe (a national *nanguan* club of traditional arts) to teach *nanguan* music to undergraduates.[24]

21. http://english.tnnua.edu.tw/releaseRedirect.do?unitID=41&pageID=6654 (accessed February 5, 2017). The introduction of College of Music on TNNUA's official website. Established in 1998, the Department of Chinese Music was Taiwan's first seven-year musical education program, from senior high school through college. For the sake of brevity, this study focuses only on collegiate curricula.

22. Chen Bo-Ru, personal interview, August 17, 2015.

23. http://www.admissions.cn/ynart/index04.htm (accessed February 2, 2017). An English introduction to the Music School of Yunnan Art Institute.

24. According to the official website of Ministry of Culture in Taiwan, Tainan Nanshengshe has been declared a national nanguan club, protecting traditional arts. http://www.boch.gov.tw/information_147_48969.html (accessed February 3, 2017).

While visiting artist models have become an ideal vehicle through which numerous Chinese music programs strengthen students' ties to other music communities, programs specializing in traditional music still encounter difficulty in attracting students due to the perception that the career prospects of graduates are limited. According to Mark F. DeWitt (Chapter 4 in this volume), many students consider traditional music important but not something they wish to major in or study formally. To protect traditional music from being "museumized" and to ensure its ongoing dialogue with other musical styles, music institutions in various countries have developed curricula that train students to be skilled in multiple roles (e.g., performing, composing, arranging, and teaching) and genres—in Finland (Hill 2009, 215), for instance. Similarly, the Department of Traditional Music at Taipei National University of the Arts, the only institution offering majors in *nanguan* and *beiguan* music in Taiwan, is considering adding majors in new indigenous genres (e.g., Hakka music and aboriginal music) in order to increase the marketability of graduates.[25] The program also features collaborative projects (involving the Department of Traditional Music, the School of Theater, and School of Dance) that combine traditional music with other performing arts.

As musicians have sought new ways to create more accessible musical performances that appeal to the public, modern Chinese orchestras, too, have invited folk artists and troupes to collaborate with them. Unlike students in programs focusing on traditional music or ethnomusicology in the United States, who may forge strong connections with the local communities they study, students in Chinese music departments are more likely to treat local genres and performance techniques as raw material with which to enrich their individual performance skills. Only those self-motivated students who already have established connections to local communities or who seek such connections for purposes of research tend to pursue community engagement per se. However, as institutions are now more concerned with making music relevant to local audiences,[26] it becomes necessary to find new forms of community engagement beyond that of the visiting artist model. The Department of Chinese Music at TNNUA, for instance, now requires students to take Music Performance and Social Service for six semesters; this is designed to enrich students' experiences in organizing off-campus events. Some feel that popularizing traditional music through outreach events may diminish the quality of performance and distort traditional forms (Wang 2012, 176–177). In any case, hosting outreach and collaborative performance inevitably requires

25. *United Daily News*, September 22, 2015, http://m.match.net.tw/pc/news/news/20150922/3155057 (accessed February 3, 2017).

26. http://www.artsjournal.com/engage/2013/06/china-thoughts/ (accessed September 15, 2015). As mentioned in this press release, community engagement is increasingly important in China. This derives from the government's belief that its arts and culture funding should benefit as many citizens as possible.

the involvement of music communities to ensure an appropriate forms of representation.[27]

As discussed in the introduction of this book, engaging with styles of music in which local communities are strongly invested is indispensable for music institutions. One example of a successful community initiative is the Performing Arts Marathon (PAM) project, organized by the Performing Arts Education Centre in the Hong Kong Academy for Performing Arts (HKAPA). Established in 2011, it is highly regarded by local communities.[28] PAM offers workshops in local primary and secondary schools and sponsors performances of local art forms such as Chinese music, *yueju* (Cantonese opera), and puppetry, as well as Western classical and popular music, outside conventional concert venues. It deepens audiences' understanding of the performing arts and strategically embeds educational outreach activities into its programs in order to cultivate young artists. As one part of the project, the Department of Chinese Music at HKAPA has dedicated itself to the promotion of Cantonese music through off-campus performances and educational programs.[29] Such endeavors that involve music communities and interdisciplinary collaboration serve as a potential model to make traditional music more accessible to a wider audience and expand students' experiences in noninstitutional contexts.

CONCLUSION

Discrepancies between Western models of pedagogy and those derived from local music communities remain an issue that Chinese music programs struggle to reconcile. More programs than ever incorporate the practices of oral/aural tradition from musical communities into institutions so as to challenge overly standardized/homogenized approaches to pedagogy. Collaborations between music institutions and broader communities through visiting-artist residencies help prevent the misrepresentation of local communities and their heritage. On the other hand, although governmental intervention and nationalist initiatives in both the PRC and Taiwan increasingly promote local musical

27. This idea was inspired by the 1990 multicultural symposium in Washington, DC, where ethnomusicologists teamed up with music educators and native culture bearers to present approaches for multicultural music education in the classroom (Volk 1998).

28. http://www.hkapa.edu/community-engagement/performing-arts-marathon-sham-shui-po/ (accessed February 2, 2017). The Star Projects/Programs (SPP) is an initiative of UNESCO Observatory RLCCE to identify projects and programs that advocate the goals of UNESCO's Seoul Agenda for the benefit of children, youth, and lifelong learners of all ages by means of arts education (http://uhka.7yl.net/page.php?id=2, accessed February 3, 2017).

29. Wu Di, trans., *Dandai yueyue chuanchen zi "mingjian" yu "xueyuan" kuaquyu jiaoliu duejie xinqushi* (The New Trend of Interactive Model between "Amateur" and "Institution" in the Inheritance of Contemporary Cantonese Music), *Journal of Xinghai Conservatory of Music*, Vol. 138 No. 1 (2015), 110–118.

styles, many students continue to view them as relatively unimportant. In an attempt to combat the perception of traditional music as "museumized" or "fossilized," some institutions attempt to increase its appeal through interdisciplinary collaborations and outreach events. The approach not only creates a more holistic musical experience for students and communities but also diversifies students' performance experiences and potential marketability, similar to the links between institutions and the music industry discussed by Talty (Chapter 5 in this volume). While some express concerns about the potential distortion of traditional music caused by a populist approach, I believe that collaborations between institutions and communities will help ensure that traditional music will be ever more relevant to musical lives into the future.

REFERENCES

Chio, Jenny. 2014. *A Landscape of Travel: The Work of Tourism in Rural Ethnic China*. Seattle and London: University of Washington Press.

Guy, Nancy. 1999. "Governing the Arts, Governing the State: Peking Opera and Political Authority in Taiwan." *Ethnomusicology*, Vol. 43 No. 3 (Winter), 508–526.

Hill, Juniper. 2005. "From Ancient to Avant-Garde to Global: Creative Processes and Institutionalization in Finnish Contemporary Folk Music." PhD diss., University of California, Los Angeles.

———. 2009. "The Influence of Conservatory Folk Music Programmes: The Sibelius Academy in Comparative Context." *Ethnomusicology Forum*, Vol. 18 No. 2, 207–241.

Ho, Wai-Chung. 2010. "Moral Education in China's Music Education: Development and Challenges." *International Journal of Music Education*, Vol. 28 No. 1, 71–87.

———. 2013. "Globalization and Localization in Music Education in Hong Kong and Taiwan." *Comparative Education*, Vol. 49 No. 2, 163–180.

Ho, Wai-Chung, and Wing-Wah Law. 2004. "Values, Music, and Education in China." *Music Education Research*, Vol. 6 No. 2, 149–167.

Keegan-Phipps, Simon. 2007. "Déjà Vu? Folk Music, Education, and Institutionalization in Contemporary England." *Yearbook for Traditional Music*, Vol. 39, 84–107.

Lau, Frederick. 1991. "Music and Musicians of the Traditional Chinese *dizi* in the People's Republic of China." PhD diss., University of Illinois, Urbana-Champaign.

———. 2008. *Music in China. Experiencing Music, Expressing Culture*. New York: Oxford University Press.

Lu, Chue-Kuan, trans. 2005. *Beiguan Yishi: Yeh Mei-Ching, Wang Song-Lai, and Lin Sui-Chih shenmingshi* [The Biographies of Three Beiguan Masters: Yeh Mei-Ching, Wang Song-Lai, and Lin Sui-Chin]. Taipei: National Center for Traditional Arts.

Mittler, Barbara. 1997. *Dangerous Tunes. The Politics of Chinese Music in Hong Kong, Taiwan, and the People's Republic of China since 1949*. Wiesbaden: Harrassowitz.

Nettl, Bruno. 1985. *The Western Impact on World Music. Change, Adaption, and Survival*. New York: Schirmer Books.

Rees, Helen. 2000. *Echoes of History. Naxi Music in Modern China*. New York: Oxford University Press.

———. 2012. "Intangible Cultural Heritage in China Today: Policy and Practice in the Early Twenty-First Century." In *Music as Intangible Cultural Heritage. Policy,*

Ideology, and Practice in the Preservation of East Asian Traditions, Keith Howard, ed., 23–54. Farnham: Ashgate.

Stock, Jonathan. 2004. "Peripheries and Interfaces: The Western Impact on Other Music." In *The Cambridge History of Twentieth-Century Music*, Nicholas Cook and Anthony Pople, eds., 18–39. Cambridge: Cambridge University Press.

Volk, Terese. 1998. *Music, Education, and Multiculturalism: Foundations and Principles*. New York: Oxford University Press.

Wang, Ying-Fen. 2012. "Lessons from the Past: Nanguan/Nanyin and the Preservation of Intangible Cultural Heritage in Taiwan." In *Music as Intangible Cultural Heritage. Policy, Ideology, and Practice in the Preservation of East Asian Traditions*, Keith Howard, ed., 161–179. Farnham: Ashgate.

Wong, Chuen Fung. 2006. "Peripheral Sentiments: Encountering Uyghur Music in Urumchi." PhD diss., University of California, Los Angeles.

Yao, Yi-Jun. 2012. "The Pedagogy of Chinese Traditional Music at the China Conservatory of Music." *Journal of Music History Pedagogy*, Vol. 2 No. 2, 179–183.

Disciplinary and Professional Experiments

CHAPTER 9

In Honor of What We Can't Groove To Yet

MICHAEL TENZER

In this chapter I advance the premise that musical transcription—the activity of listening and then visually representing aural experience—would be an effective anchoring component of future university music curricula. It is an ecumenical and wholesome practice supporting learning from beginner to advanced stages. Sharpen the skills for it, and it becomes a lifelong autodidactic reflex. It mandates collaboration between the sensate ear and the analytical mind and calls for varied modalities of analysis and theory—all criteria for reflective musical inquiry. In general, higher doses of aural/oral learning, improvisation, and creative music making of all kinds are emphatically called for in music curricula. Transcription in particular, however, is a key and perhaps underappreciated component, as it marries the aural, oral, and written. It facilitates direct engagement with any music, while cultivating notation and literacy skills that are sui generis to the Western tradition, whose invention they are.[1] With transcription, music studies can rewrite its relationship to Western music and to the literate culture of academia generally in a decentered way. But most importantly, transcription is an immersion vehicle for

---

1. The 2014 College Music Society Task Force report (Campbell et al. 2014; see also Sarath 2013) calls for a radical transformation of the curriculum starting from first principles, and much of what I say herein reflects such a position. Sarath suggests complete destabilization of the traditional model and its replacement with much greater emphasis on composition and improvisation. It has met with mixed response. See, e.g., these doubters in the music theory community: https://discuss.societymusictheory. org/discussion/264/cms-task-force-manifesto (accessed June 3, 2016).

encounters with what is musically unknown to us; a way to reach out to what we can't groove to yet.

The idea is one response to the major challenge we face: to reconfigure the dominance of European art music and its associated traditional pedagogies in the curriculum—not to cast it out, of course, but to recast it, for its own and everyone's benefit, as a major tradition among many others. Integrating more kinds of music into the mainstream and opening up to oral learning are needed for important reasons: because they better reflect the world that educated musicians will enter, and because they will present a more accessible face to all students and lure them into university music courses and activities. A third reason supersedes the two just given: the chance to embody and live inside other cultures' sound worlds is humanizing, and representing them with technologies of music notation—of whatever sort—is empowering. It can advance the various principles guiding this book. It enables the musician to bring notation to the table as a useful tool of education and archival documentation. Transcribers can catalyze their career potential as performers or composers by autodidactically accelerating their understanding of new musics. Stimulating creative listening and honing perceptual precision, transcription enhances global awareness through sustained engagement with sounds from diverse cultures.

Transcription is an ethnomusicological practice, and ethnomusicology has been separate but rarely equal in music education.[2] For many, it feels as though its moment may have finally arrived. Critic and cultural observer Edward Rothstein, a staunch champion of the Western canon, proclaimed in the *New York Times* way back in 2000 that: "we are all ethnomusicologists now" (Rothstein 2000).[3] But what would true equality mean? Academic turf is limited and not easily ceded; we have to keep fantasies of power in check. To put the best foot forward, established tradition has to be honored, and there can be no chaotic accretion of the new jostling for advantage over the old nor tossing of the baby with the bathwater. One can imagine overwhelming students if there is a vast broadening of subject matter with no unifying rationale. Innovation therefore has to be principled and not just for its own sake. Because transcription fosters engagement with literacy and notation, it has the potential to build a methodological fusion engaging both ethnomusicology and Western music topics that can reconcile us as fellow travelers. In cases where trust needs to be built between the so-called defenders of the Western canon and teachers of world traditions, transcription could command the

2. In Western art music, transcription can refer to the arrangement of a composition for new media, such as Liszt's piano transcriptions of Beethoven's symphonies or Paganini's violin *Caprices*. I don't use the term in this sense here.

3. He wrote this after the Toronto Musical Intersections conference bringing together the Society for Ethnomusicology, American Musicological Society, Society for Music Theory, and the Society for Music Perception and Cognition.

respect of all. But were transcription integrated to the extent I can imagine, the disciplinary pedagogies of both world music and the Western canon would emerge significantly transformed.

When done with awareness of inevitable flaws and biases, transcription can approach the condition of being neutral and culture blind. It refines the ear's discernment, teaches patience and precision, and fosters wonderment and respect for different ways of making and structuring music. Though transcription from recordings is by definition mediated with respect to live music, it can also be structured as a direct encounter with sound that is *unmediated* by prior knowledge or explanation. Naturally one is never free of ingrained perceptual biases, but these can be brought to consciousness and turned to good purpose. Ter Ellingson's valorization of the "experience of transcription itself" epitomizes the reconstruction the practice deserves (1992, 147). I see no reason why transcription wouldn't enrich music pedagogy in just about any context, but since my experience is in the North American liberal arts university, I argue below for its relevance there. I have used it in nearly every course I teach, including some for so-called nonmusicians, and in a variety of forms, techniques, and levels of challenge, including blind transcription of Western classical music from Bach to Stravinsky and Ligeti.

TRANSCRIPTION AND ...

The case to be made relies on one assumption and three perspectives. The assumption is that transcription is a productive thing to do. Music scrutinized note-by-note lodges in the body like a poem memorized in grade school. It is relentless in the demands it places on cognition. For beginners, it takes listening to levels of mindfulness most will have never experienced. For composers, performers, and aspiring professionals of all kinds, it separates the musical mind from the musical ego and pays obeisance to other music makers and the external stimulus they provide. The three perspectives are the dimensions of the practice in the disciplines of ethnomusicology and music theory; criteria for good musicianship and the need for embodiment (especially singing); and convictions about ethics and empathy.

... ETHNOMUSICOLOGY AND MUSIC THEORY

We tend to think of notating music encountered aurally as transcription in ethnomusicology and as ear training in music theory. The two have contrasting functions, materials, and significance in their respective fields and take different media as the sonic source: recordings in the former case and (usually) specially designed exercises or fragments of music scores in the latter.

Transcription aims to represent a performance in at least some of its aspects and is usually part of a larger research and publication project. Ear training is pedagogical and skill building. The action, however, is the same in both cases: listening and writing what one hears.[4]

Transcription was intrinsic to ethnomusicology at its beginnings but weathered doldrums once people realized, with disappointment, that it was only ever a partial representation of the music and one fraught with the danger of bias. The debate over its value is known to readers of England 1964 or any of the still accumulating reassessments (Seeger 1958, List 1974, Stockmann 1979, Ellingson 1992, Agawu 2003, Marian-Bălaşa 2005, Stanyek et al. 2014, and more). At its arrogant worst, near ethnomusicology's beginnings, transcription shoehorned "exotic" music into irrelevant metric or harmonic schemes, reflecting transcribers' assumptions that they were somehow "improving" it. In more self-aware recent times, it sank in that transcription alone cannot depict a music's significance to its makers or other aspects of meaning. The pitch-against-time grid of notation, even if modified from the Western staff or using another approach entirely, might garble even a mere surface approximation of the sound, and the more modified or innovative the notation, the more difficult it is for readers to make sense of it. Indeed, transcribed music is better seen in the context of cognition and subjectivity, in that it reflects not only the transcriber's biologically and culturally shaped percepts but also his or her position along continua of intention, expertise, experience, and insider and outsider knowledge.

For ethnomusicologists, published transcription fixes for posterity representation of an other toward which or whom today's researchers tend to be acutely aware of long-term ethical obligations. In most cases the notation is obscure to the people whose music it is. Today many think a heavy focus on transcription makes ethnomusicology less multidisciplinary and thus less relevant to other fields in the humanities and social sciences, and may risk moving attention away from live performance and music as social behavior toward static representations. Readers may have difficulty evaluating a transcription without having done the work of making their own version. The practice is not central to graduate training as it once was and will remain an outlier until something changes. We may attribute this to the anthropological bent of North American ethnomusicology as does Marian-Bălaşa (2005, 8), or to the "solipsistic" ideological bent of score analysis (2005, 22), or to inadequacy of musical notation however construed.[5] And the proof that all such doubts

4. Transcription is fundamental to jazz pedagogy and the ongoing practice of many jazz players.
5. A related point is that transcribers nowadays may rely on software (such as Transcribe!) to go after data inaccessible to the unassisted ear (as in Benadon 2006), again for research, not pedagogy, and only indirectly to improve listening perception.

prevail is in the pudding: it is absent or perfunctory in most publication now (there are exceptions, of course: see Tenzer 2000, Levine 2002, Sanyal and Widdess 2004, and others).

Despite the checkered history, nowadays concern for sound itself no longer implies disregard for social issues and frames of analysis or ethnocentrism. Learners at all levels are bound to be curious about how music is put together and eager to contemplate structural details that can be discerned only if the music is fixed in notation of some kind. Thus for current purposes the point is not to rehearse the problems of the past but to suggest that what is problematic for research can be constructive in teaching. The transcriber's bias toward hearing elements in familiar ways (e.g., pitch relationships in terms of tempered intervals or tonal harmonies) presents an opportunity to raise consciousness about the tendency and open the student up to new ways of listening. The limitations of standard notation can stimulate the invention of new or differently modified systems (that will inevitability have their own shortcomings). Notation will always undercut the integrity of music in some way but can contribute to oral learning and deeper understanding of how notation is not music itself—an illusion often too ingrained in Western music practice.

Professional music theorists are mainly concerned with composers' scores, not transcriptions, although those interested in popular and world music genres compose a growing number.[6] Popular music studies have become prominent in ethnomusicology, and this confluence of interests represents a hopeful point of intersection between the two fields. Change at the level of the core theory curriculum is still in the future, however. Clendinning and Marvin (2010)—a major textbook recently revised and published with companion workbook and DVD—sprinkles some popular music throughout its impressive forty chapters and nearly one thousand pages. There is no world music, and the book uses the familiar chronological approach to the Western tradition.[7] In fact, the inclusion of popular music makes the book somewhat more progressive than a survey of others of its ilk and reveals a clear reflection of the conservatism of the field of music theory.[8]

6. The Analytical Approaches to World Music conference, held biannually since 2010, attracts many music theorists interested in research on world music. A negligible number of music theorists attend the Society for Ethnomusicology's conferences. Equally few (or fewer) ethnomusicologists attend the conferences of the Society for Music Theory, and few aspire to include Western art music in their teaching. There can be little doubt that new generations of music professors harbor interdisciplinary urges but, like this chapter and this book, all must strike their bargain with the conservatism of the institutions and disciplines welcoming them.

7. One must remember that the majority of colleges and universities with music programs do not offer ethnomusicology or world music classes at all.

8. See http://www.collegeboard.com/html/apcourseaudit/courses/music_theory_textbook_list.html for a list of some of the books in current use. An ad hoc perusal of these books' contents reveals only very rare and modest forays into folk or popular materials. Books devoted to jazz theory are plentiful, of course. But only Cogan and

Ear training, by contrast with ethnomusicological transcription, is associated with quotidian practice and is part of music fundamentals courses everywhere, at least in the initial year or two of university. It is a highly domesticated genre of transcription oriented largely toward aural mastery of elements of European tonality (but see Friedmann 1990 and Morris 1991 for ear training for atonal music). Scales, melodies, harmonies and their basic progressions, duration series, and so on are separated out from their full music contexts and taught through dictation, aural recognition, sight-singing, class piano skills, and similar exercises.[9]

Academia often prefers the theoretical and abstract to the practical and experiential. Along these lines, music theory programs in North America commonly separate ear training classes from theory and analysis (parallel to the way literature professors may not consider it their brief to teach the mechanics of writing). Though it has champions and teachers with fires in their bellies, ear training is often considered low status service. Expectations that aural skills should be cultivated independently or earlier in life, that students ought to come to the table with everything in place, or that only those with "talent" can "really" hear well compound the problem. An economic angle, that it is cheaper for musicianship to be taught by adjunct faculty, does too.

In world music and ethnomusicology courses cultivation of aural skills and intensive listening are not usually asked for: for music students it is ear training classes where those things are supposed to get taken care of. As for non-music students, the unreflective stance is that one can't ask non-music students to go beyond a coarse level of perception. But is this really the case? To my way of thinking such a stance reinforces Western myths about who is musical and who isn't, myths that it is ethnomusicology's brief to break down. In both ethnomusicology and music theory, each for its own reasons, we see that aural learning for undergraduates is deflected or demoted from

Escot 1976, way too far ahead of its time, provides an intriguing model for what a textbook reaching for a global perspective could look like. It attracted few users then or since.

9. Curricula based on fixed-do solfège remain central to music education from childhood on in most non-Anglophone Western cultures, while the movable-do kind is sporadically taught in North America. The equivalent in Indian classical music is *sargam*, which also has its rhythm counterpart in *bols* (North India) and *solkattu* (South India), and is completely intrinsic to musical training there, not just for its usefulness in learning compositions but especially for how it prepares the musician to improvise and fortifies the ability to invent, grasp, and mentally manipulate rich vocabularies of pitch and rhythm. This system is nonpareil as effective pedagogy and has been used in limited ways in North American schools, too, by South Asianist ethnomusicologists or percussionists trained in Indian rhythm. Particularly insofar as Western music education has often been weak in rhythm training, future integration of Indian music tools (as well as solfège) would be salutary.

the prominence and value it has in the real world. Wade (2012) and the many volumes in the Oxford Global Music series begin to fill this lacuna with a variety of listening suggestions and exercises (and see Kartomi 2005 for a critical appraisal).

In the classroom, transcription can be a medium for encounter between the novice and the music. It can be something fully other than the thing ethnomusicologists may have once wished for it to be and more creative and satisfying to teach than the drills of ear training as presently construed. A curriculum with copious opportunities for dictation and transcription exercises drawn from many traditions in accordance with the instructors expertise, and with "contractual" commitments to Western tonality reimagined, would resemble what I am advocating in this chapter.

... MUSICIANSHIP AND EMBODIMENT

Being a good musician can mean many things: ability to replicate music heard (internally, vocally, or on an instrument), ability to communicate music to others with voice and body, technical mastery, quick reflexes and precision, good memory for immediate or later recall, and facility in quickly hearing relationships across long spans of music are a few. At more cerebral (but no less instinctive or embodied) levels are knowledge of repertoire, score reading skills, compositional inventiveness and improvisational skill, an ability to conceptualize formal schemas and hierarchies, and insight into structural principles. At still higher levels are expression, generosity, poise, and fellowship in playing with others. We tend to associate these capacities with experienced specialist musicians, but the potential to achieve them is a common birthright. Ethnomusicology may be a field of scholarship whose contribution is "essentially and broadly historical" (Nettl 1983, 11), but where the rubber hits the road, its most important *function* has been to help counter the conventional wisdom that musicianship is the provenance of the few.

Our mandate is teaching musicianship to everyone because musicianship is what everyone is entitled to. In the spirit of ethnomusicological credo, few would argue against the idea that the conventional distinction between musician and nonmusician is a fiction propagated by creaky social myths about talent. In important ways these myths are dying a grass roots death due to the democratizing effect of music's phenomenal accessibility in recent decades. These days many students with no formal study are excellent musicians, with diverse and long-standing experiences playing or composing at home on computers or with friends. On the other hand, a still considerable number have had musical dreams quashed by myth-subscribing childhood teachers, family members, or music-bereft public school systems and communities—and until the myths get rectified in society and public education writ large, they deserve the chance to unlearn those lessons in university.[10]

Perhaps the most important musicianship benefit issuing from transcription practice is the fact that, with some possible exceptions for very advanced learners, it simply can't be done without (at the least) rhythm embodiment and (more fully) singing to oneself aloud.[11] Transcription is always related to singing, and singing is a universal (Molino and Nattiez 2007, 357). Ethnomusicologists understand the centrality of singing, for so much of our fieldwork has been done in cultures where instrumental repertoires have vocal origins, where one sings before one plays, and where music enters the body through voice and gesture, unmediated. We have observed the natural ease of our teachers around the world in communicating music using the voice and body, and we have experienced having to "figure it out" without having it explained. In North America, reticence to sing either to oneself or before others is a social blight hindering the potential to realize a part of one's humanity. The ingredient transcription provides is its injection of literacy, writing, and cross-domain cognition, all synonymous with central values of university learning.

Initiates, often even advanced musicians, aren't necessarily going to sing simply because we ask them to.[12] We have to create, through our supportive teaching practices, the environment in which it is understood that (the bad news) the work can be done no other way and (the good news) that the moving and the singing can occur privately, at one's desk, with headphones on, deciding what is going on in the music. Results can be compared and shared with others, in class if possible, and over time confidence builds. It is naturally important for the professor to set the example in this regard and to regularly and unselfconsciously embody his or her own musicianship before the students by singing examples, moving to the music, playing rhythms, and so forth. More than this, anxiety about singing should be openly discussed, and opportunities for small group or individual meetings given to deal with different levels of such anxiety.

10. See Abril 2007 for portraits of people who face this problem.

11. Instrumentalists may use their instruments, especially if the transcription is of music for a like instrument. Wind brass and string players are accustomed to variable intonations. In such cases the instrument is tantamount to the voice. But when a piano is used as reference for transcribing a sarod, for instance, inevitably the voice will have to intervene to fine-tune intervals. When I speak here of encouraging reticent students to sing, I have mostly beginners and nonperformers in mind.

12. Some years ago I posted a syllabus online for a general studies course, then being offered for the first time, for which I had indicated that singing was a required component. Preregistration had already been open for a while, but when this information became available fully 50 percent of those preregistered dropped the class overnight. When my colleague Kofi Gbolonyo, a Ghanaian with a very different kind of socialization with regard to singing, heard of this, he practically wept. I changed the requirements, but over the years, as I offered the course repeatedly, I found many ways to encourage people to sing and transcribe at appropriate levels. See the section on content below.

As for embodiment, two simple corporeal universals—ability to entrain pulsation, and to identify repetition (of any musical element)—suffice to give the mindful listener access to perception data that can be used to construct written representations.[13] With guidance even the abject beginner can track and represent, for example, the number of pulsations in a line, the number of different lines in a verse, and so on up to the full structure of many a simple song. I have found this elementary exercise to be revelatory for those who had never considered music as structure before. Music in which pulsation can be complex for outsiders to track, such as sub-Saharan, or repetitions/restatements too complex to evaluate with respect to structural significance, such as iterating cross-rhythmic phrasings, will naturally require more of the teacher's expertise and guidance and may not be appropriate except at advanced levels. But a continuum can be constructed and intricate tasks designed and completed if the guidance and expectation of success are there. The result almost always, in my experience, is student satisfaction at having penetrated the surface of a thing as loved as music.

Transcribing some music will present insurmountable challenges even for the most skilled musicians, especially for music with thick textures obscuring individual parts. One has options in such situations, applicable depending on the student level: have the students try to crack the music's code "cold," as it were, or carefully delineate select elements (large-scale repetitions, changes of section or texture, etc.) that *can* be heard and focus on those. The latter way will yield small successes, the former invites comparison with published scholarship to open them up to how and why some music can so deceive the ears. But there is no reason to exclude anything as unapproachable a priori. I elaborate on these possibilities later.

... ETHICS AND EMPATHY

The idea of moving the study of world musics into the center of the curriculum, if taken to its abstract conclusions as a thought experiment, would destabilize the sovereignty of any particular tradition. Of course, this can't and shouldn't happen, because a student grounded in no tradition is an awful thing to contemplate. Nevertheless, for all the reasons argued, we want to push in this anti-hegemonic direction and feel comfortable in the reasons for teaching this way and in the ethical consequences for learning outcomes.

A great contribution of ethnomusicology has been to show how indelible is the link between music and identity. But education is a work of expanding consciousness and identity, and music's power to alter identity is as strong as

13. For literature on the perception of pulse and repetition, see London 2011, Lerdahl and Jackendoff 1983, Parncutt 1994, and Clayton et al. 2004.

its power to confirm it. Transcriptions that bring students into new aesthetic, sonic, and cultural spaces are especially valuable because they agitate against any complacency in their habitual selves. There is a need to separate "popular" from "world" music in this connection. Though a full discussion of this would require more nuance than space allows, in broad strokes I take the former to connote what is familiar, easy to groove to, and mass-mediated, while the latter connotes what is often distant, inaccessible, and strange, hence, as I see it, of greater pedagogical value. We want to facilitate all kinds of encounters but especially those with musical identities as different as possible from the ones we already embody. This has the value of cultivating consciousness of levels of difference that globalization may soon remove from view, if it has not done so already. Grappling with the sheer difficulty and elusiveness of the rhythmic basis of many kinds of "under the radar and off the map" music is an act of empathy and homage.[14]

Even if it is familiar, music is and should always remain strange to us, inspiring awe and wonder. In its semantic imprecision it communicates things we can never verbalize no matter how much we attempt to do so around the edges. In transcribing we are studio sketchers of music modeling nude, striving to grasp the ontology of the thing and bear witness to music with our equally naked ears. Meaning and symbolism gets drained away in the service of cognizing connections between sounds: What is this melodic interval? Can I relate this series of durations to a pulse? How might the performers be organizing these sounds in ways I cannot directly perceive? At the moment of encounter we have to experience every sound we hear as a discrete object, both alone and in relation to its neighbors, and puzzle out the logic behind these relationships. It is like constructing an empathetic portrait of someone.

Should the risk of mishearing structure in the absence of its meaning mar this otherwise sunny forecast? When we plunk students down with a recording of music from someplace foreign to their listening experience and ask them to notate it, are we failing to abide by a valuable ethnomusicology rule of thumb? There is some demagoguery limned with unnecessary anxiety for those who would pose this type of question today. We may legitimately fear misrepresenting musical features as some early ethnomusicologists once did, but decades of fieldwork and accumulated knowledge have created a safe space for error.[15] In pedagogy today, so-called egregious mistakes—not hearing the bell pattern in 12/8, not understanding that gong's metric accent is at the end rather than the beginning of the cycle—are rather learning opportunities.

The field of music theory ponders this same problem in its way. There is some struggle over how and whether to make the field less Eurocentric in terms of

14. Thanks to Yampolsky 2013 for this phrase.
15. For examples of such misrepresentation, see the many mixed time signatures and overlapped downbeats in vol. 2 of Jones 1959, discussed at length in Agawu 2003.

both membership diversity and subject matter (Gopinath 2009, Kang 2009). An argument against too much diversity is the notion that music theory works best as a supplement to musical literacy. Theories of Western music acquire meaning for musicians who know a great deal of Western repertoire and can make sense of richly theoretical descriptions depicting the musical language they can embody. Ethnomusicologists would also approve of this idea, that music theories are heuristics designed to fit each musical culture they describe. It would make equally little sense, for example, to force-feed theories of African music to students who know none of its repertoire and cannot yet embody it.

This has validity but is also a recipe for inaction: we have to take our entry points wherever we can find them. Not to minimize the rewards of listening from within a cultural competence, let us maximize respect for what the naive listener can achieve and propose new paths to such competence. Of course naive listening will always need to be supplemented with experienced insider knowledge, which it is the teacher's job to provide. We can gradually permit ourselves to jettison anxiety over cultural mishearing and substitute optimism that what beginners apprehend will beckon them on to a deeper appreciation. Such appreciation need not be a litmus test for authorization to transcribe and analyze, but a horizon gradually approachable through synergy between the student's initial discoveries and input from the teacher. These are reasons why in lieu of a "transcription curriculum," we can have an integrated practice in which each teacher guides students in approaching the music of their specialized training, allowing and correcting mistakes as they arise.

TRANSCRIPTION AND AURAL ANALYSIS METHOD

Transcription is highlighted here as a tool, not a specific reform. As practiced it would always adapt to different levels of expertise and subject matter. At some early point, however, students need to learn methods. The first thing to inculcate is awareness that until one goes to the source of the music to learn it from its creators, checks a composer's score, or reads about it in an expert's description, we can sometimes do no better than make guesses about how it is heard and understood in situ. And even then it can be undecidable, as various long-standing debates in ethnomusicology attest. But that is perfectly all right because the deductive process of discovery is fruitful. Indeed, sometimes it might be possible to discover structures that practitioners know only passively. But all decisions taken about what to represent should be based on explicit sounding evidence or, if not, at least accounted for as hypotheses and explained as such. In the process one becomes mindful of assumptions based on one's habits or associations.

Very few people can just listen and write out a full music beginning from the beginning. Offering a range of methods and problem-solving techniques, appropriate to the level of the student and the task, can help the mind and ear collaborate. Assignments can home in on precisely targeted features in the manner of quantitative problem sets. Creative exploration of different ways to notate can run the gamut of specificity from mere lettering of formal components to careful fixing of ornamental detail.

In more advanced assignments for which detail is expected, several hours per session need to be set aside. Spiral-bound staff paper is often the worst thing; oversize paper that provides plenty of room to sketch out a music as if on a canvas is more conducive. Pencils, not pens, are the order of the day; the computer graphics can wait until after one has played and sketched. One can draw the music as if painting it and be as creative with the visuals as possible; staves and notes are only one way. Calibrating the paper with proportional time markings can help if the rhythms are elusive. Grids and graphs work well for many kinds of highly metricized music. For cyclically repetitive music, once one discerns points of return, cyclic recurrences can be vertically aligned for ease of paradigmatic comparison. As in composing on a score, the eye is happy when it can scan substantial chunks at a glance and construct the temporal flow in the mind's ear.

One trains oneself to listen both for note-to-note connections and periodically recurring events, focusing on the latter at first and sketching them in so that the interstices can be filled in later. Listening can zero in on one dimension at a time—pitch, duration, phrase boundaries—and each marked down and rechecked before moving to the next. For polyphony, comprehending one line at a time is usually best. One learns to be attentive to and to mimic the variety of rhythmic values and pitches heard while also bearing in mind that two notes or rhythms that sound different can be conceptually the same to the performer(s). Always singing or playing an instrument and beating time at every step, along with or separate from the recording, brings the music into the body until it is owned and can re-emanate from the body. The search is for solutions that are as simple and elegant as possible, and the teacher will have selected ingenious music posing problems that lend themselves to revelatory answers. Students' own ears lead them on.

SIX SAMPLE TRANSCRIPTION ASSIGNMENTS

I have assigned the six questions (and others like them) illustrated in Boxes 9.1a and 9.1b in undergraduate classes for which musical training was not a prerequisite. I found that students were able to complete them successfully, often attesting afterwards to the rewards of doing so (sometimes after cursing me good-naturedly). It was as if they had always wanted to listen harder but no one ever asked them to. Multiple representational styles are, of course, possible for each question. None requires knowledge of staff notation. On the

Box 9.1a. SAMPLE ASSIGNMENTS 1–5

1. *All You Need Is Love* (Beatles).
   Start counting pulsations when the vocals enter, counting two pulsations for each "Love" and continuing steadily thereafter. Indicate the structure of one full verse and chorus, labeling each melodic segment with a letter (A, B, etc.) and showing the duration in number of pulsations.

2. *Ieiéo* (Track 45, "Le chant des enfants du monde, Vol. 13, Cameroun," 2004, Arion ARN 64639).
   The rhythm of the first eight seconds of the song is shown with the dots in the grid. This is one complete "statement" of the song. Each box represents a subdivision, the fastest pulse. After this it is all repetition of the song, but there is some variation. Add twelve more rows to the grid and fill in the dots for the twelve additional statements.

3. *Bibayak Pygmy Solo Song* (Beginning of track 2. "Gabon: Musique des Pygmées Bibayak, chantres de l'épopée," recorded by Pierre Sallée, 1989, Ocora CD 559 053).

   The singer begins with the following rhythm, in which two short durations (S) are equal to one long (L-). The hyphens show the second half of each L.

   L-SL-L-L-SL-

   It is followed by a slight variation on the same thing (one of the longs is replaced by two shorts):

   L-SSSL-L-SL-

   And this is followed by the first pattern once more. But the melodies of all three of the patterns are different. The three together make up one *complete cycle* of the melody, after which the entire thing repeats numerous times. But when it repeats the singer sometimes varies the melody. And twice—only twice—she varies the rhythm, and both times at the same spot.
       Your task is to discover how many complete cycles are sung (the last one is incomplete on the recording, so don't be concerned with it.) Represent the music in notation by making a grid similar to the one I gave you above for the song *Ieiéo*, in which each row represents a complete cycle and the number of rows is the number of complete cycles. Each row will be the same except for those two places where the rhythm is varied. Fill in dots for each note the singer sings, but whenever the melody note is different from the original cycle, mark it by squaring the dot. Finding these places will sometimes be difficult, especially the few times when the final and/or initial notes of the original cycle are varied, because this can throw off your sense of when the cycle begins. Persevere! And of course, sometimes the singer will do it just as she did it the first time—that is, with no variation.

4. Igor Stravinsky (*Le sacre du printemps: Rondes printanières*, rehearsal numbers 49–55).
   Identify the repeating four-beat rhythm introduced at the outset and the five "blocks" of timbre used in this passage. These feature 1) low strings, 2) low strings with oboe, 3) strings with French horns, 4) strings with a larger group of mixed instruments, and 5) full orchestra. The rhythm recurs continuously but with some addition or subtraction of pulsations in some repetitions and frequently swapping among the five timbres. Transcribe the entire process, indicating only the number of beats per iteration and timbre used. Show how Stravinsky has organized these simple elements into sections, sometimes articulated by changes in the basic four-beat unit and at other times by larger patterns in how the timbres are organized.

5. *Seyak/Butcherbird* (Track 1 of "Rainforest Soundwalks: Ambiences of Bosavi Papua New Guinea," recorded by Steven Feld, 2001, Earth Ear 696208010622).
   Capture the melodic contours and phrase timings of the first thirty to forty seconds of this extraordinary birdsong, labeling the separate phrases with capital letters and summarizing their pattern at the bottom of the page. Use any kind of symbols and pitch-against-time graph that you like.

Box 9.1b. SAMPLE ASSIGNMENT 6

6. *Jalajakshi* (sometimes spelled *Jalajaksha*) (Track 1, "On Record," L. Subramaniam, violin, and Palghat Mani Iyer, mridangam, Subramaniam Entertainment, Viji Records 887516271199)

   This is a Karnatak *varnam*—something like a virtuoso étude—in adi tala and Hamsadvhani raga. The composition has two large parts, each with several named subsections. We are concerned with Part 1 only.

   - Part 1:
     > Pallavi (2 tala cycles, call them A and B)
     > Anupallavi (2 tala cycles, call them C and D)
     > Mukthayi Swaram (4 tala cycles, call them E, F, G, and H)

   - Part 2:
     > Caranam
     > Chitta Swaram

   First task: In the recording (starting at 0:06) the musicians play many statements of Part 1, starting slowly and then each time faster than the previous one (they never speed up *during* a statement). At 13:06 they complete the final, fastest statement of Part 1 and then play Part 2 just once to finish, back at the original speed.

   Your job is to make a chart showing specific features of the music's rhythm between 0:06 and 13:06. You need to know that

   - For each statement of Part 1, they may repeat some parts (or combinations of them) before moving on. For example the first time they play ABCDEFGH (for a total of eight cycles), and the second time they play ABABCDEFGH (ten cycles).
   - A, B, C, D, E, F, G, and H are always played at least once; none is ever omitted.
   - Once E occurs, A, B, C, and D do not come again until the next speed level is reached. Thus combos like CDED and DEABCDE are against the rules.
   - The speed changes *only* after cycle H is played, never anywhere else.
   - Being able to recognize the eight different chunks of melody (A to H) is an absolute must for doing this assignment. To help, here are their timings for the first time through:

     A 0:06   B 0:20   C 0:34   D 0:47   E :1:01   F 1:14   G 1:28   H 1:41 (to 1:55).

   Attached is a template for the chart I want you to make, with the first two lines filled in as I expect you to do for the rest. You will add a new row for each statement. For this part of the assignment fill in columns 2 to 8. For now leave the rest of columns 9 and 10 blank; we'll get to them in the next part.

   Note that even though statement 1 ends at 1:55, the duration is 109 seconds because it began at 0:06.

   Please calculate seconds per "cycle" to one decimal place. Round off the speed to the nearest whole number. The formula for calculating the speed is [total no. of "beats" divided by total duration in seconds] x 60.

Now, why do I have "cycle" and "beat" in quotation marks in columns 5–8? See below.

   Second task: Why do the musicians play a different combination of "cycles" each time? It is not random or casual; they actually have a mind-blowing plan (that you will now deduce) displaying consummate musicianship.

   Although the music is speeding up, everything is conceived and felt *in terms of the initial tempo*. This means that each new speed is not a new tempo at all, but rather a new and faster rate of subdivision, overlaid upon the same unchanging beat rate as the original. Thus each statement has *a new subdivision rate at the original tempo*. We want to find what these rates are. But there are problems.

   - The performers' control of speed and rhythm ratios is amazing and close to perfect— but not exactly perfect. They're not machines—although they're close!
   - Measuring the timing on your iTunes or other timer may not be exact either.

You have two things to do:

1) For each statement, find out how many original cycles fit in the same amount of time. According to column 6 of the chart I provided, each cycle at the initial tempo takes 13.5 seconds. For example, suppose that (watch out, this isn't the real answer) in the fifth statement they play ten cycles. Suppose the whole statement lasts 68 seconds. How many original cycles would fit in 68 seconds? 13.5 x 5 = 67.5. Not quite 68—they are not perfect—but close enough for our purposes. So where he could have played five cycles at the original speed, he is now playing ten (he has doubled the speed). You write 5 in column 9.

2) Now for the rightmost column (column 10): the subdivision rate, calculated in terms of the original tempo. In the first statement, the rate is 4, as shown on the template. That is, Subramaniam's minimal rhythm values—the fastest notes he plays—are four to a beat. In each subsequent statement this changes. Here's how to calculate it:

[no. of "cycles" divided by no. of original cycle durations] x the original subdivision rate
or said differently
[column 5 divided by column 9] x 4

Things to always be clear about:

- the difference between speed and tempo
- the difference between beat and subdivision
- the length of a cycle, once established, never changes (actually, there are exceptions in real life—but not in the work I am giving you).

Column 1	2	3	4	5	6	7	8	9	10
Statement no.	Pallavi (Tala A, B) Anupallavi (Tala C, D) Mukthayi Swaram (Tala E, F, G, H)	End time	Total duration in seconds	no. of "cycles"	Seconds per "cycle"	Total no. of "beats"	Speed ("beats") per minute)	no. of orig. cycle durations (@13.5 secs.)	Subdivision rate relative to original tempo
1	ABCDEFGH	1:55	109	8	13.5*	64	35	8	4
2	ABABCDEFGH	3:44	109	10	11	80	44.125	8	5

* This is the only one that's the *real* cycle.

other hand, the same assignments can be effective for experienced musicians, too, since most benefit from thinking outside that box. A set of possible solutions (Box 9.2) is given at the end of the chapter.

The amount of time needed to complete the assignments varies; numbers 3, 5, and 6 typically call for dozens, if not whole weekends' worth, of repeat listening, consultation with other students, late-night sessions, and, for some, office-hour visits. All are offered as examples of how transcription can involve different kinds of inquiry and focus. Each draws attention to carefully circumscribed dimensions of the music, in effect constructing a series of filters that make the job practical (if demanding) for novices. Each could be supplemented with additional tasks or questions; or they could be taken up as small-group in-class exercises. All are offered here as stimulus to the design of similar kinds of material personalized to each teacher.

Among the classes for which I have designed work like this are a large lecture course, aimed at first year non-major students, called Musical Rhythm and Human Experience, as well as a third-year World Music Cultures course open to all and attracting a mix of majors and general students. The assignments become the major focus of the course, taking priority over papers and exams, and the integration of listening, singing, and embodiment is a topic interactively discussed in many a class period. I set aside many office hours to assist students who are new to transcription and close listening.

Specific suggestions for transcription work involving conventional or modified staff notation or other more scrupulous approaches to the details of pitch systems and rhythm are beyond the scope of this chapter and perhaps less necessary for the professional readership I am addressing. A scan of the ethnomusicology literature from Anku to Zemp will reveal possibilities. Nonetheless it bears pointing out that students consistently find transcription to be impactful and satisfying at undergraduate upper levels. There and in graduate courses I have directed large group projects such as a complete set of transcriptions for the 103 tracks of *Les voix du monde*, the remarkable three-CD set of human vocal traditions and techniques published by the Musée de l'Homme (CNRS-Musée de l'Homme 1996).[16] Devoting several sessions to group discussion of everyone's work allows sharing of the many creative approaches and solutions possible. In a graduate seminar called Musical Periodicity, students transcribe a piece of their choice and write a detailed analysis of it.

The first assignment (Box 9.1) involves a simple labeling of musical form in a Beatles song. I often include it in a worksheet with many kinds of songs, mainly Anglo-American folk songs with uncomplicated periodicities—a repertoire that even Anglo-American students, sadly, are unlikely to know. The second requires differentiating fairly straightforward changes in a repeating Cameroonian melody. Number three, a recording of a solo Pygmy singer from Gabon, sharpens awareness of change and variation in repetitive contexts. Number four, from Stravinsky's *Sacre*, is related to the first but reveals dimensions of timbre and more. The fifth calls attention to birdsong as music. The last calls on arithmetic plus close listening to uncover some rhythm relationships in a South Indian music performance; the instructions are extremely detailed, and students have been prepped with class practice in the hand gestures for counting adi tala. The performers in this case have handed us an extraordinary teaching moment: as column 10 of the solution shows, each repetition of the composition involves an incremental and systematic upping

16. This was done with a pair of Introduction to Ethnomusicology seminars in fall 2011 and 2012., each with about fifteen students (plus me, for a total of sixteen), each of whom produced three annotated transcriptions over several weeks during the term. Results varied widely with student effort and skill and the challenges the music presented.

of the subdivision rate from 4 to 5 to 6, 7, 8, 9, 10, and then by twos from 12, 14, and so on, finally arriving at 24; that is, six times the speed of the original. This is accomplished by carefully adjusting the number of repetitions of the internal parts (see column 2) and applying an unbelievable musical and technical mastery. Students can actually deduce this with careful listening and some arithmetic as described in the assignment, and may be fairly gobsmacked with the revelation of what the performers achieved on this occasion.[17] I needed say nothing further as far as urging them on to love Indian music.

CONCLUSION: NEW CURRICULUM, NEW MUSIC

Ethnomusicology's future potential in shaping university music education is to emerge from the marginality it has chafed against to welcome more people into diverse musical experience. To get there it is not a question of prevailing over the gatekeepers of European culture but rather of gradually dissolving the differences of both repertoire and method that have separated us. To flourish, ethnomusicology had to evolve idiomatic methods, necessarily in contradistinction to other music disciplines. Now, as Andrade told Brazil in 1928, it ought to cannibalize the best aspects of that which has dominated it. Here I argued for a bundle of pedagogical practices: a culture of close listening, the work of musical transcription, representation, and—because every transcription is a set of decisions about what is structurally salient—theory and analysis, too.[18] But the emphasis on aurality is modeled on the direct experience of fieldwork native to ethnomusicology and girded by belief that in the hypercosmopolitan present, even so-called nonmusician students are capable of significant, unsuspected perception. These practices are only a part of the larger picture of future music curricula, but they are the project's keystones.

One ought to harbor no illusions that where ethnomusicology has made fewer inroads and imperatives for curricular change are more abstract, people might well ask why one would fix what isn't broken. At the top of the food chain, in the world's standard-setting conservatories and more than a few universities, European classical music thrives unchallenged, and it is important for ethnomusicologists to remember this with humility. The outsider may imagine that they would look askance at a proposal to bend their curricula in the directions proposed, to say the least. And perhaps understandably so, as any anthropologist could aver: competition for places in these institutions is ferocious, and there is no shortage of students aching to enter their

17. Numerous students who enjoyed the challenge suggested that I give less explicit information on how to calculate values in the assignment text; but others (with math phobias) were grateful for it.

18. For distinctions between theory and analysis, see Cone 1967 and Lewin 1969.

gates. Wealth and prestige are concentrated here. The schools are the apples of aspirants' desires, and accepted adepts submit to a proven training formula. Some enter the worlds of contemporary music and jazz, where contact with world traditions is likely and transcription a core resource. But most do not. Considering these circumstances, idealistically advocating for the musically unknown or disadvantaged is naive and oblivious to the real world of success and striving in Western art music. It is nevertheless consolation to me that the argument offered in this chapter is a musical one, promising positive outcomes for the ears, body, and mind, and while it is formulated with reference to desiderata of the liberal university, that kind of ideology of diversity is just one part of it. It can just be, and essentially *is*, about becoming a better musician. If teachers at Juilliard, Curtis, and Yale explore transcription in the ways proposed, their students will delight them with their discoveries. And were that to happen, the news might trickle down. (But since that has proven to be a faulty model for everything from economics to cultural diffusion anyway, in the meanwhile one can hope that it will slowly trickle up.)

Fred Lerdahl (1992, 120) articulated an important insight when he wrote that "the music of the future will emerge less from twentieth century progressivist aesthetics than from newly acquired knowledge of the structure of musical perception and cognition." Lerdahl's concern was with contemporary art music composition, but the message is broadly pertinent. The music of the future is our common concern, and students will always be appropriately curious about it. It is a future to be nourished by multiple streams of world music and not only the internal histories of particular interests such as art music composition or popular music or jazz. It is our mandate to stretch what students perceive, grow their awareness of how it is enlarging their view, and foster their ability to replicate, integrate, and synthesize it in new forms. There can never be a resource richer than the traditional musics of the world for expanding our cognitive capacities—all the while beguiling us and stimulating us to know others' histories and cultures. Exposure will always be available to the curious and motivated through recordings and YouTube, but our role will be to select and discern with guidance.[19]

Above all, one should not construe these kinds of reforms as endorsement of a completely global and culture-blind approach to music in which

19. The week of May 10, 2015, as this was being written, brought news coverage of concerts and recordings by eleven-year old Joey Alexander Sila, an astonishingly accomplished jazz pianist. Born in Bali in 2003, his music education took place at home beginning at age six and consisted entirely of a diet of CDs and YouTube. Prodigal phenomena like him illustrate not only the undiminished power and allure of oral and aural tradition in the world but its resurgence through media, which allow it to leapfrog over culture and geography. The university will neither supplant nor override that allure, and trying too hard to embrace it would be disingenuous. We should embrace it appropriately because it is so fundamental but also recommit to our own strengths: writing and representation.

there would be no strict distinction between the musician and nonmusician, the West and the rest, the specialist and the generalist. That would, of course, be both ridiculous and impossible, and thank goodness. A rootless musician is useless. We will always need our cultural allegiances, our preferences, and our many kinds of expertise to guide us in guiding the next generations. And we will always be limited by the practical realities of tradition and the institutions within which we work and on which we rely. The idealism will nonetheless be instructive in isolating the values we would project: openness to all music and fealty to our musical bodies. The first instinct in any class—be it a music appreciation lecture or a doctoral seminar on the music of Pierre Boulez—can be *listen to this, figure out what you hear, and represent it.*

REFERENCES

Abril, Carlos. 2007. "I Have A Voice but I Just Can't Sing: A Narrative Investigation of Singing and Social Anxiety." *Music Education Research*, Vol. 9 No. 1, 1–15.

Agawu, V. Kofi. 2003. *Representing African Music. Postcolonial Notes, Queries, Positions.* New York: Routledge.

Benadon, Fernando. 2006. "Slicing the Beat: Jazz Eighth-Notes as Expressive Microrhythm." *Ethnomusicology*, Vol. 50 No. 1, 73–98.

Campbell, Patricia, et al. 2014. "Transforming Music Study from Its Foundations: A Manifesto for Progressive Change in the Undergraduate Preparation for Music Majors." College Music Society.

Clayton, Martin, Rebecca Sager, and Udo Will. 2004. "In Time with the Music. The Concept of Entrainment and Its Significance for Ethnomusicology." *ESEM-Counterpoint*, Vol. 1, 1–82.

Clendinning, Jane, and Elizabeth West Marvin. 2010. *The Musician's Guide to Theory and Analysis.* 2nd ed. New York: Norton.

CNRS/Musée de l'Homme. 1996. *Les Voix du Monde*, Hugo Zemp, Lortat-Jacob, B., Léothaud, G., conception and realization. Le Chant du Monde CMX 374 1010.12.

Cogan, Robert, and Pozzi Escot. 1976. *Sonic Design. The Nature of Sound and Music.* Englewood Cliffs, NJ: Prentice Hall.

Cone, Edward. 1967. "Beyond Analysis." *Perspectives of New Music*, Vol. 6 No. 1, 33–51.

Gopinath, Sumanth. 2009. "Diversity, Music Theory, and the Neoliberal Academy." *Gamut*, Vol. 2 No. 1, 61–88.

Ellingson, Ter. 1992. "Theory and Method: Transcription." In *Ethnomusicology. An Introduction*, Helen Myers, ed. New York: Norton, 110–152.

England, Nicholas M., ed. 1964. "Symposium on Transcription and Analysis: A Hukwe Song with Musical Bow." With contributions by Robert Garfias, Mieczyslaw Kolinski, George List, Willard Rhodes, and moderated by Charles Seeger. *Ethnomusicology*, No. 8, 223–277.

Friedmann, Michael. 1990. *Ear Training for Twentieth Century Music.* New Haven, CT: Yale University Press.

Jones, A. M. 1959. *Studies in African Music*, Vols. 1 and 2. London: Oxford University Press.

Kang, Youyoung. 2009. "Diversifying Music Theory." *Gamut*, Vol. 2 No. 1, 89–98.

Kartomi, Margaret. 2005. Review of "Thinking Musically: Experiencing Music, Expressing Culture" by Bonnie C. Wade. *Music & Letters*, Vol. 86 No. 2, 270–274.

Lerdahl, Fred. 1992. "Cognitive Constraints on Compositional Systems." *Contemporary Music Review*, Vol. 6, Part 2, 97–121.

Lerdahl, F., and R. Jackendoff. 1983. A *Generative Theory of Tonal Music*. Cambridge, MA: MIT Press.

Lewin, David. 1969. "Behind the Beyond: A Response to Edward T. Cone." *Perspectives of New Music*, Vol. 7 No. 2, 59–69.

Levine, Victoria Lindsay, ed. 2002. *Writing American Indian Music. Historic Transcriptions, Notations, and Arrangements*. Recent Researches in American Music, Vol. 44. Middleton, WI: A-R Editions.

List, George. 1974. "The Reliability of Transcription." *Ethnomusicology*, Vol. 18 No. 3, 353–378.

London, Justin. 2004 [2011]. *Hearing in Time. Psychological Aspects of Musical Meter*. New York: Oxford University Press.

Marian-Bălaşa, Marin, ed. 2005. "Notation, Transcription, Visual Representation." *World of Music*, Vol. 47 No. 2. Special issue.

Molino, Jean, and Jean-Jacques Nattiez. 2007. "Typologies et universaux." In *Musiques. Une encyclopédie pour XXIe siècle*, Jean-Jacques Nattiez, ed., Vol. 5. Sous la direction de J.-J. Nattiez, Alles, ActesSud / Cité de la Musique, 337–396.

Morris, Robert. 1991. *Class Notes for Atonal Music Theory*. Hanover, NH: Frog Peak Music.

Nettl, Bruno.1983.*The Study of Ethnomusicology: Twenty-Nine Issues and Concepts*. Urbana: University of Illinois Press.

Parncutt, Richard. 1994. "A Perceptual Model of Pulse Salience and Metrical Accent in Musical Rhythms." *Music Perception*, Vol. 11 No. 4, 409–464.

Rothstein, Edward. 2000. "Connections: For Western Music, the Center Holds." *New York Times*. http://www.nytimes.com/2000/11/11/arts/connections-for-western-music-the-center-holds.html. Accessed April 29, 2015.

Sanyal, Ritwik, and Richard Widdess. 2004. *Dhrupad. Tradition and Performance in Indian Music*. London: Ashgate.

Sarath, Edward. 2013. *Improvisation, Creativity, and Consciousness. Jazz as Integral Template for Music, Education, and Society*. New York: SUNY Press.

Seeger, Charles. 1958. "Prescriptive and Descriptive Music-Writing." *Musical Quarterly*, Vol. 44 No. 1, 84–95.

Stanyek, Jason, et al. 2014. "Forum on Transcription." *Twentieth Century Music*, Vol. 11, 101–161.

Stockmann, Doris. 1979. "Die Transkription in der Musikethnologie: Geschichte, Probleme, Methoden." *Acta Musicologica*, Vol. 51, 204–45.

Tenzer, Michael. 2000. *Gamelan Gong Kebyar: The Art of Twentieth Century Balinese Music*. Chicago: University of Chicago Press.

Wade, Bonnie C. 2012 [2008, 2003]. *Thinking Musically. Experiencing Music, Expressing Culture*. New York: Oxford University Press.

Yampolsky, Philip, et al. 2013. "Under the Radar and Off the Map: Three Rural Musics of Island Southeast Asia." Paper session, Society for Ethnomusicology Conference, Indianapolis.

Box 9.2 APPENDIX. SOLUTIONS TO THE ASSIGNMENTS IN BOXES 9.1A AND 9.1B.

1. *All You Need Is Love*

Verse: ‖: A A   B   C :‖
       7   7   8   7 = 29 beats total in the period
Chorus: ‖:D D   E   F :‖
       8   8   6 = 30 beats total in the period   30 + 29 = 59 total
subdivision: binary
A ("Nothing you can do"), B ("Nowhere..."), C ("It's easy")
D ("All you need..."), E, same words, different tune (could bd D'), F ("love is all you need")

2. *Ieiéo*

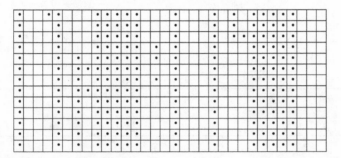

3. *Bibayak Pygmy Solo Song*

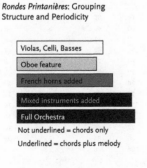

4. *Rondes Printanières*

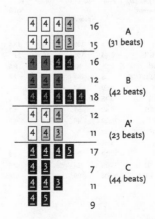

Rondes Printanières: Grouping
Structure and Periodicity

| Violas, Celli, Basses |
| Oboe feature |
| French horns added |
| Mixed instruments added |
| Full Orchestra |

Not underlined = chords only
Underlined = chords plus melody

5. Seyak/Butcherbird

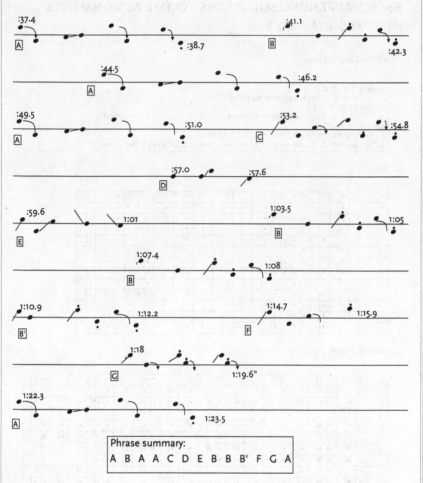

Phrase summary:

A B A A C D E B B B' F G A

6. Jalajakshi

Column 1	2	3	4	5	6	7	8	9	10
Statement no.	Pallavi (Tala AB Anupallavi (Tala CD) Mukthayi Swaram (Tala EFGH)	End time	Total duration in seconds	No. of "cycles"	Seconds Per "cycle"	Total no. of "beats"	Speed ("beats" per minute)	No. of orig. cycle durations @13.5 Secs.	Subdivision rate relative to original tempo
1	ABCDEFGH	1:55	109	8	13.5	64	35	8	4
2	ABABCDEFGH	3:44	109	10	11	80	44.125	8	5
3	AABCDEFGH	5:09	85	9	9.5	72	51	6	6
4	ABCDABCDEFEFGH	6:58	109	14	7.8	112	62	8	7
5	ABCDEFGH	7:50	52	8	6.5	64	74	4	8
6	AABCDEFGH	8:45	55	9	6.1	72	78.7	4	9
7	ABABCDEFGH	9:42	57	10	5.7	80	84.2	4	10
8	AABCDEFGH	10:22	40	9	4.5	72	95.5	3	12
9	ABCDABCDEFEFGH	11:18	56	14	4	112	120	4	14
10	ABCDEFGH	11:44	26	8	3	64	147	2	16
11	ABCDEFGH	12:12	28	9	2.9	72	166	2	18
12	ABABCDEFGH	12:38	26	10	2.6	80	184	2	20
13	ABCDABCDEFGH	13:06	28	12	2.33	96	206	2	24

CHAPTER 10

Embodied Pedagogy

Techniques for Exploring Why and How Music Matters

SONIA TAMAR SEEMAN

When we calculate the hours spent in various academic endeavors, it is interesting that teaching constitutes possibly the most time-consuming activity, yet there has been so little reflection on what we teach, how we teach, and why we teach. In this area, ethnomusicology has a great deal to contribute, especially because the nature of our subject matter and the distances (conceptual and geographic) we must bridge for students in order to reach them require careful reflection on why it is that music matters. In asking this question, I claim that (1) teaching music effectively requires conscious and conscientious shifting between far and near experiences; (2) that heightened awareness of the gap between far and near is most effectively addressed through a technique I call embodied pedagogy in order to achieve effective understanding; and (3) that the enactment of these goals in teaching any type of music class provides necessary tools for student engagement with issues outside the classroom and into the world that confronts them every day. I offer three case studies to illustrate these techniques: 1) exercises in teaching western European opera and the linkages between sound and social meaning; 2) classroom series on musical nationalism in the transition from the Ottoman Empire to the Republic of Turkey; and 3) description of our recent core curriculum reforms at the University of Texas, Austin, as another site in which these pedagogical techniques are being deployed, as well as reflecting on the harnessing of such pedagogical experiences to implement curriculum reforms among colleagues and administrators.

To break this down, I outline the components of ethnomusicology pedagogy as founded on two dialectics: moving between far- and near-experiences and structuring lectures through artificially separating the analysis of musical sound and contexts for musical performance/reception, which are eventually reintegrated. I term these techniques embodied pedagogy to achieve embodied understanding. I then describe three different teaching experiences that illustrate how embodied pedagogy, informed by far-near experiences, results in an enhanced understanding of how music works in human society and therefore the myriad ways in which music matters. The goal of this chapter, however, moves beyond the mechanics of particular core curriculum reform. The case study and reflections are intended to suggest a path towards mining historically marginalized music disciplines for innovative pedagogical techniques to better prepare students for the rapidly changing and interconnected world of this century.

FAR-NEAR EXPERIENCE AS A GUIDE FOR EFFECTIVE PEDAGOGY

Ethnomusicology as a field has unique contributions to offer music studies, contributions that enlarge the toolkit of teaching methods and also provide pathways for deeper musical comprehension. These contributions are in large part due to the ethnomusicological engagement with far-near experiences as an integral component of what it is ethnomusicologists do and how they think about the world. By far-near, I am drawing on anthropologist Clifford Geertz's distinction between experience near (spontaneous, unconscious, instinctual experience) and experience distant (conceptualized accounts of reality, made possible through reflection at a distance).[1]

Distant, or far-near, is indeed integral to the educational experience in that educators seek to enlarge students' conceptual awareness beyond the realm of taken-for-granted precepts and beliefs. Far-near is integral to ethnomusicological teaching in that educators have the challenge of teaching about musical practices that may well be outside most students' life experiences. It is useful for teaching western European, popular, and jazz traditions as well, given that western European musical traditions are likely to be as foreign to undergraduate students as Javanese gamelan. And even in cases where the repertoire might be familiar, such as a Beethoven sonata, the context of

1. From Heinz Kohut's psychoanalytical theory, Geertz argued that the nature of the anthropologists' task is one that moves between experience distant (seeking to understand an other) and experience near (one's own taken-for-granted perception of reality). The anthropologist seeks to integrate distant and near experiences in order to better represent another society's cultural practices and perception of reality (Geertz 1983, 55–70).

twenty-first-century cultural understandings are considerably different from that of mid-nineteenth-century Viennese urban audiences due to the differences in social, political, and economic contexts that have shaped cultural understanding in these periods (Nettl 1995, 82–111).

Embodied pedagogy is a second level of teaching that is necessary for the students' experience of far-near juxtaposition in such a way that they engage with a higher level of understanding. This concept puts Mark Johnson's definition of embodied understanding into pedagogical practice as an effective means for conveying what music *is* and what music *does*. In the classroom I attempt to stimulate a deeper grasp—in myself as well as students—of situated, experiential understanding of the myriad ways in which music shapes human life. Here I am taking Mark Johnson's theorization of understanding as resulting from the ongoing production of locally specific, embodied, experiential encounters.[2] Through meaningful encounters in the classroom, we set up the possibility for students' experiences to fuse into recurring structures which in turn make it possible for students to establish patterns of reasoning and understanding.[3]

Insights from phenomenological hermeneutics are crucial for illuminating how humans learn through the juxtaposition of familiar and unfamiliar experiences. Here I draw upon philosopher Paul Ricoeur's reflections on the workings of the human productive imagination encapsulated in his depiction of enlarged human understanding.[4] Ricoeur reflects on the human ability to assimilate new forms of knowledge and understanding due to the capacity of the imagination to creatively mediate the distance of the unfamiliar and the external through appropriation. The term "distanciation" in his work refers to the intentional externalization of signs, as evident in the semantic autonomy of "texts" (any assemblage of signs) that bear meanings apart from the intention of the author. Other human agents viewing them attribute meanings to such signs through appropriation; that is, making familiar meanings that

2. Philosopher Mark Johnson theorizes understanding as the ongoing production of locally specific, embodied, experiential encounters: "Any account of understanding must begin with the patterns of ongoing interaction between its physical and cultural environments and must include both our emotional responses to changes in our body and environment, and also the actions by which we continuously transform our experience" (Johnson 2015, 1).

3. Johnson's reflections draw on his earlier work on image schema with George Lakoff. For Lakoff and Johnson, image schema result from the internalization of bodily and conceptual interactions. Here "image" is not intended to refer only to the visual but rather to multimodal patterns of experience that include aural, tactile, olfactory, and taste sensations (Johnson 1987).

4. Ricoeur (1981) elaborates on Hans Georg's depictions of human understanding as a continual process by which new experiences and encounters are appropriated into the human imagination, analogous to the potentially unbounded horizon that emerges before our eyes.

were foreign to one's experience.[5] With this processual understanding of how the human imagination configures meaning, we can conceive of the classroom as a space for a variety of possible learning experiences ranging through misinterpretations and mistranslations, the reinforcement of previous beliefs, and radically transformed ways of perceiving the world. By virtue of working through a variety of musical case studies grounded in ethnographic contexts, ethnomusicologically informed classes can be consciously shaped through an ongoing dialectical experience of moving between distanciation and appropriation that has the potential to result in an enlarged understanding of the world.

Using Ricoeur's philosophical hypothesis about how humans learn, we can build upon distanciation and appropriation through exercises of embodied pedagogy. In this sense, embodied is not simply "movement," as in the artificial distinction between body and mind. Taking Johnson's notion in light of Ricoeur's distanciation and appropriation and Geertz's experience-distant/far and experience-near, embodied understanding recognizes the appropriation of external experience into one's self / one's internal understanding. Embodied understanding through pedagogical techniques can be elicited through a range of reflective as well as motoric exercises in the classroom, including in-class minute papers, think-pair-share exercises, structured debates, performance of rhythmic and melodic patterns, modeling real-life high-stakes events such as court trials, brokering peace negotiations through music, Socratic conversations, and the like. But all exercises should be aimed at increasing students' understanding of the varieties of musical sounds and effects in the world beyond their taken-for-granted assumptions. Through these methods, which I term embodied pedagogy, I challenge students to move between their taken-for-granted notions of selves, or experience-near, and introduce them to musical and other cultural practices of unfamiliar communities, thereby fostering their enlarged understanding of the world.

CASE STUDY NO. 1: TEACHING SOCIAL CATEGORIES THROUGH OPERA—CLASS, GENDER, AND IDENTITY IN BIZET'S *CARMEN*

This first case study is indebted to Susan McClary's groundbreaking analysis of gendered social identity in *Carmen* (McClary 1991, 52–67). In the classroom, we can further explore social class and gender roles in the opera itself through the relationship between the opera's characters and nineteenth-century operagoing audiences and the intersections of gender, class, and race by

5. Here it is important to note that to Ricoeur, appropriation is a fundamental yet neutral capacity of the human imagination (Ricoeur 1981, 1991).

coupling Bizet's opera with the 2001 Robert Townsend film *Carmen: A Hip-hopera*, featuring Beyoncé Knowles. Discussion of Bizet's opera includes both experience-far in space (a French opera about Spain; originally consumed by a bourgeois French audience) and temporal distance (the nineteenth century in which class relations were emergent, with a growing middle class gaining greater control over cultural production). In this, the instructor has a considerable amount of mediation to achieve, as students are less likely to be aware of their own society's class and gender distinctions, much less the differences between contemporary and nineteenth-century gender and class construction. In addition, many students have not attended opera performances, and non-majors are not likely to be familiar with operatic idioms, vocal production, narratives, and the like. Taken together, the weight of such distanced experiences needs nuanced attention to familiarize students with the material, as well as requiring that the instructor bring to consciousness students' own taken-for-granted experiences of gender and class ideologies in their own daily lives.

The following is a list of suggested exercises that elicit embodied learning by alternating between experiential learning and content-based lectures. There is no prescribed order to these components; rather, these are suggestions for types of exercises. Introducing Bizet's setting of *Carmen* can begin with a background lecture on opera, its formal structure, and its development as a sign of aristocratic prestige and privilege. To set the context for nineteenth-century changes in narrative structure and musical features associated with the gender and class positions of this opera's characters, there are several ways to open discussion on nineteenth-century changes in class formation, such as the emergence of an increasingly powerful and numerous bourgeoisie, national consciousness (evident in this opera's "orientalist" marking of Spain in contrast to the French ethno-national self-identity of Bizet's audience), musical markings of male- versus female-gendered identity through vocal range and Carmen's borderline gender marking as a mezzo soprano, a vocal range placed between soprano and contralto.

One way to bring greater awareness to students' own inculcation of class awareness and relative prestige is to treat the classroom as a mid-nineteenth-century opera house by distributing "tickets" in varying prices to each student entering the room. In addition to relative prices, each ticket indicates seating according to nineteenth-century opera hall parameters: comfortable seats in the back with access to food and beverages, middle-section seats with no access to food, and tickets that indicate that they are either to sit on hard benches or stand at the front of the stage. After beginning a portion of *Carmen*, invite students to share their ticket and impressions with their neighbor, then open up discussion on what they noticed about their neighbors and how it made them feel about people that they had thought of as social equals. Students can be asked about analogies from their own lives at events such as popular music concerts and sports events, even on airplanes. Instructors can also circulate quotes from reactionary writings, such as Berlioz's disparagement of Paris's Theatre Lyrique, or commentary on lower-class audiences in the Bastille district (Huebner 1992, 17), to stimulate discussion about how social changes were impacting operatic and other formerly elite musical genres.

After social as well as musical analysis of *Carmen*, the same modes of analysis can be productively applied to the opening scene of Townsend's 2001 remake of *Carmen* featuring Beyoncé Knowles. Students can discuss contemporary class distinctions, such as the honorable beat cop Derrick Hill as a twenty-first-century version of the soldier Don José, Beyoncé as an aspiring actress named Carmen Brown, and the rapper Blaze as the contemporary epitome of masculinity, replacing the nineteenth-century aggressively masculine toreador Escamillo. Analogies can be drawn between the stereotypical "Gypsy" forms, such as Carmen's seguidilla or the Cuban-derived habanera of Carmen's signature aria as nineteenth-century signs of alterity, and contemporary associations between hip-hop as quintessentially "masculine" and "black" as signs of racialized othering, while noting Carmen's use of rap to verbally destroy her masculine challengers. In my teaching experience, students have been very perceptive and articulate in their analysis of gender roles, racial identities, and musical forms after watching this updated version of *Carmen*, and they are able to bring these insights to bear on the nineteenth-century operatic experience.

CASE STUDY NO. 2: MUSICAL NATIONALISM—OTTOMAN EMPIRE / TURKEY AND THE CONTEMPORARY UNITED STATES

The investigation of musical nationalism provides an accessible means of exploring the role of music in shaping human experience but necessitates dialectical movement between near- and far-experiences in order for students to see the role of music in shaping their own experiences of belonging and to deepen their understanding of the broader social efficacy of musical experience. By beginning with near-experiences of how their own senses of belonging are shaped by musical and other cultural practices, I then move to seemingly far-experiences of the musical transitions from the Ottoman Empire to the Republic of Turkey, then return at the end to a reflection on both their own and Ottoman to Turkish musical experiences. Throughout, students are challenged to examine, engage, embody, and reflect on their changing perceptions through embodied exercises. These exercises are aimed at demonstrating the inherently arbitrary link between music sign and social meaning, and at pointing to the larger question of how these ideas are instilled such that they become natural and taken for granted. In this and other examples, I have found it very important to de-exoticize "far" experiences and to exoticize and estrange students' own "near" experiences. This step is crucial in order to bridge students' sense of connection to people of other societies and cultural practices and to help them see what is rather strange about their own taken-for-granted cultural practices and values. In this way, they develop a heightened awareness of differences between themselves and their classmates and roommates and those they encounter outside the classroom. Through those differences they begin to see commonalities in human engagement with music and with each other.

In the opening session, we explore the formation of national identity by interrogating students' own experiences of national belonging. By asking them to reflect aloud on how they know that they are US citizens (or not), students begin to realize that senses of affiliation are inculcated by means of gestures, signs, and sounds. Interestingly, the most outspoken students answer that they are citizens by virtue of their passports, identity cards, or birth certificates but through further discussion come to realize that those documents are external signs of legitimation that are effective only as a result of long-term inculcation of cultural behaviors that begin at an early age. University campuses are excellent contexts for this exploration since the reiteration of particular hand signals, fight songs, visual logos, and other signs are similarly effective for inculcating as well as displaying school allegiance. While beginning with a seemingly near-case study, introduction of far-experience information is useful for unsettling taken-for-granted notions of national belonging. These can range from conducting an informal poll as to when "The Star Spangled Banner" was declared the US national anthem (only since 1930, despite most people's belief that it dates to the writing of the poem in 1812 or even to the late eighteenth-century Revolutionary War period); asking students to reflect on the irony of feeling kinship with American citizens abroad, even though they may not share much in terms of values; suppositions regarding the universal musical features of national anthems (march-like, regular meter, strophic structure) compared to anthems that challenge these suppositions, such as the flowing homophonic lines of the Estonian anthem, "Maamee" (Our Land). Such discussions often lead to student disclosures regarding differences in national backgrounds and experiences. I then facilitate a student-generated list of musical nationalism descriptors that range from musical features to social and political structures and contexts and retain this list for discussion and reflections on changed perceptions at the end of the lecture series.

In the second part, I set the background for imperial uses of Ottoman Turkish music and musical reforms used in the transition to an ethno-nation state. The first part of this far-experience series includes one or two lectures in which students learn about the role of music in the Ottoman court, particular musical forms, melodic and rhythmic modes, textures, and performance structures. Here we use core course concepts to describe components of musical sound while also learning local Ottoman terms. I help students hear heterophonic textures and the development of a given melodic mode such as maqam Rast. They learn to identify changes in rhythmic patterns through embodied exercises such as singing the tonic, identifying the shift to the fifth scale degree in the unfolding of the maqam in an improvised *taksim*, and learning traditional mnemonic syllables for the strong and weak beats of a recurrent isorhythm by alternating right and left strokes on the thighs and then with frame drums. They listen closely to a live traditional performance suite (*fasıl*) in order to identify the changes in rhythms and forms and to better understand how the ensemble aesthetic of heterophony is enacted in performance. I tie these features of musical sound to larger social and political contexts, such as imperial prestige and symbolic absorption of ethnic, linguistic, and religious minorities into the imperial polity.

In the second session, we review our findings from the opening lecture. With this background now enabling students to examine at a distance their own sense of belonging, I introduce historical information on the formation of the modern Republic of Turkey, in which state officials imposed new signs, symbols, calendars, language, and music in top-down, draconian fashion within the first fifteen years. Although it is beyond the scope of this chapter to outline musical changes imposed by the new nation state, I take students through guided listening with selected examples that represent competing views of the new state supported by descriptions, song texts with translations, and images.

For the final session, the classroom becomes a parliamentary session governed by the founders of the new Turkish state. In preparation, I divide students into teams, each of which proposes one preselected musical example as part of the new pantheon of Turkish national music. Students prepare with their team by studying their selection, searching through available background information about it, and later advocating for it. Each team accrues one point per piece of supporting evidence cited, which requires referring to class readings, other listening examples, and using musical terminology appropriately. Each team can also "erase" another team's points by providing contradictory evidence if that team cannot refute the assertion. I close the session by pointing out how close their assessments were to actual debates, selections, and rejections of such repertoire in Turkey. Most of the musical examples were in fact retained in central or peripheral practices that continue to fuel contemporary debates.

The last portion of this lecture returns to the initially compiled list of musical nationalism features so as to compare what we learned about the US system and processes for inculcating national consciousness through music with what we learned about the transition from the Ottoman Empire to the Turkish nation state. Either through an in-class minute paper or open discussion, students are able to reflect on the processes and components through which musical signs inculcate senses of belonging and difference and do so on a more abstract level than when we began these exercises. In the aftermath of this exercise, students always offer insights regarding their own experiences, comparing the debate to current events in the news or reporting on something similar that occurred while attending a recent sports or political event. I end the class module with a review of features of musical national- ism and reflections on the power of music to inculcate both group belonging and distinctions between the self and cultural "others." By guiding students through embodied experiences of listening and performing, then engaging their critical thinking skills in a simulated parliamentary debate, they grasp the significance of musical sound for inculcating as well as manipulating a sense of communal belonging.

EXPERIENCE NEAR AND FAR IN MUSICAL CURRICULA: MEDIATING CHANGE

As an additional consideration, introducing such new ways of teaching poten- tially collide with canonical academic courses in music programs. On the sur- face, the methods I propose and use in my own classrooms seem to require the introduction of noncanonical genres, outside western European classical rep- ertoires. In addition, such techniques seem to relegate embodied pedagogy to ethnomusicologists teaching world music courses. However, I argue that such techniques are crucial for teaching music, *period*, regardless of genre, region, or time period, as embodied pedagogy intersects students where they live by examining how music constructs their lives as well as members of seemingly unfamiliar communities.

In my experience, those who resist the introduction of embodied pedagogy often invoke two main criticisms as barriers for introducing change: 1) there is already too much canonical material to cover; thus to introduce noncanoni- cal material and approaches lessens the amount of time for canonical content; 2) concepts such as nationalism, gender, colonialism, and the like are too dif- ficult for undergraduates to understand. For the first, most studies on flipped classrooms and critical thinking note that the tension between content and application presumes what Freire calls a "banking concept of education," which purports that knowledge is a gift to be bestowed by the knowledgeable upon the ignorant. In this model, students are viewed as empty vessels pas- sively receiving knowledge. The danger is that "the more that students work at storing the deposits entrusted to them, the less they develop the critical con- sciousness which would result from their intervention in the world as trans- formers of that world" (Freire 2006, 73). In contrast, Freire argues for viewing students as conscious beings, possessing expansive and vibrant imaginations, who are capable of learning alongside their teachers. And their teachers learn alongside them. To apply this model to music pedagogy, teachers must help students develop tools for inquiry, broader frameworks for understanding and other higher-order thinking in order to grasp canonical as well as non-canonical repertoires. While critical thinking can expand student knowledge after class, larger amounts of passively absorbed content is likely to recede from consciousness after the final exam. In addition, critical thinking enables students to continue to learn about and explore additional repertoire items, genres, performance styles, and musical forms.

To the second criticism, that students are unable to grasp abstract theoretical concepts such as nationalism, gender identity, colonialism, and the like, we can effectively apply the tenet of experience near. Students' experiences are continuously shaped and expressed through cultural signs such as dress, language, and music. As discussed above, national consciousness is clearly a process of social inculcation through experiences with signs such as flags, slogans, and musical sounds. Rather than being vague, such concepts are so near as to be intuitive and barely visible. Our job as teachers is to communicate effectively about such identity practices such that these practices become visible and thereby subject to reflection and critique.

But how are such changes to be introduced to students' already packed requirements? One solution we found at UT-Austin was to develop a first-semester course within the canonical music history sequence that introduced key concepts to be revisited and explored in-depth during the chronological music history semesters. This course begins in spring 2017 (a year in the future as I write); our plan involves juxtaposing near-far music case studies, such as Stravinsky's *L'histoire du soldat* with Argentinean tango, in order to explore the role of dance music and musical exoticism in the period of early twentieth-century modernity. While the logic of these two examples is supported by Stravinsky's use of tango rhythm, the introduction of the history of tango also helps to explain the deeper musical significance for Stravinsky's Russian—and Parisian—audiences, who were titillated at that time by the wide popularity of this new "exotic" dance.

The mechanics for introducing such curriculum changes also involve far-distant exercises, along with long-term consensus building. The timeline between developing revisions to the music history sequence in our school took over two years of concerted work, and if one counts previous attempts and brainstorming, nearly six years. The successful passage of this reform involved intensive consensus building and dialogue about concerns regarding curriculum content and priorities. In some ways it was helpful that I had an undergraduate degree in musicology, had been teaching in music departments since finishing my PhD, had been continuing to include examples from Western European art music (WEAM) in my world music courses, and continue to find as much beauty and power in WEAM repertoire items as I do in Ottoman court music, Romani wedding music, contemporary US popular genres, and the like. In discussions with colleagues, it was helpful to find commonalities in music traditions that we care about and for example to be able to draw parallels between the complexity of Ottoman Turkish maqams (256 named melodic modes!) and WEAM tonal structures. As an anthropologically trained ethnomusicologist, I found myself using ethnographic methods in seeking to understand different aesthetic systems that shape the pedagogical goals of my music school colleagues. In addition, the successful passage of these changes by our faculty was considerably eased by the support of upper administration, the report of the College Music Society (Campbell et al. 2014), and an impending NASM review while working through our curriculum committee, holding frequent meetings, and being willing to build consensus through multiple revisions of the semester sequence and its content. Certainly vertical power worked together with horizontal consensus to make these revisions possible.

MOVING FORWARD WITH EMBODIED PEDAGOGY

I offer these examples not as ideal models but as illustrations of my own efforts that inevitably require ongoing tweaking and responses to failure. I do believe that focusing on larger goals can help guide us all to be better teachers. Embodied pedagogy reminds us to integrate concepts such as critical thinking, flipped classrooms, thinking across the curriculum, and movement exercises toward the goal of increasing student understanding. Conscious integration of far-near experiences is productive in estranging students' own taken-for-granted perceptions while also generating empathy to help bridge the distance between self and perceptions of others. Integrating musical analysis with contextual associations demonstrates both the complexity of musical sound and its ability to shape human experience. Yet to effectively transform students' perception of the world around them, we must constantly de-exoticize that which seems far and hold at a new distance that which seemed near.

Ethnomusicology as a discipline has a great deal to offer music pedagogy and teaching in general. As researchers, we constantly encounter new experiences that challenge our perceptions of the world and are called upon to translate these experiences into broader and deeper knowledge of how we become human through sound. However, we in the discipline have been slow to recognize the implications of our research for pedagogy. Since our field demands that we address the question of why and how music matters, we need to allow that question to shape our pedagogy. Colleagues in canonical music programs complain about not having sufficient time in music history and music theory courses. Many of us who have been teaching world music are familiar with these challenges; we have long been required to teach courses under the impossibly ecumenical title of World Music and are expected to cover centuries and countless varied regional musical traditions in one semester. Given our focus on why music matters to human beings as a means of guiding the exploration of an incredibly vast set of musical cultures, it may well be time to employ techniques in the teaching all types of music. I propose this based on the efficacy of far-near teaching for embodied pedagogy and argue that embodied pedagogy opens up more sustainable and sustaining methods for effective teaching.

Further, such training better prepares students for encountering social issues outside the classroom, engagement with social justice issues, and a heightened awareness of transnational issues, as well as local diasporic and marginalized communities. For those in training to become professional musicians, such teaching techniques provide broad-based knowledge that prepares such students to engage with a greater variety of musical genres and styles. Those who choose applied musical fields such as archiving, music production and management, music therapy and the like gain a broader knowledge base for musical tools as well as types of musical styles that they are likely to encounter outside the classroom. Those who chose non-music career paths leave the classroom with opened ears and minds, better able to understand both themselves and others in terms of musical sound. By linking aural analytical skills with larger social, political, and historical issues, such enlarged understandings open a pathway for our students in terms of greater agency, ethical choices, and effectiveness in an increasingly complex world.

REFERENCES

Campbell, Patricia, et al. 2014. "Transforming Music Study from Its Foundations: A Manifesto for Progressive Change in the Undergraduate Preparation of Music Majors. Report of the Task Force on the Undergraduate Music Major, November 2014." Conference version. www.mtosmt.org/issues/mto.16.22.1/manifesto.pdf. Accessed January 2, 2017.

Freire, Paulo. 2006. *Pedagogy of the Oppressed*. 30th-anniversary ed. Myra Bergman Ramos, trans. New York: Continuum.

Geertz, Clifford. 1983. *Local Knowledge. Further Essays in Interpretive Anthropology*. New York: Basic Books.

Huebner, Steven. 1992. *The Operas of Charles Gounod*. Oxford: Clarendon Press.

Johnson, Mark. 1987. *The Body in the Mind. The Bodily Basis of Meaning, Imagination, and Reason*. Chicago: University of Chicago.

———. 2015. "Embodied Understanding." *Frontiers in Psychology*, Vol. 6 No. 875 (June 29), 1–8.

Nettl, Bruno. 1995. *Heartland Excursions: Ethnomusicological Perspectives on Schools of Music*. Champaign-Urbana: University of Illinois Press.

McClary, Susan. 2002 [1991]. *Feminine Endings. Music, Gender and Sexuality*. Minneapolis: University of Minnesota Press.

Ricoeur, Paul. 1981. *Hermeneutics and the Human Sciences*. John B. Thompson, ed. and trans. Cambridge: Cambridge University Press.

———. 1991. "Mimesis and Imitation." In *Reflection and Imagination*, Mario J. Valdez, ed., 137–154. Toronto: University of Toronto Press.

Townsend, Robert. 2001. *Carmen: A Hip-Hopera*. New York: New Line Television; MTV.

CHAPTER 11

Standing in the Shadows of Mozart

Music Education, World Music, and Curricular Change

DEBORAH BRADLEY

The need for curricular change in post-secondary education has long been a topic of concern within most disciplines of music. In 2014, the College Music Society (CMS) released a report recommending curricular changes for undergraduate music majors (Campbell et al. 2014). That the CMS task force chose to call their report a manifesto speaks to the perceived urgency for changes across the music disciplines: performance, musicology and ethnomusicology, theory, and music education. In this chapter, I address the need for change from a social justice perspective, focusing on music teacher education in large public and private university settings. Following from that discussion, I look at some of the historical and current impediments to change unique to music teacher education and that may be considered reflective of a culture of whiteness in post-secondary institutions. In keeping with this volume's guiding principles, the chapter concludes with examples of program revisions in music education that have begun to address the types of changes needed, along with a discussion of changes necessary to develop pedagogies of social justice for music teacher education in the twenty-first century.

DISCURSIVE FRAMEWORK

My perspective throughout the chapter reflects my concern for a post-secondary music education that embodies and enacts social justice. While social justice has become a buzzword in education over the past decade, social justice perspectives emerge from concerns related to issues of racism, gender bias, biases based on ability and dis/ability, sexual orientation, socio-economic status, language, and more. Social justice, therefore, serves as an umbrella term covering a wide range of concerns that operate systemically to produce inequities for different groups and individuals; thus, a social justice perspective brings many complex issues to the question of what constitutes appropriate curricula for twenty-first-century music majors. As Bowman writes, social justice is perhaps better thought of as a "kind of *process*—an ethical process, reliant on our capacities for reflexivity and reciprocity" (Bowman 2007, 4; italics in original).

Throughout this chapter, I discuss social justice concerns utilizing an antiracism[1] discursive framework: a "pedagogical discourse and academic and political practice" (Dei 2000, 13) within the range of perspectives that represent social justice discourses. Antiracism is "an action-oriented, educational and political strategy for institutional and systemic change that addresses the issues of racism and the *interlocking systems of social oppression* (sexism, classism, heterosexism, ableism)" (13; italics added). While my antiracism analysis focuses on race, this should not be read as prioritizing race over other forms of injustice; issues of oppression through any single lens, such as race or gender, are always already interwoven with others.

I also wish to make clear to readers that my use of the term *music education* within this chapter usually refers to degree programs serving students who seek careers as music teachers. I use the term *music teacher education* to distinguish such programs and the term *music education* to describe all music degree programs. While all music programs undoubtedly provide an education in, through, and about music, there are a host of external pressures affecting the content of music teacher education specifically. These must be taken into consideration in any discussion of change; they combine with other factors I discuss below to keep curricular changes "standing in the shadows of Mozart"; in other words, marginalized within a context that continues to prioritize the Western canon above all other forms of music and "musicking" (Small 1998).

GUIDING PRINCIPLES IN THIS CHAPTER

Although this book's main focus is change, my chapter also critiques the current situation in music teacher education as a way to "chart a path forward within the particularities of conservatory or music school culture" (Moore,

1. In the United States, antiracism is typically referred to as *critical multiculturalism*. Both terms represent similar political and education approaches to issues of social justice in education.

Chapter 1 in this volume). From a social justice and antiracism perspective, commitments to community, practical concerns for future music teachers, and concerns for global awareness are fundamental concerns and include such commitments as guiding principles. As such, while they are not categories addressed explicitly within this chapter the principles should be apparent in the philosophical discussions throughout.

CALLS FOR CURRICULAR CHANGE IN MUSIC TEACHER EDUCATION

Within the discipline of music teacher education, calls for reforms to diversify the curriculum date back to the early 1900s but became more urgent during the Tanglewood Symposium of 1967, which advocated the incorporation of a greater diversity of musical styles, past and present. Although some small changes to public school music curricula resulted from Tanglewood, the Vision 20/20 symposium of 1999 reiterated the need to motivate the discipline toward action, in recognition of the lack of substantive reforms to date. Although by the 1990s "the study of multicultural music had become a curricular norm," and technological advances had begun to affect teachers' work significantly, few of these changes were represented meaningfully in music teacher education programs. The need for MENC (the Music Educators National Conference) to undertake the 20/20 symposium was inspired by exactly the same circumstances as the Tanglewood Symposium (Mark 2000, 28). That the CMS task force has now issued a call for curricular change sixteen years after Vision 20/20 illustrates the continuing lack of substantive changes to music education curricula.

THE DISCOURSE OF WHITENESS IN HIGHER EDUCATION

European universities have played an important role in cultural production and reproduction in the Western world since the founding of the University of Bologna in AD 1088. Although the University of Karueein existed in Fez, Morocco, as early as AD 859 and is considered by many the oldest continuously operating university, and the University of Nalanda flourished in Takshashila, Bharat (India), from 600 BC to AD 500, the University of Bologna typically receives credit as the "first" university.[2] Thus, the "actual first" institutions of higher learning, along with those of ancient Greece, Persia, Rome, Byzantium, and ancient China, are not included in such lists due to their

2. https://en.wikipedia.org/wiki/List_of_oldest_universities_in_continuous_operation (accessed January 31, 2017).

"cultural, historical, structural and juristic dissimilarities from the medieval European university from which the modern [Western] university evolved." A quick browse through web pages describing these non-European institutions suggests that the subjects studied there were remarkably similar to course offerings found in colleges and universities today, including mathematics, philosophy, grammar, languages, medicine, law, and music. I do not believe that their lack of recognition results from a dissimilarity of curricular content compared to those in Europe as much as it does from what Bonilla-Silva (2008) calls the culture of "historically White colleges and universities" (HWCUs)—institutions with histories, demographics, curricula, a climate, and a set of symbols and traditions that embody, signify, and reproduce whiteness. Leaving the universities of Muslim culture or ancient India off the list of "oldest universities" represents a subtle discrediting of the scholarship and intellectual curiosity of people of color (Asante and Mazama 2002). It suggests a strategy that upholds Eurocentrism through a "powerful rhetorical device for underscoring the superiority of the West . . . to position it as 'ahead' of all others along some cosmic timeline" (Morning 2015, 193).

My point here is that calls for change in schools of music convey a need not only for curricular change but, more profoundly, institutional transformation at a cultural level that recognizes typical university music studies as indicative of the "racialized social system of white privilege" (Mills 2003, 36). This system "involves a certain kind of objectification in which formally defined credentials or qualifications become a mechanism for creating and sustaining inequalities" (Bourdieu 1991, 24). Music schools need to understand the racial assumptions that underlie classical music studies in higher education, as well as how pervasively those assumptions manifest themselves in our behaviors, our educational processes, and educational products. This is particularly crucial in music teacher education if the goal is to prepare teachers to teach in diverse settings (Howard 2006), with real understanding of culturally relevant pedagogies (Ladson-Billings 1995).

In talking about a culture of whiteness, it is important to reiterate that whiteness is not about white people; whiteness is a pervasive ideology that emerged over time and solidified during the era of colonial conquest to justify the dominance of one group over others. Whiteness is ubiquitous; it represents the societal norm of North America. The ideology of whiteness serves as a form of "social amnesia" (Peter McLaren 1998; cited in Castagno 2014) that obfuscates our implication in maintaining systems of privilege and oppression.

Whiteness as social amnesia may represent at least one reason why curricular change has thus far occurred primarily through additive measures—one new course here, one new course there. As Hayes (2015) asserts, "it has been easier for the department to 'add and stir' in regard to curricular innovation, than to examine, in a civil manner, the musical, cultural, and philosophical values that underlie our current curriculum" (5). As a result, institution-wide diversity policies within the university's culture of whiteness and departmental attempts to diversify curriculum compel us "to embrace diversity-related policy and practice uncritically and to praise any effort tagged with words like multicultural, diversity, and equality. But these are often tropes for policies and practices that do very little to advance equity or stop injustice" (Castagno 2014, Kindle 198–200). Although many individual educators aspire to make music teacher education inclusive and socially just, the traditional focus on music as aesthetic object occludes the social issues embedded in music. While the musics of the European canon form an important part of North American cultural heritage, we need to also recognize that the dominance of Enlightenment narratives in music education philosophy impede our understanding of the ways in which we are implicated in systems of oppression (Bowman 2007, 16).

Looking more deeply at these issues often creates discomfort for those unaccustomed to confronting the culture of whiteness that undergirds North American institutions of higher education. Rather than address the realities of social inequality in education, we may focus instead on the perceived beauty and universal virtues of European-derived music and thus view music teacher education as a "nice" or uplifting field of study (Ladson-Billings 1998). Token attempts at diversification, such as the addition of one course in multicultural musics or the inclusion of one world music ensemble in the music department, are similarly viewed as "nice" (or exotic) add-ons. They suggest a perceived openness to diversity that actually functions to limit possibilities for diversity. "This nice approach to diversity is consistent with, and also reifies, whiteness. As such, it cannot possibly tackle the inequity it is meant to address" (Castagno 2014, Kindle 193–195).

IMPEDIMENTS TO CHANGE AS TECHNOLOGIES OF WHITENESS

Although the 1990s witnessed an increase in multicultural resources for K–12 education, little has been done at the institutional level to develop curricula that provide teacher candidates with what is crucial: meaningful opportunities to experience diverse musical traditions or to think about the difficult questions surrounding the arts related to race, ethnicity, gender, socio-economics, ability-disability, language, and so forth. Resources alone do little to challenge dominant ideologies; Ladson-Billings (1996) asserts that multicultural theoreticians must "reexamine the ways in which their work reinforces the practice of 'weak' multiculturalism (Sleeter 1989), which leaves patriarchy, hierarchy, sexism, and racism unexamined and firmly in place, both in classrooms and in the lives of students" (254).

The language of the guidelines for music teacher education in many US State Department of Public Instruction (DPI) documents remains not only Eurocentric but in some cases implicitly restricts repertoire to the canon, focusing teacher education on the techniques of teaching band, choir, and orchestra, with only token acknowledgement of the need to study noncanonical musical practices (Bradley 2011).

In addition to stringent DPI guidelines for teacher education, music teacher education students must pass content exams before being licensed to teach. These exams do not measure musicianship skills such as creativity or improvisation but are heavily centered on formal musical knowledge (Elliott 1995), particularly the knowledge of the Western canon and its history of Western music theory. Furthermore, in the United States, e-portfolio assessments (edTPA) are now required for teacher education in thirty-five states and the District of Columbia.[3] These assessment packages are sold and administered by the textbook manufacturer Pearson.[4] Universities in some states support rather than resist edTPA through collaborative Teacher Performance Assessment Consortiums, adding yet another layer of accountability for music teacher education faculty. However, the National Association for Multicultural Educators argues that "the practice of critical multicultural education cannot, by its nature, be standardized, nor can the development of teachers who will engage critical multicultural education in their classrooms" (NAME 2014). Indeed, initial research into edTPA effectiveness suggests that despite the infusion of multicultural topics, edTPA generally "hindered critical, in-depth reflection vital to preparing teacher candidates (TC's) to teach diverse populations" (Liu and Milman 2013, 125). Thus edTPA serves as another technology of whiteness in higher education.

Music education students rely upon post-secondary institutions to teach them not only how to teach but what to teach, yet they enter their teacher education programs with a sometimes naive understanding of the complexities of pedagogy. Undergraduate music teacher education students-as-consumers demand "practical courses" in classroom management, conducting, instrumental technique, and lesson planning (to some degree in response to edTPA); they hope to graduate and be able to outpredict the uncertainties that lie ahead. Music teacher educators respond with forms of pedagogy that lead to narrow, canonical specialization (Allsup 2015, 12). Coursework in the so-called elementary and secondary music education areas often slavishly focuses on "how-to's" of teaching children to match pitch, read notation, and the like within rigid paradigms—what Regelski (2002b) labels *methodolatry*. Teacher education becomes "teacher training" in these situations. As Bowman (2002)

---

3. http://edtpa.aacte.org/state-policy (accessed January 31, 2017).
4. http://www.edtpa.com/Home.aspx (accessed January 31, 2017).

argues, "when we neglect the distinction between education and training, we risk conflating the two and accepting the latter as an acceptable substitute for the former" (64).

WHITENESS AND PHILOSOPHICAL PERSPECTIVES

Aesthetic philosophies of music have held a foundational, and restrictive, role within music teacher education; their relationship to noncanonical musics and to the culture of whiteness cannot be overlooked, given that the field of aesthetics emerged during the Enlightenment and served to justify colonial conquest (Bradley 2012). In music teacher education, calls to abandon aesthetic ways of thinking about music came to the fore of discourse in the 1990s (Elliott 1995; Bowman 1994b, 1991, 1994a; Regelski 2002a), yet music education as aesthetic education (Reimer 1970, 1989, 2003) remains a prominent—and in some places, the only—philosophy for music teacher education. As many have argued, a focus on music as works "seriously distorts our understanding of music itself" (Bowman 1994a, 51). This "history of denial . . . has put us in what is no longer a tenable position for our understanding of musical cultures, either past or present" (McClary 2000, 8). Understanding a variety of musical cultures provides a crucial foundation for teachers entering diverse classrooms and enables effective communication between teachers and students. Additive approaches to diversity, as mere acts of inclusion, however well intended, amount to tokenism and become "diversions from the 'real stuff' that remains the 'legitimate' academic core of most music programs" (Bowman 2007, 13). Single-course additions rarely challenge a dominant ideology of whiteness. Music education cannot become more socially just until it becomes more inclusive of diversity—and this means diversity of musics, peoples, voices, values, and more (15).

My goal is not to dismiss the European musical canon but to decenter it. Music teacher education must move beyond methodolatry and token multicultural courses. When students explore the ways that musicking of all kinds contributes to human life, within a curriculum aimed at challenging dominant ideologies, they begin to recognize the cultural amnesia of whiteness hiding within the enormous shadow cast by Mozart and other masters of the European canon.

COLONIALISM AND THE REPRODUCTION OF WHITENESS

The cultural amnesia of whiteness may make it difficult to recognize that our affinities for noncanonical musics emerge from the history of colonial conquest. We are complicit despite well-intended efforts to redress colonialism's aftermath of injustice (Solís 2004). Within music studies, the production and reproduction of culture over time engrains dispositions and particular ways of behaving and responding, making them seem altogether natural (Bourdieu 1991). Despite music's abilities to encourage nondominant relationships (Schippers 2010, Small 1998), our colonial heritage and assumptions about what counts as "good music" reify music schools as cultures of whiteness that nicely "provide space" for the study of other cultures and other musics, without changing any basic operating premises. Changing foundational assumptions represents the greatest challenge facing the curricular reform movement.

SUNSHINE ON A CLOUDY DAY: MOVING OUT OF MOZART'S SHADOW

If music teacher education is to become proactive in preparing students to teach music in a way that does not reify whiteness in classrooms and community ensembles but instead affirms, celebrates, and interrogates the role of music in diverse societies, then music teacher education and ethnomusicology in particular ought to work together for the types of change that both disciplines claim to value. Through collaboration, we can bring about changes that could position music studies in the forefront of serious efforts to diversify curriculum and teach for social justice.

Although single-course approaches to change have been justifiably critiqued, an optimistic viewpoint might consider them initial attempts to resist the status quo, to develop interdisciplinary cooperation and an expansion of curricula. In faculties with small music education and ethnomusicology departments, cooperation may represent the only way to move forward. As Levine's research indicates (Levine and Kohut, Chapter 3 in this volume), in small liberal arts colleges such changes often are accomplished more easily than in large institutions; however, changes are occurring within some public universities as well. For example, at Texas State University's Latin Music Studies program, approval has been granted for a minor in mariachi as part of the (undergraduate) music education degree. Texas State is designated as a Hispanic-serving institution (HSI) and operates as an "emerging research institution" (see Pedroza, Chapter 7 in this volume); thus, it may be influenced by different constraints related to curriculum. My suggestions for change in this chapter are oriented toward large public and private (typically R1) universities whose music teacher education programs march to the beat of state accountability standards and institutional bureaucracies that reinforce cultures of whiteness.

HOPEFUL BEGINNINGS

In my personal experience at two large public (R1) universities, I have not encountered the type of cross-discipline activity I believe necessary for twenty-first century music teacher education. Even so, I do not wish to disparage the small changes that have taken place at those locations. For example, at the University of Toronto, all music undergrads are required to take a course entitled Music as Culture, and music teacher education students must take at least one world music ensemble concurrently with a course entitled Music Education in Cultural Perspective. Although the simultaneity of the requirements is well intentioned, access to world music ensembles is limited, and registering for the desired ensemble in the same semester as the Cultural Perspectives course is sometimes not possible, even for students who pay close attention to course offerings and plan accordingly. This is one area in which ethnomusicology and music teacher education could collaborate proactively, so that music education students can access and participate in multiple ensembles (at schools so privileged). In return, ethnomusicology students preparing for careers in higher education might benefit from access to pedagogy courses typically restricted to music education majors. Performance, theory, history, and composition majors may likewise develop broader cultural understandings through access to pedagogy and ethnomusicology courses. A vision for change throughout schools of music involves the critical examination of subdisciplinary course content in all areas, with the goal of incorporating more diverse and socially aware content.

The Cultural Perspectives course described above serves as an example of a course that does more than add and stir; it focuses on world music pedagogies through a social justice lens, interrogating issues of colonialism, identity and representation, race, gender, and other issues of social justice (Schippers 2010). The course also strives to help students understand the privilege represented by their very presence in the music program of a prestigious university. In order to minimize concerns for cultural appropriation when studying noncanonical musical cultures, expert practitioners engage students in music-making experiences each semester that are both respectful of the culture and that address its subtleties.

During the five years I taught at the University of Wisconsin, discussions were undertaken to overhaul the music education curriculum and change the focus from pedagogical methodologies to a multicultural and social justice orientation. Although the original goal was a major revamp, extended discussion over the past five years has yielded what is probably best described as retention of the basic content of the (former) approved program but the addition of new content and experiences. Even so, students at UW-Madison will gain increased opportunities for exposure to world musics, popular musics,

diverse vocal music styles, community music experiences, jazz, and composing and arranging within a philosophy of social justice.[5] As of this writing,
the new program awaits approval from the Wisconsin Department of Public
Instruction.[6]

MOVING OUT OF THE SHADOW

The music teacher education program at the University of Washington stands
as an exemplar for moving beyond add and stir. Since the 1990s, the program
has ensured that music education students not only have access to ethnomusicology courses and ensembles but that several of their degree requirements
emerge from the collaboration between music teacher education and ethnomusicology studies. Music education students take a minimum of three credit
hours from an assortment of ethnomusicology offerings that range from an
introductory survey course of world music cultures to courses that study the
music of specific regions to ethnomusicology seminars that require students
to complete fieldwork projects in the community with local musicians.[7] As
part of subdisciplinary degree requirements, music teacher education students take an additional three-credit course entitled Ethnomusicology in the
Schools; a central component of this course involves travel to the Yakama
Native American Reservation and into surrounding Hispanic communities
for week-long residencies (homestays), so that students might dialogue musically with kids, families, and teachers living in poor, rural, or remote regions.[8]
All of the various ethnomusicology offerings engage with issues of gender,
race, class, acculturation and enculturation, hybridity, colonialism, nationalism and transnationalism, and historic and contemporary practices. In addition, through the ethnomusicology department, visiting artists offer courses
each semester; music education students must enroll in at least one of these
courses, but many opt to enroll multiple times over the duration of their
degree programs.

Though University of Washington music teacher education students
confront issues of social justice in courses such as Ethnomusicology in the
Schools and Music in Education, they are also woven into methods courses
such as Music for Children, Instrumental Music Methods, and Choral Music

5. T. Dobbs, private communication, November 6, 2014.
6. Related to this revamp, the ethnomusicology department at UW-Madison has
shrunk considerably through retirements without replacement hires and transfers
from the School of Music to other related disciplinary areas, such as African studies.
7. https://music.washington.edu/bachelor-music-music-education-instrumental-
emphasis; also, https://music.washington.edu/bachelor-music-music-education-
vocal-emphasis (accessed January 31, 2017).
8. P. Campbell, private communication, August 8, 2015.

Methods. In addition, both music education and ethnomusicology students have access to an upper level (undergraduate) course in community music that many music education students opt for and that further underscores issues of social justice.[9]

The music teacher education program at the University of California at Los Angeles (UCLA) is noteworthy because of its unique philosophy and goals. The program "prepares future music educators to teach in traditional school music programs, cultivates dispositions that encourage innovation and change in the profession, and nurtures socially responsible practices in the classroom and community."[10] The program prepares "future teachers for the large-ensemble tradition still prevalent in American schools while simultaneously challenging future teachers to become curricular innovators" (Heuser 2014, 108) through a "juxtapositional pedagogy." The program contrasts musical learning experiences typically taught in separate methods classes and "places them together in a single instructional setting to create spaces where the nature of musical thinking and learning can be explored" (108). This provides opportunities for students to "experience different styles of music learning, to reflect on the multiple processes involved in music learning, and to develop initial understandings of music psychology and music education philosophy" (108). Within the UCLA program, state-mandated "diversity requirements" are met within general education courses, but social justice concerns are introduced from the outset into music education coursework discussions. I believe the concept of juxtapositional pedagogy and curriculum development offers promise for small and large music departments alike; of special note is the way the juxtapositions acknowledge both current expectations of students and prospective employers (school boards) while simultaneously developing pre-service teachers' understandings of music's role in the life of a community. Examples of juxtapositional pedagogy include pairing the study of string ensemble repertoire with that of a mariachi group, a jazz ensemble with an iPad band,[11] and choral methods with gospel choir (113). "Individuals from the entire spectrum of music studies may participate, including those majoring in musicology and ethnomusicology," (114) each according to their respective levels of expertise. Concerns for social justice could easily become integral to juxtapositional approaches and thus reinforce the content of general education diversity coursework.

The Herberger Institute at Arizona State University provides a social justice model emerging from institution-wide concerns for broad access to higher

9. P. Campbell, private communication, August 8, 2015.

10. http://www.music.ucla.edu/music-education-concentration-undergraduate (accessed January 31, 2017).

11. iPad bands are formed by students "playing" different instruments on iPads, using apps such as GarageBand or other sound sampling technologies. iPad bands help to meet state requirements for technology in teacher education programs.

education. The issue of access is beyond the scope of this chapter but represents yet another area in which whiteness stymies institutional cultural change. For a compelling discussion of this issue, see "Listening for Whiteness: Hearing Racial Politics in Undergraduate School Music" (Koza 2008).

ASU's president issued goals for access and diversity for 2015, hoping to "maintain the fundamental principle of accessibility to all students qualified to study at a research university" and "match Arizona's socioeconomic diversity."[12] Within the Herberger Institute, a new BA in music degree program known as the "individualized track" was launched in fall 2016. It allows for students to be admitted to music studies without auditioning for a studio. Students gain admission to the program by providing evidence of musicianship on alternative instruments or in noncanonical genres. Once admitted, a musicology adviser aids students in choosing or even creating ensembles and choosing electives to support student goals. Students may take music education courses as electives within this program, ultimately enabling them to apply to the state for teacher certification.[13] "The consistent emphasis for the university and the institute is to get both the faculty and the student population to reflect the state and the nation."[14] In the music teacher education program, issues of social justice are addressed throughout music education coursework, beginning with introductory courses. The ASU program exemplifies how strong leadership can drive significant change.

One characteristic of all the foregoing examples of curricular experimentation is a shift away from aesthetic perspectives to thinking about music as a human activity both productive of and embodying culture. Once music educators begin to focus on what music does in and for human life and become less concerned with curating musical works or focusing on particular teaching methodolatries, we can move into what Brian Pertl has described as the liminal space "untethered by what went before" (Pertl 2015). Studying any of the music disciplines from the perspective of music as relationships (Small 1998) enables discussion of the embedded issues of gender, race, class, sexual orientation, ability, and dis/ability and minimizes the implied importance of canonical musics within conservatory models. Pertl's description of the Lawrence University music program and its focus on multimusicality offers an encouraging model for changing the institutional culture of the music conservatory. Although at present music teacher education students at Lawrence are required to take only one world music course, the overall focus within the

---

12. https://president.asu.edu/about/asucharter (accessed June 3, 2016).

13. Arizona offers several routes to teacher certification, including institutional recommendation (IR) via the bachelor of music (education) degree and by direct application to the state, an avenue open to students who may have another music degree. This route requires taking education courses as additional qualifications in order to meet state requirements for music teachers.

14. S. Stauffer, private communication, September 7, 2015.

program emphasizes creative and improvisational attitudes critical for teachers, much in the way the UCLA program does. Lawrence also emphasizes connections to the local community. I hope that as the program continues to develop, the same opportunities to gain multimusicality available to performance majors will be offered to music teacher education students.

In some cases, change may emerge from student initiatives; for example, student-led groups such as contemporary a cappella ensembles often require the involvement of faculty members as advisors. In these situations, faculty members may find themselves acquiring musicianship skills related to vernacular musics with which they were previously unfamiliar. As faculty become more comfortable with new styles of musical expression, they are better able to share this knowledge with students in standard music major coursework (Stewart 2015). This sort of change may represent one way to reorient institutional culture and course content from within (see Pertl, Chapter 2 in this volume).

What might an "ideal" music teacher education program for the twenty-first century look like? I imagine it would incorporate all of the best elements from the various programs discussed in this chapter, including a strong focus on social justice imbued throughout coursework, multiple opportunities to experience musics beyond the canon in meaningful ways, and pedagogies that focus on relationships in the classroom as teachers' primary concern (Ladson-Billings 1995, 1994, 2009; Vattel 2015).

Pedagogies addressing the needs of students provide a model for pre-service music teachers that will travel with them into their future classrooms. This includes respect and understanding of cultural differences gained from experiencing other musics, in conjunction with the confrontation of issues related to racism, gender bias, homophobia, socio-economic disadvantage, and so on that emerge from the music. In institutions with large ethnomusicology departments, the incorporation of such content might be accomplished through the type of cooperation between music teacher education and ethnomusicology visible in the University of Washington's program or in the cooperative approach evident in the ASU BA program. In small music departments or those without ethnomusicology faculty, experiences outside of the institution but within the local community could be sought out for pre-service music teachers and students in other music subdisciplines who could also benefit from juxtaposing classical and vernacular musical genres and from working in the community with expert practitioners.

IN CLOSING

In this chapter, I have presented arguments related to curricular change through a theoretical lens of antiracism. As such, the chapter includes critiques of current practices in order to locate opportunities from which change may emerge. Thus I have explored what may hinder change by looking at the institutional culture of whiteness that not only limits what can legitimately be taught in higher education music studies but also limits access to those studies.

Developing truly appropriate pedagogies and curriculum for the twenty-first century suggests more than changes in coursework or the inclusion of a few more genres of music. While I agree that such changes are crucial to education for the present and the future, in my argument these represent only first steps, not ultimate solutions. In order to fully move pedagogies and curricula into the twenty-first century, we need to candidly address the institutional culture of whiteness undergirding assumptions within most college and university music curricula. This in turn will allow us to critically reflect on the undesirable aspects of our current musical and instructional practices and to acknowledge the potential for current practices to miseducate—even to dehumanize. Without due consideration for what besides "the music" is being learned, skilled performances of the most beautiful of musics may be harmful in ways that are not immediately apparent (Bowman 2002, 64). Confronting cultures of whiteness includes abandoning the Enlightenment's aesthetic philosophies of music (Elliott 1995, Elliott and Silverman 2014, Guilbault 2014, Wong 2014) and fully accepting that music, as a human activity, plays a critical role in the quality of both individual and societal human life. I believe enacting curricula of and for social justice emerges naturally from this perspective. The question then becomes one of instilling in a new generation of musicians a more mature, highly active, creative, and kinder sensibility to the world; in doing so, an education in and through music can play an important role in the creation of "a society that supports its people, cares for its planetary home, thinks forward as a norm, and is filled with individuals who both think and feel beyond themselves" (Vattel 2015, para. 7).

Embracing and enacting such change, particularly within music teacher education, calls for courage in the face of strong resistance related to institutional inertia or from change-resistant colleagues who may feel threatened. At the present time, much of the work toward change falls on the shoulders of courageous individuals in music teacher education, ethnomusicology, and other music disciplines. Yet institutional examples of change already exist, as described in this chapter; these need to be studied in depth, to learn from their successes as well as their missteps.

As institutional cultures begin to shift to concerns for educating the whole student, for true diversity of both students and faculty, and embrace at the curricular level the many wonderful ways in which people make music, cultures of whiteness will slowly devolve. Thus I stand with the other authors in this volume, each in his or her own way working to bring music studies out of the shadows of Mozart, to distance them from Enlightenment-era ideologies, and into the twenty-first century.

REFERENCES

Allsup, Randall Everett. 2015. "Music Teacher Quality and the Problem of Routine Expertise." *Philosophy of Music Education Review*, Vol. 23 No. 1, 5–24.

Asante, Molefi Kete, and Ama Mazama. 2002. *Egypt vs. Greece and the American Academy*. Chicago: African American Images.

Bonilla-Silva, E. 2008. "Racism, Discrimination, Colorblindness, and the Diversity Puzzle at HWCUs." University of Wisconsin–Madison Diversity Forum, Madison, September 23.

Bourdieu, Pierre. 1991. "Editor's Introduction." In *Language and Symbolic Power*, John B. Thompson, ed., 302. Cambridge, MA: Harvard University Press.

Bowman, W. 2007. "Who's Asking (Who's Answering): Theorizing Social Justice in Music Education." *Action, Criticism and Theory for Music Education*, Vol. 6 No. 4, 1–20.

———. 2002. "Educating Musically." In *The New Handbook of Research on Music Teaching and Learning*, Richard Colwell and Carol Richardson, eds., 63–84. New York: Oxford University Press.

———. 1994a. "Sound, Sociality, and Music: Part 1." *Quarterly Journal of Music Teaching and Learning*, Vol. 5 No. 3, 50–59.

———. 1994b. "Sound, Society, and Music 'Proper.'" *Philosophy of Music Education Review*, Vol. 2 No. 2, 14–24.

———. 1991. "An Essay Review of Bennett Reimer's *A Philosophy of Music Education*." *Quarterly Journal of Music Teaching and Learning*, Vol. 2 No. 3, 76–87.

Bradley, Deborah. 2012. "Good for What, Good for Whom? Decolonizing Music Education Philosophies." In *The Oxford Handbook of Philosophy in Music Education*, Wayne Bowman and Ana Lucia Frega, eds., 409–433. New York: Oxford University Press.

———. 2011. "In the Space between the Rock and the Hard Place: State Teacher Certification Guidelines and Music Education for Social Justice." *Journal of Aesthetic Education*, Vol. 45 No. 4, 79–96.

Campbell, Patricia S., et al. 2014. "Transforming Music Study from Its Foundations: A Manifesto for Progressive Change in the Undergraduate Preparation of Music Majors." Missoula, MT: College Music Society. http://symposium. music.org/index.php?option=com_k2&view=item&id=11118:transforming-music-study-from-its-foundations-a-manifesto-for-progressive-change-in-the-undergraduate-preparation-of-music-majors&Itemid=126. Accessed December 28 2016.

Castagno, Angelina E. 2014. *Educated in Whiteness. Good Intentions and Diversity in Schools*. Kindle ed. Minneapolis: University of Minnesota Press.

Dei, George J. Sefa, and Agnes Calliste, eds. 2000. *Power, Knowledge and Anti-racism Education*. Halifax: Fernwood.

Elliott, David J. 1995. *Music Matters*. New York: Oxford University Press.

Elliott, David J., and Marissa Silverman. 2014. *Music Matters. A Philosophy of Music Education*. 2nd ed. New York: Oxford University Press.

Guilbault, Jocelyne. 2014. "Politics of Ethnomusicological Knowledge Production and Circulation." *Ethnomusicology*, Vol. 58 No. 1, 321–326.

Hayes, Eileen M. 2015. "Creativity, Improvisation, and Diversity: Oh My!" *SEM Newsletter*. Vol. 49 No. 3, 5-6.

Heuser, Frank. 2014. "Juxtapositional Pedagogy as an Organizing Principle in University Music Education Programs." In *Promising Practices in 21st Century Music Teacher Education*, Michele Kaschub and Janice Smith, eds., 103–125. New York: Oxford University Press.

Howard, Gary R. 2006. *We Can't Teach What We Don't Know. White Teachers, Multiracial Schools*. 2nd ed. New York: Teachers College Press.

Koza, J. E. 2008. "Listening for Whiteness: Hearing Racial Politics in Undergraduate School Music." *Philosophy of Music Education Review*, Vol. 16 No. 2, 145–155.

Ladson-Billings, Gloria. 2009/1994. *The Dreamkeepers. Successful Teachers of African American Children*. San Francisco: Jossey-Bass.

———. 1998. "Just What Is Critical Race Theory and What's It Doing in a Nice Field like Education?" *Qualitative Studies in Education*, Vol. 11 No. 1, 7–24.

———. 1996. "'Your Blues Ain't Like Mine': Keeping Issues of Race and Racism on the Multicultural Agenda." *Theory into Practice*, Vol. 35 No. 4, 248–255.

———. 1995. "Toward a Theory of Culturally Relevant Pedagogy." *American Educational Research Journal*, Vol. 32 No. 3, 465–491.

Liu, Laura B., and Natalie B Milman. 2013. "Year One Implications of a Teacher Performance Assessment's Impact on Multicultural Education across a Secondary Education Teacher Preparation Program." *Action in Teacher Education*, Vol. 35 No. 2, 125–142. doi: 10.1080/01626620.2013.775971.

Mark, Michael. 2000. "From Tanglewood to Tallahassee in 32 Years." *Music Educators Journal*, Vol. 86 No. 5, 25–28.

McClary, Susan. 2000. *Conventional Wisdom. The Content of Musical Form*. Ernest Bloch Lectures. Berkeley: University of California Press.

McLaren, Peter. 1998. "White Terror and Oppositional Agency: Towards a Critical Multiculturalism." In *Multiculturalism: A Critical Reader*. David Theo Goldberg, ed., 45-74. Malden, Mass: Blackwell.

Mills, Charles W. 2003. "White Supremacy as Sociopolitical System." In *White Out. The Continuing Significance of Racism*, Ashley W. Doane and E. Bonilla-Silva, eds., 33–48. New York: Routledge.

Morning, Ann. 2015. "Scientific Racism Redux? The Many Lives of a Troublesome Idea." *Du Bois Review: Social Science Research on Race*, Vol. 12 No. 1, 187–199. doi: 10.1017/S1742058X1500003X.

NAME. 2014. "NAME Position Statement on the edTPA." National Association of Multicultural Educators. Available at http://www.nameorg.org/docs/Statement-rr-edTPA-1-21-14.pdf. Accessed June 5, 2016.

Pertl, Brian. 2015. "Building the 21st Century Music Program through Cultural Rather Than Curricular Change." In *CMS Webinar Series*. College Music Society. http://dx.doi.org/10.18177/sym.2015.55.fr.10876. Accessed July 31, 2015.

Regelski, T. A. 2002a. "Critical Theory and Praxis: Professionalizing Music Education." MayDay Colloquium 2002. Amherst, MA, June 2002.

———. 2002b. "On 'Methodolatry' and Music Teaching as Critical and Reflective Praxis." *Philosophy of Music Education Review*, Vol. 10 No. 2, 102–123.

Reimer, Bennett. 2003. *A Philosophy of Music Education. Advancing the Vision*. 3rd ed. Upper Saddle River, NJ: Prentice Hall. 1st ed. 1970.

————. 1989. *A Philosophy of Music Education*. 2nd ed. Englewood Cliffs, NJ: Prentice-Hall.

————. 1970. *A Philosophy of Music Education*. 1st ed. Englewood Cliffs, NJ: Prentice-Hall.

Schippers, Huib. 2010. *Facing the Music. Shaping Music Education from a Global Perspective*. New York: Oxford University Press.

Small, Christopher. 1998. *Musicking. The Meanings of Performing and Listening, Music/ Culture*. Hanover, NH: University Press of New England.

Solís, Ted. 2004. *Performing Ethnomusicology. Teaching and Representation in World Music Ensembles*. Berkeley: University of California Press.

Stewart, Jonathan. 2015. "SIX: Fluid Leadership and Aural Arranging within the Context of Contemporary A Cappella." Ph.D. diss., School of Music in the College of Fine Arts, Boston University.

Vattel, Lucien. 2015. "Know That You Have It / Keys to a Self-Driven, Self-Loving, Self-Supporting Education." Blog post. Accessed September 04, 2015. http:// smartblogs.com/education/2015/09/03/know-that-you-have-it-ke...self- driven-self-loving-self-supporting-education/?utm_source=brief Page 2 of 3.

Wong, Deborah. 2014. "Sound, Silence, Music: Power." *Ethnomusicology*, Vol. 58 No. 2, 347–353.

CHAPTER 12

Making a Living, Making a Life

Balancing Art, Commerce, and Community as a Professional Musician

PAUL KLEMPERER

THE PROFESSIONAL MUSIC LANDSCAPE

To be a professional musician in today's marketplace, regardless of the musical style or tradition in which one performs, is in large part a balancing act. That has been my professional experience and is the underlying theme in much of the literature about careers in music, from practical how-to books to broader academic studies. In this balancing act there is an unavoidable trade-off between acquiring specialized performance expertise and diversified career skills. Which do you prioritize, and how do you find the time for both? In the past, the criteria for success were talent, perseverance, and practice on an instrument: after long years of musical training, often guided by a mentor who provided both artistic guidance and the necessary social connections, the artist followed a predetermined career path. Musicians who could not meet the rigors of this path ultimately adjusted their art to a secondary position, as a sideline or hobby scheduled around their primary work.

But the components of a contemporary musician's career have changed drastically, and the traditional path to professionalism is being supplanted by more eclectic approaches. I found that in addition to learning to play music, I had to learn how to market myself and find (or build) the community I wanted to be part of. My formal music training gave me a technical and intellectual foundation, but I relied on mentors, networking, and a variety of performance opportunities to develop my career, which in turn required pragmatic short-term decisions and the creation of longer-term goals. Conceptual divisions like professional versus amateur or artistic versus commercial didn't fit with my real-world experience, yet they were embedded in my academic training. The scholastic curriculum, rather than taking advantage of community music resources, treated them as extracurricular at best or irrelevant distractions at worst. In hindsight I recognize that community resources have been crucial in helping me adapt academic training to economic realities and be successful as a professional musician.

The twenty-first-century musical landscape has a strong "best of times, worst of times" aspect, primarily because a musician must function as a small business owner as well as an artist regardless of his or her musical skill level. Students of elite art music face the difficult job market as individual entrepreneurs alongside folk and pop artists, in a "Wild West" of unknowns, opportunities, hucksters, and changing business models. Eastman School of Music professor Ramon Ricker advocates entrepreneurial expertise as a complement to musical training, because "to be a successful music professional today you have to be pro-active . . . make something happen."[1]

In addition to musical expertise, other necessary training may include knowledge of business marketing, project management, copyright law, grant writing, as well as fluency with computer software and more. As small business owners, musicians are expected to assemble a team that will help them generate a business model, define and publicize their brand, and market their product to a receptive fan base. These skills, more than musical ability, determine a musician's chances of success. Unfortunately, curricula for music education lag behind in teaching these skills as part of preparation for a career in music.

One indicator of recent developments is the changing focus of the annual South by Southwest (SXSW) music conference, held in my home base of Austin, Texas. I've watched it grow since its inception in 1987. There has been a steady shift away from strategies for success within established paradigms (getting hired, getting signed), to strategies for how to do it yourself, be your own record label, your own publishing company, your own music business. The speakers and panels hammer home the point more fervently each year that you must create your own franchise, no matter what kind of music you play.

Even specialist musicians must be more eclectic than in decades past. The boundaries between folk, popular, and art music have increasingly blurred (globally as well as within European-based musics). Hybrid styles, nontraditional performance venues, new technologies affecting how music is performed and received: these are just some examples of the forces causing musicians to diversify their musical training. To perform regularly (three or

1. Ramon Ricker, *Lessons from a Streetwise Music Professor. What You Won't Learn at Most Music Schools* (Fairport, NY: Sundown, 2011), xiv.

four shows per week), I have had to become proficient in a variety of popular music styles in addition to jazz and classical. Fortunately, that was part of my long-term musical goals.

The market today puts increased demands on musicians and often results in a need to compromise either artistic development or career advancement. However, the current period is also unprecedented in allowing musicians to create unique career trajectories as traditional careers become less dominant. Devotion to one musical tradition, one skill set, may still make sense for some, but for economic and philosophical reasons an eclectic approach is becoming increasingly useful for many.

The balance between dedication to one's vocation (a career with diversified skills) and artistic vision involving a deep and specialized commitment to music itself is dialectical. Professional musicians often express regret that they did not focus on more specialized musical skills even as they recognize the need for diverse skills in the marketplace. This seeming contradiction reflects a dynamic tension between art and commerce. A common refrain is "If I knew then what I know now," suggesting they would have approached their career preparation differently. But musicians also recognize that musical careers are increasingly nonlinear, that they follow a serpentine or accretive trajectory, and that skills must be acquired as they are needed.

Another common adage, "success is preparation plus opportunity," is thrown around by the musicians who have jobs but with the understanding that preparation is continual and that opportunities may come from unexpected directions. In *The Savvy Musician*, David Cutler (2009) emphasizes that "every skill you possess can contribute to your professional life."[2] Peter Spellman, a guitarist and the director of career development at Berklee College of Music, suggests that "Having a sustainable career in music means continual review of your career assets and exploration of ways you can improve and enhance your services and products" (Spellman 2013).[3] Again, this suggests the importance of an entrepreneurial approach to finding one's musical identity.

Since traditional linear career models no longer apply to much of the musical economy, a project-based approach often emerges as a more realistic way for musicians to balance job opportunities with artistic goals. Angela Myles Beeching, director of the Career Services Center at New England Conservatory, sums up the prevailing view that achieving short-term goals "is the best way to work toward your long-term dream" (2005).[4]

2. David Cutler, *The Savvy Musician. Building a Career, Earning a Living, and Making a Difference* (Pittsburgh: Helius Press, 2009), 14.
3. Peter Spellman, *The Self-Promoting Musician* (Boston: Berklee Press, 2013), 225.
4. Angela Myles Beeching, *Beyond Talent. Creating a Successful Career in Music* (New York: Oxford University Press, 2005), 16.

Of the many professional musicians I have performed with who specialize in the art musics of Europe, Latin America, India, Asia, as well as folk and popular idioms, the great majority either have diversified skills (and work a variety of jobs simultaneously) or are employed in a primarily non-music job in order to survive. In my travels as a touring musician I have been struck by how similar the gigging life is around the world, regardless of musical style. In Lima, Peru, Istanbul, Turkey, and Hong Kong, I played with musicians who had graduated from music conservatories but had a patchwork income stream similar to mine and played bar gigs, short tours, and concerts, taught, and took the occasional studio session. The commonalities in our musical experiences engendered commiseration but also a kind of optimism borne of the recognition that we were in the same boat, that we were part of a global music community.

CAREER AND COMMUNITY: THE WHY AND HOW QUESTIONS

Many professional musicians, adapting to a nonlinear career path, fill in gaps in their education as commercial pressures and artistic opportunities dictate. This can mean taking tutorials, online classes, and other short, project-oriented breaks from their performance schedules. Or it can mean longer interruptions in order to acquire a new degree, certification, or skill set before returning to an active performance schedule.

The dynamic tension between art and commerce affects all facets of a musician's professional life and results in constant choices, in both the short and long term. The choices tend to be grouped (by musicians themselves, as well as the how-to books) into "how" and "why" questions. There are blueprints, formulas, and business models for success, a plethora of publications, essays, classes, and videos that delineate the how of a musical career. The why of being an artist is less clear cut and is often expressed as a subset of the how. Within this framework, your philosophy or musical identity can get reduced to branding, a strategic focus intended to establish your niche in the music business, often at the expense of pure artistic experimentation and growth.

Delineating the why question speaks directly to the issue of community. A performing artist emerges from a community, is shaped by it, and performs for it, hopefully adding to and expanding the community in the process. Beeching stresses, "As musicians, our fundamental work is community building."[5] But the tools of community-building are the tools of marketing, particularly in this era of online self-promotion and social media where a musician

5. Beeching 2005, 125.

must carefully construct an avatar-like identity for public consumption. "Your online presence should reflect your goals, your values, and what you want to convey to audiences about yourself and your music."[6] Cutler: "Marketing is an attitude—a way of life."[7] Is a musician's community real or imagined? Does it define your music with clear cultural parameters, or does your music define it over time as you evolve artistically? The answers may not be the same for everyone, even if the goal of community building remains fundamental for all artists.

Some musicians, even some music businesses (such as independent record labels, arts collectives, music venues, and merchandisers), have created viable fiscal models by starting with a clear philosophical mission, utilizing business tools without subordinating the why of the music to the how of its commercial development. These examples point to the need for finding a balance between art and commerce, a systematic part of career development. Envisioning such a plan early in one's career goes a long way toward making later time investment decisions less haphazard.

The temptation to mold your artistic identity to a marketing strategy, to commodify yourself in the process of finding your musical niche, has always been strong. This is tempered by an artist's sense of belonging to a community and the material and philosophical support it may provide. Community in this sense can mean shared information and resources, formal and informal educational opportunities, and networking for mutual benefit. Over the course of a musician's career these different aspects of community can coalesce so that all the short-term projects, all the fits and starts, eventually reveal a bigger picture, one in which the how and why questions are resolved. In 1992, I was privileged to hear veteran rockabilly pioneer Carl Perkins give a motivational keynote speech at which he said (as many have said before and since), "I didn't make a living in music, but I made a life!"[8]

A constant theme among my musical colleagues is the need to "stay up" on new music-related information, tools, and resources. Bobby Davis, director of the Austin Jazz Band, urges: "Stay on the cutting edge of technological advances. Be diverse in all aspects of music business processes."[9] Pianist Robin Smith encourages musicians to make use of web-based training such as tutorials and online courses, supplemented by regular meetings with a mentor.[10]

Types of learning vary according to the style of music one studies, but there is a generally accepted truth that formal music education is only the first step to professionalism. Experience gained through performance and apprenticing

6. Beeching 2005, 124.
7. Cutler, *Savvy Musician*, 50.
8. Carl Perkins, keynote speech, Miller Beer Convention, San Francisco, 1992.
9. Online questionnaire posted by author, June 2015.
10. Questionnaire 2015.

with experienced professionals often provides crucial additions to knowledge absorbed in the classroom. In the jazz tradition there is a recognized relationship between the "school" and the "street." Both are important components of the musical heritage, and there is creative tension between school players and street players.

Saxophonist and teacher Mark Kazanov notes that "Teachers are essential, but so is playing all the time. . . . I learned the most from the older musicians I was fortunate to play with."[11] Drummer James Fenno encourages us to "play with and listen to as much live music as possible, starting at as young an age as possible."[12] Guitarist Adrian Di Matteo notes that for him, "Advanced theory, history, performance workshops, composition classes and teaching seminars were all indispensable. Of course none of this is a substitute for real-world gigging experience."[13] Saxophonist Lee Redfield: "The best training is to shadow a professional."[14] Guitarist Alan Retamozo: "The only thing just as educational as my formal education has been playing gigs and forming relationships with other musicians."[15]

Dr. John Mills, professor of jazz composition at UT-Austin, makes an important general point about formal music pedagogy: "The only downside I see in music education is the potential misconception, on the part of teachers or students, that any system can give a student absolutely everything he will ever need to succeed. In the best case, the student has learned to continue to teach himself, as the culture and musical requirements continue to morph."[16]

Mentoring relationships are common to most commercial music scenes and to jazz performance in particular. Young musicians learn from more experienced professionals on the job how to hone their craft. Di Matteo voices a widely held feeling that this practical knowledge can and should be incorporated into formal music education programs: "Students should be exposed to the ideas of where and how music functions in various contexts (weddings, funerals, concert halls, film, etc.) and how they might actually expect to make money if that is their objective."[17]

While the economies of academic jazz programs and commercial jazz performance are separate, there has always been overlap. Commercial performers bring real-world experience to the classroom through funded programs like guest lecturer and artist-in-residence programs or through specially scheduled performances. Successful artists often have endorsements with instrument manufacturers that subsidize these academic appearances. Conversely,

11. Questionnaire 2015.
12. Questionnaire 2015.
13. Questionnaire 2015.
14. Questionnaire 2015.
15. Questionnaire 2015.
16. Questionnaire 2015.
17. Questionnaire 2015.

university jazz programs funnel skilled performers into the commercial economy of concert halls, nightclubs, festivals, recording studios, and gala event bookings.

This overlap between the commercial and academic jazz worlds has a long history and is to some extent an essential component of an art form that draws from folk, popular, and art music. But students of Western classical music, as well as elite art music traditions from around the world, are also experiencing an increased overlap between the academic and commercial economies. Examples include specialized music for weddings and other gala events, ethnic or "exotic" music contracted in restaurants, and hybrid musical projects featured in nightclubs or recording sessions, as well as big-ticket concerts and festivals. I've played in many fusion bands (fusing traditional and modern sounds) over the years as part of what was once a niche market but is now becoming quite mainstream.

The twenty-first-century globalization of culture has made boundaries between musical traditions porous. Mark Kazanov suggests that culturally, "we are now in a world market much more than we used to be. Everything is accessible and at our fingertips. Music no longer represents a culture or a specific group of people as much as it once did. Everything is much more fluid."[18] The world music market challenges musicians to expand their musical knowledge and to offer their specialized skills to a global community, mainly through new technologies.

The career landscape has also changed for musicians in terms of what economist Tyler Cowen and others see as the rise of the "Uber economy." Finding full-time work with one organization is statistically less and less likely.[19] Instead, the job market is defined more by freelancing, outsourcing, contract, and temp work (what some jokingly call the FOCT economy). A 2014 study by the Freelancers Union found that more than 33 percent of American workers are now freelancing. According to Steven Hill, senior fellow with the New America Foundation, other estimates predict that number will rise to over 50 percent by 2025.[20] Musicians, regardless of genre, are part of this larger economic trend.

Many musicians recognize that performance pay has generally stayed flat for the last thirty years (or more!), while the cost of living has steadily increased. The hoary admonition "don't quit your day job" has lost none of its piquancy. The 2015 Austin Music Census, commissioned by the City of Austin Economic Development Department, documented that of four thousand

18. Questionnaire 2015.

19. Tyler Cowen, "In an Uber World, Fortune Favors the Freelancer," *New York Times*, June 6, 2015, http://mobile.nytimes.com/2015/06/28/upshot/in-an-uber-world-fortune-favors-the-freelancer.html?_r=0 (accessed February 5, 2017).

20. Steven Hill, *Raw Deal. How the "Uber Economy" and Runaway Capitalism Are Screwing American Workers* (New York: St. Martin's Press, 2015), 30.

respondents in the music industry, more than 60 percent work two or more jobs to generate income, the second usually in a field outside music.[21]

In my travels as a touring musician from 1990 to the present, I found that the rate of $50 to $100 per player for bar, restaurant, and chamber concert gigs was standard across the United States as well as in other countries. Gala events and larger concert halls pay slightly more on average, about $150 to $250. This is true for jazz, R&B, and other popular styles but also for classical and world music gigs. I've played with many musicians trained in elite traditions who are classified as amateurs only because they have to make their income in another field and thus devote only a small part of their time to performance. An excellent oud player who specializes in Persian and Arabic as well as baroque lute music told me without hesitation: "Choose music as your career only if you have some kind of support, or if you do not mind being poor most of the time."[22]

Painting a bleak picture, we can sum up the current professional music landscape as this: Well-trained musicians come out of a music degree program having invested years to acquire specialized musical expertise and yet without the diverse skills they need. As part of a FOCT economy, they must compete against each other, finding part-time work in the academic or commercial music economies or some combination of the two (or a non-music job). This shifting landscape offers no long-term employment guarantees.

But there is a rosier side to the picture. New music technologies open up more possibilities, making it easier to compose, record, transcribe, and share music. Music consumption has expanded in many ways. World music, both traditional and fusion styles, has expanded as never before, and there are larger audiences for all forms of live and recorded music. Pianist and composer Robin Smith gave me a tour of his recording studio and noted that while his income from live shows hasn't changed in thirty years, the rise of home studios "has dropped the barrier to entry" in the world of recording. The Internet has made it possible for anyone to publish music. He now makes 40 percent of his income from recording, composing, and arranging.[23]

This situation is similar for practitioners of Western art music. A classical musician must combine specialized and general skills, find income from various sources, adapt to changes in technology and the marketplace, and find a niche that utilizes those skills while working towards a larger artistic purpose. A good example is provided by my friend and associate oboist Allison Welch, whose career in classical music parallels mine in jazz and popular music. As I was pursuing an advanced degree in ethnomusicology, she was completing her degree in musicology. I went on to work as a touring musician while she

21. Austin Music Census (Austin: Titan Music Group, 2015).
22. Interview with author, 2015.
23. Interview with author, 2015.

made most of her income as a technical writer and performer in orchestras. She performed with the Texas Early Music Project, founded in 1987 and "dedicated to preserving and advancing the art of Medieval, Renaissance, Baroque, and early Classical music through performance, recordings, and educational outreach."[24]

Over the years, her participation in TEMP evolved to include organizational as well as performance roles, and even though early music was not her academic focus, its clearly defined market allows her to draw on her academic training and fits with her artistic goals. Initially a stand-alone project, TEMP has become an ongoing part of Welch's career trajectory and vision for building community through music.[25]

If we envision a musical career as a dialectic between the how and the why, commonalities become apparent between very different career paths. Musicians who start off with pragmatic business plans find that they have to make philosophical choices early on, while those who start with an artistic vision find that its implementation requires many nuts-and-bolts compromises. In a Wild West FOCT economy, each musician creates his or her own path. At least part of the mandate of music education is to help students delineate that path.

The music section of bookstores and libraries are littered with self-help books revealing "secrets" for developing a music career. This highlights the fact that constructing such a career path is still considered an occult practice. The lack of standardized career planning, supported by academic institutions, leaves a vacuum filled by books and courses with a wide range of reputability and efficacy. Ironically enough, the publishing and marketing of self-help books itself has become a growing revenue stream for musicians! It's a pyramid scheme: to make it in the music business, write a book on how to make it in the music business. If academic institutions could systematize these practices for nonlinear as well as traditional career paths, the music education landscape could be cleared of much of the chaff.

Jazz musician Hal Galper (2000) described the changing economic picture for aspiring jazz artists over a decade ago. There are "thousands of young musicians who graduate from music schools each year without being taught the basics of how to find work."[26] But Galper also noted that there are unprecedented opportunities, if you know where to find them, such as the proliferation of "nonprofit local, regional, and national arts support organizations."[27]

This changed economic landscape affects all music; jazz musicians may simply have adapted to it earlier, as reflected in expanded curricula at institutions

24. Texas Early Music Project website, http://www.early-music.org (accessed February 5, 2017).
25. Interview with author, 2015.
26. Hal Galper, *The Touring Musician* (New York: Billboard Books, 2000), 8.
27. Galper 2000, 13.

like Berklee School of Music, University of North Texas, Eastman School of Music, McNally Smith College of Music, Humber School of Creative and Performing Arts, and other schools with advanced jazz degrees. Students are better prepared for professional decisions because of required courses dealing with career planning, music technologies, and creative adaptation to social change. Professional musicians can contribute to these courses by discussing what has and hasn't worked in their own careers.

The careers of project-driven musicians offer many insights to music pedagogy. These artists have learned by doing, tested boundaries and created new paths. Their knowledge is drawn from various sources, even if their primary focus was on a particular music tradition. A working musician's career may bridge widely different educational spheres and is pragmatically interdisciplinary. After developing a track record of this kind, a logical step for older professional musicians is to find ways to share their insights with the next generation of performers.

THOSE WHO ARE DOING AND TEACHING

The most common secondary source of income for musicians after performance is teaching. That has been my personal experience as well as that of most of the musicians I have known over my career. One result of the FOCT economy is an increase in musicians who teach and music teachers who perform; the distinction between the two groups is breaking down out of economic necessity.

Music teachers are in demand, and primary and secondary school music proficiency is rising. The Bureau of Labor Statistics predicts a 12 percent growth in employment for elementary school teachers and 6 percent for high school teachers.[28] With increasing demographic changes (such as the growth of the US Hispanic population) and more multicultural awareness, primary and secondary school music curricula also reflect greater familiarity with traditions beyond Western classical music. Cultural diversity programs are becoming one measure for a school's desirability, as reflected in school rating systems like GreatSchool.org.[29] For private teachers as well, fluency in diverse music traditions (such as jazz, blues, Latin, rock, and R&B) is not just an asset, it is increasingly expected, reflecting the communities in which they teach. Similarly, a music instructor's skill set must include familiarity with computer software, recording equipment, video editing, and similar tools that have become standard components of teaching. On a daily basis I use play-along and recording software with my students, video conferencing for long-distance

28. Bureau of Labor Statistics, http://www.bls.gov/.
29. http://www.greatschools.org.

students, as well as business software and social media for scheduling, communication, and notification of music-related events. Like many other music teachers, I post video lessons online, write educational essays and blogs, and create online links to my educational resources.

Trumpeter and music teacher David Cross notes that music programs at all levels that have funding for the arts are making advances. "Technology has revolutionized the arts as it has everything else. There is more information and there are more tools to make our jobs easier."[30] Professional players with broad musical experience who return to the academic economy enhance the teaching of college-level, high school, and middle school music students alike.

In the prevailing project-driven freelance economy, many pedagogically oriented projects arise that impact the larger music community. Independent musicians' income derives from a range of sources; personally, up to 50 percent of my income derives from cultural organizations or event preparation. Such initiatives may involve playing or writing arrangements for recording sessions (a growing market with the rise of home studios), leading amateur musicians in workshops and performances, researching and providing specialty music for cultural events, training nonmusicians in stagecraft and the use of PA systems, and other short-term projects in which specialized skills are needed. The point is that within a given community, a professional musician can wear many hats, functioning as performer, teacher, and/or cultural liaison.

INSTITUTIONS AND MENTORS

The career picture for performing musicians appears almost zen-like in its balance of opposites. Long-term goals set your trajectory, but short-term projects define your path. Specialized skills give you artistic and niche market value, but broad, adaptable skills give you a better chance of creating a stable and expanding career. An artist represents and is supported by a community, but community is also a marketing tool created so as to sell musical products. Solid training in musical performance is essential to one's career, but it is full of gaps that real-world experiences make evident.

Learning from a mentor, someone who has already trod the path, helps many musicians negotiate this balance of opposites. Apprenticing with an established performer is a time-honored way for a young musician to learn about the business of music. This relationship is enhanced when it is part of an institution (like a school), an arts production group, or an established, commercially successful band. A formal mentor-student relationship, given

30. Interview with author, 2015.

structure and value by association with recognized institutions, can be an important part of a career development.

I was fortunate to have various mentors during my high school and college years, professional players who brought their practical experience into the classroom. One in particular, jazz trumpeter Ray Copeland, suggested particular approaches to improvisation, expanded my knowledge of jazz theory, and provided insights into playing in big band horn sections as well as into the music business. Much of this knowledge is most effectively communicated through face-to-face interaction and unfortunately is still not a recognized part of a music curriculum.

The mentor-student relationship gives substance to a musician's long-term artistic goals. Both parties participate in preserving a musical tradition through a sense of "passing the torch" from one generation to the next. The direct exchange of musical knowledge leads to indirect but related exchanges that are part of building community. There can be broader social and economic effects as the musical torch gets passed: the families of students come to know the teacher, the teacher gets more students through word-of-mouth referrals, and families and friends attend the teacher's performances and help build the teacher's fan base. Musical opportunities increase for the teacher, and musical experiences become a greater part of the daily activities of everyone involved.

Mentoring is an organic part of most music traditions and bridges the gap between music technique and the more ineffable aspects of professional performance. For myself, particularly with jazz students, mentoring has been a natural connection between teaching and performance. I lead several monthly jazz jam sessions that bring seasoned professional players together with beginners. I've had musicians as young as thirteen and as old as eighty-eight onstage playing together. I'll also invite advanced students to sit in on my regular nightclub gigs. After the stage fright wears off, they learn by osmosis things that can't be taught in the classroom. Room acoustics, stage lighting, monitor speaker placement, visual cues, audience reactions, and other subtle details of professional performance are learned through this process.

Jam sessions and sit-ins are a time-honored part of jazz education, but my non-jazz students have also benefited from similar opportunities. Like a growing number of music teachers, I have taken the traditional classical recital and adapted it to the communities we live in. This may involve scheduling informal recitals in homes, coffeehouses, restaurants, or other venues. As the separation between musical traditions softens, opportunities for the reconceptualization of performance spaces increase. For example, I use a local coffeehouse for a monthly recital and encourage students in improvisatory and nonimprovisatory styles to play for each other. We mix jazz, classical, blues, folk, and world musics into the program, even original compositions.

Musicians with the goal of building community find creative ways to make music accessible when established institutions do not lead the way. Projects involving elite music traditions like Western art music are particularly instructive in this sense because institutions foregrounding these traditions have been slow to adapt to social change. An illustrative grassroots response to this situation in Austin is the Sound Bridge Project. Founder and classical flutist Lauryn Gould explains: "We wanted to find innovative and accessible ways to share our music with the community-at-large, so we founded The Sound Bridge Project (SBP). We presented chamber music concerts in nontraditional spaces and nontraditional ways. Through our events, we were able to engage the local community of performers, composers, and listeners outside of the traditional concert hall."[31] Projects like SBP are exploring ways to engage and inspire young musicians and to expand the audience for music that has become institutionally isolated. Beyond finding new venues and settings for performances, these projects challenge musicians and audiences to find ways to make music a more organic expression of a vibrant community. As professional musicians show students and their families how traditional music can be relevant, the parameters of the teacher-student dynamic expand.

Implementing mentoring as an integral part of music curricula is still at an experimental and informal stage in many institutions and communities. It requires commitment, planning, resources, and above all a vision of the powerful role music can play in shaping a young student's life. Two programs I work with exemplify how music mentoring positively affects young students. The first example addresses the issue of relevance, the adaptation of music instruction to the contemporary culture of young music students. The second example explores economic factors that restrict access for many music students.

For the past fifteen years I have taught private lessons at the Austin School of Music. The school's mission statement reads as follows: "We offer music education for today's students. We strive to make sure that your musical learning experience is customized to what YOU want to learn. . . . Our teachers make it a priority to get to know you on a personal level and to become familiar with your personal musical needs and goals so that your journey is rewarding to you. . . . Austin School of Music students learn how to play from highly skilled instructors who are also some of the most well-known working performers in the Austin area."[32] Mentorship is a central component of the school's approach to pedagogy, with an emphasis on rock, pop, and jazz as well as classical repertoire. Students learn music that is part of their family and community environment, helping them stay motivated to practice and develop their skills.

Because they learn from professional musicians, students also have more opportunity to perform locally as they progress. Over the past nineteen years,

31. Interview with author, 2015.
32. Austin School of Music website: http://www.austinschoolofmusic.com (accessed February 5, 2017).

ASM has built a successful summer program, Rock Camp USA, in which teachers guide students (ages eight to nineteen) to form rock bands, rehearse songs, and perform a concert in a local venue. The program has spread to other cities in the United States and has been widely emulated by private music schools.

With my woodwind students (saxophone, clarinet, flute), the issue of relevance derives from the students' need and desire to learn different styles of playing. This is a common issue for music teachers. Karen Berger notes that "to connect with today's students, we often need to branch out to a completely different musical idiom" (2010).[33] Most of my middle and high school students take private lessons to supplement school ensembles like orchestra, stage band, jazz band, and of course, marching band. When I first began teaching at ASM, my students mainly needed help with skills relevant to the Western classical tradition, such as reading music and mastering scales and arpeggios. Many programs at the time experienced high dropout rates because students did not find the repertoire interesting. Their main motivation was social: their friends were in band, and if their friends dropped out, they would, too. School athletics siphoned off many students after middle school. Most of my students played music only in school and did not participate in extracurricular music making.

To help motivate these students I introduced various supplemental techniques and approaches to the classical skills. For example, I taught the blues scale even to beginning students, along with the major scales. Since this scale is so prevalent in American popular music, it was familiar to them (as well as fun to play). I showed them how to create their own melodies (riffs and licks) from the blues scale, which simultaneously incorporated ear training and basic compositional skills. Many young students wanted to learn pop songs from the radio, TV, movies, as well as video game soundtracks. The blues scale exercises helped them learn these melodies by ear. I used this approach with students as young as six, with positive results. Disney and Pixar soundtrack songs are often the flavor of the day for young students, and many of these have generic pentatonic melodies, creating a teachable moment and allowing me to introduce the major and minor pentatonic and blues scales. All of my students improved their ability to learn songs by ear, and some of them became motivated to write their own songs. This was particularly gratifying with students who were bored or frustrated by the school band music and were in danger of dropping band altogether until their musical studies became more closely aligned with the other music in their lives.

A second example demonstrates the importance of the mentor-student relationship for music students who may be motivated but lack the

---

33. Karen Berger, *The Complete Idiot's Guide to Teaching Music on Your Own* (Indianapolis: Alpha Books, 2010), 34.

resources to progress. For the last four years I have worked with the nonprofit Anthropos Arts. Its mission statement is "Anthropos Arts connects at-risk youth with professional musicians, cultivating confidence, integrity, and life skills through musical instruction and mentorship. Our students receive free, individualized lessons from some of the best artists in the country. These are musicians with extensive performing, recording, and teaching experience. The lessons lead to performance opportunities at Austin's seminal venues and events, and exposure to an incredibly wide range of music—as audience and performer."[34]

Through this program I give weekly private lessons to low-income, at-risk middle school students in the Austin Independent School District. The students make a contract with Anthropos Arts and receive an instrument and lessons in exchange for commitment to practicing and performing in a final concert at the end of the semester. This is in addition to their school band commitment. The musical commitment to Anthropos tends to involve the student's family as well as band teachers because of adverse social pressures (such as parents working multiple jobs or family members in prison or suffering from drug or alcohol addiction). Something as basic as getting rides to rehearsals can be a major logistical obstacle that family and teachers work together to solve. The sense of community is very strong by the time the final concert takes place.

I personally witnessed a transformation in several of my students as their musical self-confidence and desire to learn grew stronger. Family members and teachers supported the endeavor socially, as mentioned. Musically, the effort was accompanied by a variety of teaching methods, combining instruction in the reading of Western notation with jazz-based improvisation and ear training. Anthropos concerts draw from popular and world music, so the students play jazz standards as well as Latin American and African popular songs. Since many students are from Central and South America, the repertoire is often familiar and accessible for them.

Dylan Jones, founder of Anthropos Arts, notes the high success rate they have achieved: "The benefits of our programs are profound, affecting many aspects of students' lives: overall academic success, self-discipline, self-esteem, and a pathway to college. Over the past five years, 100 percent of our senior students have graduated from high school, and more than 80 percent enrolled in college on scholarships. For the last four years, 100 percent of our seniors enrolled in college."[35] The Anthropos Arts program demonstrates that music can have an extremely beneficial effect on a student's life even if that student doesn't pursue a career in music.

34. Anthropos Arts http://www.anthroposarts.org (accessed February 5, 2017).
35. From the Anthropos Arts website.

The positive effects of music education for all students is a strong incentive for nonprofit-funded music programs targeting low-income and at-risk students, with a particular emphasis on mentoring. Austin Soundwaves, a project started by the Texas nonprofit Hispanic Alliance in 2011, provides high-quality music education to underserved youth to build "resiliency and awaken intrinsic motivation to learn, create, and achieve." Their programs include primary skills music education followed by advanced skills and mentoring.[36]

Another type of informal music mentoring I have personally participated in is work with community bands and orchestras. These give young players a chance to learn from more experienced musicians in face-to-face settings. The Austin Community College big band program, for example, brings together registered college students, volunteer professional players, and high school students, creating numerous opportunities for mentorship while playing and preserving great music for the general Austin community.[37] Programs like this have little official funding and depend to a large extent on volunteers stepping up week after week, month after month. They seem to survive mainly through the tenacious efforts of the participating musicians, family, and friends who make up the core of the community.

These examples of mentoring and community outreach are not unique. Musicians I have talked to around the United States (and internationally) are involved in similar projects. Many of these organizations and events are small and would benefit from linkages with larger institutions. They represent a creative response to the challenges and opportunities in the contemporary music scene, and they are growing.

STREET AND SCHOOL: OPPORTUNITIES FOR SHARED RESOURCES

I find the street/school dichotomy of the jazz lexicon a useful way to consider music education in general and the academic and commercial music economies in particular. School programs give you "legit chops," but street experience gives you seasoning. School gives you career credentials, but the street is a school of its own where young players absorb musical knowledge from older players in informal mentor-student relationships and interact with a variety of audiences with different tastes and expectations. In the balancing act necessitated by today's music economy, the separation of street and school appears antiquated for an increasing number of musicians. Part-time work,

36. Hispanic Alliance website: http://www.thehispanicalliance.org (accessed February 5, 2017).
37. Austin Community College Big Band, http://accbigband.com (accessed February 5, 2017).

nontraditional performance venues, and the need for diverse skills and creative adaptation are turning the division between amateur and professional, even hard distinctions between musical repertoires, into outmoded divisions. Working musicians move, out of necessity, between the academic and commercial economies, linking short-term jobs into a long-term, though often haphazard, career trajectory. Their careers demonstrate that the two worlds would benefit, artistically and materially, from being further connected.

Rapid social and economic shifts make life uncertain and often scary for anyone committed to playing music for a living. But it doesn't have to be this way, if the larger vision of building community is supported. I have found this to be true in my own career. The goal of building community (the why of the music) creates meaningful contexts for all the pragmatic choices (the how of the music) artists face as they adapt to changes in technology, demographics, and global interconnection.

An emphasis on community can provide coherence in the vacuum created by the loss of traditional linear career paths. A musician's short-term projects thread together diverse groups, institutions, and revenue sources and can create important linkages between the commercial and academic music economies. In the process of making a living, professional musicians help to delineate and expand their music community. Overshadowing the ups and downs of various gigs, the strength of this community is a lasting measure of a musician's career.

In my experience, the mentor role is a crucial part of music education. An expanded use of mentoring, connecting students to professionals in the community with a variety of skill sets, can make institutional curricula more adaptive to social and economic changes and more efficient in providing students the practical knowledge and experience they need. Because the mentor-student relationship is an organic part of most musical traditions, adaptation and innovation can enhance rather than conflict with traditional teaching methods and artistic standards.

REFERENCES

Beeching, Angela Myles. 2005. *Beyond Talent. Creating a Successful Career in Music.* Oxford: Oxford University Press.

Berger, Karen. 2010. *The Complete Idiot's Guide to Teaching Music on Your Own.* Indianapolis: Alpha Books.

Bureau of Labor Statistics. http://www.bls.gov/.

Cowen, Tyler. 2015. "In an Uber World, Fortune Favors the Freelancer." *New York Times*, June 27, 2015. http://mobile.nytimes.com/2015/06/28/upshot/in-an-uber-world-fortune-favors-the-freelancer.html?_r=0.

Cutler, David. 2009. *The Savvy Musician. Building a Career, Earning a Living, and Making a Difference.* Pittsburgh: Helius Press.

Galper, Hal. 2000. *The Touring Musician.* New York: Billboard Books.

Hill, Steven. 2015. *Raw Deal. How the "Uber Economy" and Runaway Capitalism Are Screwing American Workers*. New York: St. Martin's Press.

Perkins, Carl. 1992. Keynote Speech. Miller Beer Convention, San Francisco.

Ricker, Ramon. 2011. *Lessons from a Streetwise Music Professor. What You Won't Learn at Most Music Schools*. Fairport, NY: Sundown.

Spellman, Peter. 2013. *The Self-Promoting Musician*. Boston: Berklee Press.

Best Practices, New Models

CHAPTER 13

Progressive Trends in Curricular Change

ROBIN D. MOORE WITH JUAN AGUDELO,
KATIE CHAPMAN, CARLOS DÁVALOS,
HANNAH DURHAM, MYRANDA HARRIS,
AND CREIGHTON MOENCH

INTRODUCTION

In the recent colloquy "Studying U.S. Music in the Twenty-First Century," published by the *Journal of the American Musicological Society*, Alejandro L. Madrid expounds on the crisis in music education by examining how American music is currently approached in the academy. He writes:

> Rather than expanding the current Western music canon with a more multicul-
> turally defined American music repertory (which would still reinforce national
> boundaries and nationalistic ideologies), the academic study of American music
> can become part of a project to rethink the US nation-state and US citizenship
> from a postnational frame of mind. Instead of perpetuating the values of a
> musical canon in crisis, the study of American music should help us transform
> our understanding of ourselves as Americans.[1]

For Madrid, a cosmopolitan notion of national identity is vital to ridding music education in the United States and elsewhere of its exceptionalist tendencies. This idea can be translated into other parts of the curriculum through a conscious move away from exclusively canonical, Eurocentric repertoires and

---

1. Madrid, Alejandro. 2011. "American Music in Times of Postnationality." *Journal of the American Musicological Society*, Vol. 64 No. 3 (Fall), 699–703.

towards a more thematic, cross-disciplinary course of musical study. A post-national paradigm aligns nicely with the goals of this book project through its focus on diverse repertoires, international points of connection, and broad, inclusive frames of inquiry. We envision a future in which the study of music will train intellectually engaged global citizens in this way, with an awareness of many forms of music making, the social and historical contingencies that gave rise to them, the legalistic frames within which they operate, and the technologies that disseminate them.

This book has addressed long-held questions concerning the core requirements for Bachelor of Music degrees: Why are specific content areas (e.g., eighteenth-century song forms, part writing, jazz repertory) important? What represent the most critical components of content and the best use of music major time vis-à-vis content? How do specific courses support students' goals as future music professionals? What are the interdisciplinary possibilities within music education? Several chapters have discussed the potential of popular music pedagogy to diversify students' musical horizons. Indeed, the incorporation of noncanonical repertoires is a crucial step in the process of curricular reform, with immediate positive results in terms of the expansion of musical literacy, expanded audience engagement, and the development of new marketable skills. Such results should be supported not only from the ensemble studio and the academic classroom but also through the crafting of new degree plans and program trajectories. Since those devising music curricula must consider both the skills students need to work as music professionals generally and in their area of specialization, the authors of this chapter examine curricular elements in terms of content—pertaining to areas of knowledge, technical proficiency, conceptual understanding, and artistry—at various levels.

This chapter consists of two parts. Part 1 concerns performance and music education curricula, two of the most popular degree programs among students in large music programs. As music degrees are rigorous, it is no surprise that both areas tend to involve large numbers of requirements, often presented in a fairly rigid sequential structure. As we have seen, this issue is further problematized when the rigidity extends into course content and does not reflect the actualities of musical life outside the academy, including the degree to which musical ideas are exchanged and transmitted between musical traditions. Performance and music education degrees each include a set core of music courses during the first two years (history, theory, ear training, ensembles, lessons, etc.), then move into more specialized offerings. Reorganization of such content is necessary in order to allow for a more inclusive and student-driven curriculum that supports modern musical careers. Part 2 of the chapter reflects on the priorities of global awareness, local engagement, social justice, entrepreneurship, technology practice, the study of popular music, and technical and other skills needed by professional musicians, considering how they have been implemented in progressive music programs to date. Common themes include the importance of expanding instruction to new repertories, suggestions for enhanced collaboration between local and global communities, new contexts for performance, and new forms of audience engagement.

The curricular models outlined in Chapter 14 (whose content is closely related to this chapter) have either been discussed by pedagogues, discussed in academic literature, or experimented with already at various institutions. Graduate students in Robin Moore's 2014 pedagogy seminar at UT-Austin attempted to expand upon these ideas and apply them to typical degree plans found in conservatories and schools of music. They undertook research on existing experiments through assigned readings and discussion as well as by conducting faculty and student interviews, examining degree plans at various national and international institutions, and often contacting representatives at such institutions directly. The enhanced core model (no. 1) involves a reconfiguring of existing core-course content to reflect a more diverse, cross-disciplinary emphasis without changing the assigned coursework per se. The pluralist model (no. 2) suggests the incorporation of general liberal arts college ideals into the music degree with an emphasis on critical thinking, creative engagement, and self-driven research projects from the beginning of the program. It also requires students to diversify their interests and expertise during the first two years of study prior to specialization. The integrated music core curricula (no. 3) intends to reduce the introductory course load (theory, aural skills, and piano) into a single four- to six-credit-hour course. Doing so would make room for many new possibilities within a typical semester of music coursework. Finally, the capstone model (no. 4) works towards a cumulative degree project involving musicianship, creative fulfillment, professional development, and community outreach. These four models are not necessarily exclusive of one another; yet we believe each of these, alone or in tandem, represents a realistic and effective means of incorporating the changes discussed throughout this volume.

1. PERFORMANCE AND MUSIC EDUCATION CURRICULA

Applied curricula

For the past century and a half, music school curricula have been based on western European traditions and the study of particular kinds of music theory, music history, private lessons, ear training, keyboard skills, and participation in large ensembles. The applied practice degree in a standard music school includes extended ensemble requirements, two recitals, and many hours of private lessons. Undergraduate students spend four years and many thousands of dollars in order to pursue their dreams in such programs. At the center of applied practice degrees lies the private lesson on a primary instrument. Instead of simply preparing repertoire and honing technique in these contexts, we suggest students be given written or other assignments in conjunction with applied assignments. They could do historical research on a given aspect of the music they play, create a rendition of a piece in a modern popular style, or perform it in a public location to help overcome stage fright and/or interact more directly with the general public. They could explore a variety of musical styles and genres rather than only Western classical repertoire. They could experiment with techniques, such as improvisation, or learn to provide their own instrumental accompaniment to performances on a separate instrument. These changes would provide students with more diverse training and more space for creative initiative.

A central element of the performance degree is the requirement to give one or more recitals during time spent in coursework. The student is responsible for reserving a space to perform, preparing repertoire, organizing the program, writing concert notes, and advertising the event. Although such an experience imparts important skills, alternative options might include projects oriented toward community music making (such as conducting a concert or giving a master class), sound recording, composition, and academic research. Examples of projects that could substitute for recitals include

- composing a piece of original music, recording it, and setting up a site online from which it can be sold or disseminated.
- organizing a concert event in the community, possibly benefiting a cause of the student's choice. The student could provide all the entertainment him-/herself or book an outside group to provide some of it. The focus of the requirement would thus shift to event management and community outreach.
- writing a research paper on a musical topic of the student's choice and presenting it to a committee, perhaps in conjunction with a lecture-demo combining academic and performative components.
- recording an entire CD consisting of singing or playing in different styles of music and changing the production style and recording techniques accordingly.
- conducting a full ensemble program.

Generally as part of performance degrees students are required to participate in a large ensemble every semester. This often involves at least six hours of organized practice per week (excluding performances) for a single hour of course credit. Although there are many benefits to a student's participation in large ensembles, such as experiencing what it may be like to pursue a career in a professional orchestra, the heavy time commitment involved to the exclusion of other kinds of performance limits the student's musical training. One suggestion in terms of reform in this area is to simply decrease the number of required semesters of involvement in large ensembles. This would allow students to more freely choose which ensembles they want to participate in or to spend more time on other aspects of their education. Although such changes may decrease enrollment in large ensembles, most would continue to thrive because of student dedication to the standard model.

By the same token, greater emphasis (whether by requirement or incentive) could be placed on participation in smaller ensembles such as non-Western music ensembles, technology-focused ensembles, smaller Western chamber ensembles, and popular music ensembles, thus allowing for exposure to new repertoires. Potentially, one would have the freedom to join or even create an ensemble with an academic or didactic focus or that foregrounds noncanonical repertoire or compositional skills in addition to a performative focus. In such a context one could conduct research projects on assigned pieces, learn to improvise and compose or arrange in the style and genres of the works being showcased, and take turns conducting other students. This would impart a wide variety of new skills (see Patch, Chapter 6 in this volume). Of course, if students don't spend as much course time rehearsing for concerts in such groups, the quality of performances at the end of the semester could be compromised. One solution to this problem would be to require year-long commitments to smaller ensembles and to hold performances only at the end of the second semester. Another option would be to hold open rehearsals at the end of each semester instead of formal performances, shifting the emphasis from presentational music making to an ongoing process of learning.

Additional emphasis could be placed on participation in smaller ensembles by requiring that students enroll in a different kind of ensemble each year, so that by the end of the degree plan they would have participated in four ensembles, two small and two large (see the pluralist curricular model discussion in Chapter 14). Alternately, one could require two years in two different ensembles so that students would have more time to specialize. Incentives could be offered to students willing to participate in additional ensembles—for example, by being required to attend fewer concerts as a spectator or through recognition of their performance expertise by means of a specialized certificate.

One broader issue surrounding performance degrees is whether instrumental curricula should remain focused on the acquisition of technical skill on the student's primary instrument. This begs the related question of whether the twenty-first century musician should have one particular specialization or whether he/she should be well versed in diverse styles of music and other skills. For aspiring symphonic performers, a more traditional focus may best suit their needs. However, for others a revised course of study could be of greater benefit. Although students may not necessarily learn to play three different instruments during their collegiate career, they should at least develop flexibility on their instrument of choice. For example, a singer should be able to sing in styles other than opera, such as pop, jazz, or Broadway show tunes, and a violinist should be familiar with repertoire such as fiddle tunes or North Indian violin music. Such diverse styles could be introduced through the studio and nurtured through appropriate small ensembles.

Another aspect of instrumental curricula centers on tiered ensembles. Many music schools currently have top-tier large ensembles as well as lower-level groups for less proficient players. The tiered system works well in that it allows highly skilled individuals to explore difficult repertoire while beginners approach their music at a slower pace. The latter is especially appropriate in the case of non-majors approaching performance as a low-stress extracurricular activity. However, the tiered approach becomes problematic when amateurs are discouraged from participating altogether. Less experienced non-majors may fear an audition in which they must compete against aspiring music professionals. Conversely, music majors may feel slighted or question their own abilities if they are not assigned to a top-tier ensemble. Large ensembles also do not necessarily provide sufficient pedagogical attention to individual members. Professor Jerry Junkin[2] at the University of Texas suggests one solution to this problem. His wind ensemble program has three tiers; the top tier involves multiple, shifting instrumental assignments throughout the semester as students play in the opera orchestra, the new music ensemble, and in chamber ensembles while still participating in their home ensemble. The involvement in multiple groups exposes them to varied repertoire and experiences. Of course, the model does not provide the same sort of diverse experience to performers in the lowest tier, and the home ensemble still emphasizes largely canonical repertoire. The tiered method, however, could prove useful if expanded so as to involve all performers in a greater variety of musical idioms and to support excellence in small-ensemble groups as well as larger ones. The same model could support performance in world music ensembles; for instance, more experienced players could participate in public concerts and other events designed to attract donors and future members, while the less experienced would begin in lower-tier groups by learning about the music, special instruments, associated performance techniques, and repertoire.

The primary challenge in revising large ensemble organization within music school curricula is that large ensemble performances are attractive to donors, thus contributing to music school funding, and they often act as recruitment tools for the academic unit as a whole. Additionally, most faculty in music schools directly support large-ensemble performance through their activities as conductors or by teaching in individual studios. Any changes to the existing performance structure will therefore necessitate considerable input from all involved parties. Changes to the nature of performance degrees and

2. Interviewed by Katie Chapman, November 3, 2014.

to participation in large ensembles will involve a reconceptualization of what the music school is, how it presents itself to the community, how it attracts students, and perhaps the kinds of students it reaches out to as well. Such a shift could be designed so as to create more parity between large ensembles and others if faculty support the effort.

As part of the reconceptualization of performance programs, scholarship allocations and recruitment efforts could be used to support other kinds of performance in addition to those of large canonical ensembles. In institutions such as the University of Texas, the needs of large ensembles in terms of instrumentation are only one factor that inform scholarship allocation. Scholarship committees generally place academic standing, audition success, and individual studio needs before those of large ensembles. Often, however, the two areas overlap because if a studio runs low on trumpets, for example, the wind ensemble will probably experience a similar deficit. In any case, the instrumental requirements of small ensembles could easily be prioritized in a similar fashion once they are well established.

Individuals in the local community do not always know that small non-canonical ensembles exist. Since effective recruitment and support for them requires heightened exposure, frequent public appearances should be prioritized. This could include anything from performing in community music venues to accompanying freshman orientations so that new students are made aware of all the performance options the college has to offer. One example of a smaller group at the University of Texas that promotes itself well is the Longhorn Singers—the official show choir of the University of Texas, composed of about twenty students. They sing at pep rallies for freshman, alumni events, high school assemblies, and tailgates for football games, as well as hosting their own shows each semester. Many of their performances raise money, supporting the group financially as well as providing publicity.

As Brian Pertl (Chapter 2 in this volume) states, one must make cultural changes to music institutions in order to actively encourage experimentation with new approaches to pedagogy. As part of this effort, organizations should be willing to consider substantive transformations and should be wary of modifications to degree requirements that do not produce sufficient change. It is up to the administrators and faculty members, in consultation with students, to create the culture that supports smaller ensembles and a greater diversity of skills, and to demonstrate their importance.

Music education

The undergraduate music education degree prepares students to teach music, typically at the secondary school level in large-ensemble formats such as wind band, orchestra, and choir. Prior to teacher certification, the degree culminates in a semester (or longer) of hands-on experience in student teaching, usually coordinated between university music departments and nearby middle or high school programs. Some curricular tracks reserve the final semester of the fourth year of undergraduate study for student teaching; others require a fifth year of student teaching after four years of coursework. Although certification procedures vary from program to program and state to state, educators tend to agree that student teaching is the most important experience in undergraduate preparation for teaching careers (Rideout and Feldman 2002, 874).

Undergraduate music education curricula are understandably geared toward tangible employment goals. However, the focus on instruction in secondary school settings (often within well-established programs) may not adequately prepare future educators for the real-world challenges involved in working as a music educator. For instance, student teaching does not necessarily prepare students for dealing with issues of student recruitment and low enrollment rates or with the politics of justifying the importance of music instruction to school administrators. Education in the arts has been de-emphasized in public school curricula (Zakaras and Lowell 2008, 1–6), with many schools lacking programs in which students may cultivate the knowledge and skills needed to appreciate the arts. Recent studies indicate that active student participation in the arts has declined generally over the past four decades, possibly due to the expansion of home entertainment options and greater access to music, film, video games, and online media (Zakaras and Lowell 2008). Music teachers need to be better equipped with creative solutions to stimulate student interest and engagement in music and better prepared to combat such trends (see Patch, Chapter 6 in this volume). Additionally, the typical music education degree does not prepare students to deal with budget issues such as the strategic allotment of program funds or the procurement of additional resources. Cuts to education funding since 2008 have had a drastic effect on music school programs, and aspiring teachers should be informed about basic budget procedures, alternative grant funding opportunities, and community resources such as nonprofits dedicated to providing free or subsidized music instruction.

Music education majors generally are not trained for careers outside the secondary school environment either, such as positions in nonprofit organizations, community groups, or other alternative education platforms. With the unstable status of music in secondary schools, it is imperative that future music educators be prepared to seek employment in and/or establish partnerships beyond the public education sector. Even if they are not interested in teaching in nonprofit or community music organizations, an awareness of such institutions may impact the way they approach issues of program development and outreach. One way to increase student awareness of alternative music education platforms would be to encourage participation in community groups as part of their degree plan. This could be facilitated through coordination with a new or existing initiatives, possibly those based at the college campus itself.

Perhaps the biggest problems with undergraduate music education degrees are their heavy course load and the time it takes for majors to graduate with teacher certification. Graduating within a four-year time frame is a struggle for many students. A survey of degree plans from universities across the country reveals that majors are advised to enroll in a full course load every semester, including several summer sessions, in order to complete work in a timely fashion. For many students, working at this pace is not possible due to commitments outside the university (part-time jobs, gigging, etc.). Additionally, music education students tend to be discouraged from pursuing studies beyond the standard requirements of the degree, as any electives taken could slow their graduation further. Thus, a central challenge for reformulating the undergraduate music education degree is to streamline core courses and incorporate more opportunities for student-led curricular decisions without increasing the time it takes to graduate. Note that while the course load associated with music education degrees is especially burdensome, a surfeit of course requirements is common to many other music degrees as well, such as performance. One way to reduce time to degree for all music students would be to compress several introductory music courses (aural skills, theory, piano methods) into an integrated course or series of courses that require fewer hours of enrollment (five or less) each semester (see the proposed integrated music core curriculum in Chapter 14). Cutting back on the number of credit hours in the core music curriculum would allow all music students more freedom to enroll in elective courses and/or teaching certification courses without burdening them with the necessity of a fifth year of study.

2. ISSUES AND INNOVATIONS

The kind of successful curricular reform we envision will be the result of various institutions reaching a broad consensus over what the values and commitments of a twenty-first century tertiary music education should be. As the chapters in this volume have illustrated, there is already a lively debate about this, evidence of the growing need for reform and the variety of shapes it might take. Throughout, we have found it useful to frame curricular priorities along key issues where theoretical and ethical concerns may be most effectively addressed through practical and innovative strategies. In each of the following sections—local engagement, global awareness, and the practical concerns of professional musicians—we recapitulate some of the deficiencies of current pedagogy, and we reflect on the benefits and challenges to reform through case studies of innovative programs currently taking place at universities around the world. The case studies make clear that the priorities overlap, and that the areas in which they overlap may represent the most fruitful reforms to consider. We hope this section and the following chapter will provide examples of what the first steps toward effective reform might look like.

Global awareness

The focus of this chapter is in part one of diminishing the hegemony of European-derived art music over music education as part of a broader cultural project of decolonization. Communication between students, faculty, community, and administration and between national and international institutions will be vitally important in developing a musical pedagogy of the future and lasting curricular diversity. Expanding space for noncanonical musical experiences at students' home institutions contributes to this endeavor, helping prepare them for a more diverse array of employment opportunities and providing other advantages. The related goal of promoting increased global understanding would ultimately be best served by providing opportunities for students to meet and interact with people from musical cultures divergent from their own. Fortunately, many institutions both within and outside the so-called West are addressing this need by offering study abroad, international collaboration, and visiting scholar programs that serve as potential models to expand what an education in music can offer.

One such organization is the Global Network for Higher Music Education (GLOMUS), founded jointly by three Nordic higher education academies: the Royal Academy of Music in Denmark, the Malmö Academy in Sweden, and the Sibelius Academy in Finland. GLOMUS's mission is to foster collaborative projects that will promote intercultural communication, knowledge sharing, organizational development, and musical interaction for mutual inspiration and innovation (glomus.net). While the organization's three founding schools are based in Scandinavia, most of its current partners are in Africa: the Conservatory of Bamako in Mali, Eduardo Mondlane University in Mozambique, the University of Ghana, Tumaini University in Tanzania, the Egypt Academy of the Arts, and the University of Cape Town in South Africa. A handful of schools from the Middle East and Southeast Asia are among its partner schools, but its only current partner in Europe (outside Scandinavia) or the Americas is the University of Texas at Austin. Programs such as this could provide a model for many universities to follow as they attempt to diversify their offerings and link their programs to broader academic initiatives.

Perhaps the most notable activity of GLOMUS, which the institution itself characterizes as its flagship offering, is the biannual music camp that rotates between different participating locations. The camps typically attract anywhere from several dozen to a hundred people from partner institutions who participate in performances and research activities. Typically lasting about a week, camps offer ensemble concerts and workshops, informal jam sessions, and conference presentations. As Randall Stubbs (from the University of Tumaini) remarked during the 2011 camp in Ghana, "we are making music, crossing borders, crossing different cultures, and coming to realize that through music we can be united, doing all these things at the same time. We don't have to leave people in their own boxes by saying 'oh I just play classical, or I only play jazz or I just know traditional music' ... [camp activities provide a way] to bring music from many different places together."[3] While each participating school typically has specialized ensembles, the camp allows teachers and students to experience styles of music entirely new to them through group participation, formal music lessons, or attendance at concerts. International teaching and performing opportunities like this provide a means of compensating for the tendency toward overspecialization common to many Western music schools and creates opportunities for musicians to meet and network with others from around the world. On an institutional level it also allows school staff and administrators to exchange ideas. A participant in one of the recent camps from 2011 (who wished to remain anonymous) remarked, "It can be a life changing experience, I recall seeing a complete transformation in a young violinist sparked by meeting and collaborating with people from all over the world, [an experience] they would not have had otherwise."

GLOMUS also offers what they call GLOMAS, a global music master's degree that aspires to be "highly innovative and interdisciplinary" and "responsive to new needs arising from globalization in the field of music." GLOMAS builds on Mantle Hood's ideal of bimusicality[4] by encouraging students to develop performance skills in at least two traditions from different parts of the world. While the degree is offered currently through the RAM in Denmark and the Sibelius Academy in Finland, students are expected to travel to another GLOMUS partner for a semester and do fieldwork, either outside Scandinavia or in minority communities within the Nordic region. Among the stated degree objectives, graduates are expected to demonstrate "a high level of comprehensive musicianship that transcends cultural boundaries, knowledge of both traditional and contemporary hybrid music genres, and an ability to effective lead music ensembles and teach music across a diversity of formal and informal settings."[5]

Ethnographic fieldwork is a fundamental component of postgraduate study in ethnomusicology, yet programs vary greatly as to their emphasis on practical performance skills and an ability to lead world music ensembles.

3. https://www.youtube.com/watch?v=GWrsJ8WlZt4 (accessed August 18, 2015).
4. http://www.glomas.net/index.php?id=30 (accessed August 18, 2015).
5. http://www.glomas.net/index.php?id=30 (accessed August 18, 2015).

Nevertheless, many academic job positions require the latter. The GLOMAS emphasis on both study abroad and fieldwork do not exclude research and publication as goals but center on practical, hands-on experience with the goal of bi-/polymusicality. The program's emphasis on a diverse skill set contrasts with the potential constraints that tightly specialized degree paths have for music students on both undergraduate and post-grad levels. While there is no undergraduate counterpart to GLOMAS as of yet, it represents an example of how to craft a degree plan that allows for multiple emphases to broaden one's career options.

Another program that serves as an example of the potential efficacy of international study in music educations is in the current collaboration between the National Academy of the Performing Arts (NAPA) in Karachi, Pakistan, and the Butler School of Music at the University of Texas at Austin. The latter received a grant of two million dollars from the US State Department to fund a partnership with NAPA and the Fatimah Jinnah Women University, with four to ten exchange students from each institution participating per semester for the three-year period. Richard Boyum, the State Department coordinator, attests that "when students come here from Afghanistan and Pakistan to study, it's heartening to see them realize that we're not like what some of their leaders want us to think we are, nor do they conform to the stereotypes many of us still have of them." Boyum's sentiment is shared by officials from both participating institutions. The use of cultural exchange to improve interstate relations is not specific to music but is an important benefit that study abroad can have which is often overlooked. Collaborations between music programs and the US government suggest one way that institutions can potentially fund international study while also performing an important service for their own students and visitors.

Students visiting the University of Texas from Pakistan on exchange between 2013 and 2015 were assigned a faculty mentor who designed a course of study geared towards their individual interests. While they had a variety of different skill sets and emphases, all used their time to enhance their practical career skills including knowledge of Western harmonic theory, jazz improvisation, aural skills, and general (Western) musical literacy. One might argue that inviting students from formerly colonized regions to study Western music in the United States is not terribly progressive. But it must be remembered that Western music theory is often a part of the expected skill set of professional musicians all over the world and is something NAPA's own curriculum does not yet teach in depth. Furthermore both at home and as part of the exchanges, Pakistani students enjoyed a great deal of self-direction. While in Austin, for instance, spring 2014 participants organized ad hoc groups to perform and offered lecture-demonstrations about Pakistan's music on and off campus; they attended numerous live performances and workshops throughout the city and collaborated with local (though internationally connected) music professionals on recordings and performances. This kind of flexibility supports the "option-rich" and "project-oriented" learning advocated by many educators including the contributors to this volume.

The NAPA academy in Karachi itself provides an intriguing countermodel to music education as typically seen in North America. Their curriculum openly embraces the study of popular music as well as foreign music theory.[6] Students must take courses in both Hindustani and Western music theory, while those who study voice learn "Eastern" classical as well as pop and fusion styles. Instruction on several Western instruments is offered (violin, piano, guitar, flute) as well as on more distinctly local instruments (e.g., the sarangi). The course series for the NAPA diploma includes several units of "practical application" during which musicians jam, spend time in the studio, and write songs and compositions that incorporate influences from both classical and popular idioms. The embrace of external cultural influences and of popular culture is something many schools in the West could benefit from. As a junior faculty member from NAPA remarked, "It should be understood that in Pakistan it's really hard to get a degree in Music. This is the only academy struggling to be recognized as a degree-awarding institute." This and the fact that the propriety of music of any kind remains controversial in many Muslim majority countries, Pakistan included, makes NAPA's curriculum all the more remarkable.[7]

There are many recommendations for curricula that can be derived from observing ongoing experiments in international musical exchange. Perhaps first and foremost is for music schools to incentivize study abroad and participation in the offerings of international visiting scholars through changes to curricula. Many Western music schools offer music-oriented study abroad programs but they vary greatly in terms of their connection to the degree core.[8] Another prescription could be for more music schools to participate in international networking projects and globally oriented events such as GLOMUS. Music performance and education degrees might consider placing more emphasis on versatility or polymusicality, as per the GLOMAS mission statement that prioritizes a grounding in at least two distinct musical idioms or NAPA's course offerings in disparate bodies of music theory, and an allowance for fieldwork and study abroad as part of degree plans. The study of non-Western music theory, popular music, and independent project-oriented research on non-Western topics can all help degree earners prepare for potential careers beyond the orchestra, the academy, or secondary school education and become more engaged global citizens.

6. http://www.napa.org.pk/music-course-outline.php (accessed August 18, 2015).
7. http://islamqa.info/en/5000 (accessed August 18, 2015).
8. See, e.g., http://www.studyabroad.com/programs/music/default.aspx (accessed August 18, 2015).

Local engagement

While higher education already plays a critical role in supporting arts outreach programs of various sorts, university music programs could implement
additional steps to enhance local engagement. The first step might be to foster more direct participation in music among all university students, first by
cultivating a greater awareness of events on or off campus, and second by
incorporating more amateur music-making opportunities into the curriculum. Freeman (2014, 68–69) suggests that music majors can generate greater
awareness among the student body by networking with peers in other departments and attracting broader audiences to their own performances. Faculty
teaching music courses, especially those tailored to non-majors, could more
strongly encourage students to participate in music events of all sorts. For
their part, ensemble leaders could reach out to the general student body by
scheduling performances in highly visible public spaces and in conjunction
with social events. Departments might promote participation by organizing
cross-disciplinary music initiatives and festivals, advertising ensembles and
private lessons for non-majors (as at Lawrence Conservatory) or by incorporating hands-on music-making exercises in courses for non-majors. University
music programs might foster additional engagement among the larger campus community by incorporating performance and instruction in a diverse
range of music genres, thus creating greater alignment between audience preferences and the musical styles performed.

Music programs can work to bridge the divide between universities and
local communities by utilizing resources in the surrounding area. Campuses
are an intrinsic part of the community and music schools can greatly enhance
professional training by encouraging students to engage with community
events. For example, faculty and students could reach out to local venues and
musicians to facilitate off-campus performance opportunities (see Klemperer,
Chapter 12 in this volume). Increased contact with local venues and performers would help students develop well-rounded musical networks, and these
connections could provide the perfect platform for heuristic, entrepreneurial exercises beyond the university classroom (Partti and Westerlund, 2012,
306–308).

Providing music instruction to local populations represents another
important form of outreach. Excellent examples of this are the string projects that have emerged in several college and university music programs
across the nation.[9] These programs provide students with high-quality music

9. The National String Project Consortium is a coalition of outreach programs based
in colleges and universities across the United States that provide music instruction on
string instruments to elementary-age children. The consortium, now an independent
nonprofit, was originally founded in 1998 by the American String Teachers Association
to address the shortage of qualified string teachers. More information can be found at

instruction on violin, viola, cello, and string bass while also affording unique teacher-training and mentoring experiences to university students. However, the programs are often constrained by enrollment caps and limited numbers of instructors, instructional venues, or other resources. Departments might engage a broader audience by linking outreach initiatives to existing primary school programs or by offering instruction in a more diverse selection of instruments and repertoire. If outreach generates revenue for the music school, a greater diversity of musical offerings could lead to additional student interest and more income for student mentors.

Finally, university music programs could cultivate more local participation by requiring that music majors design and implement their own sustainable outreach programs either as (1) final projects associated with existing music courses or (2) as semester-long independent study projects for degree credit. Such initiatives could focus on underserved communities/populations in the area or facilitate amateur music making among non-music majors across the university, as discussed. Music majors would receive course credits toward their degrees while gaining valuable teaching and administrative experience through the planning, establishment, and maintenance of outreach platforms.

Practical concerns of professional musicians, student-driven projects

Entrepreneurship

Musical entrepreneurship attempts to address the crisis of underemployment and low wages common to many professional musicians by helping them develop new repertoires, new forms of artistic dissemination, new audiences, and/or new ways to engage audiences. Articulating an artistic vision and creating a work plan or promotional strategy are skills that can be developed in this way; the ability to assess a situation, identify possibilities, and pursue opportunities constitutes the foundation of an entrepreneurial attitude (Smith, 2014, 76). Creativity is key, as are collaboration and passion. Because students must devote extended amounts of time to any artistic initiative, passion becomes central to their ability to see it to completion. Finally, flexibility is also important. Becoming a lifelong learner and adapting one's entrepreneurial strategies to the changing demands of a given employment context

http://stringsprojects.org/. Brenda Brenner (2010) has written about a variation of the string project between Indiana University Jacobs School of Music and the Monroe County School Corporation that provides music instruction to all first graders at a local elementary school.

contribute greatly to the success of musicians today (Benedict and Schmidt, 2014, 84).

Because music students spend countless hours learning to perform, by the time they reach college they have already developed a variety of skills that can be useful in activities entirely separate from music. "[Musicians can] concentrate amidst distraction. They know the value of working toward long-range goals in incremental steps. They can organize their time [so as] to accomplish what is needed. They should have mastered nerves and anxiety attacks. They know how to find others with similar interests and diverse skills to put together an organization" (Smith, 2014, 68). Most entrepreneurship programs build off these core skill sets in some way.

By associating creative skills and interdisciplinary structures, current entrepreneurial experiments in music curricula are integrating student preferences and professional necessities. Some programs have managed to link their performance focus to coursework in which integral pedagogy and an eclectic range of student initiatives, sometimes entirely outside music, develop alongside the applied orientation of the program. Many of these initiatives are conceived, designed, and executed solely by students (Kaschub 2014, 127). The Prism Recital Series in Chicago, which reimagines "classical music with aspiring young artists" (primarily through the generation of spoken program notes or demonstration via excerpts), and Eclettico, a nonprofit ensemble in Michigan whose focus is education, outreach, and fundraising, are two examples of student-driven projects that have succeeded in charting alternative musical paths.[10]

As a corollary to entrepreneurship programs, music schools increasingly offer independent music business degree options with many of the same components. They enhance students' marketability upon graduation and provide community internship opportunities as well as insights into how to manage one's own career or those of others. Knowledge of topics such as copyright law, the drafting of musical contracts, how to license recorded work, how to start one's own business, and how to use the Internet as a career resource potentially benefit all graduates.

Institutions such as the Lawrence and New England conservatories have foregrounded a unique set of entrepreneurial skills in their curricula and serve as examples of curricular experiments of this kind within the United States. Both conservatories devote a significant percentage of undergraduate performance degree coursework to the cultivation of business and entrepreneurial skills. In this way they hope to counter what the Strategic National Arts Alumni Project (SNAAP) has identified as a serious deficiency in the preparation of most arts graduates.[11] The Entrepreneurial Musician course at Lawrence

10. http://thomasleepiano.wix.com/prism; http://ecletticoquartet.wix.com/eclettico (accessed 28 December 2016).

11. http://snaap.indiana.edu/snaapshot/#skills (accessed November 3, 2015).

University incorporates improvisational exercises, creative play, and interdisciplinary initiatives alongside instruction in business skills. Creative activities include dancing, other improvisational movement, or improvisational singing in an attempt to push students outside their typical "comfort zone," overcome psychological barriers, and learn to be more flexible. Lawrence Conservatory devotes considerable energy to infusing self-driven, creative activities of this type into its conservatory culture. The objective is to make open discussions and creativity a part of all classes and ensembles. Although music students are not required to take the gamut of entrepreneurial classes offered, the liberal arts and dual-degree model championed by Lawrence orients them towards diverse training. One example of a recent entrepreneurial initiative developed there is Unearth Piano: Discovering a Musical Community. This project attempts to reconceive the standard piano lesson. Each student's studies are individualized and based on their unique goals as a musician, including exposure to multiple repertoires and musical styles. In addition to private lessons, students participate in group classes that allow them to expand and share their musicality in exciting ways. Entire families are encouraged to participate in piano performance and to learn to be musical together.[12]

At the New England Conservatory (NEC), by contrast, the Career Services Center and Department of Entrepreneurial Musicianship (DEM, founded in 2010) combine to offer artist-specific services to students and alumni. The department offers a variety of courses ranging from Introduction to Entrepreneurship (required of all undergraduates) to offerings on marketing, communications, financial planning, and legal issues. Whether promoting music through website creation or the preparation of budget proposals, students learn by working on practical tasks. The DEM has 150 performers, composers, arts administrators, NEC staff, and professionals from other fields, all of whom serve as advisers. They work one-on-one with students in the introductory course and serve as mentors of subsequent projects as well. The DEM also provides access to "The Bridge: Worldwide Music Connection," providing "online access to 3,000 opportunities in music and arts administration."[13] Without losing sight of the essential purpose of a music education institution, which is the musical training of performers on their instruments of choice, NEC's entrepreneurial initiative provides guidance as to how students can overcome the many challenges they will face after graduation.

A final important feature of the NEC's Entrepreneurial Department is its Grant Program that offers students seed funding for initiatives of their own creation. It facilitates projects associated with all aspects of presenting a concert: artistic and project planning, oversight, production, and marketing. Events can take place on or off campus, allowing students to connect

12. http://anthonyvcapparelli.wix.com/unearthpiano (accessed October 7, 2015).
13. http://necmusic.edu/bridge (accessed October 7, 2015).

with diverse communities. As a result, NEC students last year earned around $85,000 through performances at weddings, corporate parties, birthdays, holiday gatherings, and other events.[14]

An important difference between the Lawrence Music Conservatory and NEC is that the former focuses on students' creative abilities conceived broadly, while the NEC focuses mainly on entrepreneurship skills centered on performance. Lawrence could be described as promoting leadership and entrepreneurship among improviser-composer-performers, much as advocated in the CMS task force document. In such a program, students ideally develop the skills that allow them not only to flourish as professional musicians but also to assume leadership roles in society at large, including as part of nonmusical careers. Yet both programs represent an outstanding response to the current deficit of practical and professional skills to which aspiring performers are exposed and to the constant changes in the artistic marketplace.

NEC's program and others notwithstanding, it is clear that undergraduate curricula in general do not adequately prepare students to secure external funding support for their endeavors. While grant-writing courses may be required of arts administration majors, they are only tangentially accessible to music majors as elective credits and are rarely promoted by advisers. In today's unstable arts economy, it is imperative that all music majors be informed about alternative funding options, administrative and legislative policies, and budgetary procedures that impact support for the arts. Freeman, for instance, suggests encouraging musicians to think about issues of funding early in their careers through a ninety-minute exercise called "A Budget for the Chicago Symphony Orchestra" (2014, 70). The purpose of the assignment is to raise awareness about the group's 45 percent annual budget deficit and its implications. Knowledge of budgetary issues seems especially relevant to music educators, as many of the tasks they perform are administrative. Middle and high school band directors, for example, function not only as teachers; directors also must oversee the allotment of funds for travel, instrument purchases, repairs, the commissioning of new repertoire, and frequently student scholarships. They must be prepared to conduct their own campaigns to solicit funds in compensation for state budget cuts (Leachman and Mai 2014).

Technology

The career paths possible with a BM or BA degree continue to become increasingly diverse in response to the changing landscape of established music institutions as well as to developments in technology and media more broadly. If

14. http://necmusic.edu/em (accessed October 7, 2015).

tertiary music programs have been slow in providing adequate training for shifting labor markets, this might be not only because of institutional inertia but also because of the speed at which technological change has taken place. Only two decades ago, the task of recording, editing, and distributing music recordings remained the domain of engineers and other specialists. Today, all these tasks can be accomplished by almost anyone with relatively inexpensive equipment. Yet formal training in music technology remains limited for the most part to specialized music production degrees, suggesting an institutional blind spot concerning the importance such training could play in the lives of musicians.

Technology shapes many aspects of musicianship and its values and practices. Partti and Westerlund (2012, 2) highlight that new technologies have ushered in an era of "digital musicianship" that places increased value on participation, musical versatility across genres, and a hybrid aesthetics that challenges notions of authenticity and authorship. These values are not new or unique to digital music, but they have been underrepresented in Western art music pedagogy. From the perspective of both personal enrichment and professional development, it makes sense to train musicians to be adept at boundary crossing and to be comfortable adapting to new musical worlds. Adopting the technologies that connect musicians to a worldwide audience is a process not only of learning to use the software but also of embracing the values associated with them.

Incorporating practical technological skills into a music curriculum poses challenges to existing curricular models. One challenge, common to many areas of a curriculum, is determining *how much* technology to teach. Berklee's performance degree, for instance, requires all students to enroll in a semester-long course titled Introduction to Music Technology. Not all programs might be willing to devote this much attention to the topic, as any time spent on technology takes time away from other content. A related issue is the question of *what* technology to teach, given the variety of valuable hardware and software available and the risk that certain skills will become obsolete. There is no single solution to these issues, but at the very least we believe all music students regardless of specialization should know something about (1) how sound is recorded and digitized, (2) how to use music notation/sequencing software, (3) how to manipulate sound in digital audio workstations, and (4) how to amplify sound for live performance. Knowledge of these skills combines an abstract understanding of digital music with its practical application. While understanding the minutiae of industry-standard hardware or software is of value, ultimately what will most benefit students is to understand abstract concepts as they relate to practice. Gary Powell, an accomplished composer, producer, and senior lecturer of music production at UT-Austin, recommends that technological assignments involve students training themselves in the particulars of any given equipment. Armed with an understanding of fundamental concepts, students should be able to problem-solve using online manuals, forums, FAQs, and trial and error. Not only will this deepen students' ability to connect abstract and practical skills, but it will also prepare them for the inevitable technological changes and uncertainties of the future.

Popular music

Educating musicians about popular music should be a central part of any music curriculum. Popular music, defined broadly as any music intended primarily for mass distribution, has permeated virtually all aspects of music making today. Given its prominence and the diversity of styles with which it is associated, instruction on this topic cannot occur in a single popular music course. Rather, it must be integrated into all aspects of curriculum, from repertoire selection in studios and ensembles to music history, composition, ear training, and theory. An embrace of popular music relates to various topics already highlighted in this chapter, such as the way such music can create ties with local communities or the way entrepreneurial musicians must navigate the waters of the commercial sphere in order to be financially successful. The following section considers how some schools currently incorporate popular music into performance, history, and professional development courses as a means of providing potential models for other institutions.

The most obvious way in which popular music can be incorporated into performance and practice is through repertoire selection in studios or ensembles. Instructors might encourage their students to view their instrument as a point of entry into multiple musical worlds, with Western art music only one of many. Introducing multiple repertoires engages students in what Frank Heuser calls "juxtapositional pedagogy," an approach that "pairs contrasting musical learning experiences ... in a single instructional setting to create spaces where the nature of musical thinking and learning can be explored" (2014: 108). Heuser suggests pairing string orchestra repertoire with mariachi pieces, choral vocal methods with black gospel, marching snare technique with world percussion, and so on. This approach reinforces the notion that pedagogical value lies not in a particular repertoire but in the abstract and technical skills required to successfully comprehend and execute it. Juxtaposing repertoire gives students multiple perspectives from which to experience music and brings into sharper relief aspects of musical aesthetics that become normalized and obscured when unexamined. The benefit of foregrounding popular music within such an approach is that it often stands in sharpest contrast to the tradition of Western art music, conceived as autonomous, universal, and timeless. It is precisely the commercial, social, and political contingencies of popular music that encourage critical engagement with music Heuser envisions. Needless to say, juxtapositional pedagogy may vary in practice depending on the students, instructors, and musical forms involved, but it accommodates a wide range of options for teachers.

Proponents of curriculum reform argue that a canonical bias in music education stifles many aspects of music making by prioritizing interpretation over creativity (Campbell et al. 2014, 2). The authors define creativity as involving qualities such as "inventiveness, interaction, the ability to synthesize new forms of knowledge from diverse sources, and the emergence of an individual voice or style within a discipline" (Campbell et al. 2014, 2). While both interpretation and creativity can be emphasized in any repertoire—for example, we can imagine improvising in the style of a Bach fugue or meticulously recreating a Coltrane free jazz solo note for note—we tend not to do these things because we attend to conventions within particular idioms. Given this, many forms of popular music are better suited for promoting creativity than Western art music. The emphasis on improvisation, on a creating an "individual voice" that both conforms to normative stylistic parameters and yet stands out is a key feature of many styles of popular music, especially those linked to music of the African diaspora. Ed Sarath is a strong proponent of jazz, broadly construed, as the ideal vehicle for teaching musical creativity because of the genre's "improvisatory core that integrates a wide array of other processes—including composition, performance, and various kinds of theoretical analysis" (Campbell et al. 2014, 3). His emphasis on musical processes and experiences shifts our pedagogical focus from "what did you learn to play?" to "what did you learn how to *do*?" Interpretation of existing repertoire will undoubtedly remain central to the skills we teach, but it should not come at the cost of other skills. Not only does training in creativity and improvisation produce better musicians, but as Sarath points out those skills have the potential transfer over to other professions, and more generally promotes a dynamism and engagement conducive to personal fulfillment in contemporary society (Campbell et al. 2014, 4; see also Sarath 2013).

Another way to incorporate popular music into music curricula is as part of music history courses. Many colleges and universities offer courses on the history of rock, jazz, African American music, or world music, all of which focus to a greater or lesser extent on popular repertoire. Such offerings provide needed curricular diversity, but too often they are conceived as less valuable for music majors than canonical Western music history, as if popular music were thematically separate from it. Professional musicians of the future would be best served by a more holistic treatment of music history, perhaps one simultaneously (dis)organized chronologically and geographically, with more emphasis on themes and issues. To accomplish this without adding extra coursework will require adding new material about popular musics *and* cutting existing material about Western art music. These changes will inevitably lead to difficult decisions about what musics to include or exclude in a given sequence, but of course all musical surveys are inherently incomplete. Our central task should be to choose musically engaging representative pieces from diverse sources and to understand them in relation to one another. Scholars recognize that all histories generate canons; rather than assume students will understand our selection criteria or that of a given textbook, we would do well to make our selection criteria explicit and transparent. We must teach not only music history but also music historiography across art, popular, and traditional idioms. The study of popular music can teach our students about important contemporary topics such as musical/cultural hybridity, difference and identity, popular dance, technology, and the modern recording industry, just to name a few that might be more difficult if not impossible to address through exclusive focus on art music.

Various curricular models may accomplish this sort of reform. One possibility would be to keep a Western art music core course or sequence but change the degree program to require that students study other musical styles as well. Berklee, for instance, requires its performers to take two history courses: a one-semester course on the European tradition and an elective on topics ranging from particular themes (film music, music of women composers), a selection of alternative repertoire (contemporary African American music, the history of rock), or a geographic focus (music of the Caribbean, American music). Another example is found at the Butler School of Music at the University of Texas at Austin, which starting in 2017 offers a four-semester music history sequence for majors. The most novel course is the introductory Music and Culture, co-taught by professors in musicology and ethnomusicology. This course "introduces students to broad concepts that shape musical practice and reception while also exploring the interconnections between canonical Western European music, popular genres, and non-Western traditions." Units in the course range from learning about different notational systems to the role of music in colonialism and globalization. Through various cross-cultural case studies, the course develops the critical skills students need to grapple with historical and ethical questions that arise in later segments of the music history sequence (Western music from the beginning of notation to 1750, 1750 to World War I, and World War I to the present).

CONCLUSION

In this chapter we've explored several proposals for enacting change to tertiary music education. Some are small, such as introducing more non-Western repertoire into existing models of instruction, while others are large, like restructuring degree programs or radically reorganizing large ensembles. In addition, the following chapter outlines a few other larger-scale reform proposals. What these all have in common is that they begin by looking at the world that today's music students will enter upon graduation and consider what skills they will need. Whether that involves greater familiarity with other music traditions, understanding the ways in which music can serve as a tool for social change, or acquiring the technological savvy to produce a demo, tomorrow's students will benefit from the concerted efforts of faculty and administrators to constantly revisit the question of what constitutes a progressive musical education.

REFERENCES

Benedict, Cathy, and Patrick Schmidt. 2014. "Educating Teachers for 21st-Century Challenges. The Music Educator as a Cultural Citizen." In *Promising Practices in 21st Century Music Teacher Education*, Michele Kaschub and Janice Smith, eds., 79–98. New York: Oxford University Press.

Brenner, Brenda. 2010. "A Unique Collaboration: The Fairview Elementary School String Project." In *Alternative Approaches in Music Education*, Ann C. Clements, ed., 201–212. Lanham, MD: Rowman and Littlefield.

Campbell, Patricia, et al. 2014. "Transforming Music Study from Its Foundations. A Manifesto for Progressive Change in the Undergraduate Preparation of Music Majors." Report of the Task Force on the Undergraduate Music Major, College Music Society. http://www.mtosmt.org/issues/mto.16.22.1/manifesto.pdf. Accessed January 31, 2017.

Freeman, Robert. 2014. *The Crisis of Classical Music in America*. Lanham, MD: Rowman and Littlefield.

Heuser, Frank. 2014. "Juxtapositional Pedagogy as an Organizing Principle in University Music Education Programs." In *Promising Practices in 21st Century Music Teacher Education*, Michele Kaschub and Janice Smith, eds., 107–124. New York: Oxford University Press.

Kaschub, Michele. 2014. "Where It All Comes Together: Student-Driven Project-Based Learning in Music Teacher Education." In *Promising Practices in 21st Century Music Teacher Education*, Michele Kaschub and Janice Smith, eds., 125–144. New York: Oxford University Press.

Kaschub, Michele, and Janice Smith, eds. 2014. *Promising Practices in 21st Century Music Teacher Education*. New York: Oxford University Press.

Leachman, Michael, and Chris Mai. 2014. "Most States Still Funding Schools Less Than before the Recession." *Center on Budget and Policy Priorities*. http://www.cbpp.org/research/most-states-still-funding-schools-less-than-before-the-recession. Last modified October 16, 2014. Accessed November 11, 2015.

Madrid, Alejandro. 2011. "American Music in Times of Postnationality." *Journal of the American Musicological Society*, Vol. 64 No. 3 (Fall), 699–703.

McCarthy, Kevin F., et al. 2001. *The Performing Arts in a New Era*. Study commissioned by the Pew Charitable Trusts. Santa Monica, CA: RAND Corporation.

Partti, Heidi, and Heidi Westerlund. 2012. "Democratic Musical Learning: How the Participatory Revolution in New Media Challenges the Culture of Music Education." In *Sound Musicianship. Understanding the Crafts of Music*, A. Brown, ed., 300–312. Meaningful Music Making for Life. Newcastle: Cambridge Scholars.

Rideout, Roger, and Allan Feldman. 2002. "Research in Music Student Teaching." In *The New Handbook of Research on Music Teaching and Learning*, Richard Colwell and Carol Richardson, eds., 874–886. New York: Oxford University Press.

Sarath, Edward. 2013. *Improvisation, Creativity, and Consciousness. Jazz as Integral Template for Music, Education, and Society.* New York: SUNY Press.

Smith, Janet. 2014. "Entrepreneurial Music Education." In *Promising Practices in 21st Century Music Teacher Education*, Michele Kaschub and Janice Smith, eds., 61–76. New York: Oxford University Press.

Zakaras, Laura, and Julia F. Lowell. 2008. *Cultivating Demand for the Arts. Arts Learning, Arts Engagement, and State Arts Policy.* Study commissioned by the Wallace Foundation. Santa Monica, CA: RAND Corporation.

CHAPTER 14

Sample Curricular Models

ROBIN D. MOORE WITH JUAN AGUDELO,
KATIE CHAPMAN, CARLOS DÁVALOS,
HANNAH DURHAM, MYRANDA HARRIS,
AND CREIGHTON MOENCH

PART 1. ENHANCED CORE MODEL

Music school curricula have limited room for new subject matter. Current course requirements in music history and theory, as well as in canonical music performance, make it difficult to expand content so as to include new academic courses or styles of performance. This complicates the creation of new models that help students develop their own interests and unique skills while still satisfying general course/performance requirements. The model presented here, inspired by Brian Pertl—that of changing the content of existing courses without changing their names—might facilitate the incorporation of students' own unique skills, creativity, and interests while bypassing the bureaucratic complications involved in proposing and approving entirely new curricula.

We have included an outline of the first two years of core content for an orchestral instrumental performance degree at a school of music, using existing requirements at the University of Texas as a model.[1] Coursework in this permutation (theory, ear training, keyboard skills, etc.) would become more topically and conceptually tied to the chronological music history sequence. Students would explore noncanonical repertory on their principal instruments, in large ensembles, and in class piano. Improvisation and

---

1. To view the original degree plan, please see http://finearts.utexas.edu/sites/files/cofa/degrees/bm_orch_inst_14-16_dg.pdf (accessed December 28 2016).

sight-reading become central features of the music theory, ear training, and class piano sequences, and theory and ear training adopt multiple modes of musical analysis (pitch-based, rhythmic, textural, timbral). The music history sequence shifts emphasis from a content-oriented structure to a thematic approach based on critical thinking and the practical application of knowledge. The revised three-semester sequence would distill historical content in order to highlight issues of social justice, the role of technology in music making, and global music awareness, among other topics. It would be more pedagogically effective because it would highlight issues surrounding all forms of music making and provide ways of thinking critically about it.

1st year

I. Lower Div. Principle Instrument—Instrument 312:
   - Strong proficiency on at least one instrument.
   - Instructors would not limit their required audition or performance material to Western canonical repertoires.
II. Approved Ensemble—ENS
   - Expand repertoires to a wider range of styles within current ensembles, and expand approved ensemble lists. At least one arrangement of a noncanonical work must be included in each concert.
   - Students are required to take both large and small ensembles appropriate to their primary instrument. Small ensembles may include world music, popular music, avant-garde / new music ensembles, or chamber music ensembles (e.g., string quartet, wind quartet, a cappella choirs).
III. Musicianship (music theory)—MUS 605A & B
   - Fundamentals of tonal theory (ear training / sight singing included under this course number).
   - Introduces more modes of analysis beginning in the second semester (pitch-based, rhythmic, textural, etc.), and explores a wider range of musical styles.
IV. Class piano I & II—MUS 201N & M
   - Fundamental keyboard skills for nonkeyboard musicians.
   - Would align with content in MUS 605—ear training, sight-reading, notation studies.
   - Weekly exploration of different scales and modes, as well as new styles of piano performance (ragtime, salsa keyboard, black gospel, the accompaniment of popular song) in addition to canonical works.
     ◦ Improvisation (individual and group).
     ◦ Sight reading (individual and group).

2nd year

I. Lower Div. Principle Instrument—Instrument 312
   - Strong proficiency on a primary instrument with incorporation of repertoire/styles of at least one secondary musical tradition.
     ◦ Juries include the performance of repertoire in a non-Western genre.
     ◦ Weekly assessments of improvisational skills, including exercises that facilitate the capability to skillfully develop a motif or a musical fragment in performance. This requirement compensates for an overemphasis on interpretive study.

II. Approved Ensemble—ENS
   - At least one non-Western European ensemble required.
     ◦ Final concert will demonstrate an ability to perform, arrange, or compose in this style (depends on students' major areas).
   - Students will take at least one small ensemble that engages with local communities, perhaps in conjunction with educational programs or off-campus concerts.
     ◦ The ensembles may feature local visiting artists and possibly collaborative recording projects.
   - Students will be asked to organize off-campus shows and outreach events in order to develop entrepreneurial skills (e.g., booking venues, promoting, teaching, fundraising, self-marketing).

III. History of Music—MUS 313 M&N
   Music history courses in the modified sequence will depart from content-driven formats to further emphasize critical thinking. We recommend that some existing content on canonical repertoire be incorporated into theory courses (such as counterpoint and harmony) in order to create more space for thematic topics (music and colonialism, music and gender, music and patronage) and units on noncanonical repertoires.
   - Coursework could involve analysis not only of scores but also of people and performances. Weekly assignments might include transcription, recording, audio editing, composing, and academic writing in order to emphasize the application of course content in different ways.
   - Instead of three semesters based on a chronological sequence, the following might provide a more flexible model, depending on the goal of the institution.
     ◦ 1st semester: general themes of the European art music tradition; e.g., basic features (pitches, modes, rhythms, meters, textures, tonality, etc.), notational forms, musical concepts and their sociohistorical contexts.
     ◦ 2nd semester: organized by theme, such as music and gender or racial studies, identity, and nationalism.

○ 3rd semester: a focus on global/contemporary topics such as musical hybridity, music and technology, the rise of classical music performance in non-Western countries.
- Final presentation. Students will choose one of the three options below (they can be combined in various ways) for a final presentation based on their concentration. This requirement is intended to help students to cultivate their own interests and develop creative performance skills:
  1. A salon-like recital combining performance, a listening guide, a reception, and a brief oral presentation on musical/historical analysis. After the recital, students will write a short reflective report demonstrating their grasp of musical concepts and their sociohistorical meanings.
  2. A fieldwork project that requires students to relate the content of their recital to local musical scenes (a liturgical context, a local performing arts initiative, live music showcases at local restaurants, participation in festival, etc.). The final presentation may require students to incorporate the use of technology (e.g., documentary film, audio recording or editing, transcription and engraving).
  3. A research paper that focuses on a musical subject/culture with a discussion of its relation to a theme or topic (e.g., music and national identity). Students will give a presentation with musical examples and a short summary about the writing process.
IV. Structure of Tonal Music (music theory)—MUS 612A & B
- A continuation of tonal theory with the incorporation of modes of analysis for musical traditions other than the Western European canon, as well as alternate forms of musical notation.
- Corresponds to MUS 313M & N in content
- Incorporates a strong compositional component in order to apply concepts practically.
- Two academic projects involving noncanonical repertory on a student's principal instrument to be performed as part of studio assignments. These will result in mini lecture-recitals.
V. Ear Training/Sight Singing—MUS 411A & B
- Designed in tandem with MUS 612.
- Utilizes improvisational exercises and student-led individual/group projects.
- Works in conjunction with music discussed in 313M & N.
VI. Class piano III & IV—MUS 210J & K
- Extends content from 612 and 411.
- Incorporates improvisation practice (groups, individual).
- Sight reading exercises include non-Western repertory.

Juries would include two or three pieces in contrasting styles, an improvisation exercise, as well as a short research report (spring semester).

2. PLURALIST MODEL. GENERAL OUTLINE OF THE FIRST TWO YEARS

This model, based on a liberal arts degree proposed by Dr. Victoria Levine, functions as a potential transition from a standard music performance degree toward one with a more diverse focus. The key difference between the pluralist model and others is that students do not declare a specialization (in performance, education, conducting, etc.) until their third year. Until that point, students take courses in multiple areas of the music school that they might choose to specialize in later. This allows them to them to explore a variety of degree options firsthand. It also expands the breadth of their performance abilities and related skills.

Core coursework in the pluralist model remains essentially the same as that of most music schools' vocal, piano, and orchestral performance degrees today. That is, it consists of classes in music history, music theory, ear training, sight-singing, ensembles, and private lessons.[2] However, the content of core courses could be expanded if desired. For example, the Lawrence Conservatory organizes its 21st Century Musicianship course around five core values, including the development of multimusicality and expanding traditional conceptions of performance.[3] Such an approach could be adapted to the pluralist model. During private lessons students might be asked to perform world music or vernacular pieces in addition to Western repertoire; this could serve as a complement to coursework such as the Introduction to World Music in the fourth semester. Music theory and ear training could incorporate materials and exercises from non-Western repertoires or other vernacular repertoires as well.

The pluralist paradigm depends on the ability of the faculty to teach core courses during the first two years on topics such as music and technology or the music business, that may lie outside their expertise. For that reason it may be necessary to transition to such a curriculum gradually. Yet the flexible structure of the model has the advantage of foregrounding areas of study, like music history, theory, and performance, that most institutions are already familiar with even if their content is modified. For example, music history might be taught through the lens of social issues and theory

2. See, e.g., requirements at the University of Texas: http://finearts.utexas.edu/sites/files/cofa/degrees/bm_orch_inst_14-16_dg.pdf (accessed October 7, 2015).
3. See https://www.lawrence.edu/conservatory/21st-century-musicianship for additional details (accessed November 11, 2015).

through performance. The pluralist model draws together several skills in the same course, underscoring their interrelations and creating a well-rounded musician.

The sample curriculum below lists each semester as corresponding to thirteen credit-hour requirements in the music school (including electives). This allows students some flexibility in their schedules to add extra ensembles, courses of interest, or university core courses as necessary, assuming eighteen hours per semester as a standard load (see Table 14.1). In addition, during the last two years in the program, students focus on their chosen specialty and have fewer required courses, so they should have time to complete other university requirements at that time as well.

First 2 years = 48–60 hours
Core: 40 hours
Music History = 3 semesters (3 hours/semester)

- This could be organized chronologically or in a more innovative way, such as through an issue-based (race, gender, etc) syllabus that includes non-Western and current musics or reverse chronological order.

Music Theory = 4 semesters (3 hours/semester)

- The theory sequence could include at least one semester of Comparative Music Theory, in which the repertoire used to study Western theory might include noncanonical pieces such as jazz standards and/or could focus on non-Western traditions, such as Indian ragas or gamelan.

Ear Training and Sight Singing = 1 semester (3 hours)

- Integrated with music theory classes after the first semester.
- First semester intended to build a foundation in practice, similar to what is already commonplace in music schools.

Ensembles = 4 semesters (1 hour/semester)

- Students would be required to enroll in a different ensemble each semester, unless extra credit hours are available and they wish to enroll in multiple ensembles as elective, in which case they could choose which additional groups to participate in.
  - They must have participated in a minimum of four different ensembles by the end of their second year.

- Students perform in at least one large and one small ensemble during this period on their instrument of specialization (or a variation).
  - Performers of instruments not central to most ensembles, such as piano, would have to play on another instrument to fulfill this requirement.
  - Large vs. small:
    - Large ensembles generally have twenty-plus students and perform canonical repertoire. Examples include wind symphony, concert chorale, opera ensemble, chamber singers, symphony band, symphony orchestra, jazz orchestra, gamelan.
    - Small ensembles more often play world, avant-garde, original, and/or noncanonical music and tend to feature soloists and improvisatory experiences. Most consist of fewer than twenty students. Examples include mariachi, recording arts ensemble, new music ensemble, North Indian ensemble, show choir.

Private Lessons = 4 semesters (3 hours/semester)
Additional elective options during the first four semesters (3-hour academic courses)
Intro to Music Business
Intro to Recording Technology
Intro to World Music
Intro to Music Education/Pedagogy
Intro to Composition
Conducting
Entrepreneurship

- It might be possible to combine Music Business and Entrepreneurship and/or Music Education and Conducting.

Following the first two semesters students would

- declare a specialization.
- plan two large projects (one each year).
  - These might include recital, a program of community outreach, music recording, marketing, composition, teaching, or a combination of such elements.

The first two years of study could be organized in a number of ways as long as multisemester courses are taken in correct sequence (these are shown in bold).

Table 14.1. SAMPLE TWO-YEAR PLAN, PLURALIST MODEL

First Semester	Second Semester
Ensemble: 1 hour	Ensemble: 1 hour
Private Lesson: 3 hours	Private Lesson: 3 hours
Ear Training / Sight-Singing: 3 hours	**Music Theory 2**: 3 hours
Music Theory 1: 3 hours	**Music History 1**: 3 hours
Intro to Music Business: 3 hours	Intro to Music Technology: 3 hours
Total: 13 hours	Total: 13 hours

Third Semester	Fourth Semester
Ensemble: 1 hour	Ensemble: 1 hour
Private Lesson: 3 hours	Private Lessons: 3 hours
Music Theory 3: 3 hours	**Music Theory 4 (Comparative)**: 3 hours
Music History 2: 3 hours	**Music History 3**: 3 hours
Intro to Composition: 3 hours	Intro to World Music: 3 hours
Total: 13 hours	Total: 13 hours

3. INTEGRATED MUSIC CORE CURRICULA

The manifesto by College Music Society's Task Force on the Undergraduate Music Major (Campbell et al. 2014, 40–43) suggests "integration" as a necessary strategy for undergraduate music curriculum reform. By integration, the authors mean that introductory music courses be taught in a classroom setting where musical creation (performance, improvisation, and/or composition) and applications of music knowledge (theory, aural skills, aesthetics, and technical skills of playing an instrument) function together as the primary modes of musical learning.[4] An integrated core curriculum of music instruction would compress a number of introductory music courses, such as theory, aural skills, and piano classes, into a single course or series of mutually reinforcing courses that transmit musical concepts and skills in a more condensed and holistic format. This integrated curriculum would cut down on the number of course hours during the first two years of undergraduate music study (see Table 14.1).

In order for the Integrated Core Curriculum model to be effective, we suggest that students meet more frequently in class formats that alternate between lecture-based instruction and hands-on application of musical concepts. For instance, students might meet three times per week in 1-hour lectures and

4. The idea for this integrated model builds upon Ed Sarath's discussion of "the Music School of the Future" and his description of an integrated music curriculum model in which all music learning is anchored in the processes of improvising and composing (Sarah 2013, 294–302).

twice per week in 1.5-hour sessions of applied practice (see Table 14.2). The most crucial aspect of the integrated core model is that students demonstrate an understanding of musical concepts discussed in lecture through creative application exercises. These might require students to express concepts through performance (individually or in ensemble format), through notation (musical arrangement and composition), or through technology (the use of notation or recording software with playback functions). Creative application exercises could be tailored so that students develop a diverse skill set in all the areas mentioned.

While overhauling the course sequence for the first two years of music study might seem daunting, one way to begin the shift toward an integrated music core could be for faculty to devise projects, assignments, and/or courses that would reinforce skills taught across several foundational courses. For example, some faculty have incorporated components of improvisation, performance, and composition within academic music courses. Professor Victoria Levine of Colorado College, for example, has developed an undergraduate music course

Table 14.2. COMPARISON OF TYPICAL UNDERGRADUATE MUSIC CURRICULUM AND INTEGRATED MUSIC CORE CURRICULUM

Typical Sequence and Hours of Introductory Core Music Courses	Integrated Music Core Curriculum
Semester 1:	Semester 1:
Music Theory & Analysis I (3 hours)	Integrated Music Core I (6 hours)
Aural Skills / Ear Training I (2–3 hours)	
Keyboard Skills I (3 hours)	
Semester 2:	Semester 2:
Music Theory & Analysis II (3 hours)	Integrated Music Core II (6 hours)
Aural Skills / Ear Training II (2–3 hours)	
Keyboard Skills II (3 hours)	
Semester 3:	Semester 3:
Music Theory & Analysis III (3 hours)	Integrated Music Core III (5 hours)
Aural Skills / Ear Training III (2–3 hours)	Music History I, correlated to integrated
Keyboard Skills III (3 hours)	core (3 hours)
Music History I (3 hours)	
Semester 4:	Semester 4:
Music Theory & Analysis IV (3 hours)	Integrated Music Core IV (5 hours)
Aural Skills / Ear Training IV (2–3 hours)	Music History II, correlated to integrated
Keyboard Skills IV (3 hours)	core (3 hours)
Music History II (3 hours)	
Total Hours: 38 hours	**Total hours: 28 hours**

on Indonesian music that combines anthropological understandings of musical events and musicological analysis with hands-on applications of gamelan composition techniques and an end-of-the-semester class performance. Class exercises reinforce student knowledge of Indonesian music and culture while also drawing upon skills in music composition, transcription, ensemble performance, and peer-directed learning.

Another step toward course integration might be for faculty to become more aware of how the classes they teach relate to those of others and to collaborate more intensively with colleagues across music subdisciplines. Pedagogical collaboration across subdisciplines could generate an awareness of courses that might be compressed into a more efficient series and provide additional insights into how undergraduate music courses could be more fully coordinated to reinforce student learning. For example, introductory courses in music theory, aural skills, and piano skills could be structured so that they correlate to the undergraduate music history sequence and vice versa.

Benefits of an integrated music core

- Fundamental music skills are taught in fewer hours than in current models.
- Music students have more opportunities to take academic or ensemble electives.
- Creative application exercises develop a broad range of music skills and deeper, applied knowledge of music fundamentals.
- Music history courses (and other courses such as private lessons and/or ensembles) could be modified to work in conjunction with the integrated core series.

4. CAPSTONE MODEL

A "big project" or "capstone" curriculum model is one in which the degree program culminates in a substantial, self-directed, highly individualized project. This approach is compatible with other curricular models we have recommended. Our suggestions are conceived with performance (BM) majors in mind, but the basic structure can be easily modified for composition majors, BA students, or others. It may be more difficult to apply the model in the case of music education majors, given the complications of state certification and extended student-teaching requirements.

The main challenge in developing and implementing a proposal of this nature is reconciling a variety of educational values or goals. Primary among these is the tension between training performers of the highest technical ability in the conservatory tradition and training well-rounded musicians for a variety of career options. We recognize that radical changes in curricula may significantly disrupt institutions in a variety of ways and thus make it more difficult to fill large flagship ensembles, meet the expectations of donors who champion particular performance programs, assure an appropriate number teaching positions for graduate students, and so on. Thus, the framework presented below strikes a balance between providing experiences crucial for the training of future musicians without sacrificing others required of standard performance degrees (see Table 14.3).

Our recommendations build on the existing BM performance structure that requires recitals in both junior and senior years but reconceives them to require a broader set of skills. The capstone involves the creation of a student professional website that reflects the entirety of the project, including the production of: professional recordings, original compositions and arrangements, sample teaching materials, recorded improvisations, and demonstrated competence with marketing, self-promotion, copyright and licensing.

Most junior and senior recitals currently consist of approximately four pieces from standard repertoire on a student's primary instrument. They contrast solo and ensemble pieces as well as a range of stylistic periods within the Western canon. The extent to which new compositions or alternative works are included varies widely depending on the student's primary instructor and institution. Our revised model continues the performance of classical repertoire but incorporates one-third to one-half "creative" material. By "creative," we mean pieces that require the student to engage in skills—such as improvisation, composition, arranging, and collaboration—beyond the interpretation of precomposed pieces. We envision these creative learning projects as student-driven, in that students will independently seek out the knowledge required to complete the project. We do not suggest that performance curricula include more instruction in composition and arranging. Instead, the educational benefit here lies in the process and the problem-solving required of students outside the classroom.

It is important to note that most of the pieces chosen for a recital may still conform to standard canonical repertoire if the student prefers this, but the

Table 14.3. SAMPLE SCHEDULE OF INTEGRATED COURSE WEEKLY MEETINGS

Monday	Tuesday	Wednesday	Thursday	Friday
1 hour: lecture/ discussion of music concepts	1.5 hours (1 hour in semesters 3 & 4): creative application of musical concepts	1 hour: lecture / discussion of music concepts	1.5 hours (1 hour in semesters 3 & 4): creative application of musical concepts	1 hour: lecture / discussion or applied practice (depending on student progress)

new model allows students the flexibility to devote up to half of the performance to alternative repertoire if they are so inclined.

The model below requires that students perform a minimum of four to six canonical pieces as well as four "creative" pieces; at least one of the latter must be outside the Western art music canon. We believe the approach satisfies the expectations of conservatory students aspiring to be symphony orchestra members while simultaneously incorporating essential new skills and experiences. Below we list performance requirements and then provide an outline of what the two-year junior/senior-year projects might look like.

Overall performance requirements

Students will give a junior and a senior-year recital, performing a total of eight to ten pieces total (four to five per recital). Of these, four to six will consist of standard canonical repertoire in addition to the following "creative" pieces:

- one work that features the student's expertise in a noncanonical idiom such as a world music ensemble, jazz ensemble, or popular music ensemble; or that constitutes an arrangement of a non-Western art piece for a solo or small ensemble performance.
- one original piece composed by the performer.
- one off-campus collaborative performance.
- one piece that incorporates prominent improvisation.

The requirements above can be combined; for example, an arrangement of nonstandard repertoire or an original composition may also include prominent improvisation and satisfy both requirements, or the original composition may be performed in collaboration with artists off-campus.

Additional requirements

- *Teaching / public speaking*: Examples include offering recital-lectures or a master class to new students; teaching private lessons; volunteering in local elementary/middle schools; etc.
- *Elective: professional preparation component*: This might involve music internships; musical or interdisciplinary collaborative projects; the creation of sound archives, perhaps in conjunction with a local music community; music therapy initiatives; scoring music for film; the organizing of a concert series; involvement in CD design and production; the composition of new musical material; or other projects approved by a primary instructor.

- *Student professional website*: The website project requires students to develop important writing, promotional, and other real-world skills while simultaneously serving as a platform for presenting their artistic accomplishments over the course of the two-year capstone. The website must include
  - videos of live performance.
  - videos of teaching.
  - studio-recorded tracks.
  - program notes for all videos and recordings.
  - scores of originally composed/arranged works.
  - promotional photos.
  - a CV/bio.

Sample two-year capstone plan

Junior year

1. Junior Recital and Live Recording: During this year, students prepare repertoire toward the fulfillment of the requirements described above and organize a recital to be recorded live. In addition to performing the selected repertoire, students develop skills associated with arrangement/composition, the booking of a performance space, concert promotion, and recording.
2. Teaching/Public Speaking or Student Elective.
3. Begin Work on the Website.

Senior year

1. Senior Recital and Studio Recording: During this year, students prepare new repertoire toward the fulfillment of performance requirements and give a senior recital. In addition, they are responsible for producing studio-recorded tracks of the same pieces and copyrighting any original works. In the process, they will become familiar with software related to recording and sound editing as well as develop skills related to rights clearance, the writing of liner notes, and product distribution.
2. Teaching/Public Speaking or Student Elective (whichever one was not completed in the prior year).
3. Complete and Present Website to a Jury.

INDEX

Society for Music Perception and
Cognition, 170n3
transcription and, 171–2, 176, *see*
transcription, cognition
see also metacognition
College Music Society (CMS), 9, 10, 37,
70, 96, 169n1, 201, 205, 274
College of William and Mary, 72 tab. 4.1,
76, 83
colonialism, 199–200, 211–14, 264, 269
Colorado College, 49, 62, 62 fig. 3.3,
62n15, 64, 64n18, 67, 275
Columbia College Chicago, 72 tab. 4.1,
87 tab. 4.4
Columbia University, 17
commercial music
courses, 96
economies, 230, 238
ensembles, 96
major, 80, 83
programs, 7, 23, 82 tab. 4.2, 83,
94, 128
scenes, 228
see also music business; music industry
community
building, 226–7, 231, 234, 239
commitment to (guiding principle),
11–12. *See also* guiding principles
of curricular
reform
cultural community of academia, 150
engagement, 163, 163n26
global, 226, 229
in music teacher education, 215, 217
outreach initiatives, 140–1, 164,
164n28, 214, 238, 245, 273
sample projects, 246
and school ensembles, 6, 151
and social justice, 207, 212
and traditional music, 160
virtual/online, 120, 123–4
compact music major, 57, 59
computer-based music, 124
Conservatory of Bamako, 252
copyright law, 12, 224, 258, 277, 279, *see*
also licensing
Cornell University, 8
Costa Lima, Paulo, 11
country music, 69, 83, 87 tab. 4.4,
89, 127–30

critical multiculturalism, 206n1; *see also*
antiracism; multiculturalism
culture of whiteness, 205, 207–12, 218
Curtis Institute of Music, 186

Dávalos, Carlos, vii–viii, 243–66
(chapter 13), 267–79 (chapter 14)
Davidson College, 49, 52, 54 tab. 3.1a,
55 tab. 3.1b, 57, 58 tab. 3.3, 67
Decoda, 43
DePauw University, 8
Dewey, John, 118, 122
DeWitt, Mark, viii, 23, 69–97
(chapter 4), 106n7, 122, 136, 163
digital
audio workstations, 261
downloads, 33
file sharing, 39–40
music/musicianship, 57, 261
Durham, Hannah, viii, 243–66
(chapter 13), 267–79 (chapter 14)

ear training
courses, 8–9, 15, 17, 25, 83, 174,
244–5, 262, 267–8, 270–2, 271
tab. 14.1, 274 14.2,
as skill, 20, 236–7
and transcription, 175, *see*
transcription
see also aural skills; chapter 9
East Asia
local musical traditions, 155. *See also*
chapter 8
pedagogy in, 155, 157
symphonic performance scene, 4
East Tennessee State University, 72 tab.
4.1, 74, 78n7, 89, 122, 127, 129
Eastman School of Music, 224, 232
electronic music, 42, 123–4, 127, 153
embodiment, *see* pedagogy, embodied
enhanced core model, 25, 245, 267–71
entrepreneurship
courses, 35, 259, 273
definition, 13, 257–60
degree programs, 86, 88 tab. 4.4,
244, 257–60
as professional skill, 12, 25, 260
and underemployment, 257
ethics, 171. *See also* social justice.
ethnicity, 2, 209

ethnocentrism, 9, 70, 137, 173
ethnomusicology and restricted
    curricula, 5–6, 47, 51
European musical instruction, *see*
    Western art music
experience ensembles, 76–7, 95; *see also*
    realization ensembles
Experiential Music Curriculum
    (U Miami), 8, 20

faculty engagement, *see* administration,
    faculty and
far-experience, 192–4
far-near experience, 192–3, 196, 201–2
Fatimah Jinnah Women
    University, 254
field-based learning, 60–1, 64, 64n18
film music, 14, 20, 264
flipped classroom, 18–19, 119, 124, 199,
    201, *see also* inverted classroom
folk music
    aural learning and, 104n5, 108
    in conservatory, 160–1
    instruction in Europe, 101–14
    courses, 61–2, 62 figure 3.3
    degree programs, 102, 157; *see also*
        chapters 4 and 5
    folk-pop, 130
    International Folk Music Council,
        see International Council for
        Traditional Music
    theory, 108n11, 109
freelancing, outsourcing, contract
    and temp work economy
    (FOCT), 229–32
funk, 4, 128

gamelan, 41, 53, 64, 192, 272–3, 276,
    see also Balinese music
genre-specific music theory, 108, 111
global awareness, 15–16, 60, 170, 207,
    244, 251, 252–5; *see also* guiding
    principles of curricular reform
Global Network for Higher Music
    Education (GLOMUS), 252–3, 255
globalization, 64, 178, 229, 253, 264
gospel music, 4, 76–7, 87 tab. 4.4, 90,
    215, 262, 268
grants
    and funding cuts, 250

NEC Entrepreneurial Department
    Grant Program, 259, *see also* New
    England Conservatory
and performance ensembles, 142
writing, 224, 260
Grinnell College, 49, 54, 54 tab. 3.1a,
    55 tab. 3.1b, 58 tab. 3.3, 66–7
guiding principles of curricular reform
    commitment to community, 11–12,
        see also community
    commitment to creative, student-
        driven projects and practices, 18–
        19, *see also* student-driven curricula
    commitment to global awareness,
        15–17, *see also* global awareness
    commitment to practical concerns of
        professional musicians, 12–15,
        see also practical concerns of
        professional musicians
    commitment to social justice, 17–18,
        see also social justice

Hampshire College, 49, 53–4, 54 tab.
    3.1a, 55 tab. 3.1b, 57, 58 tab. 3.3,
    59–60, 62–3, 67
Harris, Myranda, viii, 243–66
    (chapter 13), 267–79 (chapter 14)
Hawaii
    Hawai'inuiakea School of Hawaiian
        Knowledge, 88 tab. 4.4, 90
    music, 7, 69, 89
    music degree program, 82 tab. 4.2, 94
    see University of Hawaii
Hazard Community Technical College, 72
    tab. 4.1, 80, 81 tab. 4.2, 94,
heavy metal
    Heavy Metal Ensemble of Lawrence
        University, 42
    music, 117, 126
    opera, *Queen Boudicca: A Metal
        Opera, see Queen Boudicca: A Metal
        Opera. See also* opera
    see also rock music
hip-hop
    instruction, 12
    and turntable/laptop/iPad
        ensembles, 120
    see also Carmen: A Hip-Hopera
Hispanic Alliance, 238
Hispanic-serving institutions, 23, 140, 212